The Cambridge Companion to Mahler

In the years approaching the centenary of Mahler's death, this book
provides both summation of, and starting point for, an assessment
and reassessment of the composer's output and creative activity.
Authored by a collection of leading specialists in Mahler scholarship,
its opening chapters place the composer in socio-political and
cultural contexts, and discuss his work in light of developments in
the aesthetics of musical meaning. Part II examines from a variety of
analytical, interpretative and critical standpoints the complete range
of his output, from early student works and unfinished fragments
to the sketches and performing versions of the Tenth Symphony.
Part III evaluates Mahler's role as interpreter of his own and other
composers' works during his lifelong career as operatic and
orchestral conductor. Part IV addresses Mahler's fluctuating
reception history from scholarly, journalistic, creative, public and
commercial perspectives, with special attention being paid to his
compositional legacy.

The Cambridge Companion to

MAHLER

....

EDITED BY
Jeremy Barham

CAMBRIDGE
UNIVERSITY PRESS

CAMBRIDGE UNIVERSITY PRESS
Cambridge, New York, Melbourne, Madrid, Cape Town, Singapore, São Paulo

Cambridge University Press
The Edinburgh Building, Cambridge CB2 8RU, UK

Published in the United States of America by Cambridge University Press, New York

www.cambridge.org
Information on this title: www.cambridge.org/9780521540339

First published 2007

Printed in the United Kingdom at the University Press, Cambridge

A catalogue record for this publication is available from the British Library

ISBN 978-0-521-83273-1 hardback
ISBN 978-0-521-54033-9 paperback

Contents

Plates

Tables and figures

Music examples

Notes on contributors

Jeremy Barham is lecturer in music at the University of Surrey. In addition to Mahler, his research interests include nineteenth- and early twentieth-century music history and aesthetics, interdisciplinary and cultural studies, film music and jazz. He is editor of *Perspectives on Gustav Mahler* (Ashgate, 2005), editor and translator of Alfred Rosenzweig, *Gustav Mahler. New Insights into his Life, Times and Work* (Ashgate/GSMD, 2007), contributor to *The Mahler Companion* (Oxford, 2002) and has written on Kubrick's use of music in *The Shining* (Equinox, 2007).

Herta Blaukopf (1924–2005) was one of the leading figures in Mahler scholarship. She collaborated with Kurt Blaukopf on *Mahler, His Life, Work and World* (London, 1991) and was the editor of numerous volumes of Mahler's letters, including *Gustav Mahler – Richard Strauss. Correspondence 1888–1911* (London, 1984) and *Gustav Mahler Briefe* (Vienna, 1996). She continued throughout her life to write regularly on topics relating to Mahler and Austrian literary culture, and played a central role in the activities of the International Gustav Mahler Society, Vienna.

Stephen Downes is reader in music at the University of Surrey. Research areas include Central and Eastern European musical modernism and the erotic in music since 1800. He has published on Szymanowski, Beethoven, Rossini, Schumann, Sibelius, Mahler, Bartók, Henze and Penderecki. In 1989 he won the University of Southern California's Wilk Prize for Research in Polish Music, and in 1999 the Karol Szymanowski Memorial Medal. His latest book is *The Muse as Eros: Music, Erotic Fantasy and Male Creativity in the Romantic and Modern Imagination* (Ashgate, 2006).

Peter Franklin is Professor of Music at the University of Oxford and a Fellow of St Catherine's College; he edited the English translation (by Dika Newlin) of Natalie Bauer-Lechner's *Recollections of Gustav Mahler* (Faber, 1980). His more recent Mahler publications include *Mahler. Symphony no. 3* and *The Life of Mahler* (both with Cambridge University Press, 1991 and 1997 respectively); he also wrote the new Mahler entry for the *Revised New Grove Dictionary of Music and Musicians* in 2001.

Stephen E. Hefling, Professor of Music, Case Western Reserve University, is the author of *Gustav Mahler. Das Lied von der Erde* (Cambridge, 2000), editor of *Mahler Studies* (Cambridge, 1997) and contributor to *The Mahler Companion* (Oxford, 1999), the revised *New Grove*, and numerous journals. He serves on the editorial committee of the Mahler Complete Critical Edition, and edited the autograph piano version of *Das Lied von der Erde*. His two-volume study of Mahler's symphonies will be published by Yale University Press.

Born in Vienna, **Reinhold Kubik** has taught at the Vienna Conservatoire and in Nuremberg, Yale, Karlsruhe and London. He has written on Handel, Schubert,

Mahler, Baroque opera and editorial problems, and has published editions of Zelenka, Schubert, Zelter, Handel, Leopold Mozart, Loewe, Dvořák, Mahler (original version of *Das klagende Lied*, Fifth and Seventh Symphonies) as well as eighty Bach cantatas. Since 1993 he has been Chief Editor of the Mahler Complete Critical Edition and Vice-President of the International Gustav Mahler Society, Vienna.

The musicologist and curator **Christoph Metzger** graduated from TU Berlin with a dissertation on Mahler's reception history. He has taught in Wiesbaden, Berlin, Gent and Darmstadt, and directed interdisciplinary events such as *Musik und Licht, Minimalisms* (Akademie der Künste), *transmediale 99*, *Klangkunstforum* (1999–2001), *Musik und Architektur* (Darmstadt, 2002), and the *Baltic Biennale of Sound Art* (2004–06). He was the recipient of the AICA Award and the CEREC Award of the Financial Times, Europe (2001). He currently lives in Berlin and teaches in Cottbus and Braunschweig.

Vera Micznik teaches historical musicology at the University of British Columbia in Vancouver, Canada. She has published on issues of biography, programme, narrative, semiotics, genre, and verbal vs. musical discourse in the music of Mahler, Liszt and Berlioz. She is currently working on a book on musical discursive techniques in the nineteenth century.

Born in England, **David Pickett** was a recording engineer at EMI's Abbey Road Studios, Head of Tonmeister Studies at the University of Surrey and Director of Recording Arts at Indiana University. Currently Professor of Music at the University of North Texas, Dr Pickett is the leading authority on Mahler's *Retuschen* and an editor of the new Sibelius complete edition for Breitkopf & Härtel. A pupil of Igor Markevitch, he undertakes regular conducting engagements in Europe and the United States.

Peter Revers was born 1954 in Würzburg. He studied musicology, psychology and composition at the Universities of Salzburg and Vienna, and at the University 'Mozarteum' in Salzburg. Formerly Assistant Professor and Lecturer at the University of Music in Vienna, in 1996 he became Professor of Musicology at the University of Music and Dramatic Arts in Graz, and in 2001 President of the Austrian Musicological Society. His research focuses on Mahler, Mozart, Sibelius and the late nineteenth and early twentieth-century reception of Far-Eastern music in Europe.

Zoltan Roman is Professor Emeritus at the University of Calgary. His research has been devoted to Mahler, Webern and interdisciplinary studies focusing on the turn of the twentieth century. He has edited several fascicles of Mahler's songs for the Complete Critical Edition and is the author of numerous books and articles, including *Gustav Mahler's American Years* (New York, 1989), *Gustav Mahler and Hungary* (Budapest, 1991) and a recent contribution to *Perspectives on Gustav Mahler* (Ashgate, 2005).

Jörg Rothkamm is Assistant Professor at Leipzig University for Music and Theatre where he started a research project on the relationship between music and choreography in ballet (in collaboration with Salzburg University). In 2002 he received his Ph.D. at Hamburg University's Musicological Institute with a thesis on Mahler's Tenth Symphony (Frankfurt, 2003). He has also published on Berthold

Goldschmidt and Gustav Mahler (Hamburg, 2000), and – as co-editor – on Brecht/ Dessau (Hamburg, 2005), and Ballet (Berlin 2007).

Lewis M. Smoley is a graduate of the Juilliard School of Music in New York and Queens College of the University of the City of New York. He has lectured on Mahler at The New School for Social Research, Post College and New York University. A former radio broadcaster and producer, and staff writer of record criticism for *The American Record Guide*, his publications include *The Symphonies of Gustav Mahler: A Critical Discography* (1986), *Gustav Mahler's Symphonies: Commentary on Recordings since 1986* (1996) and the chapter on Mahler in *Music of the Twentieth-Century Avant-Garde: A Biocritical Sourcebook* (2002). He recently completed an analysis of all Mahler's works, entitled *A Complete Guide to Mahler's Music* (forthcoming).

A native of Norway, **Morten Solvik** grew up and received his education in the US before moving to Austria, where he currently lives with his wife and two children. Solvik's research focuses on the tantalizing connections between music and culture, especially with regard to Gustav Mahler and the turn of the century. He teaches music history and heads the music department at the Institute of European Studies in Vienna.

Christian Wildhagen studied musicology, philosophy and German literature at Hamburg University. In 2000 his dissertation on Mahler's Eighth Symphony was published by Peter Lang. He is cultural editor of the *Hamburger Abendblatt*, and in 2003 became principal dramatic adviser at the Hagen Theatre, Westphalia. He has published in the *Neue Zürcher Zeitung*, and worked for Bavarian Radio, the Berliner Festwochen and the Schleswig-Holstein and Salzburg Festivals. He is a member of the jury of the 'Preis der deutschen Schallplattenkritik', and since 2004 has taught at the Leipzig Musikhochschule.

John Williamson is Professor of Music at the University of Liverpool. He is the author and editor of books on Pfitzner, Richard Strauss, Bruckner and *Words and Music*. A historian who analyses, he is also interested in the aesthetics of Austro-German music of the period 1850–1950. When he finishes running the School of Music at Liverpool, he intends to return to a long-delayed project on d'Albert and a new project on the late nineteenth-century orchestra.

Acknowledgments

I would like to thank Penny Souster, Vicki Cooper and the team at Cambridge University Press for their support and advice during the production of this volume. I am also grateful to Julie Barham for advice on translations, Stephen Goss for setting the music examples, and to both The School of Arts, Communication and Humanities at the University of Surrey and the *Music & Letters* Trust for providing generous funding in support of this project. The following institutions are thanked for granting permission to reproduce material: The Pierpont Morgan Library, New York; Universal Edition A.G., Vienna and Universal Edition, London; the Österreichische Nationalbibliothek, Vienna; and the Paul Sacher Foundation, Basel. I am most grateful to all the contributors for their patience in awaiting the completion of the volume and for answering my numerous questions.

Chronology

Date	Mahler	People	Historical and cultural events
1850–9		Births of Janáček, Max Burckhard (1854), Freud, Bernard Shaw, Lipiner (1856), Conrad, Elgar, Max Klinger (1857), Puccini, Hans Rott (1858), Dewey, Bergson, Husserl (1859); deaths of Schumann and Heine (1856)	Crimean War (1853–6); Austria defeated by France at battles of Magenta and Solferino (1859); Hanslick, *Vom Musikalisch-Schönen* (1854); Darwin, *Origin of Species* (1859)
1860	7 July, Mahler born in Kalischt, on the Bohemian-Moravian border. Family moves to Iglau in December	Births of Wolf and Chekov; death of Schopenhauer	
1861			Dickens, *Great Expectations*; first edition of Heine's complete works begins publication
1862		Births of Debussy, Klimt, Schnitzler, Maeterlinck and Gerhart Hauptmann	Flaubert, *Salammbô*
1863		Births of Munch, Weingartner, Dehmel; death of Friedrich Hebbel	
1864	Learns to play accordion	Births of Richard Strauss, Alfred Roller and Wedekind	Rudolf Hermann Lotze, *Mikrokosmos*
1865	Receives first music lessons; attends primary school	Births of Sibelius, Nielsen and Otto Bierbaum	First performance of *Tristan und Isolde*; opening of Vienna's Ringstrasse
1866	'Composes' first piece: 'Polka mit einem Trauermarsch als Einleitung'	Births of Kandinsky and Satie; death of Rückert	Austria defeated by Prussia at battle of Sadowa; Treaty of Prague
1867			Ibsen, *Peer Gynt*; *Ausgleich* marking formation of Austro-Hungarian Empire; beginning of the Austrian economic 'Gründerzeit' and of liberal political domination
1868		Births of Maxim Gorky and Justine Mahler; death of Rossini	First performance of *Die Meistersinger von Nürnberg*; Eduard von Hartmann, *Die Philosophie des Unbewußten*
1869	Enters Iglau Gymnasium	Birth of Pfitzner; death of Berlioz	Vienna Hofoper opens; first performance of *Das Rheingold*
1870	Gives public concert in Iglau	Death of Dickens	First performance of *Die Walküre*; Wagner writes essay *Beethoven*

Date	Mahler	People	Historical and cultural events
1871–2	Attends Neustädter Gymnasium in Prague; plays at celebration of anniversary of Schiller's birth in Iglau Obergymnasium, November	Births of Zemlinsky, Mengelberg and Proust (1871), and Scriabin and Vaughan Williams (1872); death of Grillparzer	Franco-Prussian war results in creation of German Empire (1871); William I, King of Prussia, becomes first Emperor of Germany; publication of Rückert's *Kindertotenlieder* (1872); founding of Akademischer Wagner Verein (1872); Keller's *Sieben Legenden* (1872); Darwin, *The Descent of Man* (1871); Nietzsche, *Die Geburt der Tragödie aus dem Geiste der Musik* (1872)
1873	Plays Thalberg's *Fantasy on Bellini's Norma* at gala celebrating wedding of Archduchess Gisela and Prince Leopold of Bavaria	Births of Rachmaninov and Reger	Austrian stock-market crash, signalling decline of *laissez-faire* capitalism; Georg von Schönerer enters parliament
1874		Births of Schoenberg, Ives, Hofmannsthal and Kraus	First publication of Schopenhauer's complete works
1875	Beloved brother Ernst dies; enters Vienna Conservatoire; works on *Herzog Ernst von Schwaben*	Births of Ravel, Thomas Mann, Jung and Emma Mahler; death of Bizet; Hans Richter becomes conductor at Vienna Hofoper	First performance of Bizet's *Carmen*
1876	Wins first prizes in Conservatoire composition and piano competitions; gives concert in Iglau with fellow students	Birth of Bruno Walter	First Bayreuth Festival; first complete performance of *Der Ring*; first performances of Brahms's First Symphony; Lipiner, *Der entfesselte Prometheus*; Fechner, *Vorschule der Aesthetik*
1877	Composes movement for Piano Quartet in A minor; enrols at the University of Vienna for lectures in history, literature and harmony (Bruckner); becomes member of Wiener akademischen Wagner-Verein; matriculates from Iglau Gymnasium; works on *Die Argonauten*	Birth of Hesse	First performance of Brahms's Second Symphony
1878	Wins first prize in Conservatoire composition competition; begins work on *Das klagende Lied*; completes piano-duet transcription of Bruckner's Third Symphony with Krzyzanowski; submits overture to *Die Argonauten* unsuccessfully for the Beethoven Prize; leaves		Publication of Lipiner's essay 'Über die Elemente einer Erneuerung religiöser Ideen in der Gegenwart'; joint Austro-Hungarian occupation of Bosnia and Herzegovina

Date	Mahler	People	Historical and cultural events
	Conservatoire; enrols at the University for lectures in philosophy, literature, art history and harmony		
1879	Gives piano recital in Iglau theatre; works on *Rübezahl*; enrols at the University for lectures in art history, archaeology, history of music (Hanslick), philosophy and European history; gives piano lessons; joins the Pernerstorfer Circle; becomes vegetarian; relationship with Josephine Poisl, daughter of the Iglau postmaster	Births of Alma Schindler (31 August), Einstein and Klee	'Zweibund' establishes military allegiance between German and Austro-Hungarian Empires; festival procession in Vienna commemorating silver wedding anniversary of Emperor Franz Joseph I; first Vienna performance of *Der Ring*; Count Taafe becomes Prime Minister of Austria; Fechner, *Die Tagesansicht gegenüber der Nachtansicht*
1880	Completes *Das klagende Lied*, and composes three songs dedicated to Josephine Poisl; first conducting appointment, Bad Hall	Death of Flaubert; Hans Rott becomes insane	Issue of decree granting equal status to Czech and German languages in Bohemia and Moravia
1881	*Das klagende Lied* submitted unsuccessfully for the Beethoven Prize; conducting appointment in Laibach (Ljubljana) (operas by Donizetti, Gounod, Mozart, Rossini, Verdi and Weber)	Births of Bartók, Stefan Zweig and Picasso; deaths of Mussorgsky and Lotze	
1882	Begins work on set of five early songs; plays piano works by Mendelssohn, Schumann and Chopin at Philharmonic concert, Laibach	Guido Adler begins lecturing on musicology at the University of Vienna; births of Kodály, Stravinsky and James Joyce; deaths of Darwin and racial theorist Gobineau	Founding of Czech University in Prague; first performance of *Parsifal*, Bayreuth; Berlin Philharmonic founded; Georg von Schönerer and group of anti-Semitic German nationalists produce the 'Linz Programme' of social reform, supported by Pernerstorfer Circle; Nietzsche, *Die fröhliche Wissenschaft* (rev. 1886)
1883	Conducting appointment in Olmütz (Olomouc) (Meyerbeer, Bizet, Verdi); rehearsal conductor of chorus in Italian Stagione, Carltheater, Vienna; makes first visit to Bayreuth Festival; gives last concert as pianist, Iglau; appointed second conductor in Kassel	Births of Walter Gropius, Kafka and Webern; death of Wagner	First Vienna performance of *Tristan und Isolde*; first performance of Brahms's Third Symphony; first publication of parts of Nietzsche's *Also sprach Zarathustra*
1884	Love affair with singer Johanna Richter; becomes director of Münden choral society; composes *Lieder eines fahrenden Gesellen* and incidental music to *Der Trompeter von Säkkingen*	Death of Smetana	First performance of Bruckner's Seventh Symphony

Date	Mahler	People	Historical and cultural events
1885	Achieves major success at the Kassel Music Festival with Mendelssohn's *St Paul*; provides incidental music to *Das Volkslied*; appointed second conductor at Deutsches Landestheater, Prague (Cherubini, Verdi, Mozart, Wagner); works on First Symphony	Births of Berg and Klemperer	First performance of Brahms's Fourth Symphony; von Schönerer's Deutsch-National Verein becomes independent political party in Austria
1886	First performance of own works (three songs); conducts *Fidelio* for first time; appointed conductor at Leipzig Stadttheater, works under Nikisch (Meyerbeer, Wagner, Weber, Gluck)	Births of Kurth, Kokoschka; death of Liszt	
1887	Conducts *Siegfried*; completes Weber's fragmentary *Die drei Pintos*; becomes deeply immersed in *Des Knaben Wunderhorn*; first meeting with Strauss	Deaths of Borodin and Gustav Fechner (Leipzig)	First performance of Verdi's *Otello*; comprehensive Weimar edition of Goethe's complete works begins publication (Hermann Böhlau, 1887–1920); first edition of Klopstock's collected works
1888	Completes First Symphony, first *Wunderhorn* settings and *Totenfeier*; meets Tchaikovsky; conducts first performance of *Die drei Pintos*, Prague; receives offer of employment from Metropolitan Opera, New York; becomes Director of the Royal Hungarian Opera, Budapest	Death of Kaiser Wilhelm I	Nietzsche, *Der Fall Wagner*
1889	Death of both parents and sister Leopoldine; conducts *Das Rheingold*, *Die Walküre* and première of First Symphony, Budapest (labelled 'Symphonic Poem'); accompanies performance of three of his songs	Births of Heidegger, Wittgenstein and Hitler	First performance of Strauss's *Don Juan*; Tolstoy, *The Kreutzer Sonata*; Bergson, *Essai sur les Données Immédiates de la Conscience*; Social Democratic party emerges in Austria, led by Viktor Adler; Crown Prince Rudolf commits suicide at Mayerling
1890	Spends holiday in Italy with sister Justine; completes first set of nine *Wunderhorn* songs with piano accompaniment; becomes acquainted with Natalie Bauer-Lechner; meets Brahms	Birth of Schiele; deaths of Franck and Gottfried Keller	Brahms attends, and is impressed by, Mahler's performance of *Don Giovanni*; ascendancy of anti-Semitic Karl Lueger and his Christian-Socialist party begins; Bismarck resigns as Chancellor of German Empire; Burckhard becomes director of Vienna Burgtheater; Hauptmann, *Das Friedensfest*; founding of journal *Die freie Bühne für modernes Leben*

Date	Mahler	People	Historical and cultural events
1891	Appointed principal conductor at Hamburg Stadttheater; conducts *Tristan* for first time; composes further *Wunderhorn* songs; plays *Totenfeier* to Hans von Bülow	Birth of Prokofiev	Bahr, *Die Überwindung des Naturalismus*; Dehmel, *Erlösungen*; Wedekind, *Frühlings Erwachen*
1892	Conducts *Eugene Onegin* in presence of Tchaikovsky; conducts eighteen guest performances at Covent Garden, including first English performance of *Der Ring*; three volumes of songs with piano published (*Lieder und Gesänge*); completes set of orchestral *Wunderhorn* songs under title 'Fünf Humoresken'; two orchestral *Wunderhorn* songs performed in Hamburg and Berlin; becomes acquainted with physicist Arnold Berliner		First performance of Bruckner's Eighth Symphony; Maeterlinck, *Pelléas et Mélisande*; Nietzsche, *Also sprach Zarathustra* (complete)
1893	Revises and performs First Symphony, and orchestrates and revises *Lieder eines fahrenden Gesellen*; in Steinbach am Attersee composes more *Wunderhorn* songs and movements of the Second Symphony; visits Brahms	Deaths of Gounod and Tchaikovsky	
1894	Completes Second Symphony, (inspired by singing of Klopstock's 'Auferstehn' at von Bülow's funeral), and first revision of *Das klagende Lied*; becomes acquainted with Josef Foerster; conducts First Symphony in Weimar (called 'Titan. Symphony in Two Parts'; assumes conductorship of Hamburg Subscription Concerts after von Bülow's death; becomes acquainted with Bruno Walter	Death of von Bülow	Dreyfus affair in Paris; first performance of Bruckner's Fifth Symphony
1895	Brother Otto commits suicide; first performance of Second Symphony, Berlin; completes movements two to six of Third Symphony; affair with soprano Anna von Mildenburg begins	Birth of Hindemith	First performance of Strauss's *Till Eulenspiegel*; Polish Count Badeni becomes Prime Minister of Austria; literary journal *Pan* founded by Bierbaum
1896	Conducts first performances of *Lieder eines fahrenden Gesellen* and four-movement version of First Symphony; completes Third Symphony and *Wunderhorn* song 'Lob des hohen Verstandes'; frequency of performances of his music under other conductors begins to increase; attends *Der Ring* conducted by Siegfried Wagner at Bayreuth	Death of Bruckner	Strauss completes *Also sprach Zarathustra*; Archduke Franz Ferdinand becomes heir-apparent to Emperor Franz Joseph I

Date	Mahler	People	Historical and cultural events
1897	Converts to Catholicism; conducts in Moscow; Second Symphony and *Lieder eines fahrenden Gesellen* published; conducts farewell concert in Hamburg ('Eroica' and *Fidelio*); becomes Director of the Vienna Hofoper; conducts Viennese première of Smetana's *Dalibor*; engages von Mildenburg at Hofoper; repertoire dominated by Wagner and Mozart	Death of Brahms	Founding of the Secession; Austrian Prime Minister, Count Badeni, issues inflammatory decree equating Czech and German languages in official business: riots ensue; Lueger becomes Mayor of Vienna; era of liberal domination in Austrian politics comes to an end; first issue of Herzl's Zionist weekly *Die Welt* published; Mach, *Beiträge zur Analyse der Empfindung*; Heinrich Friedjung, *Der Kampf um die Vorherrschaft in Deutschland*
1898	Composes two further *Wunderhorn* songs; conducts first uncut *Der Ring* and *Tristan* in Vienna; takes over conductorship of Vienna Philharmonic from Richter	Births of Gershwin and Brecht; Guido Adler succeeds Hanslick as Professor of Music at University of Vienna	Strauss becomes Principal Conductor of Berlin Opera and completes *Ein Heldenleben*; Secessionist journal *Ver Sacrum* begins publication
1899	Performs his string-orchestra arrangement of Beethoven quartet in F minor op. 95 and cut version of Bruckner's Sixth Symphony; First Symphony published; completes penultimate *Wunderhorn* song 'Revelge'; begins Fourth Symphony; conducts series of first performances and new productions at Hofoper; purchases plot of land in Maiernigg for summer residence	Birth of Poulenc; death of Johann Strauss II	Kraus's satirical paper *Die Fackel* begins publication; founding of literary journal *Die Insel*, edited by Bierbaum; Haeckel, *Die Welträtsel*; Houston Stewart Chamberlain, *Grundlagen des XIX. Jahrhunderts*
1900	Conducts his retouched version of Beethoven's Ninth Symphony in Vienna; conducts Vienna Philharmonic at World Fair in Paris and first Vienna performance of First Symphony; *Wunderhorn* songs published; completes Fourth Symphony	Births of Copland, Krenek and Weill; deaths of Nietzsche and Wilde	Freud, *Die Traumdeutung*
1901	Conducts first performances of *Das klagende Lied* and Fourth Symphony; suffers serious haemorrhoidal haemorrhage; occupies summer residence in Maiernigg, composes four Rückert songs, three *Kindertotenlieder*, final *Wunderhorn* song, 'Der Tamboursg'sell', and begins Fifth Symphony; resigns conductorship of Vienna Philharmonic; meets and becomes engaged to Alma Schindler	Death of Verdi	

Date	Mahler	People	Historical and cultural events
1902	Fourth Symphony published; marries Alma Schindler; conducts first performance of Third Symphony, Krefeld; completes Fifth Symphony and further Rückert song 'Liebst du um Schönheit'; directs wind arrangement of part of Finale of Beethoven's Ninth Symphony at opening of Secession Beethoven exhibition; birth of daughter Maria Anna	Death of Zola	Eduard von der Hellen's comprehensive *Jubliäums-Ausgabe* of Goethe's complete works begins publication (Stuttgart: Cotta, 1902–12)
1903	Collaborates with Roller on *Tristan* production at Hofoper; begins Sixth Symphony; first Vienna performance of Puccini's *La Bohème*; conducts First and Third Symphonies in Amsterdam; becomes acquainted with Mengelberg and Diepenbrock; Henry Wood conducts First Symphony in London	Death of Wolf	First performance of Bruckner's Ninth Symphony; Mann, *Tristan*
1904	Conducts Third Symphony in Heidelberg, Mannheim, Cologne, and for first time in Vienna; meets Gerhart Hauptmann; appointed by Schoenberg and Zemlinsky as honorary president of Vereinigung schaffender Tonkünstler for whom he conducts Strauss's *Sinfonia Domestica*; becomes acquainted with Schoenberg; birth of second daughter Anna Justine; composes two *Kindertotenlieder*, Finale of Sixth Symphony and both *Nachtmusiken* of Seventh Symphony; conducts first performance of Fifth Symphony, Cologne; first American performance of a Mahler symphony (Fourth: Damrosch, New York)	Deaths of Dvořák and Hanslick	
1905	First performance of *Kindertotenlieder* at Vereinigung schaffender Tonkünstler, Vienna; completes Seventh Symphony; planned Vienna production of *Salome* forbidden by censors; meets Klemperer at Fried's performance of Second Symphony, Berlin; records some of own works on Welte-Mignon player piano system, Leipzig; begins Mozart cycle at Hofoper with *Così fan tutte*, in collaboration with Roller; conducts first Vienna	Births of Tippett and Sartre	First performances of Debussy's *La Mer* and Strauss's *Salome*; Vienna Secession dissolved

Date	Mahler	People	Historical and cultural events
	performance of Fifth Symphony; first London performance of Fourth Symphony (Henry Wood)		
1906	Conducts first performance of Sixth Symphony, Essen; attends first Austrian performance of *Salome*, Graz; begins, and completes, Eighth Symphony; new editions of first four Symphonies published by Universal; conducts *Marriage of Figaro* at Salzburg Mozart Festival	Birth of Shostakovich; deaths of Ibsen and von Hartmann; Hitler attends *Tristan* performance at Vienna Hofoper	Electoral reform in Austria leads to domination of Christian-Socialist, German National and Social Democratic parties; von Hartmann, *Das Problem des Lebens*; 'Mozart Year' (150th birthday)
1907	Attends concert of Schoenberg's first string quartet op. 7 and Chamber Symphony op. 9; conducts first Vienna performance of Sixth Symphony and new production of Gluck's *Iphigenie in Aulis* with Roller's set designs; death of elder daughter from scarlet fever; heart disease diagnosed; resigns as Director of Hofoper and is succeeded by Felix Weingartner; conducts final opera there (*Fidelio*); accepts contract from Metropolitan Opera, New York; meets Sibelius in Helsinki; conducts final concert in Vienna (Second Symphony); makes first trip to America	Death of Grieg	Formation of the Triple Entente between France, Britain and Russia regarding colonial differences; bill introducing universal suffrage for all males over twenty-four becomes law in Austria; Bethge, *Die chinesische Flöte*; Bergson, *L'Evolution Créatrice*
1908	Makes debut in America with *Tristan*; begins *Das Lied von der Erde* during summer in Toblach; conducts first performance of Seventh Symphony, Prague; returns for second season in America; conducts Second Symphony with New York Symphony Orchestra	Birth of Messiaen; death of Rimsky-Korsakov	Festival in Vienna celebrating sixtieth anniversary of Emperor Franz Joseph I's coronation; Austro-Hungary annexes Bosnia and Herzegovina
1909	Conducts American première of Smetana's *The Bartered Bride*; leaves Metropolitan Opera and is appointed conductor of New York Philharmonic; sits for Rodin in Paris; first French performance of First Symphony (Lassalle, Paris); meets Varèse; completes *Das Lied von der Erde*, begins Ninth Symphony and arranges Bach Orchestral Suites (first performed in New York); Seventh Symphony published; Universal gains rights to works previously with Weinberger	Death of Albéniz; von Mildenburg marries Hermann Bahr	First performance of Strauss's *Elektra*; Mann, *Königliche Hoheit*
1910	Takes New York Philharmonic on tour to New Haven, Springfield and Boston; conducts Second Symphony in Paris, during	Deaths of Balakirev, Karl Lueger, William James and Tolstoy	Origins of First World War emerge in increasingly aggressive imperialistic tendencies of

Date	Mahler	People	Historical and cultural events
	which Debussy walks out; completes Ninth Symphony; begins Tenth Symphony; honoured on fiftieth birthday by volume of tributes edited by Paul Stefan; developing marital crisis brought to a head by Alma's affair with Walter Gropius; Mahler consults Freud in Leiden, Holland; conducts triumphant first performance of Eighth Symphony, Munich; purchases plot of land in Semmering; attends performance of Schoenberg string quartets opp. 7 and 10, Vienna; begins last season in America; tour to Pittsburgh, Cleveland, Buffalo, Rochester and Syracuse		Austro-Hungary, Russia and Germany
1911	Eighth Symphony published; conducts last concert of own work (Fourth Symphony), New York; taken ill after final concert (21 February) with subacute bacterial endocarditis; returns to Europe for treatment in Paris and final journey to Vienna; dies on 18 May; buried next to elder daughter in Grinzing cemetery, 22 May; Walter gives first performances of *Das Lied von der Erde* and Ninth Symphony in Munich 1911 and Vienna 1912		

Abbreviations

The following abbreviations are used in the notes:

GMB2   Herta Blaukopf (ed.), *Gustav Mahler Briefe*, 2nd edn (Vienna: Zsolnay, 1996).

GMLW   Henry-Louis de La Grange and Günther Weiß (eds.), *Gustav Mahler. Letters to his Wife*, rev. and trans. Antony Beaumont (London: Faber & Faber, 2004).

HLGE1   Henry-Louis de La Grange, *Mahler. Vol. 1* (New York: Garden City, 1973/London: Gollancz, 1974).

HLGE2   Henry-Louis de La Grange, *Gustav Mahler. Vol. 2. Vienna: the Years of Challenge (1897–1904)* (Oxford University Press, 1995).

HLGE3   Henry-Louis de La Grange, *Gustav Mahler. Vol. 3. Vienna: Triumph and Disillusion (1904–1907)* (Oxford University Press, 1999).

HLGE4   Henry-Louis de La Grange, *Gustav Mahler. Vol. 4. A New Life Cut Short (1907–1911)* (Oxford University Press, 2007).

HLGF1   Henry-Louis de La Grange, *Gustav Mahler, Chronique d'une Vie. Vol. I. Vers la Gloire (1860–1900)* (Paris: Fayard, 1979).

HLGF2   Henry-Louis de La Grange, *Gustav Mahler, Chronique d'une Vie. Vol. II. L'âge d'or de Vienne (1900–1907)* (Paris: Fayard, 1983).

HLGF3   Henry-Louis de La Grange, *Gustav Mahler, Chronique d'une Vie. Vol. III. Le Génie foudroyé (1907–1911)* (Paris: Fayard, 1984).

ML   Alma Mahler, *Gustav Mahler. Memories and Letters*, trans. B. Creighton, ed. Donald Mitchell and Knud Martner, (London: Cardinal, 1990).

NBLE   Peter Franklin (ed.), *Recollections of Gustav Mahler by Natalie Bauer-Lechner*, trans. Dika Newlin (London: Faber Music, 1980).

NBLG   Herbert Killian (ed.), *Gustav Mahler. Erinnerungen von Natalie Bauer-Lechner* (Hamburg: Karl Dieter Wagner, 1984).

SLGM   Knud Martner (ed.), *Selected Letters of Gustav Mahler*, trans. Eithne Wilkins, Ernst Kaiser and Bill Hopkins (London: Faber & Faber, 1979).

Introduction: Marginalia on Mahler today

JEREMY BARHAM

Does Mahler matter? A history in which eighty years of screen culture and emotion commerce have interrogated, reprocessed and cashed in vast areas of Mahlerian idiolect as patois, narcotizing a society his music was to have transformed and mobilized,[1] presents a curious problem. If unorthodoxy rather than consensus is any measure of import, how is it possible or even desirable to abstract the once difficult from a repertoire in order to de-popularize it, to reclaim the margins for the formerly marginalized, even to 'rescue the history of an unfavoured [Mahler] from oblivion',[2] and yet to resist the attenuation and certain retreat into the cloistered self-interest of the initiated that assimilation into collective consciousness brings? As performance and recording gluts continue to familiarize and congeal the de-familiarizing in a game of technical and technological catch-up followed by domination, Mahler's capacity to offend historical consciences and aesthetic sensibilities now *in absentia*, and in the age of Uri Caine when the previously exterior and disjunct claim centrality and conciliation, is seriously diminished. Where then lies the musical space he so violently transgressed,[3] the sense of music history with which he toyed ironically, bitterly and comically? One who apparently resisted embourgoisement so resolutely, becomes deeply ritualized within it. The once hazardous Mahlerian experience is insulated and inimitable, glimpsed uncertainly through misted flights of imagination, submerging in the 'death' which, as sister to 'fashion and manners', characterizes the 'huge performing market in our time',[4] itself uneasily encumbered by canonic interpretative legacies.[5] While the machinery of the biographical panopticon inevitably sculpts monoliths from natural disorder, cultural musicology bathes in interpretative relativity in the conviction that, above all with Mahler, it is 'impossible to listen only to the music'.[6] Control and assumed intelligibility result from both, though problems of method and critique veering between unmediated documentary and determinist selectivity, and between absolutism and absence of judgment, are invasive. Socio-cultural and critical-historical control of Mahler thus serves and reanimates itself in a de-sensitizing hermeneutic-economic circle, evident, for example, in the archetypal narrative threads shared by several recent media appreciations[7] – the price of a limitless routine of consumption may well be as heavy as the

[1]

ludicrous idea of embargoes would be (and has been) grotesquely fascistic. Is this ideological bankruptcy, a fate that accrues from commodification masquerading as the final 'understanding' predicted by Mahler himself,[8] a fate worse than death?

If death is indeed the one universal precondition of canonization, the lingering aftermath of such sanctification is vulnerable to stagnation in the blind comfort of consuetude unless its hagiographical conditions are challenged. Like some political opponent who dies in office, Mahler was rapidly declared a saint in 1912 by his personal friend, but compositional Other, Schoenberg, who began to construct monuments, dedicating his *Harmonielehre* (1911) to the composer and celebrating with convoluted logic his own theological conversion at the altar of Mahler's thematic (non-/quasi-) banality.[9] Repaying personal and professional debts (monetary loans and testimonials) may or may not have been the incentive for Schoenberg's attempted 'validation' of Mahler's stature and technique within the suspiciously neat historical teleology constructed in his writings,[10] but to read that through external pressures a martyred Mahler had lost faith in his work, acknowledged his 'error' and become 'resigned', and to be taken systematically through the panoply of biting critical accusations to which he had frequently been subjected (inartistic means, poor voice-leading, inability to achieve true greatness, sentimentality, banality, lack of inventiveness, unoriginality, potpourri structures – though, significantly, passing over the Jewish question) suggests special pleading and might have seemed something of a poisoned chalice for Mahler's habilitation.[11] Whatever the true extent of Schoenberg's wider critical influence at this time – and Strauss's securing of the Third Symphony's 1902 première had surely been the greater proselytizing feat – the incurably romanticized, if not sentimentalized, foundations of a deeply threnodic Mahler brand, fusing music with personal circumstance and fuelled by Walter's first performances of *Das Lied von der Erde* and the Ninth Symphony, were laid here – a brand in which pervasive undercurrents of latter-day humanist faith mysticism would find palliation. Indeed Schoenberg appears sincere, if perilously uncontrolled, when confessing effusive emotional empathy with Mahler's music,[12] but a rationalist breach perhaps inevitably cordons this off from analysis. Still today, for Jens Malte Fischer the silo of emotion is nothing less than a psychological deficiency to be overcome for the sake of enlightenment: 'Those who have a merely emotional relationship with Mahler's music through the overpowering intoxication of its sound will be trapped in a position of subjugation, and will never be able to advance to a relationship of dedicated understanding'.[13] The temptation to reply that it is *only* or *primarily* from emotional investment with the sensual that other kinds of understanding of Mahler may flow is qualified by the

implications of this introduction's first observations, and by the acknowledgment that Western musical scholarship is quick to suppress experiential
immediacy and finds its relationships with more established forms of
discourse difficult to articulate.

Nevertheless, if Schoenberg was misguided about the absence of sur-
rogate Mahlerian idioms from cinema, he was right to allude – albeit with
condescension – to the 'melodramatic horror-play' in his account.[14] In
dramatizing the internal disorder of apparently stable bourgeois frameworks through episodic narrative and sensational exaggeration of emotion, the 'competing logic' or 'second voice' of the nineteenth- and early
twentieth-century cross-generic melodramatic mode thrived both on a
troubled politico-cultural inclusiveness conjoining grandiose with banal,
high with low, and on a morally heightened utopian-dystopian dialectic
of garish, externalized psychological pictograms. This cocktail of Grand
Guignol addressing the chaotic 'post-sacred era'[15] of early modernism
may not be so far removed from the physiognomics of Mahler's symphonic 'imaginary theatre',[16] with its recasting of the music-language relation
through abstraction of vocality and weighted gestures of ineffability, and
its attempt to recover meaning in obstacles, delays, problematic closure,
juxtaposition, gaps, detours, scenic spatiality and virtuosically poised
dialectics of extreme action/pathos, inanity/sublimity and desolation/
rapture. Could this at least partially explain why a mercantile, secularized
West has, despite itself, alighted with greater intensity on Mahler at certain
points in the intellectual vagrancy of its twentieth-century politico-
cultural history – for instance, in the euphoric-depressive post-war 1920s
and more radicalized, dangerous, economically insecure 1960s–1970s?
Moreover could this link, if Adorno allows,[17] absolve reticence to passion
and to consideration of the 'purposely ideological',[18] while illuminating
forgotten paths of critical integrity in Mahler reception?

In a study of the inner workings of the Hollywood industry, David
Thomson notes the 'dramatic effect exerted through time' shared by film
and a work such as Mahler's Ninth Symphony: 'there are structural affinities, in theme, reiteration, transition; in hesitation, silence, stillness and
ending'. It may be that the contemporaneous early silents of D. W. Griffith
deal in 'vastly diminished and inferior notions of life' and compare unfa-
vourably with the 'exquisite, majestic, tragic, accepting' Symphony,[19] but
these creative forms – respectively positioned at the beginnings and ends
of their generic histories – are nevertheless kindred agencies dissolving
or tensioning through their particular materials boundaries between
dreams and realities or abundance and scarcity of hope: holding out the
promise of happy endings or of 'victory to the losers'.[20] Continual listening-
again, re-attending, and understanding in the true sense of an ongoing

dialogic *process* of 'standing in the midst of' rather than an achieved monologic *state* of containment, may avert the dystopia painted at the beginning of this introduction. Revaluation may claim Mahler's music as neither deconsecrated nor beyond good and evil, neither blandly democratized nor ideologically blinkered, but as existentially constitutive and intensely Manichean, infiltrating and disquieting an increasingly broad range of cultural, political and individualized spaces in a language whose very structural-expressive rivenness is an essential condition for restoration, as its will to integration is for the broken voice: a complex 'short circuit' between different musics, historically and psychologically inflected 'like an empire nearing its end', and, 'in its ability to do many things at once . . . like the music of madness'.[21]

As editor of this volume I similarly invite readers to contemplate its contents in the spirit of ends and beginnings, as both summational and initiatory, as taking the opportunity during the time approaching the centenary of Mahler's own ending to assess, re-assess and provide a valuable base for renewal – for re-exploring the senses in which Mahler's art and our confrontation with it may continue to matter.

PART ONE

Cultural contexts

1 Socio-political landscapes: reception and biography

PETER FRANKLIN

I

In 1904 the Prussian Ambassador to the Grand Duchy of Weimar sent an anxious report to his masters at Wilhelm II's court in Berlin. It concerned the promotion of 'modern' artists like Gaugin and Rodin by the Director of Weimar's Grand Ducal Museum for Arts and Crafts, the homosexual connoisseur, soldier and diplomat, Count Harry Kessler. For the Ambassador, Kessler's modernism (something which inspired 'the known aversion of His Majesty the Emperor and King') was comprehensible only as a form of sedition on the part of 'intriguers' with partisan interests; 'an artistic opposition', he concluded, 'can, at times, easily lead to a political [one]'.[1] It is small wonder that in 1918 this same Kessler, otherwise known to music history as co-librettist with Hofmannsthal for Richard Strauss's ballet *Josephslegende*, would adopt striking language in the exercise of his later war-time position (following harrowing active service) as Cultural Attaché to the German embassy in Switzerland: 'The propaganda war has become through the engagement of the Americans more vehement and complicated. They have more money, we have the craftiness of our Jews, which I put into motion, and our more precise work. Every moment in life, every individual, becomes the battlefield of enemy parties. Nothing escapes politics.'[2]

Although he had died in 1911, Mahler was still very much a force in this complex cultural-political landscape, one that connects the ostensible stability of old imperial Europe to the chaos and dissolution of all such stability in the First World War. Indeed, one of the events in Kessler's German-liberal propaganda war in January 1918 was to be a high-profile Zurich performance of the Second Symphony under the baton of Mahler's (Jewish) former friend and acolyte Oskar Fried. Kessler's recent biographer, Laird M. Easton, reminds us that Trotsky had just abandoned negotiation in favour of world revolution – something that was a subject of lively debate, to judge from Kessler's diary entry, at the reception following the Mahler performance (it was held in Paul Cassirer's hotel suite, whose rooms had once been used by Goethe):

> The Van Goghs and Cézannes in Goethe's rooms, the peculiarly mixed, cosmopolitan party, almost as before the war, the time, the moment when

Trotsky seeks to turn the Russian Revolution into a world revolution, where
the conflict at home between the military and the civilian authority
becomes threatening, the echo of the monstrous Last Judgement depiction
of Mahler, this jumble of so many different feelings, experiences, forebodings, people, has something dreamlike, fantastic about it.[3]

Placing the musical experience amidst worldly events and anxieties,
this account also evokes much of what we think of as the expressive
character of the Mahler we have made our own. To our ears, his symphonies embrace portents and threats, contradictions and consolations,
and have an ability both to express and induce experiences of dreamlike
escape and alienation. One could almost be forgiven for thinking that
Kessler chose that particular symphony less for propaganda purposes
than for its expression and reflection of the anxieties and dreams of
sensitive Europeans like himself at that world-changing time. Yet to
make that point is also to invoke what were then already well-worn
cultural-political questions about musical meaning. Many musicians,
theoreticians and critics in Mahler's own world (he occasionally and
judiciously echoed their views) could have been expected to raise an
eyebrow at the suggestion that music might express anything beyond its
essential nature as 'music', whatever that might be. Certainly the tradition
of German idealism, filtered through the many-coloured lenses of romanticism, would have supported a belief in the ability, even duty, of Great
Art to 'transcend' the everyday world of history and politics. Schopenhauer
had famously proclaimed that 'alongside world history there goes, guiltless
and unstained by blood [*nicht blutbefleckt*], the history of philosophy,
science and the arts' – a statement that graced the score and libretto of
Hans Pfitzner's 1917 opera *Palestrina*, another work performed in Switzerland
as part of Kessler's 'propaganda war' on behalf of Germany.[4]

That Pfitzner, also a former acquaintance of Mahler's, would soon
be engaged in angry critical polemics about the dangers of 'futurism' and
the threat posed by 'cultural bolsheviks' and Jews (already marked out
by Kessler for their 'craftiness'),[5] echoes the suspicions of the Prussian
Ambassador in Weimar and the perception of Kessler that 'Nothing
escapes politics'. By the 1920s, tensions that had marked the reception
of his music during Mahler's lifetime were ever more explicitly politicized
and polarized in a Europe soon to witness the rise of fascism. On the one
hand he was a composer whose ethnic origins supposedly prevented him
from achieving the Germanic 'greatness' to which his symphonies aspired;
on the other his achievement was construed, in perhaps no less partisan
a fashion, as consisting in his modern, ironizing approach to that very
'greatness' of aspiration. Biographical readings of his life, no less than
critical analyses of his symphonies, could be political in the sense that

they might be involved variously with exercising or more critically examining forms of 'power' and the way he related to or represented them: the power of the normal, for example, that puts 'abnormal', foreign or Jewish artists in their place – or the power that underpins the most innocent-seeming pastoral fantasies that musically idealize a rural world unequally divided between aristocrats and the grateful peasants who till their land for small earthly reward.

Launched into a culture that claimed to prize the 'absolute' and non-referential qualities of symphonic excellence, it was the prodigality of the ways in which Mahler's symphonies proved susceptible of interpretation that fuelled shocked or admiring readings of their meaning. Critics and historians sought support for those readings in facts, influences and affiliations. Some of Mahler's earliest friends and proponents inevitably sought to idealize him, seeking contextual and biographical evidence for their picture of his development as mirroring that of other manifestly 'great' composers of the past. They often emphasized the spiritual and the transcendent in his music, seeing his life as a surmounting of obstacles placed in his way by imperial laws, anti-Semitism, the economic and educational inequalities of class rivalries and aspirations, or by personal pride and national identity (possessed or sought). His more articulate enemies, like the conservative Viennese critic Robert Hirschfeld, saw in all such things precisely the features of the worldly landscape in which Mahler had grown up; from that perspective his *failure* to 'transcend' them irrevocably and negatively marked his works.[6]

Yet where Hirschfeld heard in every note of Mahler's symphonies an anarchic threat to bourgeois values, the Russian critic Iwan Sollertinski – inheritor of that very Revolution that had so exercised the minds of Kessler and his colleagues in 1918 while listening to the Second Symphony – would in 1932 celebrate Mahler quite explicitly as 'the last outstanding petit-bourgeois [*kleinbürgerlich*] symphonist':

> In this sense, the problem of Gustav Mahler – understood socio-philosophically – is the problem of the death of European symphonism, in Beethoven's sense of that term; more than that, it is the problem of the fundamental impossibility of the existence of a symphonism in imperialist Europe … History condemned [Mahler] to become the last tragic representative of the Beethoven tradition.
> The bourgeois symphonism of the West was dying.
> The new symphonic culture will be created by the proletariat and – under its leadership – by its allies in the petit-bourgeois intelligentsia and the peasantry.[7]

The suspicion that both Hirschfeld and Sollertinsky might have been hearing the same things in Mahler's symphonies but interpreting them differently according to their own socio-political agendas and affiliations, might lead us to be more wary of their and others' explanations as to *why* Mahler was the way he was and to seek our own forms of possibly alternative corroboration. Questions about how his upbringing might have shaped him are intimately linked to the ways in which we seek to answer other questions about his music. What *did* he mean to express in the 'Resurrection' Symphony's Last Judgement Finale? What *were* the politics of the first movement of the Third – associated in his lifetime with workers' marches as much as with those of the military? Did Mahler's world-view change after the traumas of 1907 that seem to have prompted the dark and often elegiac visions of the last works?

In the knowledge that our own choice of historical 'facts' might be no less biased, selecting strategic vantage points from which to view the socio-political landscape in which Mahler grew up and became what he did, my catalogue will explicitly correlate 'history' with interpretation – looking where possible for what have been generally accepted as key problems concerning Mahler's creative and intellectual choices. In all cases these are critical and interpretative in nature and rooted in specific strategies and events in individual symphonies. Even over-arching issues like that concerning Mahler's specifically Jewish identity and experience demand critical attention to detailed musical manners and moments as much as to a wider 'contextual' account of laws and attitudes affecting and oppressing European Jews in the nineteenth century. Recent Israeli problems with the German texts of works like the Second Symphony – sung in Hebrew under Bernstein in 1967 – and jazz-musician Uri Caine's brilliant recompositions and paraphrases of Mahler movements, heighten and celebrate the 'Jewishness' long detected in them by Bernstein and others. All this can serve to emphasize how musicians, critics and audiences, no less than the composers they perform, write about or listen to, support and demonstrate Kessler's bitterly experienced politicization of the landscape of the ordinary.[8]

Mirroring the world (Landscape 1)

Let me propose that we might regard Mahler's symphonies as both reflecting and reconstructing the socio-political landscape of the historical world in which they were created. The important question is how the former 'mediated' the latter. We must be more specific: how might a work like the First Symphony be read in this way? Clearly there is a level on which the opening seems literally to 'paint a landscape', but if we use some of the techniques of musicologist and art-historian Richard Leppert, we might note how the naturalistic 'dawn landscape' evocation of the string harmonics is further defined, or 'set off' by the calls of *pianissimo* clarinets (mimicking distant trumpets or horns?) and actual off-stage trumpets that appear to be approaching from the far distance: evidence of human beings in the landscape; an organized and perhaps wealthy-estate-sponsored hunting party.[9] Such motifs had long been used to define pastoral romantic countryside in music. Yet we, with the conductor-composer, are in the lonely foreground, experiencing a solitary and isolated 'oneness-with-nature' in a discursive space that, in romantic novels, is usually defined as belonging to the 'hero' or 'subject' of the narrative; and of course Mahler's various programmatic and musical allusions further define this as a *German-romantic* space, painted by a German-romantic hero of the kind the composer had constructed in words in his rather stylized youthful love poems, some of which became the *Lieder eines fahrenden Gesellen*. The second song supplies the main symphonic allegro material of the Symphony's first movement: 'In the morning I walked out into the fields [*Ging heut morgens über's Feld*]'.

It is easy enough to hear a well-worn story in this musical landscape: the story of a romantic artist, alienated from the urban and material world of modernity and power, and 'escaping' into the idyllic world of a fantasized Nature where the shadow of dark chromatic clouds is dispelled by blithely unfolding diatonic lyricism. Even the appropriation of that lyricism by dancing 'folk' in the Scherzo (joined by schmaltzy petit-bourgeois sentimentalists in the second section) fits the classical–'Beethovenian' mould well enough. But what does all this euphonious good-heartedness tell us about the world of Mahler's youth and the way he might have been formed by it? Does its decent romantic Germanness conceal the anxious affirmation of a well-brought-up petit-bourgeois whose hard-working and often hard-pressed family formed part of the German-speaking Jewish community in Bohemian Jihlava (now part of the Czech Republic)?[10] Does its apparent ignorance of 'modern' problems suggest a head in the clouds, or an ambitious eye to the main chance: to the imaginative possession of that very culture of power and distantly hunting-horn players which might have seemed both nearer and more oddly distant when the talented young musician found himself transported to the grand and often anti-Semitic imperial capital in 1875? Like painted landscapes, these musical scenes are intended to be 'read'; they contain the ingredients of narratives that are further clarified in their relation to and interconnectedness with other scenes, other movements.

Both naivety and heroic aspiration resound in the grandiose Finale of the First Symphony, at whose end the hero conductor commands a veritable company of *on*-stage horns to proclaim the hymnic march of *his* appropriated Nature: as if now in possession of the site of his earlier romantic alienation. But the Symphony has one other movement, the

third (in its final version): a movement that was, from its first performance in Budapest in 1888, variously damned as eccentric or praised for
its daring modernity. This is the notorious minor-key 'Frère Jacques'
funeral march with irreverent and parodic interventions by a naturalistically notated band of Bohemian street musicians (the percussionist is
even directed to manage both bass drum and Turkish bells, like a genuine
travelling player).[11]

Nothing in Berlioz's noisy, more stagily clichéd 'Witches' Sabbath'
quite prepared audiences for this invasion of the hallowed Beethovenian
platform of great symphonic music by the foreign and unwashed. The
work was premièred in the Hungarian capital before a sharply factiona-
lized audience, a part of which saw the young Mahler as an operative
of 'Austrian' Hapsburg power in *their* national theatre. Nevertheless, the
First Symphony's mirroring of the divisions of race, taste and manners
that marked his world, had a disturbing quality that can only now be
recaptured, perhaps, with the help of Uri Caine's extraordinary reper-
formance of the third movement: as if by a band of genuine Klezmer
musicians who have wandered in off the street to find on the music
stands the discarded parts of a work they make sense of in their own
way – and better, perhaps, than many a conservatoire-trained orchestral
player.[12]

II

If the First Symphony re-sounded Mahler's world, and his relation to it
as an agent or actor within it, then the Second and Third Symphonies did
so in a way that sharpened and made more explicit the implicitly political
character and perspective of the First. At the same time they strengthened
the ambivalence about 'meaning' that reflected the ideological work
traditionally performed by the Germanic symphony as a cultural institution. Within this complex negotiation lay the concealed determinants of
the debate about 'programmatic' versus 'absolute' music which Mahler
appeared publicly to resolve in favour of the latter around 1900.[13] Mahler
the mythologized Jewish outsider had, of course, been able to determine
and forge his career not only through native wit or genius, but also thanks
to the decree that had sanctioned the economic mobility of the hitherto
ghettoized Jews in the year of his birth. That his father was able to move
to and prosper in Bohemian Jihlava from Kališt in Moravia was thanks to
a dispensation of imperial power.[14]

After the earlier German phases of Mahler's career as a conductor in
Kassel, Leipzig and Hamburg (albeit interspersed with Austro-Hungarian

interludes in Prague and, more importantly, Budapest) we must not forget that his return in 1897 to Vienna was as an employee of the Royal and Imperial Court Opera: an institution whose management was overseen by a court official, essential though box-office receipts were to its full financial well-being. The inference has often been drawn, albeit vaguely and unspecifically, that Mahler's celebrated and even notorious idealism in the opera house was opposed in some complementary way to his more subversively iconoclastic manner in the concert hall, particularly as a composer. In fact Mahler's productively tense balancing of, on the one hand, affirmation and validation of imperial power and, on the other, a radical tendency to question or undermine it, is traceable no less in his operatic work than in the manifest tensions and contradictions that define the dramatic discourse of his symphonies. His achievements in both spheres certainly raise questions about his political sympathies and affiliations in the dual monarchy of Austria–Hungary, whose controlling and organizing power was being questioned in the public arena not only by pan-Germanists and socialists but also by the many 'nationalities' that were ever more actively contesting the legitimacy of the centre's attempts to marginalize and suppress their demands for autonomy and even the right to use their own language in public debate.[15] It is difficult to gauge the extent of Mahler's sense of community with what we would now have to think of as the Czechs amongst whom he grew up as a German-speaking Jew, although there are some persuasive strands of evidence. What is rather easier to quantify is the extent of his involvement with socialists and pan-Germanists in the Vienna of his student years.

That he was on friendly terms with and even, for a time, an active participant in the circle that developed around the subsequently influential Austrian politicians Engelbert Pernerstorfer and Viktor Adler is well known and was first extensively discussed by the historian William J. McGrath in his influential book *Dionysian Art and Populist Politics in Austria*.[16] McGrath located Mahler's own group of friends, which revolved around the poet and translator Siegfried Lipiner, as closely affiliated to the Pernerstorfer circle. Mahler was a personal friend of the socialist Viktor Adler, the Jewish founder-leader of the Austrian Social Democratic Party. It came to represent the main opposition to the anti-Semitic Mayor Karl Lueger's Christian Socialist party, which inspired the admiration of the young Adolf Hitler and would nurture the prejudices and passions of many of those who would welcome Hitler's annexation of Austria in 1938. Adler's wife subsequently recorded her admiration for Mahler's preparedness to make public his vote for her husband as the (unsuccessful) opposition candidate in his Vienna constituency in 1901.[17]

Symphonic forces/symphonic spaces (Landscape 2)

The popular title 'Resurrection Symphony' has inspired many spiritually and idealistically charged readings of Mahler's Second Symphony. Yet as a mighty choral symphony alluding to and even 'improving upon' Beethoven's Ninth, it made a trenchant cultural-political statement. Its ostensibly 'spiritual' message was unequivocally glossed in the celebrated, if too little analysed, 'programmatic' sketch which he appears to have written for the edification of the King of Saxony in 1901 and communicated also to his wife-to-be, Alma Schindler, and to his sister Justine (protesting 'of course, it is only intended for someone naive'[18]): 'The earth quakes, the graves burst open, the dead arise and stream on in endless procession. The great and the little ones of the earth – kings and beggars, righteous and godless – all press on – the cry for mercy and forgiveness strikes fearfully on our ears'.[19]

This vision of an apocalyptic levelling of status and power (which must surely have suggested socialism as much as spirituality to the King of Saxony) had another twist. Elsewhere Mahler seems to have stressed the implicitly blasphemous and humanistic implications of the great reversal that follows the Last Trump, where the military trumpets and drums of divine power are banished to a strange, off-stage distance while an earthly nightingale claims the centre-stage foreground: 'there now follows nothing of what had been expected; no just man, no evil doer, no judge!'[20] No *judge*? The off-stage realm thus fades into mythology and illusion, the realm of imagined spirits and bugbears. For the King of Saxony Mahler had written: 'There is no punishment and no reward. An overwhelming love lightens our being. We know and are.'[21]

Had Mahler carried out his once-envisioned plan to have the Turkish-march in the Finale of Beethoven's Ninth announced off stage, as if by an approaching military band, then that external space might have been conclusively and uncomfortably located and dated – for a Viennese audience at least, whose collective memory of the Ottoman Turks' siege of their city in 1683 has never been entirely eradicated.[22] That musically symbolized threat, which might have been converted into an inclusive multi-national and multi-cultural brotherhood in the never-realized performance, had been present long before in the oddly unruly off-stage music of courtly celebration in *Das klagende Lied*'s 'Hochzeitsstück'. The off-stage band's anarchic inattention to the proprieties of the on-stage drama is sharply pointed by the fact that its material is fashioned out of the bones of the innocent murdered brother's musical characterization.

Then came the Third Symphony, which arguably embraces the most daring and also (perhaps inevitably) the most contradictory of Austro-Hungarian musical landscapes as seen and heard by a late nineteenth-century assimilated 'outsider'. It consequently manifested the innate tensions of Mahler's position as a Jewish intellectual socialist with his sights set on high imperial office. The triumphant final stage of his assimilation was even being plotted in the same summer in which Mahler completed the Third (1896) at his favourite lakeside retreat on the Attersee – he habitually took his holidays in Austria even while living and working in Hamburg. The route to the directorship of the Royal and Imperial Court Opera led via a strategic conversion to Roman Catholicism and a sequence of cultural-political machinations worthy of the professional politicians of the Dual Monarchy, whom he had earlier served as a kind of musical-cultural ambassador in Budapest. Mahler, the Germanized romantic idealist, passionately internalized the contradictions inherent in his aspiration to become one of the leading practitioners of European artistic culture. Perhaps that is what makes the Third so awe-inspiring and yet so perplexing. Mahler not surprisingly pointed out that the Third viewed 'the world' from a greater and more synoptic distance than had even the Second Symphony.[23]

Once again the 'symphony' is in fact an entire concert, complete with characteristic genre-pieces, an accompanied aria and a choral movement wedged between two mighty orchestral canvases. The advertised programmatic content was that of a musical depiction of the Great Chain of Being – a specifically Christianized one that leads from Man through the Angels to what Mahler hinted was an expression of 'the love of God' in the final Adagio. And yet the grandiose reconciliation performed there is questioned and even undermined by the first movement's pagan processions and elemental battle between the forces of winter and summer. The humorously figured and rudely corybantic victory of the latter over the former involved some of Mahler's most daring symphonic evocations of the lowly, everyday sounds of military marching bands, street musicians and unruly urchins. The riotous advance of these forces always suggested to Richard Strauss the sight and sound of a May Day workers' procession to the Prater of the kind that Mahler would join and accompany for a while in 1905 and whose founding father in Austria was his old friend Viktor Adler.[24] Small wonder that some of Mahler's more conservative critics heard in this music a threat not only to bourgeois propriety but also to the very fabric of society as it was then constituted.

The politics of the private (Landscape 3)

The 'humorously' childlike, yet complicatedly evoked celestial landscape of the Fourth Symphony – whose concluding song, *Das himmlische Leben*, had once figured in schemes for the Third Symphony – forms a curious tail-piece to the first three symphonies. Its consignment of the utopian dream to a remembered world of childlike fantasy also anticipates the disillusionment, or rather anti-illusionment, with which the Fifth and Sixth Symphonies flirt so boldly and even self-destructively. In one sense the landscape in which they were created had quite literally changed. The sunny Salzkammergut pleasure-lake (the Attersee) beside which Mahler billeted his party in a meadow-skirted inn during the summer holidays in which the Second and Third had been conceived, was exchanged for the more shadowy and damply forested southern shore of the Carinthian Wörthersee. Here Mahler joined the Viennese *nouveaux riches* and the successful cultural luminaries who were building themselves romantic villas on eagerly acquired plots of land that no-one had previously seen much use for. They now supported fashionable Viennese summer retreats that were well served by the Semmering railway that brought their owners direct to Klagenfurt, at the lake's Eastern tip.

It was here, in 1901, that Mahler, now Royal and Court Opera Director, brought his sister Justine, her future husband Arnold Rosé and his old admirer Natalie Bauer-Lechner to see his new lakeside house and the composition studio he had had built high above it in the densely climbing pine forest that came to represent the dark and sometimes terrifying 'Nature' that still calls, echoes and roars in the interstices of all the middle-period symphonies. Perhaps that sense of threat was linked to a realization that Mahler himself was now closer in status and social position to those far-off huntsmen whose distance had helped define the liberating breadth of the First Symphony's opening landscape.

The new presence in the lakeside villa (from 1902) of the witty and intelligent metropolitan beauty Alma Schindler, anxiously trying to play the part of his wife, must have heightened his sense of proximity to the urban world she longed for yet from which *he* had always sought to escape once the opera season was over. Did he feel himself suddenly older in her presence, a touch more melancholy and worldly-wise, when her youthfully modern and sceptical vivacity turned away from him? She certainly found his circle of friends stuffy, conservative and out of touch – something that seems to have goaded him to disengage from them and to develop an enthusiastic taste for the more 'modern' cultural world of her friends and family, of the artists of the Secession and of Zemlinsky and the young Arnold Schoenberg.

For this reason, the Fifth, Sixth and Seventh Symphonies, if outwardly more conservative in their lack of vocal movements or overt programmes, sound as up-to-the-minute and eager for life as ever – if consequently vulnerable to the lurking dangers and darkness to which I have alluded. The urban and bourgeois sentimentality of his 'love-song' to Alma in the Fifth's Adagietto seems almost designed for its parodistic guying in the closing Rondo,[25] while the celebrated mountain-side panorama of the

Sixth's first movement, rendered naturalistically present by the off-stage cow-bells, provides only temporary refuge from the relentless antitheses that it fails to resolve or from the roller-coaster psycho-drama of the Finale, at whose end we are pitched into the void.

The recapture of romantic fantasy, of his creative past and his more familiar compositional personality in the rich and mysterious Seventh Symphony seems conveniently to point to the fully regained optimism and creative energy that would apparently fuel the one symphony he wrote almost self-consciously as a Great Composer. He even described the Eighth, which ostensibly linked Catholic piety with the classically based German-literary vision of Goethe's *Faust* Part II (the 'Schlussszene'), as his 'gift to the nation'.[26] He conducted its first performance in Munich in 1910 no longer as an aspiring outsider, but as a composer at the height of his power and fame and celebrated by many of the best among his peers.

While explaining why critics of the political left have often found the Eighth's monumental affirmation historically and politically compromised, that sketched scenario does not capture the wider psychological landscape in which its first performance took place, nor, indeed, in which the Eighth Symphony would be succeeded by *Das Lied von der Erde* and the two final symphonies, whose affirmative moments are always in dialogue with disillusionment and elegy. To what extent might Kessler's observation about the potential politicization of 'every moment in life, every individual' be applicable here? Did Mahler, the successfully assimilated and culturally masterful Austro-Hungarian Jew tend latterly, like others of his kind, towards an increasingly illiberal and disillusioned conservatism? Or was it all the function of a purely subjective crisis? The psychological determinants of such a crisis might be found in the death of his daughter and the discovery of his heart condition in 1907, along with the collapse of his marriage to Alma Schindler. The torment of that drove him to seek Freud's help precisely in the period when the Eighth Symphony was being rehearsed.

The tendency to symptomatize and 'medicalize' Mahler's last symphonies – as the products of a mind unnaturally disturbed by an obsession with death or, indeed, deranged by personal tragedy – is itself political in the degree that it relies upon period criticisms of Mahler's symphonic style that were historically located and intensely bound up with the cultural politics of turn-of-the-century Europe. So too, perhaps, of early twentieth-century America, where Mahler's last four concert and opera seasons (between January 1908 and April 1911) were completed as exhaustingly compressed, high-energy campaigns in a foreign country.[27] There he was once again an 'outsider', albeit a high-status and high-earning one. The duality of his urban conducting life and rural summer retreats for composition was heightened in an extraordinary way. On the one hand, the high-octane and high-profile life of an eminent conductor in America, on the other, his new summer home in the rented first floor of a Tyrolean farmhouse with the now required composing-studio – a small wooden summer house at the edge of a nearby pine forest and overlooking a gentle valley (the razor-edged peaks of the Dolomites rising magnificently *behind* the forested hillside and out-of-sight of the studio). Here he completed *Das Lied von der Erde* and the Ninth and Tenth Symphonies.

In America, Mahler the self-made man found himself one amongst many in a land of spectacularly rich entrepreneurs and self-made businessmen who were putting up vast mansions in a 'European' manner that made the eclecticism of the Ringstrasse look relatively restrained. The Metropolitan Opera was no less a product of that aspiration to create ostentatious economic and cultural institutions whose models were similarly 'old'-European. Egged on by Alma's keen nose for the high life, coupled with her even keener sense of the aesthetic naivety and lack of style consciousness on the part of people like the Met's Director Heinrich Conried, Mahler could hardly avoid becoming something of a patriarchal luminary, some of whose public pronouncements seemed to reinforce the 'rightward'-tending reading of his later intellectual and political sympathies. His 1910 magazine interview on 'The Influence of Folk-Song on German Musical Art' is a case in point. Curiously, this turned into a reasoned (if intentionally optimistic) critique of the level of America's cultural achievement in music, one of whose vital contributions he located in 'the music of the African savage . . . the ancestors of the present American Negroes'. Accepting their 'distinguished attainments', he went on:

> I cannot subscribe myself to the doctrine that all men are born equal, as it is inconceivable to me. It is not reasonable to expect that a race could arise from a savage condition to a high ethnological state in a century or two. It took Northern Europe nearly one thousand years to fight its way from barbarism to civilization.[28]

The values expressed here seem far removed from those of Mahler's earlier Adlerian socialism. But the uncertain status of this translated 'interview' requires that we read it with care, not least as a possibly veiled critique of American cultural aspirations in general, couched in language that the conservative entrepreneurs who paid his fees might obliquely understand. It was certainly the case that the cultural superiority ostensibly proclaimed here was to be darkly compromised within a very few years, when Europe would set itself on the road to war and three decades in which barbarism would flourish and, by 1945, wreck its cities, murder untold numbers of its people and leave many of its great cultural institutions, like the Vienna Opera, in ruins. The point has to be made for the very reason that Mahler's late music seems so open to that possibility, so devoid of the complacency of a *grand seigneur* who might have set himself to producing neo-classical or neo-romantic symphonies that uncritically affirmed the status quo.

He, and they, did not. Instead, the late symphonies are characterized above all by a tone of elegiac lament whose ingredients of both realism and of 'self-indulgent' subjective urgency not only embarrass sternly objective souls who find Mahler's music too much to take, but also seem to threaten the very symphonic structures to which he clung. These provided the dialectical tools with which his last three works were constructed, yet whose own content paradoxically threatened both them and us ('Will not people make away with themselves after hearing it?' Mahler had nervously asked Bruno Walter about *Das Lied von der Erde*[29]). In the Adagio movements of the Ninth and Tenth symphonies that threat is constantly renewed, as in the piled-up dissonance of the devastating chromatic 'scream' that marks both the climax and a violent act of vandalism upon the musical argument of the first movement of the Tenth; the structural 'recapitulation' that follows almost inevitably assumes the character of a protracted coda, a dying-away into silence.

It is fascinating, in the light of the wider reception and criticism of early twentieth-century symphonic composition, that the music of the last two symphonies is outwardly 'absolute' by one set of criteria, but irredeemably committed to intensely detailed expressive meaning by another. The private–public tension becomes almost an irresolvable contradiction at the heart of these works, whose manuscript scores bear strategically placed verbal or poetic keys to the music's import. These have suffered the same fate of marginalization or deliberate suppression as the fragments of poetry (at least in English translation) Mahler appears to have left on Alma's bedside table during his last summer, when marital and emotional crises shadowed the completion of the Ninth and sketching of the Tenth Symphony.[30] As if realizing the intentionally negative assessment of some of his most articulate detractors, the late music appears expressively articulate and nuanced down to the level of the smallest chromatic passing note or dissonant suspension. Heralded in the last movement of *Das Lied von der Erde*, with its complex interaction between 'expressionless' narration, stylized evocation and impassioned engagement, the Ninth and Tenth symphonies face the impossibility of their own discursive extension as much as of their persuading Alma unequivocally to return his love or their deceased eldest daughter to come back to them.

The images that Alma has left us of Mahler weeping on the floor of his composing studio or having collapsed on the landing outside the door of her bedroom (where he was clearly no longer invited to sleep) have fed readings of the last two symphonies' traumatic and possibly psycho-sexual origins that have inspired prudishly irrational distaste. They might equally inspire attention as incomparably eloquent indicators of the working of what one might call the internal politics of subjective psychological stability in Mahler's culture and class. But the intimate subjective landscape, in which we ourselves cannot avoid being figured as questioning recipients and critics, is also once more overlaid with the imagery of a wider socio-historical world – like that of the brave New York fireman whose funeral procession, glimpsed from a New York hotel window, seems to have inspired the doom-laden, muffled drum strokes in the Tenth's Finale.[31] Mahler himself, no less than the King of Saxony in the Second Symphony's Last Judgement scenario, is not only the privi-leged spectator but also, by implication, one of the participants, even the imagined deceased – one amongst a whole host of fallen heroes whose elegy he wrote in music that seemed to harbour prophecy when *Das Lied*, the Ninth Symphony and, eventually, the Tenth were heard and reheard in a rapidly changing world. As that world reconstructed itself as irrevoc-ably different and removed from the one in which those works had been conceived, they seem no longer merely to have reflected but even, for a time, darkly to have made sense of the 'jumble of so many different feelings, experiences, forebodings, people' that Harry Kessler found him-self unable to disentangle from the experience of the Finale of the Second Symphony in 1918, when talk of world revolution and military and civilian conflict had filled the air like the smoke and screams from the trenches of the Great War. The uncertainly assimilated outsider now seemed to speak for that world, not only as its elegiac apologist but also as its critic and victim, movingly confirming Kessler's observation that '[e]very moment in life, every individual becomes the battlefield of enemy parties'. The tense discourse of Mahler's subjectivity was as political as that of his more public negotiation with the forms of a culture that had never quite accepted him.

2 The literary and philosophical worlds of Gustav Mahler

MORTEN SOLVIK

Any thorough understanding of Gustav Mahler and his music must probe the complexities of his thoughts about life and existence. Mahler's pursuit of these fundamental questions went far beyond idle speculation, haunting his personal reflections and informing his artistic project with a nearly obsessive quality. In significant ways, Mahler's works represent a response to this existential inquiry, an extension of an overriding need to somehow fathom the universe.

The composer as thinker

The intensity of Mahler's intellectual interests struck virtually everyone who knew him. The recollections of such friends and acquaintances as Natalie Bauer-Lechner, Richard Horn, Anna von Mildenburg and Richard Kralik all make noteworthy references to Mahler's effusive tone in conversations about life and art.[1] Bruno Walter, for a time Mahler's assistant and one of the most philosophically inclined of his conversation partners, referred to his private time with Mahler in Hamburg as mainly preoccupied with 'confessions of the soul, philosophy, and music'.[2] Mahler's uncanny ability to grasp new concepts and develop intriguing perspectives impressed them all. As Walter also pointed out: 'Friends of his, professionally occupied with natural science, were hard pressed by his deeply penetrating questions. An eminent physicist whom he met frequently could not tell me enough about Mahler's intuitive understanding of the ultimate theories of physics and about the logical keenness of his conclusions and counter-arguments.'[3]

As befitting his inquisitive personality and searching spirit, Mahler nurtured an infatuation with reading: 'I "devour" more and more books! They are, after all, the only friends that I take along with me! And what friends! God, if I didn't have them! ... They are becoming ever more intimate and consoling to me, my true brothers and fathers and loved ones.'[4] The intensity of this engagement in reading signalled not only the importance of ideas to Mahler's well-being, but also a certain need to escape from the exigencies of daily life, providing a palliative to the reality that surrounded him while bringing him face to face with the deeper questions that concerned him. Delving into a book frequently meant nothing less than pondering the very essence of nature, art and the human condition.

At bottom, Mahler searched for reassurance in the notion of a meaningful existence, that life had a distinct and higher purpose and that death represented nothing more than a transition. It was an assurance not easily won. For all the fervour of these philosophical and literary pursuits he remained deeply sceptical about ever finding an answer to his query. Mahler faced a deeply disturbing set of challenges to the transcendental urge at the fundament of his world-view. Perhaps most problematic was his perception of nature, the site of idyllic beauty and eternal truths that nevertheless also served as a grim reminder of the shockingly gruesome underbelly of life. As Bruno Walter observed:

> When his heart was lifted, he was capable of reaching the heights of belief;
> a strong, calm faith was not his lot, however. The suffering of the creatures
> struck him too painfully in the heart; murder in the animal world, the evil
> men perpetrate upon one another, the susceptibility of the body to illnesses,
> the constant threats of fate – all of this constantly shook him from the
> assurance of his beliefs and he became ever more aware of the problem
> of his life: how the suffering of the world and the evil of the world could
> be reconciled with God's grace and omnipotence.[5]

The central dilemma of a seemingly uncaring God would accompany Mahler throughout his life. Already at the age of eighteen he penned the following dramatic lines:

> Oh, that I might behold this earth in its nakedness, lying there without
> adornment or embellishment before its Creator; then I would step forth and
> face its genius. 'Now I know you, deceiver, for what you are! . . . Out of
> the valley of mankind the cry goes up, soars to your cold and lonely heights!
> Do you comprehend the unspeakable misery here below that for aeons
> has been piling up mountain-high? And on those mountain peaks you
> sit enthroned, laughing! How in the days to come will you justify yourself
> before the avenger, you who cannot atone for the suffering of even one
> single frightened soul!!!'[6]

Thirty years later Mahler explicitly formulated the same sentiment in – as he put it – a 'burning indictment aimed at the Creator' and continued: 'in every new work of mine (at least for a time) there arises once again the call: "That you, [are] not the Father of this world, but its Czar!"'[7]

The sense of betrayal and desperate reckoning evident in these words marks both a deep scepticism on the part of Mahler and a fervent need for a higher power, a tangle of hope and despair that is a hallmark of Mahler's mindset. Most crucially, Mahler brought his philosophic musing, with all of its aspirations and contradictions, to the heart of his artistic project. Out of this conflict there emerged an overwhelming urge to formulate a musical response – indeed, a musical answer – to this profoundly serious topic. Referring to the first movement of the Second Symphony he once wrote: 'Here, too, the question is asked: *What did you live for?* Why did you suffer? Is it all only a vast, terrifying joke? – We *have* to answer these questions somehow if we are to go on living – indeed, even if we are only to go on dying! The person in whose life this call has resounded, even if it was only once, must give an answer.'[8] Mahler's compulsion to give an answer – to compose – in the face of such riddles forms a crucial component of his musical personality and intellectual make-up. To understand why he even contemplated such an undertaking, we have to examine his early development as a thinker, more particularly his experiences as a student in Vienna.

Student days

The climate that surrounded Mahler when he arrived in the imperial capital in 1875 pitted the defenders of the liberal, rationalist achievements of the Ringstrasse era against the demands of a younger generation that held to a more mystical view of life in which intuition and inspiration were called upon to forge a path to the future.[9] The artistic, political and social debate awakened in Mahler a strongly intellectual vein in his character, and it was not long before he became deeply involved in his setting. While completing his musical studies at the Conservatoire of the Gesellschaft der Musikfreunde, the young student enrolled for additional courses at the University of Vienna. Matriculation records show him registered for, among other courses, Early German Literature, Art History, and the History of Philosophy.[10] Similar interests emerged in his contact with fellow intellectuals. In 1878 Mahler joined the so-called Pernerstorfer Circle, a group of young thinkers that promoted a pro-German blend of artistic idealism and social change. A few years later he co-founded the Saga Society, a gathering of friends whose activities included recitations of the *Nibelungenlied*, the *Edda*, and other German sagas. The mission of the Society emphasized living in the spirit of the German medieval hero in the hopes that a 'new world view should come into being, an artistic, poetic one opposed to the modern scientific one' in the hopes of founding a 'new and magnificent culture'.[11] Siegfried Lipiner, another founding member and one of Mahler's closest friends from this period, became a leading figure in university life, exhorting his fellow students in a widely hailed speech to reinvigorate the present with a quasi-religious conception of reality: 'to comprehend ... the world as a work of art'.[12]

As confrontational and passionate as the stance of Mahler and his friends may have been, it bore the marks of a curiously reactionary nostalgia for the ideals of the romantic past. No one embodied these traits more clearly than one of its most vocal spokesmen, Richard Wagner (1813–83). A prolific essayist, Wagner used his prominence as a composer to promote an aesthetics of artistic creativity taken largely from Arthur Schopenhauer (1788–1860) that reified the artist as a privileged visionary. According to this view, the great work of art represented the mystical manifestations of existence in its truest, most original form, beyond the world of appearances. It is clear that Mahler had a thorough grasp of the writings of both Schopenhauer and Wagner and that he embraced their transcendental vision of art.[13] Reflecting on the creation of one of his own compositions, he once remarked: 'But now imagine such a *large* work that, in fact, mirrors the *entire world* – one is, so to speak, only an instrument upon which the universe plays'.[14]

In addition to this artistic message, Wagner also emphasized the glorious achievements of German culture, a chauvinistic stance that did little to disguise the ambitions of a broader political agenda. Wagner's philosophical perspective was, of course, lent enormous credence by his undeniably ingenious compositions, in which the overwhelming power of art and the timeless lore of German legend – wrought in so many of Wagner's own music dramas – seemed to confirm the legitimacy of his vision. For Mahler, and for many aspiring thinkers and artists, Wagner appeared nothing less than a prophet of a conception of existence with an irrefutable claim to truth. Wagner's seething anti-Semitism, rampant nationalism and prickly personality could not diminish Mahler's admiration for the 'Master', whom he praised not only as a profound thinker but also as one of a handful of truly great men in the history of humanity.[15]

Perhaps not surprisingly, coming of age under Wagner's shadow had a direct bearing on Mahler's conception of himself as an artist. His first musical efforts during these formative years show him – like the Master – writing his own texts: the libretto for an opera, *Rübezahl*, based on a German fairy tale; the words to his own cantata, *Das klagende Lied*, based on elements from works by Ludwig Bechstein and the brothers Grimm; as well as numerous poems, later examples of which transmuted into the *Lieder eines fahrenden Gesellen*, written under the influence of the folk poetry collection by Arnim and Brentano, *Des Knaben Wunderhorn*.[16] In utilizing self-composed texts based on Germanic folk sources as the point of departure for his own musical compositions, Mahler took up projects fully in keeping with the political and artistic leanings of his immediate surroundings. Though later works would depart from this patently Wagnerian model, literature – and German romantic literature, in particular – would continue to play a central role in Mahler's oeuvre.

Literary taste

A striking demonstration of this persistence can be found in the textual sources that Mahler employed directly and indirectly in his compositions. The following overview provides a sample of literature cited in Mahler's works, either as sung texts or as references in programmatic descriptions. Table 2.1 shows an overwhelming preponderance of German literary works whose authors flourished in the early nineteenth century.

A broader look at Mahler's reading habits makes it clear that he pursued an extraordinarily wide range of interests, extending from classical antiquity to the latest developments of early twentieth-century physics and covering many of the novels, dramas, poems, and philosophical tracts in between.[17] A sample of the authors he is known to have read provides an indication of this diversity: Aristotle, Plotinus, Shakespeare, Spinoza, Sterne, Cervantes, Kant, Schiller, Novalis, Schopenhauer, Eichendorff, Grillparzer, Ibsen, Dostoyevsky, Wilde and Wedekind. For all of this breadth, Mahler nevertheless nurtured a particular fondness for the likes of Novalis, Jean Paul, E. T. A. Hoffmann, Hölderlin and, above all, Goethe.[18] It was with these and other like-minded authors that he felt most at home, writers that for the most part set out to explore more thoroughly the realm of human emotions, the magical powers of nature, and such topics as the folk, the German Middle Ages, religious experience, and art itself. In their pursuit of a subjective view of the world they relied on intuition and feeling to provide a deeper perspective on life. Inherent to this aesthetic project was a belief that art, by virtue of its mystical essence, was capable of bridging the gap between the material and ideal realms, that the creative act was both transcendental and revelatory.[19]

While this description begins to suggest a profile of Mahler as an intellectual, set within the composer's immediate surroundings this world-view seems remarkably outdated. Not only did most of his favourite authors stem from an earlier time, the literature and philosophy of his own day clearly had other agendas. Already towards the middle of the nineteenth century literature had started to embrace 'realism', an attitude that would grow enormously in importance in the coming decades. Even in the Biedermeier era one finds a tendency to focus on the everyday life of

Table 2.1 *A sample of literary sources in Mahler's works (by date of birth of author)*

Author	Biographical dates	Literary work	Mahler's oeuvre
T'ang Dynasty (618–907)			
Mong-Kao-Jèn	689–740	selections in *Die chinesische*	*Das Lied von der Erde*
Wang-Wei	701–761	*Flöte* (ed. Hans Bethge,	
Li T'ai Po	701–762	1876–1946)	
Chang Tsai	765–830		
Hrabanus Maurus	c. 780–856	'Veni creator spiritus'	Symphony No. 8
St Francis of Assisi[a]	c. 1181–1226	(Latin hymn)	
Dante Alighieri	1265–1321	*The Divine Comedy*	*Symphony No. 1
Tirso de Molina [Fray Gabriel Téllez]	1571?–1648?	'Serenade' and 'Phantasie' from *Don Juan*	Early songs
Friedrich Gottlieb Klopstock	1724–1803	'Aufersteh'n'	Symphony No. 2
Johann Wolfgang von Goethe	1749–1832	Final scene of *Faust II*	Symphony No. 8
Jean Paul (Friedrich Richter)	1763–1825	*Titan, Siebenkäs*	*Symphony No. 1
Friedrich Hölderlin	1770–1843	'Der Rhein'	*Symphony No. 3
E. T. A. Hoffmann	1776–1822	*Fantasiestücke in Callot's Manier*	*Symphony No. 1
Clemens Brentano (ed.)	1778–1842	*Des Knaben Wunderhorn*	*Wunderhorn* songs, Symphony Nos. 2, 3, 4
Achim von Arnim (ed.)	1781–1831		
Jakob Grimm	1785–1863	*Der singende Knochen, Von den Machandelboom*	*Das klagende Lied*
Wilhelm Grimm	1786–1859		
Joseph von Eichendorff	1788–1857	[not specified]	*Symphony No. 7
Friedrich Rückert	1788–1866	various collections of poetry	*Rückert* songs, *Kindertotenlieder*
Ludwig Bechstein	1801–1860	*Das klagende Lied*	*Das klagende Lied*
Nikolaus Lenau	1802–1850	'Der Postillion'	*Symphony No. 3
Victor von Scheffel	1826–1886	*Der Trompeter von Säckingen*	*Der Trompeter von Säkkingen*
Richard Leander [Richard von Volkmann]	1830–1889	'Frühlingsmorgen' 'Erinnerung'	Early songs
Friedrich Nietzsche	1844–1900	'Das trunkne Lied' from *Also sprach Zarathustra*	Symphony No. 3
Gustav Mahler	**1860–1911**		*Das klagende Lied, Lieder eines fahrenden Gesellen*

[a] The attribution to Hrabanus Maurus is disputed. Mahler believed this text to be by Francis of Assisi; see letter to Friedrich Löhr from July 1906 in GMB2, p. 333.
*programmatic reference

the bourgeoisie. As these topics grew more common, there emerged, too, a sense of conflict between one's inner urges and the dictates of society. The growing political assertiveness of the middle class after the social uprisings of 1848 and the advances of technology and industry no doubt played a part in the growing influence on literature of societal issues, practical concerns, the role of the state, and the individual's experience of these factors. German 'naturalist' literature took up these themes and, in the materialist spirit of the times, began moving towards a world-view devoid of transcendence. Exploring 'reality' opened up a new awareness of the dark recesses of the human psyche, neuroses, sexual pathology, the hypocrisy of society, morality and the limits of acceptable behaviour. To be sure, there were also authors who sought to resist these implications at the end of the century. Some saw the timeless values of a glorious past tinged with a nationalist or religious ethos as a bulwark against the chaos of the present, some resigned in bitter-sweet recollection, still others responded with a renewed search for beauty.

Virtually no one, however, returned to the ideals of the romantic past, a fact that Mahler himself well recognized. This helps explain a notable absence of the writers of his own generation among the authors Mahler admired. Richard Dehmel (1863–1920) and Stefan George (1868–1933), for example, whose texts inspired many a musical work at the turn of the century, show up nowhere on Mahler's reading list. Absent, too, are numerous prominent contemporaries in Vienna, such as Arthur Schnitzler (1862–1931), Karl Kraus (1874–1936), Hugo von Hofmannsthal (1874–1929), and Hermann Bahr (1863–1934), all of whom lived in the same city and, remarkably enough, had virtually no contact with him. Mahler's avoidance was hardly accidental, as evident in his sarcastic references to 'Maeterlinck's dreary, tipsy thoughts inspired by cheap liquor' and 'Bierbaum's tavern humour',[20] or in forbidding Alma to read Oscar Wilde[21] and calling Gerhard Hauptmann's *Das Friedenfest* 'a dreadfully realistic thing'.[22] The literary avant-garde of the turn of the century, whether engaged in realism, naturalism, modernism or other currents of the time, tended to focus on issues that lay far from Mahler's preoccupations as a composer and thinker. The social criticism, sexuality, sensual perception and other earthly topics that often served as the mainstay of artistic production, fell beneath Mahler's standards of what was considered worthy of such treatment.[23] To him, such pursuits amounted to an absorption in the petty cares of daily existence that lacked seriousness, suitability of content, and often even the requisite craftsmanship: 'This prattle of the moderns that art does not need the highest skill in its execution is completely senseless. On the contrary, such a thorough-going application of all artistic means is needed from the main sketch to the last details of completion of an artwork in a manner that these gentlemen Naturalists – Impotentists! – have never even dreamed of.'[24]

There was not a little irony in this, as many of these 'modernists' harboured a profound admiration for Mahler. Hauptmann, for one, noted in his diary upon meeting the composer: 'Made the acquaintance of Gustav Mahler yesterday. Outstanding mind. Demonic force of nature. Stamp of great genius unmistakable.'[25] Schnitzler praised him in very similar tones: 'In the face of such great works I do not so much have the feeling: This is a greater artist than I am, – rather: This is an artist; I am not.'[26] While acknowledging such acclaim, Mahler at bottom felt very isolated and intellectually far removed from his contemporaries. In a letter to Alma he writes: 'I have always struggled to be understood, appreciated by my equals, even if I don't end up finding them in my lifetime'.[27]

The philosophical debate

Mahler's critique of such artists – in their choice of topic and in their unwillingness to grapple with what he considered the larger issues – helps us position the composer in the philosophical debate at the end of the nineteenth century. Once again, Mahler's intellectual isolation comes to the fore. At this time, German philosophy was characterized by a fundamental conflict between materialism and idealism, a conflict one can trace back at least in part to the writings of Immanuel Kant (1724–1804) a century earlier. In his investigations of what we can know, Kant drew a primal distinction between the objects of the world as they appear to us on the one hand and the true nature of those objects (the thing-in-itself) on the other. In laymen's terms, a distinction between the material and the ideal realm. Kant's *Critique of Pure Reason* (1781) served as an admonition against serious inquiry into this second sphere as humans could never, properly speaking, acquire knowledge of matters metaphysical. Though it denied the possibility of transcendental inquiry, Kant's epistemology nevertheless posited the existence of an ideal world, a point not overlooked by romantic philosophers a few decades later. Friedrich Wilhelm Schelling (1775–1854), for instance, saw the divide between nature and spirit bridged by the creative artist, whose works constituted a revelation of inner being in its truest form. Especially after the mid-nineteenth century, this transcendental philosophy stood in ever sharper contrast to the principles of natural science. Notable advances in scientific inquiry had led many thinkers to conclude that a materialist view of existence was perfectly capable of describing the universe and its behaviour, that with observation, theoretical models, and verifiability, it was not necessary to seek an ultimate rationale beyond the world of objects. The radical sensualism of Ludwig Feuerbach (1804–72), for instance, argued that the world of experience represented the sum total of reality, that the metaphysical urges apparent in idealism and religion were but a human yearning for immortality, an *a priori*, and thus unfounded, projection.[28]

The pre-eminence of the materialist stance among the cultural elite helps explain the artistic concerns of the avant-garde at the turn of the century as well as Mahler's resistance to these tendencies. It would be wrong, however, to conclude that the composer simply refused to consider their position. Mahler's unruly spirit and inexhaustible curiosity about the world around him led him on a constant search through the gamut of philosophical speculation, including a significant foray later in life into the realm of science:

> Up to the end of his first creative period he was a true Romantic, relating to joys and sorrows, nature and God, in the most subjective possible manner. Now, he tried his hardest to be objective ... The man who fashioned this terrifying musical image of a world without God [the Sixth Symphony] had begun searching for God in books. He had lost Him in the world, which appeared to him increasingly mysterious and gloomy. Where was this God whose gaze he had sometimes met? Previously he had searched for him in Spinoza, Plotinus, and other philosophers and mystics. He now moved on to scientists, and to browsing among biological works, seeking in the cell that which eluded him in the universe.[29]

Mahler tackled this new approach with characteristic vigour, reading and even commenting on recent developments in physics.[30] Nevertheless it is revealing that, while genuinely interested in such advances, Mahler did not let the plausibility of scientific and materialist approaches to existence stand as sufficient explanations for the inner workings of the universe.[31] Instead, in his choice of authors and in his interpretation of their works, he searched for a middle ground. One of his favourite books, *Die Geschichte des Materialismus* (1866) by Friedrich Albert Lange (1828–75), was a tract that allowed scientific explanation as a mode of representation while denying it its ultimate sufficiency with regard to consciousness and spirit. Significantly, Mahler's interests in other philosophers of the time reflected precisely this same syncretistic mindset. The likes of Gustav Theodor Fechner (1801–87), Hermann Lotze (1817–81) and Eduard von Hartmann (1842–1906) – all of whom Mahler read with great enthusiasm – argued for the validity of scientific inquiry while positioning these findings in the realm of appearances behind which lay a deeper, more essential reality. The writings of these late idealists rescued the concept of spirit without denying positivist science and further validated Mahler's larger artistic-philosophic mission.

Mahler's need to address the thinking of his day also applied to literature. Despite a tendency to favour authors of the early nineteenth century, he did not dismiss more recent work categorically. One contemporary he particularly admired was Peter Rosegger (1843–1918), author of numerous tales drawn from the timeless wisdom of the folk.[32] Two further examples can be found in Leo Tolstoy (1828–1910) and Fedor Dostoyevsky (1821–81), Russian writers who lent great impetus to the German naturalist movement with their critique of society and careful examination of the human psyche. For all of their hardened realism, both writers were, however, like Mahler, unwilling to relinquish the notion of redemption, a force beyond daily existence that might save us from the human predicament or lend meaning to our strivings.[33] It is perhaps revealing that Mahler's enthusiasm for yet another founder of the naturalist movement, Henrik Ibsen (1828–1906), was notably cooler. While recognizing *Peer Gynt* as a great work, Mahler otherwise referred to the playwright as exercising a negative influence.[34] Mahler also managed to keep an open mind where he suspected true ability. His less than enthusiastic response to *Dorian Gray* by Oscar Wilde (1854–1900) did not prevent him from attending *The Importance of Being Earnest* a few years later and finding it very witty.[35] Wilde's *Salome* likewise stymied him, but he had no trouble conceding having learned much about it from Strauss's opera.[36] A further example of Mahler's receptiveness to recent literature can be found in *Frühlings Erwachen*, a scandalously modern play by Frank Wedekind (1864–1918) about the awakening of sexual awareness among a group of ill-fated teenagers. Mahler attended the first production of the work in Berlin directed by Max Reinhardt with Wedekind in the cast; he was surprised at his own rather positive reception of the work, but also wondered aloud what might have become of this talented writer in different company.[37]

Philosophy and music

Ultimately, many of Mahler's interests in the world of ideas found their reflection in his musical compositions. As we have seen, a vital component of his self-understanding as a composer lay in art's claim to a vital perception of truth, one that for him occupied the same epistemological sphere as religion or science. Thus, his speculations as an intellectual were inextricably bound to his artistic activities in the common task of unravelling the essence of life itself. This intermingling of philosophy and music helps to explain the world-embracing ambitions of his symphonies as well as the prominent use of texts in many of these works; the frequent programmes, movement titles, Lied quotations, and vocal passages provide verbal indications of the composer's musico-philosophic aims.

To shed light on the intricacies of the interaction between text and musical gesture and to see how Mahler's literary preferences resurface in his musical thinking, let us take a closer look at the Second Symphony.[38] The massive Finale of this work paints a vast canvas of redemption, echoing a reassurance of life after death proclaimed by a large choir to words ostensibly by Friedrich Klopstock but largely penned by Mahler himself:[39]

Auferstehn', ja auferstehn' wirst du,	Rise again, yes you shall rise again,
Mein Staub, nach kurzer Ruh!	My dust, after a short rest!
Unsterblich Leben! Unsterblich Leben!	Life immortal! Life immortal!
Wird der dich rief dir geben.	Will grant you he who called you.

Here the redemptive gesture could hardly find a more explicit rendering than in Mahler's adaptation of Christian symbology.[40]

Preceding this grand closing gesture stands a movement of deep personal faith, a song for alto and orchestra entitled 'Urlicht' ('Primeval Light') that invokes the soul's desire to return to God. Tellingly, these aspirations are met with a grave challenge before giving way to warmth and radiance at its close:

Ach nein! Ich ließ mich nicht abweisen!	But no! I did not let myself get turned away!
Ich bin von Gott und will wieder zu Gott!	I am of God and want to return to God!
Der liebe Gott wird mir ein Lichtchen geben,	The dear Lord will give me a lantern,
Wird leuchten mir bis in das ewig selig Leben!	Will light my way to eternal, blessed life!

Mahler's literary source for this personal testament is revealing. As in other symphonic movements and in many of his songs, Mahler turned to a collection of German folk poetry published in three volumes by Achim von Arnim and Clemens Brentano in 1806 and 1808 entitled *Des Knaben Wunderhorn*. While it might seem counterintuitive that the composer would find appropriate texts for some of his largest and most ambitious symphonies in poems of such direct simplicity, this is precisely what he felt he needed: 'I have committed myself utterly and with complete awareness to the type and tone of this poetry (which distinguishes itself considerably from every other type of "literary poetry" and could almost be more properly called nature and life – that is, the source of all poetry – than art)'.[41]

This unmediated, naïve expression of ages-old wisdom rang far truer to Mahler that the prettified or sophisticated verses of art poetry.[42] The immediate and almost mystical source of meaning appealed to Mahler's concern for communicating a profound message.

While Mahler holds out the promise of eternal life in the final two movements, transcendence does not come without a bitter struggle. His strategy here, as in so many of his symphonies, takes us to the heights of deliverance only after a crisis of faith. To complicate matters, it is a crisis that comes to us with a smile on its face, a jest that only gradually reveals its horrible message. The innocuous-sounding bearer of bad tidings, the Scherzo, includes, in this case, a lengthy instrumental quotation of another *Wunderhorn* Lied. The song 'Des Antonius von Padua Fischpredigt' ('Saint Anthony of Padua's Sermon to the Fishes'), parodies a light-hearted country dance, the Ländler, while telling the story of a preaching saint:

Antonius zur Predigt	Anthony goes to preach
die Kirche find't ledig!	and finds the church empty!
Er geht du den Flüssen	He goes to the rivers
und predigt den Fischen!	and preaches to the fishes!
. . .	. . .
Die Predigt geendet,	Once the sermon is over,
ein Jeder sich wendet!	each one goes back.
Die Hechte bleiben Diebe,	The pike stay thieves,
die Aale viel lieben,	the eels amorous,
die Predigt hat g'fallen,	the sermon was pleasing,
sie bleiben wie Allen!	they all stay the same!

The unsung text lurking behind the symphonic movement casts a disturbing shadow on the promise of resurrection to follow. More than highlighting the comical scene, the seemingly humorous tone mocks the fruitless attempts of the holy man to awaken a sense of ethical behaviour in the animals that have congregated at his feet. Predictably, these creatures forget the pious message as soon as the sermon is over, revealing the disturbing gap between religion and the amoral machinations of the natural world. Ridiculing the saint and his hopeless enterprise calls into question the very articles of faith that Mahler articulates in bringing the symphony to its affirmative close.

The sardonic humour very much in evidence here served Mahler as a vehicle for capturing the hopelessness of human enterprise. Such bittersweet commentary on one's own attempts at coming to terms with the meaning of life held a special place for Mahler, a type of 'decontamination of life by means of the humour of the tragedy of human existence'.[43] Indeed, there are many literary references capturing this combination of the ridiculous and the sublime from among Mahler's favourite authors, most prominently the romantic generation of the early nineteenth century, who, despite holding an idealist world-view, took a far from naïvely innocent view of reality. These writers frequently did their best to project a subjective perspective on life full of the doubts and contradictions of the individual psyche. The techniques employed by E. T. A. Hoffmann and Jean Paul, for instance, include scrupulous attention to banal detail, ridiculous situations, insertion of extraneous information, and wry comments on human nature. The end result, often humorous and bewildering, conjures up the instability and confusions of an unreliable subject and an inconsistent world. The text enacts contradiction and, like so much of Mahler's music, becomes a cipher for the ineffable, volatile phenomena it is trying to capture.

We can return briefly to the Second Symphony for another example of textual reference, this time of a far more directly philosophical nature. In a sketch to the first movement Mahler marks a subsidiary theme that appears for the first time at bar 129 (rehearsal 8) 'Meeresstille'. While perhaps suggesting Goethe's poem of the same name or Mendelssohn's overture,[44] a much more likely candidate upon closer inspection is Schopenhauer's *Die Welt als Wille und Vorstellung*, one of Mahler's favourite books. Schopenhauer's philosophy of life revolved around the concept of an essence fundamental to all forms of existence that he called the 'Will'. Like all manifestations in the material world, humans are enchained to this primal force and subject to the blind pursuit of life; it is this blindness that prevents most of humanity from attaining oneness with the universe, a state of being reserved only for artists of genius and individuals capable of abnegating the will and thus dissolving their individual selves. Schopenhauer describes this latter state in the closing pages of his book:[45]

> But we now turn our glance from our own needy and perplexed nature
> to those who have overcome the world, in whom the will, having reached
> complete self-knowledge, has found itself again in everything, and then
> freely denied itself ... Then, instead of the restless pressure and effort;
> instead of the constant transition from desire to apprehension and from joy
> to sorrow ... we see that peace that is higher than all reason, that ocean-like
> calmness [*Meeresstille*] of the spirit, that deep tranquillity, that unshakable
> confidence and serenity, whose mere reflection in the countenance, as
> depicted by Raphael and Correggio, is a complete and certain gospel.
> Only knowledge remains; the will has vanished.[46]

In Mahler's symphony the passage in question seems an island of serenity in this unruly movement, a glimpse of transcendent peace in a score that Mahler explicitly described as a representation of the struggles of life and the questions we must pose about the meaning of mortality.[47]

The Second Symphony and virtually all of his works are fraught with an awe for existence and a deep awareness of its fragile nature. True to Mahler's misgivings, the imminence of tragedy looms large in his music, hope aspires to redemption in the face of annihilation. With relentless honesty, Mahler unmasks his most intimate hopes while simultaneously unleashing the doubts that threaten to pull him under.[48] Though most symphonies attain transcendence in the end, they do so only after a bitter struggle and a mockery of the grand gesture, ultimately calling into question the validity of the entire project. These works are less about the overcoming tentatively achieved in the finale than the crisis that precedes it, less about the answers that console than the questions that both fascinate and horrify.

There is far more to say about the thinker lurking behind the composer in Mahler. Fundamental to any such consideration, however, is the seeming paradox that bridges the gap between the persistent idealism of the composer's world-view and the prophetic quality of his artistic achievement. As we have seen, Mahler generally favoured literary and philosophical sources from an earlier age and, resisting the thinking of many of his contemporaries, refused to accept the notion of a material world devoid of spirit:

> Actually I cannot understand how it comes that you – with a musician-poet's soul – do not believe = [and] know. What is it then that delights you when you hear music? What makes you light-hearted and free? Is the world less puzzling if you build it out of matter? Is there any explanation to be got from you seeing it as an interplay of mechanical forces? What is force, energy? *Who* does the playing? You believe in the 'conservation of energy', in the indestructibility of matter. Is that not immortality too? Shift the problem to any plane you choose – in the end you will always reach the point where 'your philosophy' begins to 'dream'.[49]

While this position may at first seem to echo an outdated world-view, Mahler's music was not born of a reactionary attempt to impose the simplicity of a bygone era onto the confusions of the present.[50] Far more, in grappling with the materialist perspective of his contemporaries Mahler sensed insufficiencies that he could only partially overcome, trapped, as it were, in an artistic mission torn between conviction and dread. By embracing precisely the dilemma that arose from his fervent need to invest life with deep significance, Mahler laid bare a compelling and often frightening landscape of the soul. The fractured self, the incomprehensibility of the cosmos, the implications of a godless universe – the topics and expressive gestures of Mahler's art anticipated the concerns of generations to come.

3 Music and aesthetics: the programmatic issue

VERA MICZNIK

Evaluating a composer's aesthetics of music and its relation to programmes is fraught with difficulties, not least because the historical meaning of aesthetics as a discipline has undergone changes since its early, 1750 definition by Alexander Baumgarten: 'Aesthetics (a theory of liberal arts, of inferior mode of knowledge, the art of beautiful thinking, in a way analogous to thinking about reason [logic]), is the science of sensual cognition'.[1] It was thus conceived as a philosophical category denoting the knowledge of the beautiful through the senses (a lower form of knowledge than logic, which deals with intellectual concepts). By the middle of the nineteenth century, as universalist philosophical aesthetic theories distanced themselves from professional criticism, the demise of the metaphysics of the beautiful became inevitable. Music criticism which centred more directly on the musical works themselves, and addressed more practical questions of knowledge and meaning was able to come closer to elucidating the inner workings of music, and thus became more influential in the aesthetic tastes of the time. This situation was recognized by none other than Eduard Hanslick, the aesthetician of 'absolute music' when he wrote in 1854: 'Formerly, the aesthetic principles of the various arts were supposed to be governed by some supreme metaphysical principle of general aesthetics. Now, however, the conviction is daily growing that each individual art can be understood only by studying its technical limits and inherent nature.'[2]

Adorno situates this distancing of the fundamental theoretical problems of aesthetics from the specific, more concrete studies of art later in the century, in Benedetto Croce's introduction of 'radical nominalism into aesthetic theory',[3] while Carl Dahlhaus also states that the metaphysical foundation of aesthetics 'came to an end around 1900, surrendering its constituent parts to historical studies or philosophy of history, to technology or psychology of art', only to be revived again in the 1920s in a new, phenomenological, incarnation.[4]

A possible resistance to the notion that philosophical aesthetic ideas may underline Mahler's works has not deterred critics' interest in exploring these relationships. An overview of the main nineteenth-century philosophical and aesthetic trends cited as having a possible impact on Mahler is summarized below.

[35]

Aesthetic theories

Early nineteenth-century German aesthetics had praised 'absolute' instrumental music's emancipation from imitation of passions or language, placing music above all other arts for its ability to 'signify' on its own with no reference to the real world, in a general, 'immeasurable', 'realm of the infinite'.[5] Among its representative figures, Mahler admired Jean Paul Richter and E. T. A. Hoffmann, whose irony and sense of humour became part of his musical language,[6] while Hegel's aesthetics did not seem to preoccupy him, perhaps due to the philosopher's favouring of vocal music over the imprecision of pure instrumental music because 'a text provides . . . definite conceptions and thereby rescues consciousness from that dreamier element of feeling without concepts'.[7]

Whether directly influenced by Schopenhauer, or only through his philosopher friend Siegfried Lipiner and later through Nietzsche's philosophy, we know that Mahler read and admired his work.[8] Schopenhauer's aesthetic conception, somewhat like that of the early romantics, considered that music articulates the 'innermost nature of the world' – the will – without the mediation of reason, ideas or representation: 'unlike all other arts . . . [music] acts directly on the will, that is, on a listener's emotions, passions, and affections, quickly elevating and transforming them'.[9] Because of this, music stands highest among the arts, and even higher than philosophy which is only 'translating into concepts and words what music says intuitively'.[10] It is very likely that some of Mahler's statements, such as 'the important question [is] *how*, or perhaps even *why*, music should ever be explained in words at all' might have been influenced by Schopenhauer.[11]

Mahler's early fascination with Wagner's ideas has been widely discussed.[12] Wagner's aesthetic theory in *Music and Drama* displayed some similarities to Hegel's, in that his proposed union of music and dramatic text within the new concept of 'music drama' aimed precisely at an ideal balance between feeling and understanding which he considered to be missing from each of the two media in separation. Though his symphonic conception of music drama relied on a profound recognition of the practices and meanings of 'absolute' instrumental music, his need to fertilize it with the textual component removes him from absolute music adherents. It was only later, through reading Schopenhauer, and in the context of *Tristan und Isolde* and the essay *The Music of the Future*, that he modified his views to promote the supremacy of music, thus giving back to music its 'metaphysical dignity'.[13]

The philosopher Friedrich Nietzsche, whose writings Mahler certainly knew,[14] shared Wagner's interest in Greek tragedy and, in the years between *Tristan* and *Parsifal*, his love for Schopenhauer. Like Schopenhauer,

Nietzsche had great disdain for programmatic or illustrative music which he articulated in his early philosophical work *The Birth of Tragedy* of 1872: 'music itself in its absolute sovereignty does not *need* the image and the concept, but merely *endures* them as accompaniments'.[15] Although he renounced both Wagner and Schopenhauer later in life, Nietzsche's position on the superiority of 'absolute' music never wavered, and as late as 1887, in *The Will to Power*, he again expressed his scorn for words in relation to music: 'Compared with music all communication by words is shameless'.[16]

Despite the above, we might agree with Adorno's statement that, at least by Mahler's time, there was a 'fundamental difficulty, indeed impossibility, of gaining general access to art by means of a system of philosophical categories'.[17] The general philosophical aesthetic theories, rather than influencing directly the making and the reception of music, would have left their imprint on the aesthetic debates of the time in a different way, through more concrete and practical discussions of musical works and tastes voiced by musicians and critics themselves. One of the most influential late nineteenth-century manifestations of this mutation from universalist philosophical aesthetics to nominalist debates focused on how particular works produce meaning, was the politically partisan debate in the public music critical arena between the representatives of 'absolute' versus 'programme' music.

The remainder of this chapter will attempt to unravel the issues involved in the evaluation of Mahler's apparent inclinations towards absolute or programmatic music positions as articulated in the reception history of his works, through an examination of this reception and through readings of the music. Rather than provide an answer or side with one solution or another, I will suggest ways of broaching the issue – calling on theoretical ideas from literary criticism and semiotics – which accommodate Mahler's and his own contemporaries' beliefs (insofar as they are recoverable), as well as today's more relativistic approach to truth and evidence in aesthetics and semantics. Such a multi-textual approach to 'the case of Mahler' is intended to advance the understanding not only of his music, but also of the different ways of thinking critically about the relationship between music, programmes and historical evidence.

'Programme' versus 'absolute music'

Amongst the most ardent promoters of the theory of programme music, Franz Liszt and his music historian acolyte Franz Brendel postulated, like Wagner, that instrumental music had reached an impasse because it lacked the ability to communicate 'precise ideas'. Liszt proposed that a verbal programme attached to his symphonic poems would restore the 'poetic' dimension to 'absolute music', the definition of ideas which the composer wanted to communicate through his music.[18] To a certain extent this theory returned music to the position of an incomplete art in need of extra-musical textual ideas to make itself understood. Countering this and other theories which distrusted the ability of music to signify on its own, and more concretely than in the 'spiritual realm of the infinite' propounded by earlier metaphysical idealists such as E. T. A. Hoffmann, Hanslick's *On The Beautiful in Music* resituated the essence of music in pure 'musical sound in motion' (melody, harmony, rhythm),[19] thus encouraging a reappraisal of the symphony as an autonomous instrumental genre in the 1870s.

The historical and critical assessment of Mahler's works cannot be understood outside the prevailing late nineteenth-century paradigmatic dichotomy of 'programme' versus 'absolute' music, which by the 1880s had become so entrenched that Mahler and Richard Strauss were seen, rightly or wrongly, as situated on opposite sides of the debate.[20] Influenced by this situation, critics and scholars have long been obsessed by the thorny issue of classifying Mahler's aesthetic beliefs and his music as either 'absolute' or 'programmatic'. Sides taken within this dichotomy have varied throughout the generations, and continue to be negotiated even today. There is good reason for this: 'the case of Mahler' presents us with one of the most complex networks of corroborating and contradictory musical, aesthetic and documentary evidence, as well as misinformation, which – depending on when and by whom it is interpreted – have led to a wide variety of conclusions. When the complexity of this problem is acknowledged, it provides grounds for fruitful discussion and ingenious interpretations. Donald Mitchell's recent statement, for example, that (during the 'Wunderhorn' Years (1888–1901)) 'the tension generated by Mahler trying to pursue two opposed ideologies simultaneously, one dedicated to the path of the symphonic poem, to the programmatic idea, the other to the path, the tradition, of "symphony", unpolluted by programmatic affiliations or associations',[21] at least recognizes the antinomy of the problem, even if it does not provide a solution. But alongside such thoughtful attempts to come to terms with the issue, one unfortunately still encounters unqualified statements such as 'Mahler's symphonies are long, complex, and programmatic', which instead of clarification, promote further confusion.[22]

Perhaps in asking whether Mahler's music is 'absolute' or programmatic' we are asking the wrong question, since this polemic, as Carl Dahlhaus has pointed out, is rather academic, and belongs to the ideology of reception.[23] A better path of discovery might be to pursue the question of why and how this whole issue became so much more crucial to the interpretation of Mahler's thought and works than to that of other contemporary composers. Perhaps it is possible to understand from 'the case of Mahler' that the so-called objective proofs invoked in supporting historical or aesthetic questions – the documentary evidence including letters to critics, Natalie Bauer-Lechner's recollections, Alma's writings, suppressed programmes, inscriptions on the scores, and Mahler's text-based symphonies – shape our questions in the first place. In other words, had Mahler not left behind the wealth of verbal simulacra of his thoughts, but only non-texted music, we would not have asked the same questions and in the same ways. Recognizing and addressing this issue not simply as a paradox, but as a productive act in the hermeneutic circle,[24] according to which we must go back and forth between evidence and the interpretation of the text, will certainly lead to a closer elucidation of the relationship between production and reception.

In approaching this subject, most Mahler scholars have employed a positivistic historicist methodology which privileges gaining knowledge and 'truth' about a work through 'recapturing' as accurately as possible the composer's views, and the contemporaneous cultural context, facts, comments and situations. Aside from the paradoxical illusion that there is only one truth to be recaptured, the initial problem of this is that the cultural, ideological, political conditions perceived to exist at a certain moment in time, while often influential, are not related to the artist and the work of art in a deterministic, causal fashion; rather, when translated through human subjectivity into an artistic medium, they can manifest themselves in the most unexpected configurations. Secondly, the statements made by composers or their contemporaries can be contradictory, and hence, depending on which sources one reads, the ensuing conclusions may support opposite sides of an argument. Thirdly, aesthetic and musical interpretations are historically contingent practices, that is, they are founded on yet further sets of intersubjective assumptions and conventions of the interpreters that should be taken into consideration. For these and many other reasons, the notion of 'truth' needs to be challenged, and countered with the recognition that every statement owes its explanation at least in part to the contextual or contingent status of both the person who made the statement and of the reader/scholar who interprets it: in other words, to both parties' competence and contextual paradigms. Readings of contemporary 'evidence' might give us some valuable information about what Mahler himself and other people thought publicly of his music, about his and his contemporaries' conception of 'absolute' or 'programmatic' aesthetics, but will not tell us 'the truth' about Mahler's music or indicate a precise way of interpreting it. Ultimately, as Adorno observed, 'truth content – quality – does not fall prey to historicism. History is immanent to artworks.'[25] Mahler inscribed his historical moment and aesthetic position in the music, and the only way that we can get closer to its understanding is by reading (interpreting) critically both the evidence and the music.

Assessing the evidence

Because of the absolute-programme-music dichotomy, some of the earliest critical reactions to the unusual musical characteristics of Mahler's works presumed the existence of underlying, suppressed programmes. Typical in this respect were, for example, the reactions of the Swiss critic William Ritter to Felix Weingartner's performance of Mahler's ostensibly non-programmatic Fourth Symphony in Munich on 25 November 1901: 'The first movement could be Daniel in the lions' den, Orpheus slaughtered by the Maenads ... It's nothing but acrobatics and the performance of a lady in tights in a menagerie';[26] or that of the *Allgemeine Zeitung* critic referring to the Finale of the Symphony: 'The grotesquely comic means something in the theatre, but, in a symphony, it must at least be justified by a precise programme'.[27] So affected by the controversy were those times that both Strauss, the paradigmatic representative of programme music, and Mahler, who claimed not to belong to that trend, ended up defending 'purely musical logic'.[28] Even Hanslick, the doyen of 'absolute music', contaminated by this same debate, read programmes in Tchaikovsky's *Pathétique* Symphony, although none had been provided by the composer. Yet, unlike Ritter, he was grateful that 'the composer lets the music speak for itself and prefers to leave us guessing rather than force a laid-out course upon himself and us'.[29]

The contradictory evidence Mahler left behind, especially his obvious vacillation about programmes transmitted through sources of varying reliability, contributed to the confusion over his 'absolute' or 'programmatic' stance. Despite the programmes that Mahler provided for the early symphonies, the first biographical-analytical studies, such as, for example, that by Ludwig Schiedermair (written under the composer's supervision), make clear that Mahler wanted to promote himself as a composer of 'absolute music'. Schiedermair certainly echoes Mahler's wish to be presented as such when he comments 'To believe that Mahler wanted to put down precise facts in his works amounts to misunderstanding the composer entirely'.[30] On the other hand, as Peter Franklin has recently pointed out, 'Insufficient attention has perhaps been paid to the corresponding strength of his [Mahler's] public commitment *to* programmaticism during the same period'.[31] Franklin, like many others, rightly emphasizes the opposite kind of evidence: the numerous programme outlines for the early symphonies that Mahler promoted to his friends and to critics, as well as all the titles and inscriptions found on his early autograph manuscripts, which together seem to support Mahler's alleged reliance on programmes. However, can evidence alone provide answers to this dilemma?

The reception of Mahler's First Symphony will demonstrate both the beginnings of certain interpretive trends and the mercurial way in which evidence was construed. At its première on 20 November 1889 in Budapest, after having referred to the piece as 'a symphonic work' or 'symphony',[32] Mahler performed it with a generic title: 'Symphonic Poem in two parts', wherein four out of the then five movements simply bore tempo indications, while only one, the Funeral march, was labelled 'À la pompes funèbres'.[33] In an attempt to clarify Mahler's attitude towards the fashionable topic of programme music, the preview in the local newspaper *Pester Lloyd* by the critic Kornél Ábrányi (father), which, according to La Grange, must have been written in consultation with Mahler, explains the differences between 'pure music', 'programme music' and 'dramatic music'.[34] The author places Mahler somewhat beyond these categories, emphasizing that he expresses ' "impressions" and "passions" which create an entirely personal spiritual world' which 'contains everything, from naive illusion to doubt and skepticism'. Like Mozart, the writer assesses, this spiritual world reaches an 'absolute purification and liberation', and like Schumann, Mahler attains to 'resignation' and an 'objective conception of the world which protects him against all the vicissitudes of life'. Despite establishing a non-programmatic context for the work, Ábrányi provides some quite general programmatic suggestions prompted by the music itself, using images and concepts, in a Schopenhauerian or Nietzschean sense, that remain within the more general language associated with 'absolute' music rather than prescriptions of how the music would have been composed: the title of the Symphonic Poem could simply be *Life*, since it illustrates all aspects of existence, from the 'rosy clouds of youth' of the first movement, the tragedy that bursts forth in the fourth movement 'The Hunter's Funeral', to the Finale's 'victory' in 'philosophical resignation', 'eternal truth' and 'harmony'.

In the review written for the *Pester Lloyd after* the performance, August Beer manages to read in some detail the rich and diverse musical meanings communicated by each movement's musical topoi, through which he characterizes the two parts of the 'Symphonic Poem' indicated by Mahler from the outset: he hears the general 'pastoral, idyllic mood' of the first three movements, consisting of 'a poetic forest scene, a fanciful serenade', and 'a merry wedding roundelay', followed by the second part, outlining a 'funeral march and a Finale of high drama'.[35] Even though it criticizes the 'formlessness' of the first movement and the Finale, insofar as this interpretation relies mostly on the critic's perception of what Mahler might have attempted to communicate through his musical materials, and does not claim a programme where the composer did not supply one, it gives a convincing account of the music's meanings through conventionalized musical topics that we might agree with even today. However, the one 'substantial fact' for which he reproaches Mahler is that 'the work lacks a unifying underlying note'. He writes:

> Even in a symphonic poem, although it permits of incomparably greater freedom in form and layout, we require the music to be self-contained and to show a corresponding tendency for a specific train of thought to predominate, whether this be the illustration of a poetic idea, or a sequence of mental and physical events standing in a causal relationship to each other.

He sees a 'large gap' between the first three-movement section and the last two movements, and thus suggests that 'Mahler's composition gives the impression that a programme for this music was only subsequently projected' which 'serves to close ... [this] gap'.[36] One can see here that Mahler's mere mention of the genre of symphonic poem created generic expectations; its lack of unity, therefore, is blamed on the absence of a satisfactory programme. No such demands would have been required from a five-movement symphony, whose movements would not have been necessarily expected to tell a coherent story. But once started in the direction of the programmatic proposition, it is not surprising that for subsequent performances Mahler became caught into providing more and more programmatic details, such as associating the Symphony with Jean Paul's novel *Titan*.[37]

    More attentive readings of the above evidence also point out the ways in which the theory of 'music as autobiography' developed early on, partly because of the prevalent nineteenth-century view that works of art reflected their author's feelings and state of mind, and partly as an alternative in support of Mahler's anti-programmatic stance. In the absence of a programme at the time, Ábrányi's proposition that Mahler's Symphonic Poem was a statement about the composer's 'entirely personal spiritual world', about 'Life' which 'contains everything, from naive illusions to doubt and skepticism' could easily be linked with the composer's later comments which served as the basis for further interpretations of his music as 'autobiographical'. The famous remark Mahler made to Natalie Bauer-Lechner that 'My two symphonies [First and Second] contain the inner aspect of my whole life; I have written into them with my own blood everything that I have experienced and endured – Truth and Poetry in music ... Creativity and experience are so intimately linked for me'[38] as well as many similar affirmations that life experiences and composition are connected (for example, 'Only when I experience

something do I compose, and only when composing do I experience'[39])
have led to interpretations of Mahler's music as programmatic in a different
way – as portraying his life experiences. These statements form the basis not
only for Richard Specht's theory of Mahler's music as autobiography,
applied even to the later works,[40] but also for today's similar arguments,
such as, for example, Stephen Hefling's with regard to Mahler's Ninth
Symphony.[41] Yet knowing how these statements originated might suggest
alternative readings. Mahler's likening of his 'musical autobiography' with
Goethe's *Dichtung und Wahrheit* could be interpreted as his acknowledgment that, just as Goethe's ambiguous title blurs the line between reality
and fiction, or draws attention to the impossibility of separating the reality
of an artist's life from his creation, his own works (and perhaps those of
other composers) relate only fictionally to life experiences. Furthermore,
Mahler made numerous comments to critics *discouraging* them from
making any association between the music's meanings and extra-musical
situations:

> I should regard my work as a complete failure if I felt it necessary to give
> men like yourself even the slightest indication of the emotional trend of the
> work . . . The parallelism between life and music may go deeper and further
> than one is at present capable of realizing. – However, I am far from
> requiring everyone to follow me in this. I gladly leave the interpretation
> of details to each listener's imagination.[42]

The contradictory nature of such 'metaphorical hints' of 'what [the
composer] sought to manifest musically'[43] suggests that they should
carry no more 'objective' authoritative power in relation to the creative
process than other interpretive strategies we might use for reading
Mahler's mind and his music.

   Finally, it is surprising that of all the attempts to explain the 'incomprehensible' meanings of Mahler's symphonies through the palpability
of the linguistic medium (programmes, score inscriptions or letters), the
contribution to programmatic meanings of those verbal hints that would
have been closest to the music – the texts of the songs he used in the first
four symphonies – has been insufficiently discussed.[44] An interpretation
of how the verbal content of the songs might have been 'translated' and
incorporated into the music, and then transmitted, at least in part,
through the new symphonic medium is, indeed, complex. Yet in the
First Symphony, the first movement's 'programmatic' ideas of 'nature',
youth and walking are all present in the musical materials to which the
text 'Ging heut' morgens übers Feld' is set, just as the sarcastic futility of
St Anthony's empty preaching to the fishes captured in the *perpetuum
mobile* of both the melody and the musical accompaniment of Mahler's

Wunderhorn song remains present when the same music is heard instrumentally in the third movement of the Second Symphony. And what better way of communicating textual ideas than through the words of songs such as 'Urlicht', 'O Mensch!', 'Es sungen drei Engel' or 'Das himmlische Leben'? It seems that while searching for his own compositional voice, Mahler was trying to reconcile his attraction towards the simpler, folk-like, alternatively witty, ironic and tragic *Wunderhorn* aesthetic with the serious, grandiose and dramatic tradition of the symphonic genre. Through the inspiration of the song texts as means of musically capturing that world, his method of composition at that stage seemed to involve incorporating those meanings into the song settings and then placing them within the generically distinct symphonic medium, and thus lending them new semantic dimensions. The multi-faceted ways of exploiting or combining the intrinsic musical meanings of these and other referential musical materials constitute the essence of the 'signature' language that Mahler was in the process of creating for himself.

That Mahler was insecure and even uncomfortable at first with this method of composition, however, is demonstrated by his complete unwillingness to reveal the connection between the First Symphony and the *Gesellen* songs, which had already been composed at the time of the Symphony's première but had not been performed in public. One might even surmise that, out of fear of being accused of lack of originality, Mahler's continual efforts to provide new credible programmes for the Symphony could have been designed to distract attention from the actual sources of the musical ideas. It was only when he no longer had a choice, that is, when the songs and the Symphony were performed in the same programme in Berlin on 16 March 1896, that he gave up this symptomatic concealment of the connection and allowed the critic Max Marschalk openly to mention it, although in a letter of 14 January 1897 he still asked Marschalk not to refer to the ' "Fahrenden Gesellen" ' episode of [his] life, since 'the connection with the First Symphony is purely artistic'.[45] In the case of the well-known 'Bruder Martin' tune, however, the quotation technique was laid open: he bluntly quoted the source, counting on people's recognition of the tune and on their inference of meanings of grotesque distortion from the fact that he set it in the minor, scored it for low strings, and transformed it generically from a children's song into a funeral march. The message sent out this way was that it is not the source of inspiration that matters, but what you do with it. The case of the Funeral March showed the public what an elaborated musical meaning can be achieved through the manipulation of material within intramusical systems of reference. It is also at this time that he acknowledged to Marschalk that he was inspired by Moritz von Schwind's woodcut *The*

Hunter's Funeral Procession, while insisting that it was only the 'mood' that was relevant to the understanding of the music.[46] Interestingly it might not be mere coincidence that after the Berlin performance the programmatic titles for the Symphony disappeared.

Despite his careful and consistent dissociation from the representatives of 'programme music' (including his famous speech condemning programmes in 1900[47]), and despite his apparent abandonment of programmes after The Fourth Symphony, Mahler's own vacillation about providing and withdrawing programmes in the early symphonies certainly contributed to the perpetuation of programmatic interpretations of his later symphonies. To be sure, as Franklin notes, he did publicize his programmes, but awareness of the detailed circumstances under which he did that, and of other factors that were more likely to have impinged on the composition process, such as the textual supports, should prevent us from over-emphasizing the role of those programmes in our understanding of the music, and, instead, encourage us to consider them in their precariously dynamic relations with the music. The aesthetic compromise of providing programmes *only* for the early symphonies may be indicative of his temporary insecurity and desire for the recognition and success of his works. This publicity was no longer necessary for the later symphonies once audiences had become more familiar with, and accepting of, his instrumental musical language.

More recent theoretical formulations

Ultimately, the issue of programmes in Mahler's music cannot be clarified without a better critical-theoretical differentiation of the relationship between what Jean-Jacques Nattiez calls the domains of the 'poietic' (the making of the work) and the 'esthesic' (the reception of the work). Dahlhaus, who was among the first musicologists to take this division into account in dealing with the 'programme'-versus-'absolute' aesthetic paradigm, recognized that the two aesthetic positions occupy opposite extremes of a continuum, and articulated a workable distinction between them by placing them in the domain of reception. Thus he stated that 'the reception and aesthetic interpretation of a work must hold to the published text, not to the anecdotal history of origins, which is a composer's private business'.[48] In other words, the question of programmatic versus absolute music does not ask whether the work was conceived programmatically or not, but rather whether or not the composer decided to impose on its reception a certain programmatic reading through attaching an explanatory programme to the public score of an instrumental piece: it is a matter of reception, of what belongs to 'the final text'.

The issue, then, is to distinguish between different kinds of 'program-matic' references according to their place in the 'poietic' (genetic) or 'esthesic' (reception) process, with the understanding that one may or may not be relevant to the other. To the first kind of programmes belong possible (known or unknown) external sources for the composer's inspiration (such as Mahler's later rejected programmes); to the second belong titles, prefaces and programmes that the composer attached to the score to guide the listeners in their perception, as well as interpretive programmes or stories devised freely by recipients from the music to help them articulate the logic of a composition. A third category which falls in between, consists of attempts to match a discovered supposed source of inspiration for the composition of a piece (a moment of genesis) with an analysis of the final piece (which belongs to reception). Here, for instance, stand Hefling's ana-lysis of Mahler's 'programme' for the first movement of the Second Symphony based on Adam Mickiewicz's epic poem *Dziady*,[49] and readings of Mahler's First Symphony according to Jean Paul's novel *Titan*.[50]

A concept from literary theory is pertinent here: Gérard Genette's notion of 'paratext' – 'that which accompanies the text', a 'threshold', an 'undefined zone between the inside and the outside [of the text], a zone without any hard and fast boundary'.[51] In this useful classification of the paratextual categories, programmes would be part of the 'productions' that accompany the text, 'to ensure [the text's] ... "reception" and consumption', while all the genetic documentary information contained in letters, confidences, and implicitly in sketches or inscriptions on the scores, would belong to the 'private epitext', whose participation in the work's 'textuality' needs to be included, yet should not be allowed in hierarchical fashion to suffocate the actual 'text' – the musical or literary work as presented to the public.[52]

More importantly, however, seeing the programme as the 'paratext', as part of a 'package' for 'marketing' the musical text, helps us understand the historical dimension of the idea of 'programme music' in the evaluation of Mahler's works. Insofar as in his time a programme would be given to a critic or would appear in programme notes, it *would* belong to the text Mahler intended for public consumption. Yet insofar as he decided not to include it in the printed score, it no longer belongs to the 'text' that was left to posterity. Thus the 'text' itself has a historical dimension, that is, it changes with the times. This does not mean that the 'text' that Mahler offered to his contemporaries must have a privileged status over the one we are offered – the two can coexist and inform one another. Understood in this way, both the 'inside' and the 'outside' of the text, 'text' and 'context',[53] past and present, participate equally in the network of signs and codes, in the semiosis of the text's production of signification. Textuality is thus a *performance* of the subject who undertakes the task of interpretation.

All context (political, historical, literary, cultural, genetic, and so on) constitutes a layer participating in the process of textualization, and which thus needs to be considered. Variants, annotations, prefaces, sketches, editorial notes all belong to the text. Analysis of the 'clueless' final score no longer concerns itself with only intrinsic explanations, but incorporates knowledge of the private pre-compositional information, the epitext. A textual network could be established as follows for reading the 'story' of the first movement of the First Symphony (see Figure 3.1).

Several intersecting intertextual semiotic codes can be accessed to enlighten its meanings. Similar to that of Raymond Monelle in the case of the fifth movement of the Third Symphony,[54] my approach is to steep the logical formation of the textual codes as firmly as possible in semiosis: that is, in conventional practices that explain how concepts or signifieds can travel from one semiotic field to another, and in tracing back the semiotic processes through which they relate. Whilst accepting the notion of a general textuality in which cultural networks tease one another out, and ideas float back and forth in heuristic play, it seems to me important in the discussion of programme music to be able to demonstrate if and how the 'poietic' concepts relate with those of reception, and argue why some programmatic readings are more plausible than others.

For example, in judging the programmaticism of the first movement of the First Symphony according to the 'biographical code', its origins could be seen to have been connected with Mahler's affair with Johanna Richter. Such a statement cannot be deduced directly from the musical work, but rather through a series of denotations and connotations moving back and forth between past and present. We know *a posteriori* from Mahler's published letters that the composition of the *Gesellen* poetry and songs was contemporaneous with Mahler's romantic involvement with, and suffering for, Johanna Richter. Various other codes can be identified, especially through intertextual references to other works. Among them, the formal structure of monothematic sonata form which here serves to emphasize the song melody, the introductory '*creatio ab nihilo*' coming from the generic tradition of the symphony, especially Beethoven's Ninth, and codes of musical representation of nature, as exemplified, for example, by Wagner's Prelude to *Rheingold*.[55] For the rest of the Symphony one can distinguish other codes, both musical and extramusical: generic mixture of Ländler and waltz in the second movement, the well-known grotesquely distorted version of the children's canon *Bruder Martin*, interspersed with the 'Klezmer' music and with death-connoting quotations from the last *Gesellen* song, and finally, the 'struggle to victory' topical scenario of the last movement. Even from such a minimal reading of the music's own meanings, if one felt a need for anchoring music in real life, one could build a story around a fictional individual, 'a hero' in the romantic sense, or, if leaning towards music as biography, around the life of the composer. Yet these meanings would belong to 'reception' rather than to the 'production' of the work, because they are incorporated in the music itself and open to many other interpretations. Finding 'internal' programmes or narrative patterns that resemble by analogy structures from other media – plot archetypes of the kind Anthony Newcomb locates in the Ninth Symphony,[56] readings arrived at in the light of the concepts of 'story' and 'discourse' from literary theory, or interpretations of musical discursive topics resulting from genre associations[57] – insofar as they can be argued on the basis of the musical substance, can enrich the scope of our understanding and perception. Knowing from documents some of the chronology and the details of the creative process, as well as the history of reception of the work, Mahler's own 'programmes' seem also to belong to reception, and therefore it is by *not* giving them precedence over our own interpretations that we leave the hermeneutic circle open.

Not being strictly bound by, or privileging, 'evidence' does not mean that criticism and aesthetics dealing with programmes lose their anchorage in a historical perspective, or become fictional. Instead, this allows us to be more open-minded and flexible in interpreting them, and to create plural textualities that intersect in imaginative and unexpected ways. Musical semiotic chains have their own logic, grounded in culture and history through long processes of bindings or deferrals of signifieds and signifiers which attach themselves to one another and grow into new ideas. Awareness of the positions from which interpretation is carried out should be maintained as much as possible, and totalitarian or exclusionary statements should be avoided. In so doing doors are kept open for future generations to engage in new readings. Adorno best captured the dilemma between music and programme, materiality and spirituality in Mahler's music, writing:

> [Mahler] is particularly resistant to theorizing because he entirely fails to acknowledge the choice between technique and imaginative content . . . To understand him would be to endow with speech the music's structural elements while technically locating the glowing expressive intentions . . . Mahler can only be seen in perspective by moving still closer to him, by entering into the music and confronting the incommensurable presence that defies stylistic categories of program and absolute music . . . Instead of illustrating ideas, [his symphonies] are destined concretely to become the idea. As each of their moments, tolerating no evasion into the approximate, fulfills its musical function, it becomes more than its mere existence: a script prescribing its own interpretation.[58]

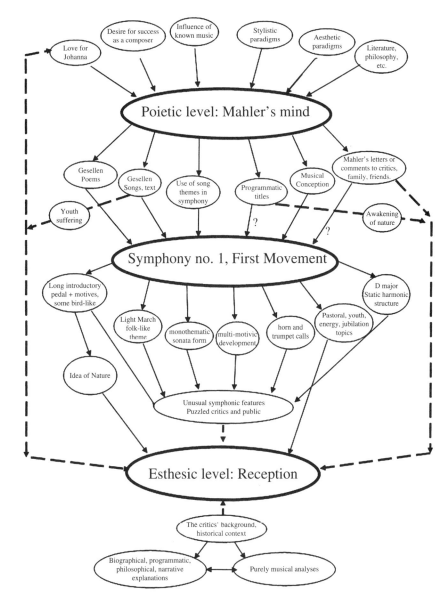

Figure 3.1 Textualities in the First Movement of Mahler's First Symphony.

Mahler the creative musician

4 Juvenilia and early works: from the first song fragments to *Das klagende Lied*

JEREMY BARHAM

According to various sources, the compositions of Mahler's childhood and student years (up to 1880) were both numerous and generically diverse.[1] In speculative 'catalogues',[2] the well-documented abortive opera projects *Herzog Ernst von Schwaben*, *Die Argonauten* and *Rübezahl* are listed alongside less familiar or less credible references to four early symphonies, songs, song fragments, chamber and piano works (including the *Polka mit einem Trauermarsch als Einleitung* which Mahler 'composed' at the age of six or seven). That the vast majority of these 'works' have not survived is due partly to the fact that many, such as the piano pieces in 'Wagnerian' style which Mahler played in 1875 to his prospective piano professor Julius Epstein, were probably never notated. Of the remainder, including those works deriving from his three-year period of study at the Vienna Conservatoire (1875–8), nearly all either have been lost or were deliberately destroyed by the composer. According to Conservatoire records, Mahler won respectively a unanimous first prize for the 'first movement of a quintet' and a non-unanimous first prize for a 'scherzo for piano quintet' in the 1876 and 1878 composition competitions.[3] Bauer-Lechner mentions a prize-winning piano suite and violin sonata, neither of which appears in Conservatoire records.[4] According to Carl Hruby, Bruckner recalled a 'symphonic movement' replaced by an andante 'sonata movement' in an annual Conservatoire examination,[5] while Richard Specht wrote of a prize-winning string quintet,[6] Alma Mahler referred to 'a movement of a quartet for a competition',[7] and Ludwig Karpath recounted that Mahler competed unsuccessfully in the Conservatoire's annual song competition (probably in either 1875–6 or 1876–7).[8]

Paul Banks argues on convincing stylistic grounds for the attribution to Mahler of a Symphonic Prelude located in the Österreichische Nationalbibliothek in the form of a piano arrangement of a score copied by Mahler's student colleague Rudolf Krzyzanowski.[9] However, apart from this, whether by accident or design Mahler left only one complete movement and three fragments of undisputed authorship from this period in his life: the former for piano quartet in A minor, and the latter

Plate 4.1 'Es fiel ein Reif in der Frühlingsnacht'. Reproduced with kind permission of the Pierpont Morgan Library, New York

comprising the opening section of a 'scherzo' movement for piano quartet in G minor and two incomplete song settings of 'Es fiel ein Reif in der Frühlingsnacht' and Heine's 'Im wunderschönen Monat Mai' (illustrated in Plates 4.1 and 4.2).

Plate 4.1 (cont.)

Plate 4.2 'Im wunderschönen Monat Mai'. Reproduced with kind permission of the Pierpont Morgan Library, New York

Songs and song fragments

The four-stanza version of the poem 'Es fiel ein Reif in der Frühlingsnacht' most closely resembling Mahler's text was originally written by the poet and folk-song collector Florentin von Zuccalmaglio (1803–69) – possibly as

Plate 4.2 (cont.)

a romantic elaboration from authentic folk sources – and published by him
in 1825 in the journal *Rheinische Flora*.[10] Mahler's early attraction to this
type of text – in this case a bitter-sweet narrative of the ill-fated elopement
of two lovers – is perhaps symptomatic of his later fascination with the

Wunderhorn collection. However, it is difficult to trace specific musical links with the *Wunderhorn* style in this setting's hesitant combination of diatonic simplicity and widely vagrant tonality shifting from D minor to F♯ major via hints of D♭ major and E minor. More interesting is the strong stylistic contrast displayed between this and the other, presumably contemporaneous, fragmentary setting (orthography and content suggest for both manuscripts an early composition date nearer to 1875–6 than 1878–9). As has been noted elsewhere,[11] Mahler's decidedly un-Schumannesque 'Im wunderschönen Monat Mai' shows him dabbling, with some competence, in a Wagnerian chromaticism of the kind that he seldom called upon in later life. Here he seems to be thinking from moment to moment, eliciting from Heine's text an entirely unexpected sensuousness, subverting the Schumann model in a wash of pre-modernist tonal and structural freedom, perhaps in an attempt to explore and assert a sense of burgeoning identity. It seems significant that of all his earliest fragmentary compositional efforts, these are the only ones to have survived. They perhaps provide the first evidence that Mahler's youthful search for a musical voice would require negotiation with both a Wagnerian legacy made all the more burdensome by his own veneration of his predecessor, and a simpler folk heritage whose re-presentation had somehow to be integrated with the high-art aspirations of a musical sophisticate. Negotiating these twin impulses would be a difficult but immensely enriching one for the mature Mahler and for the wider development of early modernist musical culture.

Mahler's awareness of this problem is suggested in his assessment of the songs he wrote at this time as 'inadequate' due to his 'wild' and 'excessive' imagination and the difficulties of achieving something significant on such a small scale.[12] However, as was sometimes the case in later life, it was not long before Mahler found the inspiration for artistic accomplishment in the promise of emotional fulfilment. His first completed songs, from February and March 1880, were settings of three of his own poems for tenor voice and piano, prompted by romantic involvement with their dedicatee Josephine Poisl, the daughter of the Iglau Postmaster. Of the '5 Lieder' listed on the title page of the manuscript the last two lack song titles, indicating perhaps the point at which the relationship ended: two additional poetic texts written by Mahler for Poisl at this time – 'Vergessene Liebe' and 'Kam ein Sonnenstrahl' – may have been designated for inclusion in the set.[13]

In a major leap beyond his previous endeavours, these settings prefigure some of the principal concerns and practices of Mahler's mature Lied technique: the orchestral allusions, broad sweep and dramatic contrasts of 'Im Lenz'; the reliance on unifying ostinato rhythms, drones, rhythmic-motivic ideas and expressive appoggiaturas in 'Winterlied'; and the deceptive *faux-naif* folk tone of the yodelling 'Maitanz im Grünen'. The performance directions of this last song notably include the *echt-Mahlerian* term 'keck' (cheeky or pert) and the earliest reference to the Austrian folk dance whose rhythmic, thematic and structural content became such a fundamental and idiosyncratic means of connecting symphony and song: 'Im Zeitmaß eines Ländlers'.[14] In ethnographic sublimation of the kind of folk material he had known since childhood, such as his reputed favourite song 'At se pinkl házi' ('Let the Knapsack Rock'),[15] and which he may well have encountered with Josephine in and around Iglau, Mahler both honours this music's traditions with bagpipe drones underpinning rustic diatonicism, and subverts them, whether with knowing mediant shifts from D to F (one of Mahler's signature tonal relationships) at moments of textual condescension ('Ah, Hansel, you haven't got one! [a sweetheart] / Then look for one!' (bars 24–9) and 'Oh look at silly Hans! / How he runs to the dance!' (bars 65–70)), or in a subtle re-engagement with Schumann's world in the final recessive marking 'wie aus der Ferne' (bar 86) – the first of many indications of Mahler's spatial preoccupations. This is clearly not a folk song but rather an image of one, already filtered through the complex intermixture of ethnic and political baggage carried by Mahler from an early age as an assimilationist, German-speaking Bohemian Jew walking through a Central European landscape that was at once deeply in his blood and intellectually alien. It is not surprising therefore that the conflict of nostalgia and faint disdain for the innocence of the round dance is present so early in Mahler, and that this 'simple' song, like the following account of his experience of Bohemia in early 1880s, written by his childhood friend Fritz Löhr, is historically emblematic of burgeoning cultural ambivalence:

> There [the vicinity of Iglau] in the height of summer we would go for walks lasting half the day . . . to villages where the peasantry was in part Slav . . . to where authentic Bohemian musicians set lads and lasses dancing in the open air . . . There was the zest of life, and sorrow too . . . all of it veiled by reserve on the faces of the girls, their heads bowed towards their partners' breast, their plump, almost naked limbs exposed by the high whirling of their many-layered bright petticoats, in an almost solemn, ritual encircling. The archaically earthy charms of nature and of nature's children, which Mahler came to know in his youth, prepared the ground for his creative work and never ceased to vitalize his art.[16]

Mahler recognized the wider structural potential of this music, for, transposed from D to F major and with some textual alterations, additional accompanimental chromaticisms, and a sophisticated array of constantly changing performance instructions, it became the song 'Hans und Grethe', the third item in Volume 1 of *Lieder und Gesänge* (later known as *Lieder und Gesänge aus der Jugendzeit*), published in 1892; and this in turn became the inspiration for the 'Kräftig bewegt' second movement of the First Symphony.

With 'Im Lenz' and 'Winterlied', the twin poles of Mahler's influences were beginning to coalesce even further into a distinctive literary and compositional style. In the former, the dialogue between narrator and love-sick, first-person protagonist familiar from later *Wunderhorn* settings, is played out in an unmistakably orchestral context of glissandi, high repeated chords, tremolandi and horn evocations (bars 14–15 and 43–4). More important, perhaps, is Mahler's greater degree of control over a still comparatively wide-ranging tonal pattern (F major/D minor–A♭ major–C major, to the more diffuse final section travelling from F♯ minor back to A♭ major). What helps to counterbalance these wanderings is an overriding *dramatic* structure articulated primarily through deft moments of transition between the alternating narrative voices of each verse: for example, evocative pauses (bars 13 and 42) and the sudden harp-like incursion at bar 27. Seen alongside the sometimes strained harmonic relations, these nevertheless suggest a miniature song trying to break through its own expressive and structural limitations.

'Winterlied' continues the Mahlerian themes of isolation and alienation, but, with arguably even greater mastery of the materials, it represents the young composer at his most assured and Schumannesque (its striking image of peering dejectedly into the warmth of a room from outside links this song with *Dichterliebe* and the scherzo of Mahler's Second Symphony[17]). The seemingly unstructured, through-composed text assumes shape both through the principal articulatory points in the music (the shift to C minor at 'In the cold snow' (bar 30), when the narrator 'sings' to his beloved, and the varied reprise of the piano introduction at bar 61), and by a gradual intensification of texture through infiltration of the symbolic semiquaver spinning-wheel figure and an upward dynamic arc to bar 58, the last vocal phrase 'Gone for ever!' Across these boundaries Mahler cleverly manipulates the gentle double-appoggiaturas of the opening bars so that they become more heavily dissonant in between the increasingly impassioned vocal invocations of bars 30–58. If the earlier shift to C major at bar 24 seemed a somewhat forced way of eliding with the C minor of bars 29–30, the masterstroke comes with the unexpected but fulfilling return to F major and the spinning wheel (bars 59–61) for the concluding piano postlude – a homage to Schumann in its ambiguous consolatory-resignatory response to the anguished *Stimmungsbrechung* of bars 57–8. In this early song Mahler seems to have found the beginnings of a structurally convincing and expressively meaningful resolution to the problem of how to unify the folk- and art-music impulses – the age-old dialectical tension of nature and culture.

Piano quartet

By contrast, the principal tension underlying the movement for piano quartet, the sole representative of a compositional genre to which he would never return, was that between the requirements of his own creative imagination and those of his Conservatoire professors; and this tension in turn foreshadowed a much larger one of profound importance for the composer's development: that between acknowledgment of, and deviation from, structural-generic models.

Evidence confirming the precise date of composition of the piano quartet movement is scant and conflicting. I have summarized it elsewhere, concluding that 1877 is the most probable year of its completion.[18] Most discussions of the movement have predictably discerned in it evidence of the third founding ingredient of Mahler's emerging compositional practice: the style and structures of the central, Austro-German, high-art instrumental music of Beethoven, Schubert, Schumann, Brahms and Bruckner which Mahler would have regularly experienced in his early years in Vienna.[19] However, the lone status of the movement and its apparent endorsement by Mahler himself[20] have increased the desire to detect in it intimations of his own later instrumental style and language.

Whilst Newlin and Ruzicka, taking their cue from Stefan,[21] primarily address the quartet's possible thematic prefigurings of the Sixth and Ninth Symphonies, Mitchell, Stahmer, Banks and I have been more concerned with its contentious structural features. Eliciting polarized responses from critics and analysts, the quartet's formal design, whilst described by Newlin as 'lucid' and by Stahmer as demonstrating the composer's 'keen instinct for the rupturing [*Brüchigkeit*] of form in the closing years of the 19th century', is for Mitchell 'direction-less' and an unsuccessful 'flouting of classical "sonata" practice'.[22] While all of these comments have elements of truth about them depending on perspective, my quasi-Adornian reading of the movement's tonal and formal strategies counters Stahmer's assertion that the work consists only of a 'string of sections strongly tied to tonic keys' and therefore has no '"dramatic-harmonic" formal plan'.[23] Although Banks, like many others, acknowledges the sometimes mechanical way in which Mahler 'manufactures' music through excessive repetition of motivic ideas (see especially bars 110–35) – a technique probably instilled by the composition professor Franz Krenn from 'superficial observation of Beethoven's and Schubert's methods'[24] – he also recognizes that the piece's most unusual and distinctive ploys are to be found in harmonic events and strategies such as the strongly dissonant D pedal under chords of Eb^7 and Ab in bars 84–5, the false relations F–F♯ and D–D♯ in bars 104–5,[25] and the shift to F♯

minor at bar 174 of the recapitulation, rendering it, rather than the exposition, the site of greater tonal contrast. This line of argument can be expanded to suggest that the quartet in fact adumbrates three idiosyncratic elements of Mahler's mature, large-scale structuring method: the initial presentation of thematic or harmonic 'dramatis personae' whose differing attributes may only be exploited at a much later stage; the broader exploration of *fields* of tonal conflict (in this case, major versus minor modes or flat-side versus sharp-side keys) rather than local, densely argued key oppositions; and the dramatic intensity of playing fulfilled and thwarted formal/generic expectations against each other.

The first and last of these are exemplified in the ambiguity of the relatively monotonal 'exposition', where the character and function of the three identifiable themes (beginning in bars 3, 42 and 54) are blurred. What at first seems like a slow introduction becomes strongly thematic and expositional through its extended and varied repetition and contrapuntal combination (it also includes a solitary statement of the third theme (bars 32–4) which seems to serve no purpose other than briefly to introduce a future *dramatis persona*); what might have formed a convincingly resolute first subject (the A minor *Entschlossen* theme at bar 42) is surely too brief and inconclusive; and the ensuing third theme is surely too distinctive and substantial in character to form a mere codetta to the exposition, its brief opening foray into F major offering the first notable, if momentary, appearance of an alternative key area. The impression rather is that this entire opening part of the movement (bars 1–66) is a preparation for the movement 'proper' which begins with what textbooks would describe as the development section (bars 67–150), and this is not dissimilar to what would happen, albeit on a much larger scale, in later, ostensibly 'sonata-form' movements such as the opening ones of the First and Third Symphonies. Given this ambivalence, the preparation for, and the moment of 'recapitulation' (bar 151) is inevitably problematized, for what is being reprised is arguably of a preliminary rather than an expository nature. A closely related ambiguity pertains, for example, to the 'recapitulation' of the first movement of the Third Symphony. In the quartet movement the 'problematic' reprise is curiously preceded by an extended tonicization of the subdominant D minor (bars 116–38) through a thirteen-bar A pedal, followed by the introduction of a new theme (bar 139) conceivably constructed from the incipits of the first and third themes. The harmonic lead-in to the reprise is equally noteworthy: over an E♭ pedal a diminished seventh changes to the dominant seventh of B♭, the Neapolitan of A minor, with which it shares two common pitches (A and C) and to which it simply shifts without resolution.

Example 4.1 Piano quartet, bars 209–11 in harmonic reduction

In the 'recapitulation' itself, the incursion of the F♯ major section (bars 174–89) is significant not so much because it signals the continuing presence of developmental processes (by no means uncommon in nineteenth-century sonata-form reprises), but more because, dominated by the third theme, it occurs *before* the appearance of the second theme. This reordering has the effect of casting the putative transitional function of the second theme into further doubt, enhancing its thematic status and reifying the artificiality of formal components, especially transitions within supposed 'recapitulations'.

Rather than there being an absence of clear tonal strategy as Stahmer suggests, Mahler offers an intriguing alternative approach to harmonic organization in the movement. In the 'exposition' this is configured around the opposition between the predominant minor mode and various brief or promised but thwarted turns to the major: C at bars 20–2, B♭ at bars 38–40, C/F at bars 50–6 and F at bars 62–3. One of the key elements involved in this suppression of major-mode brightness is the repeated last-minute withdrawal of 'positive' harmonic fulfilment from an important rising bass figure (bars 38–42 and 65–6), a quintessential Mahlerian procedure which recurs at two important structural moments later in the movement (bars 188–9 and 213–15). Before the long pedal-point 'preparation' for the reprise, the 'development' section has shifted the arena of conflict to one between flat- (D and G minor) and, for the first time, sharp-side tonalities (E and F♯ minor), occurring either side of a central passage of intense textural and thematic activity in tonic and subdominant (bars 92–101). The 'recapitulation' performs an expected unifying function, but not in any orthodox sense: the seemingly incongruous inserted passage beginning in F♯ minor (bars 174–89) in fact serves to integrate the combined interplay of the first and third themes which took place in the first half of 'development' with the sharp-side tonalities from the second half of the 'development'. Then, through the successive casting of the third theme (and its combination with the first theme) in sharp-side keys A major, B minor and F♯ minor (bars 202–9) *and* in flat-side keys F major and D minor (bars 210–15) via an extremely deft Neapolitan trick (see Example 4.1), both the flat-sharp and the major-minor conflicts seem to become crystallized (perhaps 'resolved') into a nodal point of the work's structure.

Finally, two important passages in the movement seem temporarily and unexpectedly to rupture the structural seams of the music in different ways. Elsewhere I have characterized bars 92–101 as a moment of what Adorno might have termed 'breakthrough':[26] a textural and figurational intensification, perhaps arising out of Mahler's own virtuosic keyboard practice, is combined with the incursion of what appears to be a new unison theme in the strings (a 'dramatis persona' which was briefly prefigured in bar 69) but whose octave leaps and overall shape could be seen as an extension or breaching of the structural limits of the movement's first theme. That this radicalized 'breakthrough' nevertheless consists of two symmetrical thematic statements in subdominant and tonic (the main tonal axis of the movement) separated by a two-bar virtuosic climax of triplet double octaves in the keyboard, and is placed virtually at the mid-point of the movement, may exemplify both Mahler's early sensitivity to structural proportion and his desire to challenge the confines of tradition. A foreshortened reminder of this 'breakthrough' is heard immediately after the integrative nodal point in the 'recapitulation' referred to above. As if in answer to the impossible questions posed by the demands of conventional cyclic formal processes, Mahler dissipates or 'composes away' the potentially disruptive effects of this already truncated second 'breakthrough' by the evasive and enterprising means of a violin cadenza which suspends musical and temporal progression and leads to the sullen coda.

There is certainly plenty of evidence in this quartet movement to explain why Mahler may have considered it 'the best' of his student works. It would also have been fascinating to see how Mahler might have dealt with this music's tonal, thematic and structural unfinished business in subsequent movements, a long-range procedure he would later carry out so often in his symphonies. Unfortunately the twenty-six-bar scherzo-like fragment for piano quartet in G minor located in the same folder of early compositions and thought by some to be linked to the completed movement, offers little clue. Enguerrand-Friedrich Lühl's 1994 'completion' of the fragment and Alfred Schnittke's 'paraphrase' of it in his *Klavierquartett* of 1988 offer varied responses to unanswerable questions.[27]

Das klagende Lied

A contributory factor in the emerging compositional fluency evident from the Poisl songs may have been their chronological and musical proximity to Mahler's first large-scale work, *Das klagende Lied*, with which both 'Im Lenz' and 'Winterlied' share distinctive, and potentially symbolic, melodic content.[28] Certainly in the case of the former song and probably in the latter too, the cantata provided the source material for the self-quotation,[29] and this process offered an early indication of Mahler's subsequent explorations of the relationship between compact song structures and extended dramatic canvasses.

The compositional context and chronology of *Das klagende Lied* are convoluted and open to dispute, and this is principally because the work was revised three times, the most drastic result of which was the deletion of the original first movement, 'Waldmärchen'. Assessment of the reasons for this cut and its impact on the remaining music has led to some interesting debates about Mahler's compositional aesthetic and the identity of the work, which have been re-emphasized by the International Gustav Mahler Society's publication in 1997 of a critical edition of the original three-movement 'version'.[30] Table 4.1 outlines the work's genesis, revisions and performance history.

In accordance with the notion of *Fassung letzter Hand* and in view of purported structural, dramatic and narrative weaknesses in the three-movement structure, there are those who believe that the revised bipartite version of the work supersedes its tripartite predecessor.[31] In opposition to this, others have pointed to the fundamental musico-dramatic role of 'Waldmärchen' in maintaining the structural and narrative integrity, as well as the thematic coherence, of the whole work.[32]

Resisting the dogmatic exclusivity of an 'either–or' position, and acknowledging that Mahler retained confidence in the three-movement structure for at least twelve years and that the extent of the revision far exceeds conventional notions of *Urfassungen* and *Fassungen letzter Hand*, I have advocated viewing the bipartite and tripartite cantatas more as different 'works' than as different 'versions' of the same work.[33] If part of the reason for Mahler's radical revision was the practical desire to get the cantata published and performed, this should encourage preservation of the original as an invaluable source of insight into the young composer's idealistic and unconstrained creative aesthetic – an ethical perspective which reinforces the embargo on attempts at hybrid performances such as that of Boulez's 1970 recording. That said, if the numerous revisions made by Mahler in the light of his intervening compositional and directorial experience constitute genuine improvements to the presentation of the music, then it may never be possible to arrive at an optimum performance of the tripartite work. In addition to the removal of 'Waldmärchen', the movement titles, and, temporarily, the off-stage orchestra, the results of Mahler's revisions included those noted in Table 4.2.[34]

Table 4.1 *Chronology of composition, revision and performance of*
Das klagende Lied

1878–80	Mahler works on the text	Variously called: (i) 'Ballade vom blonden und braunen Reitersmann' (1878) ['Ballad of the Blonde and Brown Horseman'] (later 'Waldmärchen') (ii) 'Ballade' (1878–9; three-part text consisting of 'Waldmärchen', 'Der Spielmann' and 'Hochzeitsstück') (iii) 'Das klagende Lied' (1880)
1879–80	Mahler works on the music	(i) Quotes music in 'Im Lenz' (February 1880) (ii) Short score of second movement 'Der Spielmann' dated '21 March 1880' (iii) Reports completion of composition in a letter of 1 November 1880[a]
1880–91	Fate of the original three-movement work	(i) Copyists prepare full score (the only extant MS source of 'Waldmärchen')[b] (ii) Mahler enters the work unsuccessfully for the Beethoven prize of the Gesellschaft der Musikfreunde (1881) (iii) Mahler unsuccessfully offers the work for performance to the Allgemeiner Deutscher Musikverein festival (1883); rejected by Liszt[c] (iv) Mahler presents the work without success for consideration by the publishers Schott in Mainz (1891)
1893–1906	Revisions to the work and performances in Mahler's lifetime	**First revision (1893):** (i) Begins revising all three movements while in Hamburg, ultimately leading to: excision of 'Waldmärchen', off-stage orchestra in other two movements and all movement titles; other changes to orchestration and replacement of emotive or pictorial performance directions with more conventional terms (ii) Mahler prepares score of revised bipartite version[d] **Second revision (1898–9):** (iii) As a result of publishing contract with Waldheim, Erberle & Co., Mahler makes further revisions including restoring off-stage orchestra, though without original bitonal and polymetric effects; vacillates about use of boys' voices (iv) First publication of bipartite work (Weinberger, 1899 or 1902[e]) (v) Mahler gives first performances of bipartite work, Vienna 1901 and 1902 (boys' voices not used) **Third revision (1906):** (vi) Mahler makes further revisions after his 1906 performance in Amsterdam (vii) Most revisions incorporated into posthumous score published by Universal (1913), though not the optional use of boys' voices
1934–98	Posthumous performances and editions	(i) Alfred Rosé gives first performance of 'Waldmärchen' (Brno, 1934) and first broadcast of hybrid tripartite work[f] (Vienna, 1935) (ii) Boulez gives first American and British performances of 'Waldmärchen' and makes the first recording of hybrid tripartite work (1970) (iii) Edition of 'Waldmärchen' published by Belwin Mills (New York, 1973) (iv) Revised bipartite work published as Volume 12 of the Complete Critical Edition (ed. Rudolf Stephan, Vienna: Universal, 1978), restoring optional alto boy's voice (v) Original tripartite work published as Supplement Volume 4 of the Complete Critical Edition (ed. Reinhold Kubik, Vienna: Universal, 1997) (vi) Kent Nagano gives first performance of original tripartite work in Manchester and makes first recording (1997); subsequent performances given in Germany, France and America (1997–8)

Notes to table 4.1 (*cont.*)

[a] SLGM, p. 65.
[b] Given by Mahler to his sister Justine at some point after 1894. Currently housed in the James Marshall and Marie-Louise Osborn Collection, Beinecke Rare Book and Manuscript Library, Yale University (MS507).
[c] See Reilly, '*Das klagende Lied*', p. 39.
[d] Currently housed in the Dannie and Hettie Heineman Collection at the Pierpont Morgan Library, New York. See Reilly, '*Das klagende Lied*', pp. 43–5, for the chronology of these revisions.
[e] See Reilly, '*Das klagende Lied*', p. 31, for explanation of the discrepancy.
[f] That is, 'Waldmärchen' together with 'Der Spielmann' and 'Hochzeitsstück' of the revised bipartite work.

Table 4.2 *Mahler's revisions to* Das klagende Lied

Vocal forces	Reduction of the number of vocal soloists from six (SATBar, boy soprano and alto) to three (SAT) plus an optional boy alto
Deployment of vocal soloists[a]	(a) Indecision over assignment of solo voices, for example 'Der Spielmann' from bar 152: variously labelled 'Bar. Tutti', 'Alt', possibly 'T Bar. Chor' and finally assigned to solo tenor which remained in revision (b) Vacillation over use of boy's voices, for example solo 'Ach Spielmann' in 'Hochzeitsstück' from bar 259: 'Sopran.' changed to 'Knabenstimme' in original tripartite MS; revised in bipartite work to 'Alto solo' with note: 'Where possible, to be performed by a boy's voice'
Orchestral forces	(a) Reduction from two piccolos to one (b) Increase from two oboes to three (third oboe doubled by existing cor anglais) (c) Change from two clarinets in B♭ and A to two clarinets in B♭ doubling on C and E♭ and addition of third clarinet in B♭ or C (doubled by existing bass clarinet) (d) Addition of contrabassoon (doubled by existing third bassoon) (e) Removal of natural horns (*Waldhörner*) (f) Removal of cornets in F (*Pistons*) (g) Removal of one of two bass tubas (h) Reduction of harps from six to two
Off-stage orchestral forces	(mostly replacing obsolete and/or military band instruments) (a) Replacement of flutes in D♭ with flutes in C (b) Addition of two oboes (c) Removal of bassoons (d) Addition of four horns in F (e) Replacement of four bugles (*Flügelhörner*) in B♭ (1 2 and 3 doubling on trumpets in F) with two trumpets or bugles (*Flügelhörner*) in B♭ (f) Removal of two cornets (*Pistons*) in E♭

Deployment of orchestral forces	(a) Substantial revoicings such as
	   (i) 'Der Spielmann' from bar 45
	   (ii) 'Der Spielmann' from bar 381
	 (b) Minor reorchestrations, primarily to thin out textures, for example 'Hochzeitsstück', bars 207–12
	 (c) Clarifying rhythms by use of shorter note values and intervening rests, or by replacement of triplets/dotted rhythms with sharper rhythms, for example
	   (i) 'Der Spielmann' from bar 85 (lower woodwind), bar 182 (oboe)
	   (ii) 'Der Spielmann' from bar 249 (lower strings and horns)
	   (iii) 'Hochzeitsstück' from bar 83 and bar 302 (off-stage orchestra)
	   (iv) 'Hochzeitsstück' from bar 223 (double basses) and bar 312 (lower strings)
	 (d) Removal of indications of spatial dislocation, for example 'Der Spielmann', alto solo bar 341 *(von ferne)*, whole orchestra bar 391 *Wie von Ferne*, but introduction of stopped horns to suggest distance ('Hochzeitsstück' from bar 136)
	 (e) Removal of obsolete instruments, for example, muted natural horns (*Waldhörner*) replaced with open horns in E ('Hochzeitsstück' from bar 171)

Table 4.2 (*cont.*)

	(f) Simplification of instructions for off-stage orchestra ('Hochzeitsstück', bar 79)
	(g) Incorporation of off-stage material within main orchestra, for example 'Hochzeitsstück', bars 130–2 (sustained dim. seventh chord)
	(h) Removal of bitonal and polymetric passages involving off-stage orchestra, 'Der Spielmann', bars 222–30 and 'Hochzeitsstück', bars 345–8
Choral writing	(a) Increased contrapuntal textures, for example 'Hochzeitsstück' from bar 40
	(b) Thinning out of textures, for example 'Hochzeitsstück' from bar 126
	(c) Increase in clarity at climax points through uniform diction and rhythm, for example 'Hochzeitsstück' from bar 442/2. (Text, dynamic contour, pitch and length of phrase are also altered with climactic point arriving on new word 'Weh!', bar 451)
Tempo indications and performance directions	(a) Reduced fluctuations, for example 'Der Spielmann', from bar 391 (*rit., molto rit., Langsamer, Gemessen* deleted)
	(b) Greater precision of tempo relationships, for example 'Hochzeitsstück' bar 13
	(c) Removal of 'romanticized' and potentially programmatic performance directions: *Mit sehr geheimnisvollem Ausdruck* [with very mysterious expression] at the beginning of 'Der Spielmann' becomes *Sehr gehalten* [very restrained]; *Religioso* at bar 73 of 'Der Spielmann' is deleted; *Mit höllischer Wildheit* [with infernal wildness] at the beginning of 'Hochzeitsstück' becomes *Heftig bewegt* [intensely agitated]
	(d) More detailed, and generally more extreme, dynamic indications, for example 'Der Spielmann' from bar 45; 'Hochzeitsstück' from bar 377
Text	Addition of clarifying text in the absence of 'Waldmärchen', for example 'Hochzeitsstück' from bar 159: three extra lines further questioning why the King is so 'pale and silent' during the festivities

[a] Bar numbers refer to the 1978 critical edition of the bipartite work.

Whatever the combination of sources from which Mahler assembled his text,[35] the content and tone of its chivalric Kain-and-Abel story, presumably set in a mythical old Germany, of brothers fatefully vying for the hand of a queen and the keys to the kingdom, are folk-like and redolent of Wagnerian/Weberian quasi-archaicism. Mahler almost certainly came to know *Der fliegende Holländer*, *Tannhäuser*, *Lohengrin* and *Der Freischütz* in his student years or earlier, and played through excerpts from *Götterdämmerung* with student friends Wolf and Krzyzanowski, an opera whose catastrophic ending is not dissimilar to that of *Das klagende Lied*.[36] Although he did not hear *Parsifal* until 1883 in Bayreuth, he would have been familiar with its middle-high German literary sources as well as other mythological epics of the period from lectures attended during his first year at the University of Vienna, 1877–8. Mahler wrote his text in a stanzaic, ballad-like form whose primarily third-person narrative contains many rhetorical questions addressed to the protagonists, and in which even first-person passages are recounted by proxy from beyond the grave through the bone flute. This approach avoided operatic identification of character with singer – solo vocalists and choir sharing not only in the unfolding of the narrative but also in the bone flute's enunciations. Although, as with some later works, the text provided a helpful framework, it also presented Mahler with the challenge of marrying verse structure and recurring refrains with large-scale musical development and coherence. In answer to this he devised some intriguing responses.

Notably, *Das klagende Lied*, commonly labelled a cantata, belonged to one of the least well-defined of late nineteenth-century generic traditions. Although precedents exist among the output of Beethoven, Schumann and Brahms, on account of its strong narrative thrust and its mythic-tragic content, it is more like an expanded form of German ballad in the tradition of Zelter, Schubert and Loewe. After all, this was the original designation of the text, the eventual title's only generic reference is the word 'Lied', and Mahler himself would later draw heavily on the narrative ballad tradition in his solo songs.[37] With its multi-movement, yet through-composed, form, its highly theatrical, scenic character and the predominance of the orchestra throughout, the work found Mahler already experimenting with generic fluidity through blending various instrumental, vocal and stage practices.

Fiske and Banks draw attention to elements of key symbolism, Leitmotifs and contrasting harmonic types familiar from Wagnerian, and earlier, operatic traditions, and it does seem that 'Waldmärchen' begins with an extensive 'overture' of sorts (bars 1–126), duly presenting a number of themes, figures and moods that will become prominent during the course of the movement. However, much like the structurally intractable opening of the Third Symphony, this series of linked *tableaux* (marked out by thematic material, tempo or figuration at bars 1, 30, 50, 70, 88, 98 and 115) also compromises the sense of where the true 'beginning' of the musical drama is located. What tends to hold this opening, and the entire movement, together are pervasive pedal points (a feature of the whole work) and a nucleus of oscillating harmonic shifts stemming from the opening horn and clarinet figures, involving semitonal and mediant relationships (see Example 4.2) which function as either colouristic devices or signifiers of structural transition. These shifts challenge the firmly diatonic, pedal-orientated harmony of much of the movement, which, together with the main sectional divisions' inflexible adherence to the text's stanzaic form through a repeated downward scale figure heard at all but two of the refrains (bars 145, 188, 237, 285, 364, 498 and 600), suggests that Mahler was somehow denying or suppressing late-Wagnerian influence in the work. A brief examination of the setting of the final verse and surrounding music problematizes this view.

At the presumed point of the fratricide when the elder brother laughs, having drawn his sword (from bar 487), a striking series of musical events ensue:

Example 4.2 'Waldmärchen', oscillating harmonic shifts

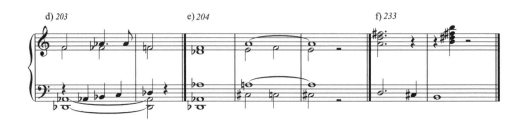

Example 4.3 'Waldmärchen', harmonic oscillation, bars 495–7

- previous unstable chromaticism coalesces to E♭ minor via the progression F♯m →
  dim. seventh on E♭ → E♭m (bars 486–8)
- a driving horn rhythm begins (bar 488), strongly reminiscent of the melodrama in
  the 'Wolf's Glen' scene of Weber's *Der Freischütz*
- a pungent distortion of the signature harmonic oscillation is heard in bars 495–7
  (see Example 4.3)
- an intense combination of four principal themes or Leitmotifs occurs in bars
  488–502 (lower strings bar 488, upper woodwind bar 490, trumpet bar 495, choir
  bar 498)

Example 4.4 'Waldmärchen', bars 587–9 in reduction

- a radical change of texture takes place in bar 503 signalling the younger brother's dream world/death; mediant shift from previous B♭ minor (bar 499) to G♭ major (bar 505), underpinned by semitone bass descent G → G♭
- for the first time in the movement the signature oscillation is given harmonic direction and quasi-resolution (bars 506–7) with the progression G♭ → A⁷ (as German aug. sixth) → D♭ (2nd inv.); repeated in bars 512–13
- the theme most closely associated with the oscillation (viola, bars 520–1, oboe bars 524–5) is now absorbed within a single chord (G♭)
- the movement's static opening 'frame' or *tableau* returns (bar 543) to close the 'book', now with rocking horn figures that end on harmonically stable rather than unstable sonorities (compare bars 543–4 and 545–6 with bars 1–3)
- the bass begins a long chromatic descent from A♭ to D, bars 551–89, underpinning lush, *Tristan*-like harmonic shifts: C♯⁹ → C maj⁷ bars 571–2, C⁷ → F♯m bars 573–4 (these bridged by descending melodic 'quote' from *Tristan*, oboes bars 572–4), F♯m → Am (over F♯ pedal) bars 575–6 (creating first of several appearances of 'Tristan' chord: bars 578, 581, 584–5), ending with the chromatic and mediant-based progression shown in Example 4.4 under second descending *Tristan* 'quote', violins bars 587–9
- the final harmonic shift: G functions as Neapolitan to F♯m, bars 590–3, returning music back from late-Wagnerian dream world to quasi-archaic, chorale/chant-like texture and ubiquitous closural descending scale

The undeniable late-Wagnerian allusions here are framed in the context of a nostalgic dream passage of loss, and reflection on tragic past events: 'Why, O flowers, are you heavy with dew? To me they look like tears!' Music of this type will not recur until the point in 'Hochzeitsstück' when the king is struck dumb through guilt at the impending revelation of the minstrels' bone flute (after a ten-bar passage of intense major–minor ambivalence from bar 149), a final citation of the 'Tristan' chord occurring at the climactic point of the revelation itself (from bar 341): 'O horror! Can you hear the dread tale of foreboding?' By casting Wagnerian chromaticism in this light, Mahler may seem to offer an oblique encoding of the difficulty of simultaneously 'containing' or assimilating this legacy whilst intimating both a desire to move beyond it and a sense of 'guilt' about doing so as, in his case, the creative 'sibling' compelled to turn the tables on the venerated elder figure: aesthetic and psychological impulses, life and art, intertwine.

Many of the basic harmonic techniques of 'Waldmärchen' are employed in 'Der Spielmann' and 'Hochzeitsstück', and if on the one hand Mahler seems less obviously constrained by the verse structure of the text in these movements, on the other hand the first movement's sometimes abrupt shifts from one narrated 'scene' to another and its evocation of spatial differentiation and varieties of temporal flux via bold manipulations of key, texture, tempo and figuration are continued and intensified in the next two movements, particularly through the extraordinary use of the off-stage orchestra. A theatrical tendency which Mahler would later transplant into symphonic contexts, evidently this multi-dimensionality was already well advanced in conception given the radical, Ivesian mixture of metres and tonalities brought about by the first appearance of the distant band between the reported construction of the bone flute and the narrating voice's warning not to play it ('Der Spielmann', bar 222).

The first revelation of the crime, and the first example of 'first-person' narrating, is significantly assigned to a boy alto, marked *von Ferne* (bar 341) – an indicator of temporal as much as spatial separation – and preceded by a dazzling sequence of textural vignettes preparing for the moment of otherworldly transmogrification: a 'supernatural' brass cliché of diminished chords and tritone relationships (for example A♭ maj^7 → Dm, bars 307–9), a passage of rippling dream music inscribing a C^9 chord (bars 316–19), a chromatically inflected collage of nature sounds (bars 320–35), and a melodramatic shift from F major to E♭ minor (bars 335–6). At the point of revelation, Mahler introduces sustained string tremolandi, a sonority that would often come to signify moments of high tension or unearthliness in future symphonic contexts. The last 123 bars of the movement are constructed over two vast pedal points – E♭ (bars 386–435) and C (bars 439–end) – which both anchor and energize the contrasting senses of intermediate closure and expectancy, as the first-person narrative is taken up successively by the more powerful adult alto voice (bar 440) and the full choir (bar 460), and is combined with third-person narrative (from bar 438) in a sustained and expansive full-orchestral texture.

'Hochzeitsstück', whose energetic opening gives the impression of an operatic final act, is notable for the robustness and theatricality of its orchestral writing, perhaps not unexpected in the part of the narrative where final retribution and disaster are played out. The deployment of the off-stage orchestra is crucial here in helping to define the trajectory of the drama and in uniting the worlds of past and present, dream and 'reality' with cataclysmic consequences. The first sign of unease can be detected in the very opening theme in which B♭ major struggles to maintain a presence amongst rapid turns to the minor (B♭ bar 6, A♭ bar 13, E♭ bar 15), and a familiar mediant shift to G♭ (bar 7). Later the extended appearance of the off-stage group (from bar 89) is subtly infiltrated or brutally undermined by music of present immediacy (for example, bars 98, 103 and 122), and this presages the all-important point of reversal where the horns of the off-stage band appear to cross over into the narrating sphere, interrupting the festivities with a portentous sustained diminished seventh chord (bar 140) in preparation for the minstrel's first revelation. From then on the boundaries between inner and outer worlds, reminiscence and 'actuality' become increasingly uncertain. The festivities have receded in the king's consciousness as he 'listens' to the tale but they gradually return in the form of the off-stage ensemble from bar 317 until reality comes crashing in as he snatches the flute, and is addressed directly by it. Here, as if to emphasize the difficulty of psychological suppression and the uncomfortable disparity between 'reality' and consciousness, the only other passage of off-stage bitonality occurs, at the end of one of the most chromatically unstable tonal periods (from bar 324) and at the vocal climax ('Can you hear the dread tale of foreboding?', bar 344); the material that had been exclusively assigned to the distance is for the first time appropriated by the main orchestra (bar 353): narrative perspectives of past and present, and psychic worlds of inner reflection and outer immediacy, are forced together. The tale is now related by a boy treble and signifiers of distance are abandoned. Again a vast Brucknerian pedal (E) supports the final 117 bars of the work, providing balance to the preceding active and at times dislocated harmonic structure and textures. The effect of the last *Langsam* section (from bar 482) reminds one of the concluding *tableau* of a stage melodrama in which the actors strike motionless poses and reflect solemnly on events. It may be no coincidence that the work ends in the same tonality as the piano quartet movement and the Sixth Symphony, and with a similarly brutal closing stroke that was to clinch the latter's sense of unremitting tragedy. In *Das klagende Lied*, the first work in which Mahler recognized his true voice, lay the source of many of the structural and expressive hallmarks of his idiosyncratic, mature vocal and symphonic practice.

5 Song and symphony (I). *Lieder und Gesänge* Volume 1, *Lieder eines fahrenden Gesellen* and the First Symphony: compositional patterns for the future

ZOLTAN ROMAN

Mahler was a prolific composer neither in quantity nor in his choice of genres, and the diversity evident in his early music was not to recur. The 'early' compositions that were published in his lifetime include four markedly different works or groups of pieces. His hybrid cantata-oratorio *Das klagende Lied* is discussed in Chapter 4. The five pieces in Volume 1 of *Lieder und Gesänge* (*aus der Jugendzeit*, as the title's later, unauthorized extension has it) comprise a group of miscellaneous solo songs with piano accompaniment. *Lieder eines fahrenden Gesellen* is a set of four, apparently similar songs in that they, too, were initially written for voice and piano. But these pieces constitute a true cycle, and were to be turned into the composer's first orchestral songs. This, the 'first period' of Mahler's creativity came to a close with the First Symphony, again a cyclic work that was to be recast. He took some ten years to write these works, beginning with the text of *Das klagende Lied* in 1878, and ending with the 'Symphonic Poem in two parts', the original, five-movement form of the First Symphony, in the spring of 1888. Those years saw him advance from an adolescent, unemployed graduate of the Vienna Conservatoire to the threshold of the international musical stage as director-designate of the Royal Hungarian Opera. Indeed, that lofty position was to play an important part in securing Mahler's first appearance as a composer of consequence with the première of the 'Symphonic Poem' in 1889.

Lieder und Gesänge, Volume 1

Having brought out a piano-duet arrangement of Bruckner's Third Symphony with Rudolf Krzyzanowski in 1880, and a revised version of Weber's opera *Die drei Pintos* in 1888, Mahler at last saw his own music published in the three slim volumes of the *Lieder und Gesänge* in 1892. The first volume contains five songs on poetry by three different writers; estimates of their dates of composition vary widely from 1880 to 1887.[1]

The earliest one of the five songs is 'Hans und Grete'. Its original version titled 'Maitanz im Grünen' was one of three songs Mahler had optimistically headed as *5 Lieder für Tenorstimme*, 'dedicated to Josephine'. They were his first love songs; they were not to be his last. 'Maitanz' was composed on 5 March 1880, at a time when the young musician was leading the woeful existence of the unemployed in Vienna, and pining after Josephine Poisl, the postmaster's daughter in Iglau. Aside from its key, 'Maitanz' (in D major) is all but identical with 'Hans und Grete' (in F major and E♭ major for high and low voice, respectively).[2]

The text of this song is of more than passing interest, typical as it is of Mahler's love for folk (or folkish) poetry. At the same time, it is prophetic of the enigmatic relationship he was to have with his texts in general. A decidedly 'folkish' song in all respects, 'Hans und Grete' is identified as a *Volkslied* in the table of contents shared by the three song fascicles. The printer's copy of the song reveals that Mahler added the epithet as an afterthought, and then under the title. Yet there is no evidence to indicate that either the text or the melody is by anyone other than the composer himself.

If the poem of 'Hans und Grete' provides us with a telling glimpse into Mahler's relationship with folkish lyrics (to be developed fully in his long association with *Des Knaben Wunderhorn*), the texts he set in the remaining early *Lieder und Gesänge* hint at musico-poetic sensibilities which set him apart from his illustrious forerunners and contemporaries, in matters of taste as much as in his treatment of the borrowed poetry. His sole settings of verses of indisputable literary excellence are the two unfinished Heine songs, begun during his days at the Vienna Conservatoire. The closest he was to come to using poetry of at least comparable quality during the next four decades was with the verses of Friedrich Rückert. Similarly, while other composers of his own and of preceding generations showed marked preference for the lyrics of stylistically contemporaneous poets, Mahler neglected his literary coevals. But most notably, while earlier and contemporary composers treated a received text as largely inviolable, only rarely did he leave a text completely unaltered.

'Frühlingsmorgen' and 'Erinnerung' are settings of poems by Richard von Volkmann (1830–99), a physician who published copiously under the *nom de plume* 'Richard Leander'. The texts of 'Serenade' and 'Phantasie' were taken from Ludwig Braunfels's German rendering of the *Don Juan* play of 'Tirso de Molina' (*recte* the Mercedarian friar Gabriel Tellez, 1571–1648). Mahler invented each of the four song titles; though he made only minor changes in the borrowed verses, he created the entire second strophe of 'Phantasie'.

As is the case with the 'early' works in general, musically, too, the first five *Lieder und Gesänge* represent a microcosm of stylistic-technical

Example 5.1 'Frühlingsmorgen', piano accompaniment, bars 9–12

Note: Unless the inversion has special significance, chord symbols appear in root position. Chords or words in parantheses supply essential context.

characteristics which adumbrate, to varying degrees, most of those found in his later works. Two examples, selected for their harmonic and structural properties, will suffice to illustrate.

Tonality and harmony always rate careful consideration in Mahler's music; they have an especially important, musico-poetic function in his vocal works. While key relationships will be of greater interest in connection with the larger – especially cyclic – works, harmonic manipulation plays a role even in the smallest pieces, whether as architectonic device, as a signal for mood change, or to project something of hidden ideational import. 'Frühlingsmorgen' contains interesting, if somewhat uneven, foretokens of Mahler's later harmonic practices. The simple, essentially tonic–dominant world of the song is obscured at times by such devices as widely spaced dissonant aggregations, and simultaneous harmonies on different steps of the scale. As a rule, nearly continuous tonic or dominant pedals tend to mitigate such tonal disturbances. But in Example 5.1 the tonic pedal, though certainly present, is diffused and intermittent enough to allow the 'tone cluster' (functionally a secondary dominant) in bar 9, and the bi-level harmonic structure in the next bar (with the effective resolution postponed for another bar and a half) to be heard clearly, if fleetingly.

One of the reasons why recognition of Mahler's importance for the development of musical style in the twentieth century has grown so rapidly is that well-nigh none of it is 'strict', conceptually or technically pedantic, or predictable. This is especially true of form in his music. Consequently, when used with reference to Mahler's solo vocal music, the traditional terminology that had been pertinent to the art song for so long is often little more than a suggestive approximation, and practically never an accurate description. This observation is best supported by the fact that over one half of his songs are 'variations',[3] and every one of the remaining songs displays at least traces of the process.

In the following section on the *Lieder eines fahrenden Gesellen*, we shall encounter one of the truly complex song structures among Mahler's early works; later on, we shall see the same principle at work in the First Symphony. But for now, 'Serenade' and 'Phantasie' may serve as examples which illuminate by being exceptions to the rule. Lyric inserts in a stage play, the texts (doubled in length by the composer in the second instance) readily lent themselves to subdivision into regular stanzas. In all of his vocal works, it was here that Mahler came closest to pure strophic form, and it is chiefly for this reason that these two pieces are among his least inspired songs.

Before we leave the five miscellaneous songs published in 1892, a brief discussion of their accompaniments is in order. Although Mahler is properly regarded as a pioneer of the orchestral song, nearly one third of his total output in this genre has only a pianoforte accompaniment. Moreover, most of his later vocal works were initially composed with an appropriate keyboard accompaniment (as distinct from a short-score arrangement for piano). In general, the early pianoforte songs have an idiomatic accompaniment, one that tends to be undemanding of the pianist. It is largely voice-supporting and plays a subordinate role, though simple chordal passages are rare. There is occasional linear interest and some sharing of the melodic material between voice and piano. But two of the songs deserve attention beyond such simple facts, for they appear to foreshadow Mahler's instrumental-colouristic thinking in his song accompaniments and, as well, illustrate the type of problem that tends to arise with some frequency in dealing with this composer's music.

In the first edition, 'Serenade' displays the parenthetical phrase '(with the accompaniment of wind instruments)' under the title; 'Phantasie' calls on the pianist to 'imitate the tone of a harp', adding in a footnote: 'The accompaniment of a harp may possibly be suggested for this song'. The problem is that of the three annotations, only the advice to the pianist of 'Phantasie' appears in the manuscript, and although a printer's proof – so often the decisive evidence in such cases – is extant for 'Serenade', it lacks the subtitle printed in the first edition. What, then, are we to surmise of Mahler's wishes for these two accompaniments? Lacking additional sources, we may choose to accept the 'circumstantial' evidence of the printer's proof for 'Serenade': the fact that Mahler failed to make such a critical addition to it (as he did, albeit in a different context, in 'Hans und Grete') suggests that it is of spurious origin. By the same token, the lack of a printer's copy for 'Phantasie' shifts the burden of proof on to the first edition, and since both annotations were clearly meant only to guide, it seems reasonable to retain them in a modern edition.

Lieder eines fahrenden Gesellen

The two aspects of the *Lieder und Gesänge* just discussed, namely form and accompaniment, quite naturally lead us to the *Lieder eines fahrenden Gesellen*. For this set of four songs is a striking 'transitional' work between the early, exclusively piano-accompanied pieces and the later – certainly in their definitive guise purely orchestral – Lieder. But just as importantly, the *Lieder eines fahrenden Gesellen* virtually exploded the miniature formal world of the earlier collection. Though not necessarily longer, these Lieder are more intricate. Furthermore, they make up a cycle – a sort of 'super form' that *is* both more expansive and more complex. But to begin, we must deal briefly with two related problems which continue to confront the historian with ambiguities: the cycle's work history, and the provenance of its texts.[4]

The extant autograph text-sketches (for 'Die zwei blaue Augen von meinem Schatz', numbered and dated as 'I' and '15. Dezember 1884', and for 'Ich hab' ein glühend Messer', 'II' and '19. Dez. 84.') and Mahler's oft-quoted letter to Friedrich Löhr, penned on New Year's Day 1885 ('I have written a cycle of Lieder, six of them for the present'),[5] together raise the question: did Mahler write four more poems and set all six to music by 1 January, or had he merely completed the poems and called *these* 'Lieder', with customary German licence?

Three of another five poems the young composer wrote between August and December 1884 include the image of the wayfarer. Clearly, the idea had been in his mind for some time before he set to work on writing the texts for the *Gesellen* Lieder. When 'Die zwei blauen Augen' was still meant to open the cycle, one of the other poems could have been the 'closing' Lied he promised to send with his letter to Löhr; its last strophe rings 'right' for a cycle of cheerless wayfarer poems:

> Was ruhest du mein müder Fuss?
> Fahr' weiter stillen Leids Gefährte!
> Über alle Schönheit ich wandern muss,
> Ach, über die grüne, grüne Erde.[6]

One of the unsolved puzzles presented by the first editions of the cycle (published in 1897) is the date 'Dezember 1883'[7] printed under the composer's name. I have no doubt that the year has to do with the text of the cycle's opening song, 'Wenn mein Schatz Hochzeit macht', and with the hoary dispute about the young composer's 'discovery' of *Des Knaben Wunderhorn*. The received date of 1888 has long been discredited by the indisputable derivation of Mahler's text from one of the *Tanzreime* in the anthology, and by other, persuasive circumstantial evidence.

Recent literary scholarship has confirmed that conclusion by identifying an 1883 edition of the collection as the most likely source for Mahler's *Wunderhorn*-texts, and it was in May of that year that Mahler first visited Kassel, the spiritual and commercial centre of the *Wunderhorn*-cult; he moved there in August. It seems reasonable to suggest that he may have bought (or received as a gift) a copy of the new edition of the anthology already in 1883. We also know that he was in love with Johanna Richter by December of the same year;[8] and in the same month one year later he wrote the poem of 'Die zwei blauen Augen'. Evidently, both the year and the month imprinted on the first editions possessed extraordinary significance for Mahler even in 1897, and the desire to 'commemorate' them may have been strong enough to move him knowingly to propagate a false date.

While we may assume that Mahler composed the music of the *Gesellen* Lieder in 1885,[9] the orchestration of the cycle is more difficult to date. The type of paper used for the extant manuscript of the score points to 1891 or later. Then, in a letter dated 9 April 1893, the composer offered a 'Geschichte eines fahrenden Gesellen' 'with orchestral accompaniment' to an unidentified singer.[10] And finally, there can be little doubt that Natalie Bauer-Lechner saw Mahler *revising* that same score in January 1896.[11]

Though a tangled assortment of socio-musicological questions bears on Mahler's decision to orchestrate the *Gesellen* Lieder, a relatively simple technical reason arose from the need to translate vertically and horizontally complex musical structures into intelligible (that is to say, optimally transparent) musical sound. The following analysis of the cycle's third song, 'Ich hab' ein glühend Messer', provides us with a glimpse into these structural complexities. While such intricacy is not uncommon in Mahler's vocal music, here it is distinguished by the fact that it had to be validated and anchored, textually as well as musically, within the ideational and technical parameters of a musical cycle.

The vocal-melodic material of the song breaks down thus (except where otherwise indicated, the melody is derived from the orchestral score) (see Example 5.2).

With the addition of instrumental segments and basic harmonic analysis, the formal diagram of the song looks like Example 5.2.

Manifestly complex as a whole, this schema conceals a structure of amazing flexibility, allowing for a number of formal interpretations:

(1) A traditional-formal reading (one that coincides with the accompanimental articulation) divides the song into two asymmetrical parts: I (A^1A^2 B^1 C^1; 32 bars) and II (b_1 B^2 B^3A^3 C^2; 48 bars). Yet that asymmetry is contra-indicated in a number of ways. The four major dramatic and syntactic vocal sections are grouped in an ideally designed balance of tensions: first 'halves' that are both *similar* (repetition as AA and BB) and *disparate* (A *versus* B) are balanced by

Example 5.2 'Ich hab' ein glühend Messer', vocal-melodic material

rh = rhythmic shape
int = intervallic configuration

second 'halves' which reverse that relationship (B *versus* A followed by C and C). But as befits a closing section, C² is weightier: it is longer, and encompasses a wider vocal range.

(2) Two-part divisions are discernible also around three symmetrically determined, yet different 'central points':

(i) According to the number of bars (2 × 40; see ▌ in **Table** 5.1). In this division b₁, an apparently insignificant, rudimentary motive, serves to 'bridge' the two parts.

(ii) The song's mixed metre gives rise to two symmetrical divisions:

(a) According to the number of beats (crotchet; see ▲ in **Table** 5.1). Mathematically, the dividing line falls mid-way through bar 44, but musical sense relocates it to the end of the bar: here begins a new accompanimental texture which introduces the first vocal section of Part II.

(b) According to the number of pulses (quaver; see • in Table 5.1). As numerical and musical subdivisions fall within a semiquaver of each other, we may consider the dividing line to be at the end of bar 39 (this division shows similarities with both 1 and 2(i) above).

(3) The five-bar segment of the song which encompasses the three symmetrical dividing lines (40–5) forms a substantial instrumental module between Parts I and II. Yet it is readily expanded by sight and sound to include everything between C^1 and B^2. The result is a fifteen-bar 'bridge' between the two vocal parts, a major interlude that is a veritable musico-poetic 'centre of gravity'. If we regard prelude and postlude as discrete segments, we get the overall subdivision:

Prelude (1–4; 4 bars) Part I (5–30; 26 bars)

Interlude (31–45; 15 bars)

Part II (46–74; 29 bars) Postlude (75–80; 6 bars)

This figure represents an optimal combination of the best features of the asymmetrical (that is, traditional-formal) and symmetrical ('modern')

Table 5.1* 'Ich hab' ein glühend Messer', formal diagram

Part I

Section									
	Bars	1–4 instr							
	Key	Dm							
	Harmony	I							
A^1 ($\frac{9}{8}$ time sig.)	Bars	5–6	6–7	7–8	8–9	9–10	10–11		
	Melodic material	$(a_1$ –	$a_2 [\alpha_1 + \alpha_2]$ –	b_1 –	b_1 –	$b_2)$			
	Key	Dm							
	Harmony	I		VI II^7	V				
A^2	Bars	12–13	13	14–16	16–17				
	Melodic material	$(a_1 - a_2 [\alpha_1]$ –		b_3/α_2 –	$b_2)$				
	Key	Dm							
	Harmony	I		VI IV	$I_4^6 V^7$				
B^1	Bars	18–19	20–1	22	23	24–5			
	Melodic material	$(c_1$ {rh$_1$ int$_1$} –	c_2 {rh$_1$ int$_2$} – $b_3 [b_1/b_2 + b_1/b_2])$ –	instr					
	Key	Dm							
	Harmony	I	V° I Gm: V						
C^1	Bars	26–7 –	28	28–9	29–30	31–2			
	Melodic material	$(d_1$		b_1	$b_1)$	instr			
	Key	Gm							
	Harmony	I I^7 I$_4^6$ (VII^7 of V I^6)		(r)	(r)	I			

Table 5.1* (cont.)

Part II

Section		
	Bars	33–9 instr
	Key	Gm
	Harmony	I
	Bars	40 41 42–5
	Melodic material	• b_1 [β_1 + ■β_2] – instr (3 + ▲1)
	Key	Gm/G /C
	Harmony	(I) (V)
B^2	Bars	46–7 48–9 50–1 52
	Melodic material	(c_3 {rh_2 int_1} – c_4 {rh_3 int_3} – b_3) instr
	Key	C
	Harmony	V I_4^6 V V^7 I or: G/Gm I IV I Np. of G/Gm
B^3	Bars	53–4 55–6 56–7 57–8 58–9
	Melodic material	(c_5 {rh_3 int_1} – c_6 {rh_3 int_2} – b_1 – b_1 – b_1
	Key	C
	Harmony	V I_4^6 V^9 IV^7 VII^7 IV^7 or: G/Gm I IV I^9 or: Em I^{11} (no root) $Np^7 V^{7(o)}$ $Np^7 V^7$ Np^7 $I^{(\sharp 3-\text{natural }3)}$
A^3	Bars	60–1 62 63 63–4 65 66 67
	Melodic material	(a_1 – [$\frac{4}{4}$ b_3[b_1 + x + b_1 + b_1 + b_1]) instr time sig.]
	Key	Em
	Harmony	I $\sharp VI^7$ I^7 Np^7 $E^\flat$m: [II^7 V---------------------- (I, Np, IV, VII, V of V)]
C^2	Bars	68–71 71–2 72–4 75–80
	Melodic material	(d_2 – b_3 – d_3) – instr
	Key	$E^\flat$m
	Harmony	(V)---(bar 78: I)------

*This basic diagram is derived predominantly from the vocal melodic material; motivic variants are not so identified. Purely instrumental segments are marked with 'instr'; 'rh' stands for rhythmic shape, 'int' for intervallic configuration and (r) for repeat.

subdivisions. In addition, it simulates an ideal analytical construct, one that is as faithful as it can be to the *sound* of the piece of music it purports to represent, considering the well-known (and ultimately insuperable) limitations of 'translating' sound into symbol.

Given the weight of each *Gesellen* Lied, Mahler had to create a strong tonal scheme in order to make the encompassing cyclic 'form' a convincing

Example 5.3 First Symphony, Second Symphony and *Lieder eines fahrenden Gesellen*, comparison of tonal frameworks

● = original keys; M,m = Major, minor; b, mi, e = beginning, middle, end; tr. = transposed

one. As is clear from the printer's copy of the pianoforte version, sometime between late 1895 and 1897 he transposed the two middle songs up by a minor second and a minor third, respectively. Analysis reveals that it was this late decision that caused the *Gesellen* Lieder to jell as a true musical cycle. Moreover, the key scheme provides important clues to its work history.

The fact that Mahler transposed only two of the four songs implies that he was drawing on experience gained in the ordering of the large-scale, cyclic tonal structures of the First and Second Symphonies. The years during which these two works evolved (about 1884–94) subsume the entire period from the song cycle's inception to its long-delayed orchestration – but not to the revision of its key scheme.

If we consider the opening and closing keys of each *Gesellen* Lied and of each symphonic movement as being of equal structural moment, the similarities between the tonal orders of the song cycle and the symphonies is evident from Example 5.3.[12] Two such sets of coincidence are rendered at least unlikely by the following observations.

First, the high degree of similarity between the two pairs of key sequences would not exist if the second and third songs had remained in their original keys. Secondly, the regular cyclic recurrence of a given key, characteristic of the symphonies, materialized in the *Gesellen* Lieder only *after* the transposition of the middle songs. However, the rate and direction of the *overall* tonal progression common to the cycle and the Second Symphony had always been an integral part of the cycle's design. Given the late date of the Symphony's Finale, therefore, it seems not unreasonable to wonder whether Mahler's decisions concerning the Second Symphony may have been influenced by his experience with the song cycle. And admitting such a possibility makes virtually *any* chronological permutation of the *Gesellen* Lieder and the two symphonies plausible.

First Symphony

Necessarily conjectural as the foregoing comments are on the ties that appear to bind the *Lieder eines fahrenden Gesellen* and the Second Symphony, connections between the song cycle and the First Symphony are both abundant and beyond argument. Not surprisingly, some of these connections arise from their shared, convoluted chronology.

Unhappily, there exists no evidence to document the inception of the First Symphony. If we believe Guido Adler (Mahler's lifelong friend and supporter, and an eminent music historian), it fell in the same year as that of the *Gesellen* Lieder, namely, 1884.[13] But then both works disappear from sight for about four years, until we find the young musician writing to his friend Löhr in evident elation in March 1888: 'So! My work is finished! . . . I must out into the open . . . For six weeks, I have had nothing but the desk in front of me!'[14] The remark about 'six weeks' suggests that all his work on the Symphony was done after the middle of January. To be sure, he had been desperately busy until then with the creative and production work on Weber's reconstituted *Die drei Pintos* (première on 20 January in Leipzig).

If it is justified to describe *Das klagende Lied* as one of the most impressive 'opera 1' in post-classical music, the First Symphony surely deserves similar recognition. Moreover, just as that hybrid vocal-orchestral work seems unclassifiable, the traditional generic label is an uncomfortable fit for this piece, despite its apparently 'symphonic' character. At least in part, this is due to the unprecedented concentration with which it compounds such 'new' aspects of symphonic music as non-traditional structure (in itself relatively commonplace since Schubert, Schumann, Berlioz and Liszt), parody (already employed by Berlioz), and the instrumental reuse of vocal materials (well established since Schubert). Yet a full explanation for the uniqueness of Mahler's First Symphony must, I think, be sought in the totality of his symphonic conception. While the focus here is necessarily on the first one of a *series* of works (all unique in one way or another), the mostly linear stylistic development of Mahler's oeuvre, and the availability of much first- and second-hand information from later years, make for a practicable quest.

Symphonic music after Beethoven had been increasingly characterized by a contest between the architectonic type and the dynamic forces inherent in the material. The growing ascendancy of variational relationships caused the 'type' to become less important than the 'form' generated by the thematic material. As his letter to the critic Max Marschalk in the spring of 1896 shows, Mahler saw clearly the ongoing evolution of the symphonic idea:

> Now we are . . . at the great cross roads which forever separate . . . the mutually exclusive paths of symphonic and dramatic music. – Just compare a Beethoven symphony with Wagner's tone structures, and you will perceive the essential differences. – . . . Wagner made the *expressive means* of symphonic music his own, just as now the symphonist . . . will gain ground again in his resources.[15]

He was also keenly aware of his own unique contribution. In a remark to Bauer-Lechner in 1895, we see the idea of a new symphonic concept materialize out of the in-progress Third: 'That I call it a symphony is, in the literal sense, unfounded, for it does not keep to the inherited form in any respect. But symphony means to me simply to erect a universe with all resources of the available technique. The ever-new and changing content itself determines its own form.'[16]

Recognizing this newness, and his willingness to assume the mantle and burden of a pioneer, constituted two sides of Mahler's overall symphonic concept; the intensely personal (not to say autobiographical) nature of the creative act, and the current questions surrounding programme music, represented two others.

During the summer of 1893 (that is, before he had completed the Second Symphony), Mahler was already looking back:

> My two symphonies sum up the entire content of my life . . . And if one were able to read it well, my life would have to be revealed to him as actual fact. With me, creating and experiencing are linked to such an extent that if my existence were henceforth to flow as peacefully as a brook in a meadow, I could never again . . . make anything good.[17]

Such trenchant statements notwithstanding, the critical line between 'life' and 'music' continued to be elusive. In his often faltering attempts to locate it, Mahler kept returning to the First Symphony, its programmatic connections with the *Gesellen*-Lieder, and the experience behind it:

> 1896: the Symphony commences beyond *the love affair*; . . . the external experience formed the work's *motivation*, not its content.

> 1897: please, my dear friend, leave the '*fahrenden Gesellen*' episode of my life alone. (The *connection* with the I. Symphony is a purely *artistic* one.)[18]

Although Mahler's apparent vacillation was caused by chronological-psychological distancing, a much broader ambivalence underlay it, one that was part and parcel of the *Zeitgeist* for a young, progressive composer of the age. It concerned the problem of programme music. In his middle period, he began to sound defensive about earlier 'transgressions', such as in the case of the First Symphony:

> 20 March 1896: at the time my friends persuaded me to provide the
> D major with a kind of programme, in order to facilitate its understanding.
> So I thought up this title ['Titan'] and explanations after the fact. That
> I omitted them on this occasion was not only because I do not consider
> [the work] fully or ... appropriately characterized by them, but while it
> was something that I had experienced, the public was badly misled by it.[19]

Soon he took pride in being recognized by Arthur Seidl (a 'friendly' critic) as someone who was different from the most popular 'programme' composer of the day:

> 1897: You have characterized my goals ... quite appropriately: ... my 'music
> arrives at the programme ultimately as its final ideal clarification, whereas
> with Strauss the programme is provided as the given task'.[20]

But when all is said, and Mahler's understandable denials and dissembling notwithstanding, we need have no doubt that he did, indeed, write 'programme' symphonies. The totality of his symphonic music stands as a grand autobiographical record of unique personal expression.

Before we look at the First Symphony's opening movement, it is necessary to consider briefly the original second movement, the andante 'Blumine'. Though Mahler was no stranger to indecision about the overall plan of large works, only twice did he eliminate movement-sized sections, both from early compositions. But while the case of *Das klagende Lied* was an aesthetically and musically complex one, 'Blumine' presented a simpler problem.

It is not unreasonable to wonder today why Mahler included 'Blumine' in the First Symphony at all. While it had undoubtedly served Scheffel's popular *Der Trompeter von Säkkingen* well, its symphonic existence is justified neither by the quality of the invention, nor by the treatment of the material. Two explanations offer themselves: either the young composer felt inordinately attached to music that reminded him of happier times in Kassel, or, hard-pressed to complete the Symphony in 1888, he included the piece as a 'suitable' slow movement. In either case, he soon realized his error: though the piece is still in place in the score he 'renovated' in 1893, and though some feel that its removal deprived the Symphony of a 'typical' slow movement,[21] he omitted it for the work's fourth performance in 1896 and, as far as we know, never considered it for publication.

Judging solely from the differences that characterize various analyses of the first movement of the First Symphony, we could conclude that this is an exceptionally problematic piece of music. However, closer scrutiny of such disagreements with respect to the overall form, the nature and function of the 'introduction', or the nomenclature and origin of the thematic material reveals that they are due chiefly to the inherent inadequacies of a conventionally formulaic approach to this music. Not only are the traditional boundaries of 'exposition', 'development' and 'recapitulation' blurred here, but also the architectonic conventions of academic sonata form are subjected to far-reaching reinterpretation and modification (nevertheless, custom and convenience dictate that I retain the conventional terminology for at least the main sections of 'sonata form'). The first sixty-one bars of the Symphony will serve to illustrate the need for a fresh view of the movement.

This section is usually described as an 'introduction' to the 'first movement proper'. Yet a detailed examination of it and of its uses readily shows that, in the overall musical-technical and aesthetic context of the work, it is no more a conventional 'introduction' than are similar sections in, say, Schumann's D Minor and Bruckner's Ninth Symphonies – or in Mahler's Ninth some twenty years later. Indeed, the 'exposition' is under way from the first note of the movement, and that with its most fertile component.

On the motivic level, the 'introduction' presents (and immediately manipulates) the germinal unit of the entire Symphony: the interval of the fourth. To mention but two of many links: the derived fourth-motive (bars 7–9) returns transformed in the Finale (bars 385–95), while the stylized cuckoo-call (bars 30–2) recurs in two different guises in the funeral march (bars 21–2 and 48–9).[22] Structurally, four materially and functionally well-differentiated variants of the section occur in the work: as an initial expository area (the opening sixty-one bars); as a concentrated articulating device (reduced to the 'ticking' fourths), bridging two major thematic subsections in the middle of the 'exposition' (bars 104–8); as a full-scale intra-movemental referent providing the entire first part of the 'development' (bars 163–206); and as a major inter-movemental, recapitulatory-cyclic gesture, introducing the restatement of the second thematic group in the Finale (bars 428–57).

The 'introductory' sixty-one bars constitute an equally important ideational element of the first movement. The Nature-painting aspects of the section (headed by Mahler 'Wie ein Naturlaut') serve to prefigure in elemental sound that which will be projected by the melodic material rested from its associations in the second *Gesellen* Lied ('Und da fing im Sonnenschein/gleich die Welt zu funkeln an', and so on). 'Rested from', for the specific order and meaning of the ideas and images was at no time intended to be taken over into the symphonic movement. This is evident from the order in which Mahler reused the pre-existent material, and as well from his otherwise baffling selection of motives and phrases. Direct quotes add up to only seventy-three of the song's 127 bars, most of them in the three subjects of the first thematic group: bars 62–9 (cellos); 84–106 (mostly first violins, with motivic interpolations by first flute and oboe); and 117–35 (mostly second violins, with substantial contributions from the first violins, and lesser ones from flutes and oboes).

Because of the nature and origin of the melodic material, the second section of the 'exposition' (bars 62–162) is monothematic and developmental; both of these aspects are confirmed in the section that follows it (this is usually described as the 'development'). In addition to the expected, ongoing manipulation of the song material, it incorporates a complete exposition of the freely invented, ternary second thematic group (horns in bars 208–18; cellos in 220–4 and 231–5).

It should not surprise us by now that the end of the 'development' is elusive. Indeed, *if* this movement has a 'recapitulation' at all (and the unceasing manipulation of a diversity of melodic material that far exceeds the sonata 'norm' makes one wonder), it has two starts. The first one (commonly held to be the beginning of the 'recapitulation', for reasons that seem to be limited to the forceful return of the tonic key at this point) occurs at bar 358, with the onset of a brief variant version of the first subject of the *second* group, that is to say, material that is neither from the 'exposition' nor yet whole. On the other hand, in bar 383 the first subject of the first group is brought back in a manner which combines the salient characteristics of its twofold 'exposition': it is in the tonic (as were bars 62–9, borrowed from the very opening of the underlying song), and its music is derived from the second strophe of the song (as were bars 108–16, although there in the dominant). To be sure, here the music slides into the recapitulatory mode, as it were; but this is only superficially different from the kind of recapitulation we find in the first movement of Brahms's Fourth Symphony, a work completed some three years before Mahler's First. On any account, then, a claim on behalf of this structural point as the beginning of such 'recapitulation' as may exist in this movement would seem to be hard to dismiss.[23]

Certain aspects of the movement's modulatory scheme also arise from its deep roots in a song, thus contributing to the vulnerability of a putative sonata form. Even though the movement ends in D major, the four major subsections of the 'exposition' (that is, the 'introduction' and the three subjects of the first group) regularly return to – and chiefly move in – A major, despite brief excursions into other keys. This, generically 'strophic', behaviour recalls 'Ging heut' morgen über's Feld' in a number of ways. The first subject of the first thematic group (bars 62–9) begins in D major, and the second subject (bars 84–106) in E major, before they both continue in A major: the brief tonal arches imitate the song's subsectional tonal relationships. Secondly, although D major is first secured only with the exposition of the second group in the 'development' section, it returns regularly thereafter; thus, the symphonic movement seems to consist of two tonal 'halves', one each in A and D majors. This is reminiscent of the large-scale tonal relationships in the song, where the first half is in D major, the second in B and/or F♯ majors.

Clearly, already in the first movement of his First Symphony Mahler retained the traditional structural and tonal relationships of the 'sonata form' only as an overall, flexible framework. The following, brief comments on the remaining three movements will suffice to show that these, too, had been conceived and executed according to the same principle.

The composer called the three-part second movement a 'Scherzo' at the early performances of the work. The fact that only the 'Trio' designation of the middle section survived publication may indicate that Mahler recognized the distinctly Ländler-inspired style of the music. The oft-mentioned affinity to (if not 'derivation' from) 'Hans und Grete' of the movement's various motivic fragments and rhythmic attributes is, in truth, little more than a matter of a shared style between song and symphonic movement. Neville Cardus's thought-provoking suggestion that Mahler derived the main subject of the movement by rhythmic transformation from the opening phrase of the first movement's first subject has failed to attract attention.[24]

The so-called 'funeral march', the virtual slow movement, is also in a tripartite form. Mahler's symbolically pregnant, much-discussed use of the 'Brüder Jakob' canon in the outer sections notwithstanding, the musico-poetic masterstroke of the movement (if not of the entire First Symphony) is the very literal derivation of the middle section from the second part of 'Die zwei blauen Augen von meinem Schatz', closing song of the *Lieder eines fahrenden Gesellen*. Unlike in the case of the first movement, here the borrowed musical material is not 'rested' from its context in the song cycle. Rather, the 'song without words' character of this episode and its structural placement explicate and resolve the ambiguity that was created at the end of the song cycle. There, the implied finality of the protagonist's escape from reality through sleep (or 'is this', as Eichendorff-Strauss mused in 'Im Abendrot' some sixty years later, 'perhaps, death?') seemed to have been contradicted by the cadential six-four chords. Now, in the third movement of the First Symphony, the return of the 'funeral march' unambiguously signals a return to a painful but concrete reality.

According to the Symphony's 1893 programme, it is the outcry of that 'most deeply wounded heart' that we hear at the opening of the last movement. Here Mahler succeeded in balancing the demands of a 'narrative' overall form and a recognizable (if predictably distorted) symphonic finale. Though 'vocal' (chorale- and aria-like) material is used prominently, it is subordinated to the architectonic scheme.

The totality of the First Symphony, and of all such works thereafter, reflects the freedom with which Mahler approached the extra-movemental form. The resulting unique symphonic canon readily accounts for works of widely differing sizes (that is, with two, four, five or six movements) and greatly variegated movement types (in other words, the symphony as 'universe'). In the case of the First, then, its make-up from three song- and dance-dominated (and thus more suite-like) movements and an essentially symphonic finale cannot be dismissed as the flawed creation of a young and inexperienced composer, an attitude that was not uncommon even among the sympathetic critics following the first performance, and whose condescension lingered on well into the twentieth century. In the event, it inaugurated an epochal development that consummated romantic symphonic music by merging its dual streams and created a storehouse of musical-technical and aesthetic ideas, devices and procedures which were to inspire the multi-faceted renascence of the genre in our time.

6 Song and song-symphony (I). *Des Knaben Wunderhorn* and the Second, Third and Fourth Symphonies: music of heaven and earth

PETER REVERS
(*translated by* JEREMY BARHAM)

'Storytelling in song': Mahler's songs from *Des Knaben Wunderhorn*

It would scarcely be an exaggeration to suggest that Mahler's compositional 'genetic code' can be located in his Lieder output. Many of Mahler's songs show a distinct ambiguity: even the texts of folk songs or children's songs often contain a note of tragedy, farewell, separation or death. Songs on the subject of war or military life, for example, often depict grotesque and disturbing images. It is particularly in the songs of *Des Knaben Wunderhorn* that Mahler emphasized an unmediated proximity to life, and he was well aware that his choice of texts contrasted sharply with the Lied tradition up to that time. In a letter to Ludwig Karpath from 2 March 1905,[1] Mahler revealed not only his distinct awareness of being the pioneer of a new Lied aesthetic but also his attempts to return to the roots of artistic creativity, and to unveil these as yet untouched by the controlling power of the artistic process – something which is also expressed in his textual additions to the poems. His vivid description of the *Wunderhorn* texts as 'blocks of marble'[2] should be understood in the sense of their being raw or natural materials which first require individual moulding and shaping.

Since there are particularly close links between the *Wunderhorn* collection and the first *Gesellenlied*, Mahler must have encountered the anthology at the very latest during his time in Kassel (1883–5). In 1895 Mahler was given a copy of the three-volume first edition (Heidelberg 1806/08) by Anna Bahr-Mildenburg, for which he was effusive in his thanks: 'It is so lovely that its contents are almost new to me, that I am not mistaken after all and that I am composing one or other song for the second time. All that is due to you.'[3] The relationship between the piano and orchestral version of Mahler's songs has until quite recently been subject to conflicting interpretations. It has now been established that the piano versions can each claim independent status. Only the group of nine early *Wunderhornlieder* were composed exclusively as piano songs. The majority of the *Wunderhorn* songs nevertheless exist in two formats, and the piano version of 'Es sungen drei Engel' (1895) appeared after the orchestral version (the fifth movement of the Third Symphony). Although Mahler produced all the orchestral *Wunderhorn* songs in piano versions as well, and although fourteen of these fifteen songs were published during his lifetime, shortly after his death Universal Edition had the piano editions brought into line with the orchestral versions, and these 'adapted piano versions' formed the basis of all performances until 1993. It was only during the course of Renate Hilmar-Voit's and Thomas Hampson's work on the Critical Edition of the *Wunderhorn* songs that Mahler's piano versions were reconstructed. The differences between the versions include dynamics, phrasing, tempi, even pitch and duration, and not least the sung text. Conversely, instructions appear in the piano versions which could be interpreted as plans for orchestral adaptation (for example, the indication 'Trompetenmusik' in the piano version of 'Trost im Unglück' or the comment in 'Zu Straßburg auf der Schanz" that, with the help of the pedal, low piano trills were to 'imitate the sound of muffled drums'). Another important performance practice issue is the substantially reduced string section of his 'chamber-music-like songs' compared with that of his symphonies,[4] and those orchestral songs which Mahler reworked into symphonic movements are especially significant. Bauer-Lechner recalled that in 1901 Mahler 'was busy reworking the instrumentation of "Das himmlische Leben"',[5] so that it matched the Fourth Symphony's substantially larger orchestral apparatus. Mahler did not just expand the smaller orchestra of the song version with additional instruments, but in fact completely rescored it. 'Each instrument must be used only in the appropriate place, and according to its own individual qualities';[6] this demand should serve as a guide, particularly for performances of his orchestral songs, and with particular reference to instrumental dimensions.

For example, Mahler initially wrote the song 'Urlicht' (19 July 1893) as an independent orchestral song, a version which only became known in 1998 from the Critical Edition. The song went through two subsequent reworkings: as the fourth movement of the Second Symphony, and as the version that appeared in 1899 with other orchestral *Wunderhorn* songs under the title 'Urlicht – Alt Solo aus der 2. Symphonie'. These three versions at times reveal marked differences in orchestral forces and instrumentation. In the Second Symphony, the distinctive instrumental sound of the song's introductory eleven-bar chorale for horns, trumpets, bassoons and contrabassoons, marked *sehr feierlich, aber schlicht* (*very solemn, yet simple*), is pushed even further into the background of the orchestral body. At this point, music is removed from linguistic

Example 6.1 'Urlicht', alto line bars 14–20, 22–6 and 54–62

b.14-20

Der Mensch liegt in gröss - ter Not! Der Mensch liegt in gröss - ter Pein!

b. 22-6

Je lie - ber_ möcht' ich im Him - mel_ sein,

b. 54-62

zart drängend *mit steigerndem Ausdruck*

Ich bin von Gott und will wie - der zu Gott! Der lie - be Gott, der

58 *rit.* *molto rit.*

lie - be Gott wird mir ein Licht-chen ge - ben, wird leuch - ten_ mir

expression and belongs to a different transcendental world, from which, as if from a distance, it steals into the reality of human suffering addressed in the subsequent text. The form of the song reflects the path from human uncertainty to salvation in a variety of ways. In the first place, the song's opening is very distinctive. In the first two bars the lines 'O Röschen rot' ring out like a motto. This open-ended statement represents the ambivalent symbol of the rose which in biblical interpretation stands for both the hope and the fragility of humankind. The wind chorale fills this 'empty semantic space' with an aura of religiosity, and only after it has faded away in bar 13 does the voice, embedded in a subdued string texture, enter again with the words 'Der Mensch liegt in größter Not!' The beginning of the chorale is not quoted until the end of the first verse, where the longing for heavenly existence first finds expression, and this is taken up again at the end of the song with the words 'ewig selig Leben'. What the chorale intimated at its first appearance is made clear through specific textual allusions at its resumption. It allows one to glimpse – vaguely at first – that vision of unending peace and divine salvation, that human self-consciousness addressed towards the end of the poem: 'Ich bin von Gott und will wieder zu Gott'. That all human suffering is eradicated in this statement is shown not least by its particular motivic shaping. The allusions to the realm of suffering with which the alto solo began are unmistakeable, and the metaphor of light invoked in the song title is thus clarified (Example 6.1).

While the chorale in the fourth movement ('Urlicht') remains in a gentle, intimate mood, in the Finale it forms part of the distinctly theatrical intensifying passages at bars 160 and 192 onwards. It is patently obvious that the song movement is integrated into the Second Symphony's cyclical structure, that it does not lie 'outside the schematic plot of the symphony ... but has a clear dramaturgical function in preparing for the Finale, as a lyrical and entirely recessive point of inertia [*Nullpunkt*] before the latter's dramatic explosion'.[7]

Specific instrumental characters play a decisive role in many of the *Wunderhorn* songs. The unison beginning of 'Zu Straßburg auf der Schanz'' is a signal-like gesture representative of that extra-territorial element which bursts apart the delineated world of rigid military discipline from the outside and serves as the real catalyst for the soldier's desertion. The military drum and march vocabulary contrasts with the nature-like motives of this introductory alpine horn section. Both horn and drum roll are sounds symbolic of the human condition: on the one hand a longing for freedom and home, and on the other hand a military code that precludes any emotional sentiment. The dramatic tension of the song essentially derives from the conflict between these two worlds.

With their immediacy of expression, those songs whose texts deal with war, the military, persecution and repression are among the most significant of the *Wunderhorn* collection. Like 'Zu Straßburg auf der Schanz'', 'Lied des Verfolgtem im Turm' is defined by the conflict between expressive characters: a prisoner's impassioned outburst of expressive freedom is set against the naively coaxing song of a girl vividly describing that freedom. Mahler again uses a series of musical vocables: call-like patterns and yodelling sounds for the girl, and fanfares and signals for the prisoner. The two seemingly opposed spheres of expression nevertheless have close motivic and tonal links.

This song is one of a group of dialogue songs which prompted a long-standing misconception in performance. Its implicit 'division of roles' has frequently resulted in the allocation of male and female voices. This is substantiated neither by the score nor by performance traditions during Mahler's lifetime, and in fact contradicts the concept of dialogue songs. For rather than a dialogue between independent individuals, there is an inner dialogue, reflecting various emotional states, modes of thinking or expression, and psychological conflicts within one individual. In an entirely radical way, far exceeding the Lied traditions of the nineteenth century, Mahler thus gives voice to the oppositions of this world: on the one hand, the sentimentality, the coarseness and the ordinariness of life, and on the other hand the suffering, pain and brutality of existence. The allusions to the banal lead at times to 'shock effects that are already modern. Ceaselessly torn between mockery and nostalgia, these episodes also reflect the multicoloured spectacle of everyday experience, of its ambiguities and contradictions – a true image of life in all its heterogeneity.'[8]

The tetralogy of Symphonies 1–4

Mahler's description of his first four symphonies as 'in their content and structure ... a perfectly self-contained tetralogy'[9] inevitably brings to mind associations with music drama. This suggests a compositional process of epic proportions in which the intimation of varied time-frames is an essential element. There are many different motivic and thematic connections between these symphonies, and Mahler himself stressed the 'particularly close relationship ... between the Third and the Fourth', a fact he judged 'so unusual and remarkable' that he even had 'misgivings about it himself'.[10] But the tetralogy also forms an over-arching eschatological scheme which corresponds to certain aspects surrounding the works' origins. For example, Mahler described the inspiration for the Finale of the Second Symphony as a religious-metaphysical lightning bolt. He summarized the key event, the funeral of Hans von Bülow, as follows: 'Then the choir, up in the organ-loft, intoned Klopstock's *Resurrection* chorale. – It flashed on me like light-ning, and everything became plain and clear in my mind! It was the flash that all creative artists wait for – "conceiving by the Holy Ghost"!'[11] Religious implications thus surface in Mahler's own verbal descriptions of his music. The metaphysical claims of his overall symphonic concept become clear from his letter of 26 March 1896 to Max Marschalk, in which, before going on to address some of the profound questions of human existence, he wrote of the first movement (*Totenfeier*) of his Second Symphony 'it is the hero of my D major symphony who is being borne to his grave, his life being reflected, as in a clear mirror, from a point of vantage'.[12] Mahler was in no doubt that his Second Symphony grew 'directly out of the First',[13] thereby emphasizing an evolutionary, rather than self-contained, narrative structure for which traditional formal demarcations were of limited relevance. Moreover, from his First Symphony onwards, Mahler developed a unique musical logic, based on evolving development and a parataxis of concise motivic-thematic building blocks, that largely replaced the dialectical principle of sonata form. Mahler himself said to Natalie Bauer-Lechner that compos-ing was like 'playing with bricks, continually making new buildings from the same old stones'.[14] Musical experiences from childhood and youth were of primary importance for his compositional vocabulary.

These 'basic musical objects, types and idioms'[15] frequently alluded to universal, and thus inter-subjective acoustic experiences, pointing to the world of real sounds and acoustic materials.

Compositional clarity: *Totenfeier* and Mahler's Second Symphony

> I demand that everything must be heard exactly as it sounds in my inner ear. To achieve this, I exploit all available means to the utmost . . . It doesn't do, in these matters, to have preconceived ideals which simply do not correspond with reality.[16]

The meticulous way in which Mahler pursued optimum clarity in the presentation of his musical ideas is apparent from his numerous retouchings and instrumental alterations which he even made to published works. For Mahler, the detailed formulation of timbre was also an integral part of musical structure. The reworking of the symphonic poem *Totenfeier* (1888) as the first movement of the Second Symphony (1894) gives an important demonstration of how Mahler attained the greatest possible musical clarity. A comparison reveals that Mahler's translation of his compositional ideas into notation was far more complex in the Symphony than in *Totenfeier*. In revising the score, Mahler left nothing to the habits of interpreters, whom he considered had always had a reputation for 'slovenliness' (*Schlamperei*). His sound-world is always precisely articulated, and in a certain sense he composes the interpretation of the music in its notation (Example 6.2).

The genesis of the Second Symphony reveals the fundamental importance which song had as a source of inspiration for Mahler's symphonic writing. Mahler later described the piano version of the song 'Des Antonius von Padua Fischpredigt' (8 July 1893) as a 'preliminary study for the Scherzo of the Second'.[17] Eight days later, the score of the third movement (which was originally planned as the second) was completed in sketch; the fair copy of 'Urlicht' is dated three days after this (19 July 1893). On 30 July Mahler completed the sketch of the Ländler movement (which was originally to be placed fourth). Mahler dated the fair copy of the *Wunderhorn* song 'Des Antonius von Padua Fischpredigt' 1 August, that is to say *after* completing the sketch of the Scherzo movement. The conception of the work thus started with the inner movements, over whose ordering Mahler nevertheless vacillated for a long time. The reworking of *Totenfeier* into the first movement and the composition of the Finale did not take place until spring and summer 1894.

The precise role of programmatic ideas in the Second Symphony is not easy to ascertain, for Mahler offered several different descriptions of the

Example 6.2 (a) *Totenfeier*, violin and viola parts, bars 31–7; (b) Second Symphony, first movement, violin and viola parts, bars 31–7

work's content. While *Totenfeier* is clearly linked to the First Symphony in a letter of 26 March 1896 to Max Marschalk, the first movement of the Second, according to Bauer-Lechner, depicts 'the titanic struggles of a mighty being still caught in the toils of this world: grappling with life and with the fate to which he must succumb – his death'.[18] In the programme notes Mahler provided for the Symphony's Dresden performance on 20 December 1901, the theme is one of remembrance before the coffin of a loved one: 'We are standing beside the coffin of a man beloved. For the last time his life, battles, his sufferings and his purpose pass before the mind's eye.'[19] The lack of uniformity among programmatic accounts can be attributed to the fact that they do not so much present a self-contained sequence of events as pose fundamental existential questions. In this respect the question of whether Adam Mickiewicz's *Dziady* formed the literary basis of *Totenfeier* (for which there is no conclusive evidence) is also of secondary importance.[20]

Differences in structure and musical dramaturgy between *Totenfeier* and the later symphonic movement are also evident. For example, the intensely dramatic quotation of the main theme during the development

Plate 6.1 *Totenfeier*, bars 249–59. © Copyright 1988 by Universal Edition A. G., Vienna.
Reproduced by permission, all rights reserved.

(from bar 244), emphasized by *ff* tam-tam strokes, is presented much less forcefully in *Totenfeier* (Plate 6.1).

The assembling of the inner and outer movements (summer 1893 and spring/summer 1894 respectively) cannot have been merely fortuitous, but left traces in the dramaturgy of the work. In the first place there is a curious discrepancy in the first movement between the ostensibly clear demarcation of formal sections and an autonomous dramatic construction characterized by breakdowns and sudden losses of energy. This is particularly evident in the unexpected onset of a dynamically forced *katabasis*[21] at the end of the first movement (bars 441–5). This was anticipated at the end of the development (from bars 316 and 329) where the latter collapse is articulated especially through the 'undomesticated and almost operatic, crude violence of its rhythmic and orchestral power'.[22]

When Adorno said that the first movement 'generally shows the collapsing tendency',[23] this doubtless referred to a significant aspect of the musical content that can only be understood in relation to the Finale. For both of the breakdowns specified above involve a collapse of the energy that has gradually built up from bar 254 and which, in bars 282–9, anticipates a passage in the final movement (bars 301–9). In that movement, the *katabasis* (bars 311–23) immediately precedes a variant of the subsidiary theme which, together with the 'extra-territorial' interjections of the off-stage orchestra, conjures up an apocalyptic soundscape. Since the meaning of the passage is clearly defined by the subsequent vocal statement 'O glaube, mein Herz o glaube. Es geht Dir nichts verloren' from bar 561, the inner significance of the *katabasis* figure and the aforementioned quotation from the first movement is revealed: they point to the *peripeteia*[24] from the collapse of the real world into apocalypse, to a trust in God which develops into certain salvation after the 'Großen Appell' (bars 448–71) and the reprise of the main theme in the unaccompanied choral entry at 'Auferstehn' (from bar 472).[25] As with the Finale of the First Symphony, the underlying sonata form is shrouded here in a complex network of reminiscences and anticipations. The former are found particularly at the beginning of the movement, which recalls the outburst from bar 465 in the Scherzo, described by Mahler as a 'death-shriek'. The fact that the first crucial anticipation (bars 26–42) follows immediately after this – the motive intoned at the end of the Finale to the words 'Sterben werd' ich, um zu leben' – makes it clear from the outset that the movement's form is entirely determined by its transcendent content. The paratactic construction of the Finale's opening is divided into three sections: (a) *fff* outburst ('death-shriek'): bars 1–25; (b) anticipation of the 'Sterben werd' ich, um zu leben': bars 26–42; and (c) 'Kleiner Appell': bars

43–61. These are clearly separated by the *Cäsur* marking (bar 25) or general pause (bar 43), but the opening passage as a whole lacks the distinct thematic profile fundamental to the process of exposition. Nevertheless, Mahler carries out all the more obviously an 'exposition of content', in which essential stages in the movement's dramaturgy are presented in condensed manner. The Finale strikingly exemplifies the degree to which formal categories of sonata form are emancipated from the primacy of motivic-thematic processes and instead merely form the supporting foundations of an overriding dramatic progression. The development section (bars 194–447), with its blatant march-like character, also refers back to the first movement. The 're-formulation' of the Finale's main themes into march themes not only underlines the dynamic formal function such sections have had since time immemorial, but also signals the relentless forward-moving process which will achieve its greatest dramatic highpoint in the apocalyptic vision. The extent to which the Finale's form is shaped by a scenically inclined dramatic conception is revealed not least by the difficulty of accommodating both the 'Großen Appell' and the ensuing choral entry into the conventional framework of sonata form. In the spatial disposition of its sonorities and its signal-like qualities, the 'Großer Appell' clearly recalls the corresponding passage in the exposition (from bar 43), and is thus mediated thematically. But with the idiosyncratic suspension of all dynamic progression, and a literally 'transcendent' (*'entrückten'*) sonority, Mahler creates a completely detached, 'insular' atmosphere, marked by the liberation of time and space and the removal of all subjectivity's powers of subjugation.

The scherzo movement, based on the *Wunderhorn* song 'Des Antonius von Padua Fischpredigt', offers a counter-example to this. Its 'aimlessly circling'[26] semiquaver movement was described by the composer as a terrifying vision of 'life ceaselessly in motion, never resting, never comprehensible'.[27] Though seemingly beyond human control, it is still possible for the relentless march of time to be halted, at least temporarily, by an intense subjective intervention (the *fff* orchestral outburst described by Mahler as a 'cry of disgust'[28]), and for it to yield to an expressive and lyrical trumpet cantilena. Here Mahler vigorously deploys that kind of dynamic process which, through the sheer power of the compositional act, enables an individual to embody his 'own temporality structured around personal events'.[29] The variety and complexity of differing temporalities are among the outstanding innovations of Mahler's early symphonic writing. The 'suspension of temporal thinking in terms of event and history'[30] in the 'Großen Appell' of the Finale, and the highly dramatic subjective intervention in the chronologically ordered temporality of the scherzo movement, are just the twin poles between which a broad spectrum of 'lived temporalities' extends: time appears in Mahler not only as steady flow, but also to a large extent as a complex of 'discontinuous, spontaneous, creative acts'.[31]

The Third Symphony

Aspects of temporal structuring also contribute to the unique formal principles of the Third Symphony. The abrupt parataxis of differing 'temporal ruptures'[32] is treated with particular suppleness in the third movement, the 'animal piece' based on Mahler's *Wunderhorn* song 'Ablösung im Sommer', revealing in microcosm the extent to which the temporality of the subject dictates the progression of the movement. In a radical juxtaposition, 'measured time' as the inexorable passing of the present, comes face to face here with a nostalgic invocation of the past as the expression of the individual and his own particular temporal domain. Both the 'metronomic' pulse and the harmonic structure in which leading-note movement and cadence-like progressions are avoided, create the impression of 'lifeless, mechanical motion', and this is further intensified by the 'stubborn repetition of the opening bird-call motive' (clarinet, from bar 3).[33] In contrast to this, the posthorn episodes function as the quintessence of the 'Other',[34] timbrally articulating an apparent distant idyll in the tone of the instrument itself whose connotations of promised but deceptive idyll are specifically adopted by Mahler from earlier works such as 'Die Post' from Schubert's *Winterreise*.

Precisely because the posthorn episodes are 'bordering on the mawkish or even kitschy',[35] because they allude so directly to the realms of the Lied and fashionable cantilena, their termination seems thoroughly disenchanting. Through the trumpet's military signal 'Abblasen' (bars 345–6), reverie is forced to give way to reality as if in some film scene. This corresponds with the mood of the song text: compassion for the cuckoo which has fallen to its death is not thematized here, but rather the laws of nature within which the fate of a single individual is of no significance. More than in the other movements of the Symphony this portrayal of the natural world transcends any identification with individuality. Instead it represents an unalterable principle – neither progress in the sense of the 'gradation of existence' which Mahler was broadly aiming to illustrate in the work, nor something dependent on overpowering causality.

The category of the grotesque is frequently mentioned in connection with the third movement, and this derives principally from the movement's crucial aporia between the inarticulate, instinctual realm of the animals (set in the familiar sound-world of the children's song) and the posthorn dream world. Both seem familiar but scarcely compatible. They contain characteristic images which allude to the real world (children's song, military signal, posthorn) but do not constitute a logical drama-turgical structure. According to Mirjam Schadendorf, a fundamental feature of the humorous art work is that 'what is being portrayed turns out to be completely meaningless'.[36] Fragments of reality are indeed evoked, but at the same time they are divested of their ability to construct a coherent domain of reality. Instead of an overarching synthesis of the two poles of expression, conflict prevails. Nevertheless, this is how the scherzo fulfils that 'mode of artistic ambiguity' which Esti Sheinberg defines as the basic element of the grotesque, whose disunity is 'a stagnant condition to which there can be neither solution, nor classification'.[37] The bewilderment Krummacher ascribes to the end of the movement results from the denial of any reconciliation between the two heteroge-neous expressive worlds: 'A sudden irruption follows the last, slowly fading posthorn episode. The movement continues with persistent flut-tering noises, only to switch unexpectedly into a terrifying outburst.'[38]

There is a clear parallel between the temporal conflict of song and posthorn episode and the first movement's polarity of 'forward-moving', march-like temporality and its stemming in the funeral-march sections (bars 27 and 164) and dissipating passages for percussion alone. A key semantic position is occupied in this context by bars 14–17 (horns 1 and 3) in which Mahler clearly anticipates the beginning of the fourth move-ment (the Alto solo Nietzsche setting). The text's account of the awaken-ing of the individual from sleep and dream to awareness of the innermost aspects of the world corresponds not only with the programme of the Symphony, whose last five movements are inscribed with the phrase 'What the . . . tells me', but also with Mahler's literary and philosophical disposition, which was not exclusively rooted in Nietzsche but also integrated fundamental ideas of Schopenhauer and Wagner. The 'me' in Mahler's movement titles is an artistic vision which finds expression only in the medium of music, and the 'telling' manifests itself in two different ways: on the one hand as an autonomous formal process which funda-mentally expands and modifies conventional formal models whilst not completely invalidating them; and on the other hand in a tendency towards linguistic expression, as exemplified in the song movements.

The meaning of the songs in Mahler's Third has been interpreted in diverse ways. Donald Mitchell has described 'Das himmlische Leben', the Finale of the original seven-movement programmatic conception, as the 'fons et origo'[39] of the Symphony and has attempted to corroborate this analytically. The ultimate elimination of the song from the symphonic cycle can be explained not least in terms of the metaphysical orientation of the work's spiritual claims. He clearly recognized that the 'tapering, topmost spire'[40] signified by 'Das himmlische Leben' was scarcely compatible with the dream-like perception of a 'gradation of existence'. It was also essential for Mahler to communicate the ideas of becoming and gradual development at the root of the programme in an overarching dramaturgical structure. His famous remark that 'the eternally new and changing content determines its own form'[41] refers not to traditional formal categories but to the expansion that results from superimposing other dramaturgical processes, especially narrative structures. Precisely therein lies the apparent contradiction between Mahler's claim that the first movement contained 'the same basic groundplan' as classical works,[42] and Adorno's identification of the formal process as 'no more than a husk'.[43]

This is immediately apparent from the introductory bars (1–26). Here the resolute opening *ff* horn melody (whose sociological, psychoanalytical and political content has been amply demonstrated by William McGrath[44]) is presented with little sense of being a starting point for further structural development or a process of growth. The formal authority ostensibly claimed by the horn introduction is revealed as a chimera, for the clear four-bar antecedent phrase is followed by a vain attempt to build a meaningful high point at the note B (bars 7–9), and leads to a continuously descending melodic line which comes to a standstill on A (bars 11–13). Thus the supposed 'consequent phrase' lacks not only motivic pliability but above all developmental potential. Before the anticipation of the *misterioso* beginning of the fourth movement (from bar 15), its inconsequential dissipation elides into a harmonic progression that likewise will be of crucial importance in the Nietzsche song: F major – A minor – F♯ minor – A major (bars 11–14), which is slightly modified to become F major – A minor – F♯ minor – A minor in bars 11–14 of the fourth movement.

Like the exhortations 'O Mensch!' and Gib Acht!' in the fourth movement, the subsequent funeral march (from bar 27) here brings a thoroughly human sphere of experience into play. Its hesitant beginning scarcely leads one to expect development. However much the *aufwärts stürmende Gang* (rushing, upward movement[45]) of the lower strings (from bar 38) promises increased intensity, and however much continuity of thematic structure seems to prevail in the horns from bar 61 and the trumpet from bar 83, these expectations remain unfulfilled. The barely developed horn melody repeatedly succumbs to the pull of the tonic D (bars 69, 71, 73 and 77–9), by which it becomes completely paralysed. The following introductory march (bar 136) anticipates the principal theme of the movement but turns out to be indecisive and fragmentary.

The inversion of expected temporal processes has been central to the unfolding of the movement thus far. Rather than achieving a dynamic sense of progression, the music continually lapses into a state of decay. The condensed funeral march at bar 164 fulfils with greater intensity the potential for forward movement apparent from bar 57 of the first variant, which temporarily bursts through the rigidity of the funeral-march idiom until its impetus is cut short by trumpet fanfares, and the music once again sinks into the low register. This breakthrough nevertheless proves to be of some consequence for the movement's dynamic profile, for Mahler generates from this critical situation a gradually emerging, multi-levelled exposition, permeated by march idioms, which unfolds in a series of 'dynamic waves' to bar 368.[46] Nevertheless by the end of the section it is questionable whether any goals have been achieved. The march impulse is suddenly halted at the beginning of the development section (bar 369) by a diminished-seventh chord and with that part of the horn introduction directly associated with the fourth movement's 'Midnight Song' – the motive at the words 'Tief ist ihr Weh!' – after which follows further material previously heard in bars 58–75.

The transition to the recapitulation (bar 643) demonstrates how Mahler often stages formal processes as 'soundscapes'. It re-establishes structural sequence in an exaggerated, obtrusive manner, adhering to traditional generic conventions like no other formal division. The recapitulation restores structural order like a strong-man act after the complex parataxis of marches in the development which increasingly abandon its initial lyrical character and whose extended procession of diverse timbral groupings necessitates an unusual form of closure. The forced march dynamic, above all from bar 530, dissolves thematic integrity and generates a chaotic vortex of activity which finally abandons any melodic or timbral thematic identity: the 'destructive annihilation of the very material itself'[47] becomes the development's central quality.

The recapitulation does not so much constitute the resumption of previously established thematic material at a new, higher level, but rather begins by following the exposition almost exactly. If the whole movement up to this point has been characterized by a refusal to achieve goals, and if extensive dynamic growth could only be maintained with difficulty in the march sections of the development, then at first the recapitulation 'regresses' to a stage of musical development established long before. Once again the essential programmatic dichotomy between a dynamic principle and sleep, rigidity or lifeless Nature comes to the fore in the introduction to the recapitulation, which is substantially shorter than that of the exposition. The forward-pressing and occasionally exuberant qualities of the funeral march are reduced, and by taking up at bar 703 the variant of the trombone solo which first appeared at bar 424 in the development, Mahler synthesizes previously distinct structural sections, replacing the previous epithet *sentimental* with the romantic gesture of the turn (bar 724). Once more Mahler's music signals retrospection, the apparent backward glance to an expressive mood disengaged from any temporal dynamic. Nonetheless, by opening up the world of D major (from bar 710) he points forward to the tonality of the final movement, and this is made even clearer by the turn figure which also assumes significance within the Finale's thematic material.

The Fourth Symphony

Compared with the previous two symphonies, the Fourth both has reduced instrumental resources and dimensions, and is less metaphysically ambitious. Mahler's comment to Bauer-Lechner that he 'only wanted to write a symphonic Humoresque'[48] relates to the original six-movement conception which was to contain three *Wunderhorn* songs ('Das irdische Leben', 'Es sungen drei Engel' and 'Das himmlische Leben'). But the 'Humoresque' genre was important more as the starting point for a specific compositional procedure. Mahler's ideas were fundamentally influenced in this regard by Jean Paul's concept of humour, and he can be linked in this with Schumann for whom humour constituted an expressive category inextricable from the compositional process. Musical humour's main stylistic resources include various 'articulations, unmediated affective ruptures, stubborn repetitions of empty figures, quotations, reminiscences and allusions, rhythmic-metric disorder, structural ambiguities, deformations of phrases and periodic structures' and so on.[49] All this obviously requires a high degree of structural transparency, and places corresponding demands on performers. In his Fourth, Mahler anticipates a chamber-music conception of symphonic texture, and this is particularly noticeable in the second movement, which according to the composer 'was the only one to remind him stylistically of an earlier work of his – the Scherzo of the Second. It offers new content in an old form'.[50] The contrast between the measured introduction (wind instruments, horn, C minor) and the first thematic group on strings (from bar 7) in this movement immediately recalls Mozartian instrumentation. But the opening of the movement also comprises the interleaving of two open-ended phrases (bars 1–8 and 7–14) in which the first thematic group is primarily defined by different extensions of the same head motive (Plate 6.2).

Plate 6.2 Fourth Symphony, second movement, bars 1–11. © Copyright 1963 by Universal Edition (London) Ltd, London. Reproduced by permission. All rights reserved.

Example 6.3 Fourth Symphony, second movement, oboe and bassoon (bars 3–4) and oboe, flute and piccolo (bars 185–91)

The tendency to build variants through the corresponding repetition of marked diastematics can be seen in the horn introduction (bars 1–9) which is later taken up by the oboes (bar 23) but continued with a motive from the first thematic group (bar 25). Mahler is attempting here a method of combining motives which renders obsolete the distinction between thematic material and contrapuntal figures. Of course this precludes strongly periodic, self-contained thematic construction. Instead themes must be extremely open in order to allow the exchange of their individual constructive elements whilst preserving rhythmic-metric identity. This notably occurs in the three-bar thematic variant in the first violin (from bar 31) in which Mahler combines heterogeneous elements, namely the modified head of the theme's second phrase (bar 11), and the third bar of the first phrase.

While in such cases the temporal structure of the variants is preserved, the trill motive from bar 3 undergoes a 'metric displacement'[51] which in many ways points to similar compositional techniques of Stravinsky (Example 6.3).

Mahler effects not so much a return to the elegance of classical phrase structures as a defamiliarization and montage sometimes suggestive of neo-classical tendencies. The diverse role of the solo violin is also marked by defamiliarization. According to Mahler's instruction, the solo violinist 'has to have two instruments at their disposal, one of which is to be tuned a tone higher, the other at normal pitch'. Together with the expressive indication *wie eine Fidel* (*like a fiddle*), this *scordatura* tuning suggests a folk-inspired idiom, but at the same time shows that the solo violin is used not for its 'symbolic meaning'[52] but as an evocation of the authentic street culture of the fiddle.

The displacement of the tonic at the beginning of the first and second movements is striking. For example, the B minor introduction of the first movement, with its jingling fool's cap, persistently denies itself the tonic key, its reprise at the beginning of the exposition's closing section (from bar 72, followed by the first theme in the tonic G major), breaking through the 'almost pedantic adherence to the rules' claimed for the work by Mahler.[53] The exposition is in fact remarkably self-contained, and even the development (bar 102) starts off as if it were a repetition of the exposition. Mahler thus primarily fulfils a cyclic principle, and this is also characteristic of the innumerable thematic variants (particularly of the first theme). His highly innovative concept of a kind of music which repeatedly returns to both thematically and tonally familiar regions whilst extending them in entirely unexpected, if not bewildering, ways, becomes particularly apparent at the beginning of the first movement's recapitulation. The emphatic head of the first theme (bar 234) dissipates after only a few notes and fades to *ppp*, before the actual recapitulation – apparently completely indifferent to the preceding events – resumes the musical progression at bar 239 with the end of the antecedent phrase.

This dramaturgy of, on the one hand, a pointedly cyclical form, and on the other hand, numerous 'irritants' which counter any sense of expectation, becomes particularly crucial in the final movement with its plethora of motivic-thematic interrelationships. It is noticeable that several fragments of 'Das himmlische Leben' are anticipated in the first three movements, and that therefore Mahler far exceeds 'the kind of cyclic unity usually found in nineteenth-century music'.[54] He concentrates thematic and tonal development like a spiral which only finds its true fulfilment in the song finale. In this journey towards the Finale with its predominant tonal centres of G major, E minor and E major, an extremely important part is played by the third movement. Its double-variation structure is couched in waves of successive tempo increases, three sections of raised intensity – each of which is nevertheless reduced to the initial *piano* dynamic (bars 84–92, 188–221 and 263–88) – and finally an explosive breakthrough (bar 315) which unveils 'a radiant E major soundscape in which the horns anticipate the melody of "Das himmlische Leben"'.[55] The structural positioning and specific formation of this breakthrough shed light not just on its semantic dimension but also on Mahler's innovative stylistic methods. The second theme of the movement is the bearer of the aforementioned waves of intensification, whose high points (bars 89 and

210) introduce a chromatically descending line akin to the rhetorical figure 'passus duriusculus' – an interpretation corroborated not least by the expressive indication *klagend* (*lamenting*) at the beginning of the second theme (bars 62 and 175). Immediately before this, the first theme had ended in complete timbral stagnation (bars 55–61), an idea that Rudolf Stephan accurately described as a forerunner of the *Klangfarbenmelodie* employed by Schoenberg less than ten years later in the third of his *Five Orchestral Pieces*, op. 16.[56]

The remarkable effect of the breakthrough in bar 315 derives not only from the first long-term appearance of the E major tonal area of the Symphony's conclusion, but also from the radical contrast between two sound-worlds. The sweeping, dynamically forced tutti sound, energized by harp and string arpeggios, acts as a foil to the subsequent anticipation of the final movement (from bar 320), and this is preceded by a passage of extremely subtle cross-fading of woodwind against strings, harp and horns in which Mahler reduces diastematics to an absolute minimum. Inner meditative calm and a forceful outburst of sound converge to a structural and semantic focal point, forming the unique culmination of the Symphony's finale-orientated construction. Mahler nevertheless refrains from any obvious *per aspera ad astra* aesthetic. The breakthrough is not followed by a majestic conclusion to the movement but fades in the final bars *Gänzlich ersterbend* (*dying away completely*). The seemingly unburdened heavenly life in the final movement is not only one in which all experience of suffering is extinguished. It appears more like a withdrawal and a simplification, a denial of all strenuous symphonic effort, a mystery in sound that ultimately retreats from any sense of compositional staging: 'Sehr zart und geheimnisvoll bis zum Schluß' ('very gentle and mysterious until the end') (bar 122).

7 Song and symphony (II). From *Wunderhorn* to Rückert and the middle-period symphonies: vocal and instrumental works for a new century

STEPHEN E. HEFLING

(*Kindertotenlieder* No. 1, 'Nun will die Sonn' so hell aufgeh'n!', vocal line, bars 74–84)

'Hail the joyous light of the world!' In his classic monograph *Gustav Mahlers Sinfonien*, Paul Bekker adopts this concluding line from the first of the *Kindertotenlieder* to epitomize Mahler's middle period.[1] Ironically, Bekker's assessment would remain valid today had he not evaded the ambivalence in Mahler's – not Rückert's – partial repetition of that line: Mahler's minor mode and bitter musical rhetoric indeed yield 'quaking emotion' (*mit Erschütterung*; see above). Such affective duality is characteristically Mahlerian; he never fully resolves it. Yet Bekker maintained that the Fifth and Seventh Symphonies manifest *Freudenlicht der Welt*, whereas the blackness of the Sixth is merely material, not spiritual. Mahler's colleagues Guido Adler and Bruno Walter concur regarding Symphonies 5 and 7; both, however, knew better about the Sixth.[2] Since then, Adorno's famous 1960 critique of Mahler as 'a poor yea-sayer'[3] has precluded whitewashing the Fifth and Seventh. And today Adorno's contention that 'the Finale of the Sixth Symphony has its pre-eminence in Mahler's oeuvre because, more monumentally composed than all the rest, it shatters the spell of affirmative illusion'[4] may seem entirely plausible.

As director of the Vienna Court Opera, Mahler assigned himself a staggering workload: a hundred performances annually, full artistic administration plus, beginning in 1898, the Philharmonic concerts. In February 1901 he collapsed in a haemorrhage so severe that 'I thought my last hour had come'.[5] Personally and artistically, Mahler's life was transformed. He dropped the Philharmonic and halved his opera performances. Then within a year the forty-year-old bachelor betrothed and impregnated Vienna's most beautiful girl,[6] twenty-two-year-old Alma Schindler. This rush to have children was Mahler's response to his recent brush with death, as Stuart Feder has shown.[7] But during the summer composing holiday of 1901, well before courting Alma, Mahler made issues of life and death central to several new compositions: his last *Wunderhorn* Lied, 'Der Tamboursg'sell', three songs from Rückert's 400-odd *Kindertotenlieder*, and four independent Rückert settings – each composed one day and orchestrated the next. He also began the Fifth Symphony.[8]

Mahler was ready for new creative paths. He already recognized the Fourth Symphony as the culmination of a tetralogy,[9] today called the *Wunderhorn* symphonies. Moreover, the Fourth's masterly formal strategy together with its advances in contrapuntal and motivic development, ironic musical discourse, and immediacy of intimate utterance clearly mark it as the gateway to Mahler's second maturity.[10] These evolvements would prove crucial to all of his subsequent compositions.

In Rückert's poetry Mahler found the intimate utterances of an individuated personality, in marked contrast to the folkish, stock *Wunderhorn* characters who had inspired the urbane yet generic marches and Ländler (frequently tinged with irony) of his earlier songs.[11] And Rückert's worldview matched Mahler's in several respects; it also overlapped with the pan-psychic philosophy of Gustav Theodor Fechner, which influenced several of Mahler's symphonic worlds, including the Second and Third.[12] Mahler marvelled at 'how close in feeling Fechner is to Rückert', and the poet indeed influenced the philosopher.[13]

According to Fechner, the entire cosmos is an inwardly alive spiritual hierarchy extending from atoms up to the deity; Rückert also sees all-encompassing unity in both the simplest aspects of existence as well as the complex systems of culture. A universalist, Fechner posits no distinction between the saved and the damned; and there is none in Mahler's 'Resurrection' Symphony (1894): wings won through fervent striving of love bear us 'to the light no eye has penetrated'. The Finale of Mahler's Third (1896) embodies the notion that God and love are equivalent. And for Rückert, dying in love leads to an afterlife of eternal light, even as Fechner believes that death releases us into the third stage of being, where we merge as one with waves of light and sound. Moreover, Rückert was an orientalist, and Eastern literature strongly influenced his own poems, including two that Mahler selected in 1901.

The Rückert Lieder

Just such a Lied is 'Ich atmet' einen linden Duft' ('I breathed a delicate fragrance'), apparently the first of the summer's harvest.[14] Ostensibly the subject could not be simpler: delight in the gift of a lime branch. But as in the ancient Persian and Turkish lyrics he knew well, Rückert's repetitions and wordplays create a floating, opalescent quality hovering between the sensual and the spiritual. Liquescent l's and wordplays on *linden Duft* abound. Such ethereal fluidity informs both the musical substance and transparent scoring of the song. (Indeed, all Mahler's Rückert settings are virtually chamber music, and he insisted on performing them in a small hall with reduced strings.)[15] Pentatonic scales reflect the poem's oriental overtones in much of the lilting ostinato accompaniment, slightly blurring the tonal focus, and culminating in the concluding 'added-sixth' chord.[16] Lines, rather than harmonies, prevail throughout, proceeding with sensuous ease. Such subtleties indeed mark a new beginning, foreshadowing the summer's concluding masterpiece, 'Ich bin der Welt abhanden gekommen' ('I am lost to the world'), and the late style of *Das Lied von der Erde* (The song of the earth, 1908).[17]

'Blicke mir nicht in die Lieder' (14 June) is the shortest and simplest Rückert Lied, the most like *Wunderhorn* poetry,[18] and the wittiest. Mahler hated eavesdroppers while composing; thus its text – 'Do not look at my Lieder! . . . Your curiosity is betrayal!' – is 'as characteristic of Mahler as if he himself had written the poem'.[19] Mahler captures Rückert's image of the busy worker bees in an ostinato buzzing throughout. Although the poem suggests a traditional strophic setting, Mahler's line repetition, tonal motions counter to textual divisions, and reprise of the 'motto' phrase with different words (see especially bars 22–43) yield a song artfully unpolished and seemingly still in progress; it fades inconclusively into the bees' buzz.

Mahler's most direct response to the February crisis is 'Um Mitternacht' ('At midnight'), the most dramatic and problematic of his Rückert Lieder. Throughout the first four stanzas the isolated protagonist is trapped in spiritual anguish, which Mahler reflects in austere, static music sparsely scored for combinations of solo winds: time stands still at midnight.[20] Rückert's final stanza turns from despair to religiosity. But here Mahler's overwhelming *deus ex machina* unleashes his 'Resurrection' chorus in miniature,[21] a magnificent magnificat that virtually swamps the singer. Evidently Mahler misread Rückert's ending (in Harold Bloom's sense).[22] Gerlach, for example, deems this one of Mahler's several Nietzschean artistic usurpations (including the Fifth and Eighth Symphonies): 'The goal, from which Mahler spared neither the piety of the

Brucknerian chorale nor the dignity of Christian hymns, is the Man of the Future, the "Overman" in a world without God'.[23]

At holidays' end, he was suddenly inspired to compose 'Ich bin der Welt abhanden gekommen', his most extraordinary independent Lied. Calling it 'feeling that rises to the lips but does not cross them', Mahler declared 'It is my very self!'[24] Here he conveys Rückert's (and Schopenhauer's) Buddhistic withdrawal from worldliness, appropriating the techniques of 'Ich atmet'. Yet paradoxically, these procedures now saturate the song with an organic coherence previously matched only by portions of the Fourth Symphony. Everything grows from the pentatonic cell and the arching melodic contours of the title line (bars 11–14). For the poem's final lines ('I live alone in my heaven, in my love, in my song', bars 54–9) Mahler closely paraphrases the end of the Fourth's slow movement (fig. 13 ff.) – a serene moment marked 'sehr zart und innig' ('very sweetly and intimately') that fades 'gänzlich ersterbend' ('dying completely') just before the onset of 'Das himmlische Leben' ('Heavenly life'). Mahler described this Andante as 'the smile of St. Ursula' (from the poem of the Finale), whom he associated with the tenderness of his mother; he also compared it to 'the scarcely noticeable, peaceful smile of the slumbering, departed children of mankind'[25] – thus, it reflects the ongoing polarity of birth and death. This *gänzlich ersterbend* music would soon return, transformed, in the famous Adagietto of the Fifth Symphony.

The last of the Rückert Lieder, 'Liebst du um Schönheit' ('If you love for beauty's sake') was a 'privatissimum' from Gustav to Alma in the summer of 1902, when their marriage was already under stress. The poem lists and dismisses three of the couple's concerns: Mahler's appearance, his age and his disdain of material goods. The music, which Mahler never orchestrated, was conceived explicitly for Alma in an intimate, nostalgic and retrospective style unlike anything else he had written, or would.[26]

Kindertotenlieder

The chronology of the *Kindertotenlieder* now appears settled: the first, third and fourth date from 1901, the second and fifth from the summer before the January 1905 première.[27] Rückert's *Kindertotenlieder* lament his loss of two young children in 1833–4. Mahler's multiple motivations for setting these texts have been explored by psychoanalyst Stuart Feder. In brief: memorialization of his eight deceased siblings; anticipatory mourning of his own death; identification with his parents, especially his father; and symbolic representation of his own wish for children, negatively expressed because death and birth had been closely paired for

Mahler since infancy.[28] That pairing is discussed frequently by Mahler's favourite philosopher of music, Arthur Schopenhauer: 'Birth and death belong equally to life, and hold the balance as mutual conditions of each other, or, . . . as poles of the whole phenomenon of life'. Accordingly, the Hindu god Shiva, who represents destruction and death, bears both a necklace of skulls and the *lingam*, or phallus – the symbol of procreation as the counterpart of death.[29]

From Rückert's 425 *Kindertotenlieder* Mahler selected five of the best. The first four explicitly embody imagery of darkness and light, while the last does so implicitly by progressing from storm to eternal rest.[30] The life–death polarity thus symbolized becomes the cycle's overriding theme. Mahler highlights it variously, particularly through his signature device of major–minor modal shifts (for example, 'Freudenlicht der Welt'). Such modal associations are central to the unifying tonal scheme – d–c–c–Eb–d/D – which arrives somewhat consolingly in D major. In other respects the *Kindertotenlieder* continue the tradition extending from Schubert's *Winterreise* to Mahler's own *Lieder eines fahrenden Gesellen*, whereby tragic background events engender a series of psychological vignettes lacking narrative continuity and concluding somewhat ambiguously. Also traditional is the significance of the 'accompaniment', which may reveal more than the vocal part. Modern, however, is Mahler's 'dual-purpose' concept of songs employing either piano or orchestra.

Mahler sets the three 1901 *Kindertotenlieder* strophically with variants, following his principle that 'there should be no repetition, but only evolution'.[31] The fluent linearity emerging in 'Ich atmet' einen linden Duft' is everywhere apparent. But in stark contrast to that Lied, 'Nun will die Sonn' so hell aufgeh'n' ('Now will the sun rise as brightly'), marked 'Langsam und schwermütig' ('Slowly and dejectedly'), contains no musical brightness; indeed, following a bleak four-bar ritornello in sparse two-part counterpoint, the title line descends rather than rises, unfolding a tritone and landing upon a plaintive half-diminished-seventh chord (θ7) that will punctuate each strophe.[32] The response, 'as though the night had seen no misfortune', is a tortuous chromatic ascent 'with restrained voice' over a lullaby accompaniment (cf. 'Wie ein Wiegenlied' in No. 5, bar 100 / fig. 8 + 9). Therewith arrives the cycle's first, ironic, minor-to-major shift: the protagonist remains unconvinced about 'Freudenlicht der Welt', and in the expanded interlude following the third strophe his suppressed rage emerges through deformation of the lullaby motive. The only flicker in the darkness is the glockenspiel, a harbinger of deliverance from the Second Symphony.[33]

The second song, 'Nun seh' ich wohl, warum so dunkle Flammen' ('Now I see well why such dark flames') (1904), is the most subtly complex. Rückert's poetic conceit is the alternation of darkness and light projected upon the child's eyes, which, mutely expressive yet misunderstood in this life, have become stars in the sky for eternity. Ignoring the Petrarchian sonnet structure, Mahler proceeds quasi-strophically, with musical rhetoric that intensifies the first song's ambivalent polarity of *Freudenlicht* versus despair. Motivically, the arching contours make this the *Doppelgänger* of 'Ich bin der Welt abhanden gekommen', but here the descending contour often surpasses the ascending. The song's tonal allegory is C minor striving unsuccessfully towards major. Volatile throughout, the music never achieves full cadence or background linear closure. Optimistic major passages portend ecstasy, yet always relapse into the regretful minor motto phrase ('Nun seh' ich wohl . . .').

The third and fourth songs are straightforwardly strophic (ever with subtle variants). Pursuing C minor, 'Wenn dein Mütterlein' begins with musical imagery of soft footsteps approaching the poet's study at night. All remains hushed until 'there, there where your beloved little face would have been' releases uncontrollable grief that swamps the poetic metre and forces the remaining text into one long, lamenting phrase collapsing back into C minor (fig. 3 / bar 33). The second strophe ends similarly 'mit ausbrechendem Schmerz' ('with sorrow bursting forth'), but the postlude denies closure, stopping on the dominant.

Although not without passing shadows, 'Oft denk' ich, sie sind nur ausgegangen' ('Often I think they've merely gone out') is in bright, warm E♭ major, and the poet-father has ostensibly accepted that the children are not coming home. Yet the singer's last words – 'the day is beautiful on those heights!' – bring an unexpected, hyperbolic climax strongly redolent of denial.

Mahler's Finale whips up four strophes' worth of D minor turbulence (partially derived from the first song's interlude). But he avoids the near-realism of a traditional storm scene, because this tempest is an interior one: the children are already gone.[34] Obsessively repetitive like the poetry, the music blusters ahead without pause between stanzas. While avoiding literal repetition, Mahler also prevents his variants from relieving the turmoil ('With restlessly painful expression' heads the score).

Finally the storm abates, yielding to abundant serenity via masterly minor-to-major transition punctuated by the celestial bells (fig. 8 / bar 93 ff.), and through transformation of the roiling quavers into a lullaby ('wie ein Wiegenlied'; cf. No. 1). As in the Fourth Symphony's *gänzlich ersterbend* transition to 'Heavenly Life', Mahler delicately evokes a return to maternal shelter – 'they rest as in their mother's house'. (Originally he substituted 'Mutter Schoß' ('mother's womb') for Rückert's 'Mutter Haus'.)[35] Thus accepting, not overcoming, the sorrow of the birth–death polarity brings Mahler's *Kindertotenlieder* to a close.

'Der Tamboursg'sell'

This chilling song of an ambitious young soldier facing the gallows for crimes unspecified seems like the rogue's march for Mahler's *Wunderhorn* persona. Beneath his extraordinary success Mahler probably felt guilt about siblings and rivals left behind, and sacrificing his health to ambition; hence his identification with the drummer-boy, who accepts execution unquestioningly.[36] A funereal tread with characteristic dotted-crotchet/quaver rhythm dominates this last and gloomiest of the *Wunderhorn* Lieder. Although shaped by poetic stanzas, the musical abundance exceeds the bounds of strophic form. For the last two stanzas – six farewell salutations and a final outcry – the tonality drops symbolically from D minor to traditionally fateful C minor.

Affinities between 'Der Tamboursg'sell' and the funeral march of the Fifth Symphony notwithstanding,[37] Mahler henceforth avoids wholesale plundering of his songs; the Rückert settings do not expand symphonically as the *Wunderhorn* had. The Fifth Symphony's opening movement, arguably Mahler's most complex funeral march, required different materials.

Eternal recurrence? The Fifth Symphony

Scherzo

> Mahler said: 'The task of contemporary creative musicians would be to combine the contrapuntal skill of Bach with the melodiousness of Haydn and Mozart'.[38]

When Mahler expounded this daunting agendum to Schoenberg's circle in 1905, he had already accomplished it in his Fifth Symphony. But the task had not been easy. Mahler commenced with the scherzo, which he found 'enormously difficult to work out because of the structure and the highest level of artistic mastery that it demands in all interconnections and details'.[39] Its polyphonic complexity proved difficult to orchestrate, yet ultimately he achieved 'three-dimensional' depth plus clarity.[40]

Portions of it may have been sketched earlier: a preliminary plan from 1895–6 for the Fourth Symphony includes 'Die Welt ohne Schwere – D-dur (Scherzo)', although the finished Fourth contains no such movement. However, 'The world without cares' – better translated 'without gravity' – certainly fits the Fifth's complex yet buoyant scherzo;[41] as Mahler also told Natalie:

> 'It is kneaded through and through such that no little grain of corn remains unmixed and unchanged. Every note is of fullest liveliness, and everything revolves in a whirling dance'. He also compared it to a comet's tail. 'There is nothing mystical or romantic about it; it comprises only the expression of unheard-of power. It is man in the full light of day, at the zenith of life'.[42]

Later he offered Alma a slightly different description:

> oh heavens, what are they to make of this chaos that eternally gives birth to a new world, which perishes again in the next moment – of these primeval sounds, this foaming, roaring, raging sea, of these dancing stars, of these breath-taking, iridescent, flashing breakers?[43]

All of these characterizations reflect the language of Nietzsche, whose *Fröhliche Wissenschaft* extols '"light feet, "dancing", "laughter" – and ridicule of "the spirit of gravity"'.[44] And Zarathustra, Nietzsche's prophet of the Overman, exhorts:

> Come, let us kill the spirit of gravity [*Geist der Schwere*] . . . Now I am light, now I fly, now I see myself beneath myself, now a god dances through me
> . . .
> I say unto you: one must still have chaos in oneself to be able to give birth to a dancing star. I say unto you: you still have chaos in yourselves.[45]

In his 1905 *Gustav Mahler* (of which Mahler approved), Richard Specht also senses the 'mood of sovereign power' in this music; Specht reports Bruno Walter's comparing it to Goethe's poem 'An Schwager Kronos' ('To Coachman Kronos').[46] Therein life is likened to a coach journey; Father Time is the driver, and the rider is a young Achilles urging Kronos forward to a quick and ecstatic end in the underworld:[47]

> Down then, down faster!
> Look, the sun is sinking!
> Before it sinks . . .
> Snatch me, drunk with its last ray,
> A sea of fire
> Foaming in my eyes,
> Blinded, reeling
> Through hell's nocturnal gate
> Coachman, sound your horn,
> Rattle noisily on at a trot . . .[48]

Here Goethe (whom Nietzsche greatly admired) anticipates aspects of Zarathustra's 'going under' (*untergehen*) – the journey of over-rich,

creative souls who sacrifice themselves to the present on the earth, holding back nothing: 'Like the sun, Zarathustra too wants to go under'.[49]
And the sound of the horn – both 'obbligato' solo and choir of four – is
the scherzo's most prominent timbre. Indeed, portentous horn blasts
twice abruptly halt the whirling (figs. 10 + 1 and 27 + 11 ff.).

The robust main theme of this longest of Mahler's scherzos is a stylized
Austrian waltz, whilst the two trios evoke the lighter French *valse*.[50] The
scherzo's second subject resembles Baroque *ondulé* string writing, and is
sometimes treated quasi-fugally. Mahler's sophisticated 'kneading through
and through' transforms the musical kernels far beyond their origins, such
that they become difficult to distinguish, as do several of the movement's
formal divisions.[51] Although evolving continuously, the music proceeds
altogether unpredictably, culminating in the frenzied waltz of the coda
(fig. 30 + 9 ff.). Yet the numerous disjunctions never dispel the immense
power of this self-renewing chaos, recalling Nietzsche's eternal recurrence –
'the eternal hourglass of existence . . . turned upside down again and again,
and you with it, speck of dust!'[52]

In summer 1901 Mahler was planning 'a rule-abiding symphony in four
movements, each of which is independent and self-contained, and they are
connected only in related mood'.[53] But this changed radically, yielding three
large parts (*Abteilungen* in the autograph), whereby the first two movements
are inseparably intertwined, material from the fourth returns in the fifth, and
the scherzo is the powerful pivot between these two pairings.

This unique structure reinterprets the archetypal Beethovenian struggle *per ardua ad astra*, most famously achieved in *his* Fifth. Mahler bows
to Beethoven's 'fate' motto in his opening trumpet call,[54] but otherwise
proceeds altogether differently. This new Fifth spirals gradually and
uncertainly from the gloom and irony of its first two movements (C♯
minor and A minor) through the scherzo's boundless energy (D major,
yet occasionally darkly tinged) to the famous Adagietto, a world apart in
tonality (F major), timbre (only strings and harp), and interiority. The
ensuing Finale virtuosically juxtaposes and combines lyricism with heady,
occasionally boisterous joy – yet its jubilation seems less than entirely
fulfilling. The symphony's overall ascent from C♯ minor to D major is
unquestionably a structural and symbolic progression towards brightness. Adumbrated in the funeral march's first eighteen bars, this semitone
conflict becomes overt with the emergence and dissolution of the second
movement's D major chorale. The scherzo makes D major the likely
ultimate goal, but D becomes irrevocable only with the resurgence of
the chorale near the Finale's end.

Whereas Mahler's Fourth appropriates classical form and the choral
finale as backdrops for its individuality, the Fifth sidesteps tradition, both

in its movement structure and by eschewing the dialectical paradigm of sonata form. All movements are rondo-like; rather than finality, they suggest that perhaps their distinctive refrains and interrelated couplets might cycle on endlessly – rather like the Nietzschean recurrence of all joy and sorrow.

Part I

Mourning and rage – *Trauermarsch* and *stürmisch bewegt* – are the topics of Part I. Their pairing intertwines the first- and second-movement rondos: the 'Leidenschaftlich Wild' ('passionately wild') Bb minor outburst of the funeral march's first trio initiates the pattern of disjunction.[55] But the crucial connection is the recurrence of the march's second trio in the second movement's secondary material (at figs. 5, 12, 20 and 23). Thereby the funeral march remains an active presence throughout the agitated second movement.[56] Moreover, nearly all sections of this movement brusquely erupt in a chromatic squall, augmenting the disruptiveness already manifest in the funeral march, which had collapsed in anguish shortly before its close (fig. 18, 'Klagend' ('bewailing')). Rage rather than mourning drives the corresponding crisis of the second movement ('Wuchtig' ('with full force'), fig. 24 ff.). In the wake of it, however, emerges a full-blown chorale (fig. 27, very briefly foreshadowed at fig. 18–6) that builds towards the D major 'Höhepunkt' ('high point'). Predictably, collapse ensues; nevertheless, beckoning *Freudenlicht* – just what was lacking in the first three *Kindertotenlieder* – has appeared.

Thus, Mahler designed Part I to be overcome by the Scherzo's 'unheard-of power': grief and resentment play no further role in the Fifth, and the spirit of gravity has been left behind.[57] Yet this scherzo is not an unalloyed victory. Willem Mengelberg's score records the following, probably from conversations with Mahler: 'Forced joyfulness, he wants to forget it, the sorrow, but cannot yet, it has a forced effect – cloudy ground coating, here and there even a dance of death [*Totentanz*]'.[58]

Part III: Adagietto and Rondo-Finale

Only once did Mahler perform the Fifth's Adagietto apart from the entire symphony.[59] But this quietly ecstatic interlude has become his best-known music, largely for the wrong reasons. Usually treated as an elegy lasting ten to fourteen minutes, the Adagietto is actually a love song that Mahler performed in seven to nine minutes, as did his trusted colleagues Bruno Walter and Willem Mengelberg.[60] As Mengelberg noted on his conducting score: 'N. B. *This Adagietto* was Gustav Mahler's *declaration of love* to *Alma*! Instead of a letter he sent *it* to her in manuscript . . . (*both of them told me this!*) W. M.'[61] Laced with appoggiaturas and allusions to the 'glance' motive that inevitably recall *Tristan and Isolde*,[62] the Adagietto culminates in a transformation of the meditative passage that, as noted above, closes both the Fourth Symphony's slow movement and 'Ich bin der Welt', where the text is 'I live alone in my heaven, in my love, in my song'. But what had been deathly serene – 'gänzlich ersterbend' in the Fourth, 'Innig . . . pp . . . ohne Steigerung' ('intimate, *pianissimo*, without intensification') in the song – now becomes passionately ecstatic in the Adagietto: '*ff breit viel Ton! Drängend*' ('*fortissimo*, broad, lots of tone! Urgently'). It is perhaps the most erotic and idealistic moment in all of Mahler. Thus, as in Schopenhauer and Wagner, Eros and Thanatos are for Mahler paired opposites. In marrying Alma, his fervent hope was to unite 'his very self' with hers, in love, song and renewal of life – but no longer alone.

The Rondo-Finale opens unassumingly – yet these introductory shards yield a vast structure astonishingly rich in contrapuntal interplay. But Mahler immediately signals that the spirit of gravity will not prevail: the bassoon tune in bars 5–6 quotes his satirical *Wunderhorn* song 'Lob des hohen Verstandes' ('Praise of lofty intellect') – a singing contest between a nightingale and a cuckoo, judged by a long-eared ass. The ensuing oboe phrase, however, is a diminution of the chorale melody from the illusory 'Highpoint' of the second movement.[63] The rondo's refrain, lyrically shaped in overlapping two-bar units, stems from the scalar descent at the end of the chorale. And the first couplet (fig. 2) revives the Baroque quaver motion of the scherzo's second idea: this becomes the subject of genuine fugal episodes employing a variety of countersubjects – one of which again alludes to 'Lob des hohen Verstandes' (figs. 3 + 11 and 25–13).

All of this is *fröhliche Wissenschaft* – joyous science, in Nietzschean parlance. Yet the up-tempo Adagietto as second couplet (fig. 7 + 14, etc.) is surprising: intimate yearning becomes jaunty tunefulness; the military-band trills in its last appearance (fig. 29) seem cruelly parodistic. But for Zarathustra 'all things are entangled, ensnared, enamored';[64] thus even rapture must be overcome. Although less anguished than movements 1–3, the Rondo-Finale is likewise in perpetual flux. Repeatedly the drive towards fulfillment is thwarted, often by blunt deceptive cadence, and abrupt shifts without transition abound (for example figs. 4 + 12, 6 + 9, 12 – 11, 13 – 4, 13, 21, 23, 27 – 11).

To wrest a happy ending from this ceaseless ferment would require, in Adorno's terms, a major breakthrough; for many, Mahler's concluding chorale (fig. 32) does not suffice.[65] Near the end of Part I the chorale intimated redemption. Now, as it arrives in full, the context lacks sanctity. Moreover, its relation to the Finale's frivolous opening becomes obvious: the religious topos has been secularized. As though acknowledging this,

Mahler diminishes the chorale's power just before the coda (fig. 34–12 ff.), thereby forestalling total jubilation. And the coda's clatter of triangle and cymbals rivals the raucous peasant dance concluding Tchaikovsky's Fourth.

Lack of conclusive resolution suggests everything could happen again. According to Zarathustra, eternal recurrence means 'if ever you wanted one thing twice, if you ever said "You please me, happiness! Abide, moment!" then you wanted *all* back'.[66] And Nietzsche's finale to parts 1–3 of *Zarathustra*, 'The Seven Seals', is itself a rondo, its refrain concluding '*For I love you, O eternity!*'[67] Such a reading of Mahler's Finale would explain its ambivalent, even flippant entangling of the quotidian with the transcendent. In any case, as La Grange observes, in the Fifth Mahler surpasses himself 'in instinctively assuming the uncertainty, the doubts, the secret anguish, the fundamental ambiguity, that marked his time and still weigh so heavily on ours'.[68] His writing such a work at the turn of both the twentieth century and his own fifth decade is hardly coincidental.

Tragedy immutable: The Sixth Symphony

The subtitle 'Tragic' is Mahler's own, as is the well-known précis of the Sixth's Finale: 'It is the hero, on whom fall three blows of fate, the last of which fells him as a tree is felled'.[69] The Sixth's conclusion and overall structure differ fundamentally from the Fifth's: there are four movements of traditional stamp, and the dialectic of sonata form is central to the first and last. It is as though the condensed classicism of the celestial Fourth were inverted and expanded into a tragic vision ending in a nihilistic void. All movements but the Andante are in A minor, the key of stormy agitation in the Fifth (and later in *Das Lied von der Erde*). Mahler is the consummate symphonic dramatist in the Sixth, and its dark outcome is by no means certain until the recapitulation in the Finale.[70]

Allegro energico, ma non troppo
The grim military realism and frequent, rapid shifts of mode in Mahler's penultimate *Wunderhorn* song 'Revelge' – the grisly tale of dead soldiers aroused from the field and led to victory by their drummer – foreshadow the marches in all three A minor movements of the Sixth, as well as its motto overall: major to minor above a fateful flourish of drums. In the first movement, following a heavy A minor march of nearly sixty bars grouped in twos, the motto first appears (fig. 7–4). From it emerges a pallid wind chorale (*pp*) portending transition, but still tonic-bound.

Thereafter the soaring F major second subject reportedly representing Alma[71] ('Schwungvoll', fig. 8) is as surprising to this movement as she was to its composer. Two ample periods of the 'Alma' subject (with a perky mini-march interlude) close the exposition in exhilaration. Adorno (predictably) considers this contrived; however, even Walter and Adler found the Alma theme weak.[72]

Two features of the bipartite development are remarkable: relative absence of the motivic and contrapuntal virtuosity prominent in the Fifth, and close adherence to the original tonic of A minor in its first half. It marches on, with increased fixation upon the motto rhythm and intermixture of second-subject motives (fig. 19 ff.). After seventy-five bars, however, the scene rapidly changes (fig. 21 + 3). Wispy parallel triads in the violins and celesta float above a D pedal, and cowbells emerge, symbolizing for Mahler 'world-withdrawn isolation' (*weltferne Einsamkeit*) – the last sounds of living beings heard by wanderers high in the mountains.[73] Twice the motto sounds, off-tonic, distant, ineffectual. Then the tonality glides to E♭ (furthest remove from A minor, fig. 23); second-subject and chorale ideas calmly unfold, and closure in this Alpine reverie seems at hand. Yet it vanishes more suddenly than it arrived: B major is asserted by third-relation, and the march resumes, becoming minor and more intense as the transition approaches the recapitulation.

With bravado the principal subject returns in A major (fig. 28), which is quashed five bars later – the motto writ large, *sans* drums. The literal reprise (fig. 33) precipitates an extended transition, but the second theme, considerably truncated, catches hold only during a subdominant digression (fig. 35 + 5 ff.). Thus a coda must determine the outcome of the movement.[74] And this coda does so through intensified developmental activity and by replenishing the second subject – first sardonically (at the point corresponding to the cowbells' entry, fig. 40 + 5), then dazzlingly in A major as the 'chorale', now in the brass, finally sounds like one. Yet uncertainties remain – most notably a final major–minor gesture at the second theme's highpoint (fig. 45–2).[75]

Scherzo

The Sixth's movement order – scherzo before Andante or vice versa – is a complex issue. Briefly: Mahler's autograph score reveals he originally intended the scherzo to precede the slow movement. But immediately following the public dress rehearsal (Essen, 27 May 1906), terrified by what he had unleashed, Mahler suffered a severe panic attack. He then reversed the inner movements for the première, thereby mitigating the stark contrast between the Andante and Finale. And he deleted the Finale's third symbolic hammer blow (fig. 165–7).[76] Nor did Mahler rescind these alterations in the two subsequent performances he conducted. Nevertheless, in 1963 the Kritische Gesamtausgabe adopted Mahler's original Scherzo–Andante sequence, which thereafter became common (and is followed here). Recent researchers have vigorously challenged this, however,[77] and today one encounters both versions.

The backdrop to the Sixth's scherzo – an eerie admixture of Ländler, march, and '*altväterisch*' ('old-fashioned') trio – is the Dance of Death, an ancient cultural topos common to the visual arts, literature and music (*Totentanz*, tarantella, 'Death and the Maiden', etc.).[78] Regular quavers interspersed with semiquaver diminutions in $\frac{3}{8}$ are the Ländler element; the heavy tread in A minor with pedal bass and dotted rhythms derives directly from the first-movement march (explicitly quoted at bar 16; cf. fig. 2). This macabre extension of the first movement's affect is chilling, even demonic. The meagre, highly repetitive material drives 'wie gepeitscht' ('as though whipped') all the way through the motto reference (bar 72) to the first trio, which absorbs yet alters the scherzo's pulse. Significantly, the trios are in F and D – the tonal centres of the first movement's 'Alma' theme. She reports that the trios' unusual tempo and metrical changes ($\frac{3}{8};\frac{4}{8};\frac{3}{4}$) imitate the 'arrhythmic games' of their children tottering on the sand. 'Ominously, the childish voices became more and more tragic, and at the end died out in a whimper'.[79] So indeed the movement closes, coloured by modal shifts of the motto.

Andante moderato

Both nostalgia and the need to escape it suffuse the Andante; hence 'the afflicted tone of the *Kindertotenlieder*' in its bittersweet main theme.[80] The ubiquitous lullaby accompaniment derives from the cycle, as does the 'Freudenlicht der Welt' phrase-ending (fig. 49–1, and also bar 9). Indeed, 'as though the night had witnessed no misfortune' could be the movement's title. Many features underscore its yearning, chief among them the antinomic deployment of E♭ – antipode to A minor (and previously tonal centre of the first movement's cowbells episode) – through subtle, wistful modal oscillations and tonal departures discussed below.

The music generates a flexible form perhaps best described as rondo-like:[81] three appearances of the main theme (bar 1, figs. 55, 60–1) sandwich two episodes of forty-four bars each. Yet this scheme is considerably diffused by the intricate motivic connections spanning the movement's sections. The first episode commences bleakly, but also a semitone above the original tonic. At length E minor brightens into E major (fig. 53), ecstatically tinged – now the herd bells are nearby rather than far distant below. But this pastorale soon collapses back into E♭ (fig. 54 ff.). The second episode (fig. 56) brings a stronger surge towards escape: the latent anguish beneath this pallid music erupts in the movement's first *fortissimo* tutti, ominously in C♯ minor (fig. 59). But no: *et in Arcadia ego*. The will to fulfillment rejoins (with symbolic cowbells), rhapsodically transforming the main theme in the new key of B, perhaps to vanquish the pensiveness of the original tonic. But unexpectedly, E♭ returns: the mounting rapture can no longer prevail. The deceptive cadence at fig. 62 signals final resignation, and the music quickly evaporates.

Finale

The post-Kantian era witnessed an extensive privileging of tragic art, which emphasizes the contrast between freedom and fate.[82] Many of Mahler's favourite writers contributed to this trend, but Schopenhauer and especially Nietzsche best illuminate the tragic outcome of the Sixth. In the background looms the Kantian sublime – awe, even terror, yielding aesthetic delight beyond the merely beautiful. For Schopenhauer, tragedy teaches withdrawal from the world.[83] For Nietzsche, life is to be fully embraced in all its weal and woe. His *Birth of Tragedy* declares that in Dionysian art 'we are forced to look into the terrors of the individual existence – yet we are not to become rigid with fear'; the artist, through Apollonian artifice, reshapes horror into the aesthetically sublime,[84] as Mahler had done in earlier works. But in concluding the last book he published, *Die Götzen-Dämmerung* ('Twilight of the idols'), subtitled 'Or, How One Philosophizes with a Hammer', Nietzsche goes further; tragedy is an orgiastic embrace of life, not to achieve liberation, but rather 'in order to be *oneself* the eternal joy of becoming, beyond all terror and pity – that joy which included even joy in destroying'. Nietzsche then quotes from *Zarathustra* a section now entitled 'The Hammer Speaks': 'if your hardness does not wish to flash and cut and cut through, how can you one day create with me? For all creators are hard ... Only the noblest is altogether hard.'[85]

The terror of the Sixth's conclusion is precisely its unrelentingly bleak hardness; as Bruno Walter observed in 1912:

> What is peculiar about the Sixth Symphony is that its terrible, hopeless gloom is presented mercilessly without any human sound ... The man who fashioned this terrifying musical image of a world without God ... had lost him in the world, which appeared to him increasingly mysterious and gloomy.[86]

'At the moment of tragic catastrophe', Schopenhauer writes, 'we become convinced more clearly than ever that life is a bad dream from which we have to awake'.[87] Perhaps this image informs the uncanny opening of the Sixth's Finale, a disoriented A♭ augmented sixth quivering with mildly atonal sonorities from which soars and falls a violin line of destiny uncertain – brutally interrupted by the all too familiar motto. Variants of this introduction also mark the development, recapitulation and coda of the vast sonata form (figs. 120, 143, 164). Thereafter follows (except in the coda) a lengthy episode of 'world-withdrawn isolation', including cowbells. – Ascetic withdrawal, or Dionysian abandon?

The exposition's A minor march (fig. 110) is the first movement *reviditur*, commingled with the ghastly irony of 'Revelge'. Similarly, the D major second subject (fig. 117) recalls both tonality and *Sehnsucht* of the 'Alma' theme. Immediately it cadences, the murky introduction interrupts (fig. 120) – our first hint of the drama's endpoint. As in the first movement, the Finale's development (fig. 124 ff.) is bipartite – organized around the famous hammer blows. Nevertheless, the hammer itself is symbolic ornamentation: Mahler added it only after completing the autograph fair copy, and initially contemplated five strokes rather than three.[88] As always, Mahlerian drama is substance and structure, not merely sonic colour. D major had been a potential fulfillment field (Adorno's term) in both the second subject and the recent interlude. Thereafter the resumption of forward motion brings dominant preparation of D (fig. 126–3 ff.) lasting well over a full minute – 'The maddening sting of these pains' pierces us just at the moment when, in Dionysian ecstasy, we anticipate the indestructibility and eternity of infinite primordial joy, as Nietzsche puts it.[89] 'Joy flares high at the edge of horror' is Adorno's paraphrase.[90] Panic collapse, negative fulfillment, hammer or no: a deceptive cadence has never disrupted more powerfully. The second blow (fig. 140) is similar, but shorter, less focused preparation (fig. 139 ff.) weakens it, just as Alma observes.[91] Out of this chaos the uncanny introduction precipitates recapitulation, again thwarting expectations of fulfillment in D.

But first to arise, phoenix-like, is the secondary material (fig. 146, V/B♭). Thereby Mahler invokes the tradition of the tragic reversed recapitulation:[92] the reprise will close with the principal march material. Adorno is right: 'epic expansion attains tightest control', for henceforth a positive outcome is impossible: it is too late. Tragic inevitability gives rise to tragic dramatic irony – the spectators sense the outcome while the actors do not. As the music waxes ecstatic, the timpani hammer out the motto rhythm (fig. 151–4), foretelling the inevitable. Yet the mania persists, only to succumb to the relentless A minor march (fig. 153). When, therefore, the secondary material reappears in tonic major (fig. 162 + 11 – possibly dominant of D?), the irony is almost unbearable. As in classic tragedy, *we* know what fate demands; the music seems not to, except, again, for the timpani.

When the curtain falls, the hammer has spoken, smashing the idol of fulfillment; no Dionysian joy remains. Adorno believes 'the music's abandonment to unbridled affect is its own death, the unabated vengeance of the world's course on Utopia'; for Samuels it constitutes the suicide of the romantic symphony. In any case, as at the close of *King Lear*, utter devastation prevails.

'Was kost' die Welt?': The Seventh Symphony

The Seventh defies all expectations; therein lies the measure of its success. If no longer 'the Cinderella among Mahler's symphonies',[93] it remains his most perplexing work. From the grouping of movements to the details of each, disjunctions and paradoxes abound. The seeming lack of overall relation or progression among the five movements and its uproariously 'cheerful' conclusion are a world apart from the Sixth's tight construction and black conclusion.

Indeed, Mahlerian polar contrasts are perhaps nowhere sharper than between that tragic Finale and the archly stylized, even rococo, self-sufficient *Nachtmusiken* of the Seventh, actually written the same summer (1904) that Mahler finished the Sixth and *Kindertotenlieder*. This unusual gestation became central to the Seventh as we know it; the following summer Mahler was unable to continue. Then, returning home from an excursion,

> I got into the boat to be rowed across [from Krumpendorf to Maiernigg]. At the first stroke of the oars the theme (or rather the rhythm and character) of the introduction to the first movement came into my head – and in four weeks the first, third, and fifth movements were done.[94]

Thus, the remainder of the Seventh was composed to sandwich the two *Nachtmusiken*.

Nachtmusiken and Scherzo

'The shadow of the Sixth ... becomes the realm of shadows of the [Seventh's] three middle movements', Adorno observes. Tragic aspiration has vanished, replaced by retrospective romanticism gently tinged with irony.[95] The first *Nachtmusik* 'is a nocturnal journey', reports Alphons Diepenbrock, 'a march with a fantastic chiaroscuro ... and the fantastic colors lead one's fantasy out of oneself and into the past, awakening a vision of peasants and soldiers'.[96] Tellingly, the Sixth's harrowing major–minor motto is thrice casually dismissed (figs. 72–2, 92–2, 111), and its cowbells appear in the context of carousel music (fig. 103 + 2 ff.). Indeed, the abundance of sonic symbols is bewildering: distant horn calls and responses, chipper military fanfares, wind band music, and birdsong all come and go.[97] Formally simplistic, the piece is a fantasy world far from the grim realism frequent in Mahler's marches.

'The second *Nachtmusik*', writes Peter Davison, 'is not so much intimate as about intimacy in the context of the universal, a serenade about all serenades', in which nature provides the backdrop for the human drama.[98] It is music 'composed within quotation marks', to borrow from Adorno, opening with an ironic allusion to both melody and harmony (θ7) of the *Tristan* prelude: no Wagnerian angst will disturb Mahler's indirect discourse on love.[99] This wistful refrain may appear unexpectedly almost anywhere, temporarily halting the music's momentum. Atmosphere and character are foregrounded during this leisurely stroll; plucked accompaniments often merge into and subtly displace the melody, punctuated by a real guitar and mandolin. Although the ternary structure modulates gently in the middle section (B: fig. 187 ff.; A', fig. 207–3) the rest scarcely departs from pastoral F major. Tonic (fig. 202 + 7) and thematic reprise (fig. 207–3) are askew, indicating indifference to grand structure. The piece is built, as Davison notes, 'from fragmentary images of musical and amorous convention ... ironically dissociated from their customary function'. And whenever it verges on intense emotional immediacy (for example figs. 183 and 213 ff.) 'the music quite literally retreats behind the conventional'.[100] The fantasy fades in imitation of falling asleep.

'Schattenhaft' ('shadowy'): Mahler's unusual performance indication sums up the D minor scherzo he placed between the two *Nachtmusiken* – a vignette of hell and demonic glee.[101] In certain respects this is the impotent *Doppelgänger* of the Fifth's 'development scherzo': whereas that distended waltz transformed the course of the entire symphony, this one only grows progressively nastier, proffering no transcendence. The entire *perpetuum mobile* remains largely fixated on D minor/ major, wherein its volatile energy frequently short-circuits into flashes and fragmentations, punctuated by various snaps, slides and shrieks (*kreischend*, fig. 161). Overall form, articulated by themes, is vitiated by interrelation and deterioration of motivic materials.[102] The treatment accorded the charmingly nostalgic trio epitomizes the whole: no time for such respite. Quickly infested by scherzo elements in its first appearance (fig. 134 ff.), the trio is fragmented and parodied with shocking vulgarity near the movement's end (fig. 164–6).[103] Shortly thereafter the music disintegrates, its parting shot a rude D major *ff* pizzicato viola chord.

First movement: Langsam – Allegro

'Hier röhrt die Nature' ('here Nature roars like a stag in rut') was Mahler's characterization of the Seventh's opening tenorhorn solo.[104] The principal kernels for this B minor introduction are already present in the 'boat sketch' mentioned above, and two additional sketchbook leaves contain the core of the exposition's first thematic group, in E minor and its dominant (figs. 6 and 10 + 4 ff.).[105] Particularly noteworthy are the propulsive dotted quavers and crotchets, the arrestingly angular minorseventh melodic contours, and the unusual θ7 sonorities that open the work. The latter are inversions of the famous 'Tristan' chord, closely related to the major 'added-sixth' chord derived from the anhemitonic pentatonic scale, that Mahler had mined so extensively in 'Ich bin der Welt'. And the famous stacked fourths occurring harmonically and motivically (for example figs. 4–5, 6–4, 10 + 4, 33–2) share the same origins. Hemitonic pentatonic scales (*Hirajoshi, Kumoijoshi*) also play a role, as does the augmented triad. These plus numerous neighbour-note dissonances constitute the first movement's strikingly modern-sounding vocabulary, 'a kind of supermajor' (Adorno) foreshadowing Mahler's late style.[106]

Like its components, the principal theme is driven and disjunct, as is the closely related material in the dominant. The second subject, which arrives unexpectedly via deceptive cadence (C major, fig. 15–4), is as voluptuous as the first was agitated, its indulgent sensuality prolonged through the rubato of a diva. But a falling-fourth trumpet call truncates the cadence, leading to a substantial modified repeat of the exposition (fig. 18 + 4), in E minor and its dominant. Both Beethoven and Brahms had played this card in developments, with finesse; here it is disruptive, and subsequently perplexing in its subjugation of the second subject (fig. 24 ff.).

Another trumpeted rupture (fig. 26) ushers in the development proper (fig. 28 + 5), via another harmonic deception. Presently, bumptious rehearsal of the principal materials yields to a reflective breakthrough: two static, intimate episodes based on distant fanfares and solemn transformation of an introductory march motive (figs. 32–1, 37 + 1; cf. 3–3) are linked by a lyrical G minor interlude (fig. 33 + 5). Initially the recapitulation occurred at fig. 39 + 5; instead, following the second episode Mahler interpolated a B major transfiguration of the second subject – a celestial highpoint that captivated the symphony's earliest critics.[107] But this, too, is denied closure, as return of the introduction inaugurates a process of variation and incremental intensification, whereby the functions of reprise and coda are blended, and the movement's climax (complement to the B major passage just noted) begins at fig. 62–4 – a chillingly militaristic treatment of the principal idea.

Rondo-Finale

Questioned by the Swiss critic William Ritter regarding his ground plan for the Seventh, Mahler replied: 'Three night pieces; in the finale, broad daylight. As foundation of the whole, the first movement.'[108] The foundational role of the first movement remains puzzling. However, the Finale's 'broad daylight' is dazzling to the point of unease; nothing

Mahler wrote has elicited as much controversy. A C major conclusion to the symphony was hardly to be expected, and its harmonic complexities yield to rampant diatonicism. Moreover, many hyperbolic gestures, including allusions to Wagner's *Meistersinger* overture (especially bars 15–22 ff.) and Mozart's *Seraglio* Janissaries (figs. 234–2, 269), suggest burlesque. And the eclectic range of topoi is extraordinary – fanfare, march, serenade, minuet, gypsy music, etc. The rondo's first wrenching 'transition' (C // Ab, fig. 230–5) is stupefying; it returns to prepare the work's bizarre final cadence. Indeed, deceptive cadences of various sorts abound, and frequently harmonic, thematic and metric articulations do not coordinate.[109] In short, the disjunctiveness characteristic of earlier movements here reigns supreme.

Precedents are found in the Fifth's Finale. Here as there, the notion of eternal recurrence seems to inform the rondo's avoidance of closure; its refrain appears seven times, like that of Zarathustra's 'The Seven Seals'.[110] But the Seventh's Finale goes much further than the Fifth's in questioning notions of structure, centrality, continuity, development and triumphant apotheosis. As Scherzinger notes, it 'challenges tradition precisely by making its own guiding logic – the denial of its ordinary functions – progressively more audible'.[111] There is something of Zarathustra's extravagant recklessness in it: 'For courage is the best slayer, courage which *attacks*; for in every attack there are drums and full brass [*klingendes Spiel*] ... for it [courage] says, "Was that life? Well then! Once more!"'[112] Much of the Finale seems ironic, particularly the grandiose cyclic return of the first movement's main theme (fig. 280–1 ff.) – 'a triumph over a conflict that was never really there in the first place'.[113] Apparently Mahler anticipated the endlessly overlapping circles of irony characteristic of post-modernity.

At the first rehearsal of the Finale he summarized it thus: 'Was kost' die Welt?' ('What does the world cost?')[114] The German adage he was quoting responds: 'Ich kauf' sie mir!' ('I'll buy it for myself!') – thus, a hyperbolic expression of exaggerated elation. But the overall response of the music seems to be the sacrifice of traditional positive affirmation, of *Freudenlicht der Welt* as Rückert knew it. Thus, the Seventh is the post-tragic, ironic, riotous counterpart to the Sixth. But as usual, Mahler's next symphony would assume a very different world-view: '"For what" remained the agonizing question of his soul', Bruno Walter writes, 'each of his works was a new attempt at an answer. And when he had won the answer for himself, the old question soon raised its unassuageable call again.'[115]

8 The 'greatest' and the 'most personal': the Eighth Symphony and *Das Lied von der Erde*

CHRISTIAN WILDHAGEN
(*translated by* JEREMY BARHAM AND TREFOR SMITH)

The 'greatest' and the 'most personal'

Whenever Mahler had completed preliminary work on a new composition he lost no time in letting friends and relatives know about it. Attributes he would thereby bestow on his works are revealing – and in such cases Mahler was certainly not sparing with superlatives. 'It is the most significant thing I have done yet'[1] was for example his assessment of the Finale of the Second Symphony. He called the Third Symphony 'my most individual and my richest work'.[2] Whatever the degree of understandable enthusiasm resonating from such comments, it was rare for Mahler's judgements to be final. He appeared to sense each new composition as having reached a yet higher stage of development, successive completed symphonies always seeming his best to date.

There are only two notable exceptions to this. In order to express the aspirations and significance of the Eighth Symphony in words, during its composition in 1906 he wrote, 'Just imagine the universe beginning to ring and resound. There are no longer human voices, but planets and suns circling above.'[3] He upheld the judgement that it was his 'greatest' work even when writing his important and substantial later works. At the beginning of October 1909, two months after the draft score of the Ninth Symphony had been completed, he called the Eighth 'my most important work',[4] and in the summer of 1910 he spoke once more of his 'greatest achievement'.[5] Mahler bestowed a similarly positive, if subtly differing, attribute on the work which immediately followed: *Das Lied von der Erde*. Completed in 1908 it became and remained for him 'the most personal thing I have done so far'.[6] If the Eighth constituted the external, 'objective' highpoint of his compositional achievements, to which all his earlier symphonies were 'only preludes',[7] then *Das Lied von der Erde* brought about a radical turn towards the subjective with its extreme internalizing of expression and the intimacy of its feeling and experience.

This sudden shift, comparable to that from third-person to first-person narrative, manifests itself at almost every level: in tone, style, harmony, instrumental forces, orchestration, and not least in the choice of text and the structural character of the composition, such that the work is generally thought to usher in a third period in the development of Mahler's output.

The *magnum opus*

The Eighth Symphony is exceptional on account of its scoring (three choirs, eight soloists and an orchestra of well over a hundred musicians), which has few equivalents in musical history. The work's intermixed instrumental-vocal character represents a prototypical 'vocal symphony' which, as Mahler said to Richard Specht, 'is sung right through from beginning to end'.[8] The texts on the other hand influence the overall structure in such a way that the usual four-movement pattern is replaced by two strongly divergent 'Parts'. As if to emphasize this outward lack of uniformity, the hymn 'Veni creator spiritus' and the final scene from Goethe's *Faust* embrace two poetical works which were not only written in different languages but also date from periods over 1,000 years apart.

These divergences from the established symphonic norm contributed to the work's special status and may even have induced Mahler to consider it 'the greatest thing I have ever done', a phrase which by ingenious coincidence conferred on the Eighth a rank similar to that which Goethe had conferred on *Faust* in his repeated references to it as his 'chief concern' and 'magnum opus'.[9]

Origins: 'As if it had been dictated to me'
With no other work did Mahler so emphatically stress the overpowering character of the inspiration which had taken hold of him. He admitted: 'I have … never worked under such compulsion; it was like a lightning vision – suddenly the whole thing stood before me and I simply had to write it down, just as if it had been dictated to me'.[10] The remarkable speed with which the writing progressed in the summer of 1906 seems to substantiate his account, and Mahler's vivid 'dictation' metaphor was one in a long line of similar comments.[11] Conversely he remained aware of the responsibility to put what he had 'received' down on paper in an appropriate way. But this rational part of the creative process paled in comparison with his endeavour to attribute authorship of his acknowledged *magnum opus* to a so-called 'higher' authority, to that creator-spirit – beyond the grasp of rationality – to which the Whitsuntide hymn of Part I immediately calls with the opening words 'Veni, veni, creator spiritus!'

When Mahler began work in mid-June 1906 only the use of the medieval hymn at the beginning was certain. This text had fallen into his hands by chance, as so often happened, in a communion or prayer book of dubious origin, but he quickly abandoned the plan to translate the hymn into German and proceeded to set the Latin text to music. It soon became obvious, however, that his structural conception of the music was diverging from the text in hand. He made do with a few instrumental interludes, but at the same time had a search for a liturgically authenticated version of the hymn carried out at the Vienna Hofoper. When this was finally found in the middle of July, he noticed serious discrepancies with his first source ('this wretched liturgical tome'[12]) and braced himself for extensive alterations to his already completed sketches. To his 'utter astonishment', however, he noticed an unexpected correlation between the sketches and the complete hymn text. 'Each of the new words' – amounting to at least two and a half verses – 'fitted naturally into the whole'.[13] He told many of his trusted friends about this experience and in accordance with Mahler's theory of the work's 'higher' authorship, the myth was born that he had intuitively composed the missing verses. Bruno Walter later celebrated this as a 'miraculous act of empathy and anticipation'.[14] In reality it was more prosaic, particularly since Mahler dealt with the hymn text very freely anyway, to suit his requirements. Three weeks later, on 15 August, the sketches were finished, and by the beginning of September, a more detailed short score of Part II was ready, which was to be based on the final scene from Goethe's *Faust*.

This choice of text replaced initial plans to follow the hymn with three separate movements: an Adagio entitled 'Caritas', a Scherzo with the title 'Christmas games with the little child' (after two *Wunderhorn* poems) and a final hymn to the power of 'Eros'.[15] Although traces of this idea are preserved in the second part, nothing seemed more suitable to Mahler 'as a response'[16] to the hymn than the allegorical intensity of the end of *Faust*, a drama which had preoccupied him throughout his life.

First performance

The Munich première on 12 September which had been fought for against countless organizational problems turned out to be a supreme triumph for Mahler as conductor *and* as composer.[17] With the Eighth he finally achieved the resounding success that had eluded many of his earlier symphonies. Otto Klemperer, who together with Oskar Fried and Bruno Walter assisted Mahler, recalled: 'Nowadays one can hardly imagine interpretation in its ultimate perfection ... He always wanted more clarity, more timbre, more dynamic contrast. During rehearsals ... he turned to some of us in the auditorium and said: "If after my death, something does not sound right, then change it. You have not only the right but the duty to do so".'[18]

Expectations were aroused in endless press reports.[19] According to the *Münchener Stadtschreiber*[20] the first performance was overwhelming in its fulfilment of these expectations: 'The success of the evening was extraordinary, and met with the approval of the entire musical world ... The final scene left behind an unforgettable impression culminating in a rousing apotheosis for Mahler that lasted several minutes.' Thomas Mann wrote a hymn-like paean of gratitude to Mahler, enclosing with it a copy of his novel *Königliche Hoheit* (1909): 'It is ... a mere feather's weight in the hand of the man who, as I believe, expresses the art of our time in its profoundest and most sacred form'.[21]

The universal symphony

The superlatives which clung around Mahler's declared *magnum opus* from the outset and which stand out in Mann's tribute could easily lead to a misinterpretation of the Eighth as the typical product of megalomania. Persistent use of the questionable epithet 'Symphony of a Thousand' has been one result of such doubtful interpretation.[22] However, closer examination of the work reveals that the gigantic increase in resources was simply the outward reflection of much deeper spiritual desires – an aspiration which can justifiably be called 'all-embracing'. Mahler sought to sketch out in his music nothing less than a symbol of the universe in sound.

As if Mahler wanted to bring about a great synthesis of Western music, the Symphony includes Baroque fugal techniques alongside the solemn tones of the chorale and the hymn. His appropriation of a Wagnerian musical language is just as masterly as the occasional recourse to the unpretentious style of the German Lied: 'The symphony must be like the world. It must embrace everything' he said to Jean Sibelius in 1907, the year the work was completed.[23] Far more than an interplay of sounds composed according to principles of absolute music, Mahler's symphonic 'world' is a mirror of his whole experience framed by the programmatic expression of his world-view.

The vocal element of the work retains links with cantata and oratorio traditions. But the inclusion of a choir within the symphonic context cannot be discussed without reference to the model of Beethoven's Ninth and subsequent works by Mendelssohn, Berlioz and Liszt. This diversity of formal and historical references appears to be an essential characteristic of Mahler's idea of the universal symphony, which goes beyond the fulfilment of traditional norms in using *every* available means of musical history to express his beliefs. Analysis of the word–music relationship shows how the two parts of the Symphony, which seem to be opposites in so many ways, are bound into one 'whole'. Mahler consciously creates connections between them through explicit compositional cross-references and a relatively circumscribed stock of melodic ideas – so-called *Leitthemen* (principal themes), a dense network for which Thomas Mann's eloquent expression 'magic relationships' (*Beziehungszauber*) is no less relevant than for Wagner's music dramas.[24] In this way, Mahler establishes a web of compositional *and* spiritual references spanning all appearance of conflict.

Principal themes and ideas

His setting of the texts is supported by five main ideas, articulated as religious intercessions in the hymn and portrayed symbolically in the *Faust* poem. These form the essential elements of the work's inter-denominational message and metaphysics:

(1) The idea of 'love' as a creative and redemptive world principle.
(2) The concept of a 'higher grace' which acts beyond the realms of rational and moral justifiability.
(3) The confronting of the above with the weakness and the 'inadequacy' of earthly human existence, resulting in:
(4) A 'striving' caught up in ceaseless 'activity', and a desire for divine enlightenment. According to Goethe's poetic allegory, these together lead to:
(5) Purification of the soul and 'rebirth', to a continuation of existence after death.

The idea of human inadequacy is directly expressed at parallel places in both parts: in the lines 'Infirma nostri corporis / Virtute firmans perpeti' ('Our weak frames / Fortify with thine eternal strength') the hymn evokes the relationship between man and the mortal frame of his body, his earthly entrapment. Part II takes up these thoughts in the lines of the 'more perfect' angels: 'Uns bleibt ein Erdenrest / Zu tragen peinlich' ('We retain an earthly cloak / Hurtful to wear'). Through a virtually identical musical setting (Mahler's direction is 'Like the same place in Part I') the frailty of existence is correlated with *Erdenrest* (earthly cloak), which according to Goethe's symbolism impedes the soul's ascent to the *höhern Sphären* (higher spheres).

The plea for enlightenment and 'ensouling' (4) is also the main purpose of the Whitsuntide hymn: a key verse in Part I runs: *Accende lumen sensibus!* Although the Pater Profundus's prayer leads straight through into the cry 'O Gott! Beschwichtige die Gedanken / Erleuchte mein bedürftig Herz!' ('O God, calm my thoughts / Give light to my impoverished heart!'), Mahler primarily sees the figure of Faust as the quintessence of creative man, striving for enlightenment and embodying a universal creative idea in individual form. This allowed him to be placed alongside that divine creator-spirit which the work invokes at the outset in the first verse of the hymn: 'Veni, creator spiritus / Mentes tuorum visita / Imple superna gratia / Quae tu creasti pectora' ('Come, Creator

Example 8.1 'Veni creator spiritus' theme, Part I, bars 2–5

Example 8.2 'Accende' theme, Part I, bars 261–5

Spirit / Dwell in our minds / Fill with divine grace / The hearts of thy servants'). (Example 8.1.)

   This central equation of striving, creative humanity and the creator-spirit of the hymn is brought about through the reuse of the 'Veni creator spiritus' theme at a crucial point in Part II. Largely unaltered, it returns for the first and only time as an answer to Gretchen's vision of the purification of Faust's soul in the final scene ('Sieh, wie er jedem Erdenbande / Der alten Hülle sich entrafft' ('See how he sheds the earthly leaven / Tears off each shroud of old untruth')) (Part II, fig. 168). The individual thus points beyond, towards a higher sphere of which he is also a part; he joins the hierarchy of all existence that extends 'upwards' to the one all-conditioning Absolute, the creator god, who grants mankind the divine enlightenment and redemption he desires: an act of divine grace (2), which manifests itself as love. Mahler integrates the impulses of sensual-earthly love, *Eros*, and the hymn's theological notions of *Caritas* and *Agape* (1), the latter revealed in the central passage of Part I with the powerful invocation: 'Accende lumen sensibus / Infunde amorem cordibus!' ('Illuminate our senses / Pour love into our hearts!'). (Example 8.2.)

   According to Anton Webern, Mahler illustrated this passage at the final rehearsal in Munich (11 September 1910) as follows: 'here is the bridge leading to the conclusion of *Faust*. This passage is the axis of the entire work.'[25] The 'Accende' theme is heard almost in its original form in the angels' lines: 'Gerettet ist des edle Glied / Der Geisterwelt vom Bösen / "Wer immer strebend sich bemüht / Den können wir erlösen"' ('Saved, saved now is that precious part / Of our spirit world from evil / "Should a man strive with all his heart / Heaven can foil the devil"'). What was shaped in Part I as a collective plea for revelation, takes on a *scherzando* character in Part II now that Faust's soul has been saved from the devil, and the angels' act of salvation is thereby interpreted by Mahler as one of caring love.

Long sections of the distinctly monothematic music of Part II are based on metamorphoses of the love theme, and through this Mahler expresses compositionally what Goethe's poetry presents in a series of allegories of the idea of love. He elicits from this theme the *schwebend* (floating) and *pianissimo* melody accompanying the Mater Gloriosa's appearance in the middle of Part II (fig. 106), and wrote to Alma about his conception of this figure:

> That which draws us by its mystic force, what every created thing ... feels with absolute certainty as the centre of its being, what Goethe here – again employing an image – calls the eternal feminine ... you are quite right in calling it the force of love. There are infinite representations and names for it ... Goethe himself reveals it stage by stage, on and on, in image after image, more and more clearly as he draws nearer the end: in Faust's impassioned search for Helen ... through the manifold entelechies of lower and higher degree; he presents and expresses it with a growing clearness and certainty right on to the mater gloriosa – the personification of the eternal feminine![26]

The Mater Gloriosa is the extreme personification of the principle of an all-ensouling love (1), whose enlightening force had earlier been petitioned in the hymn of Part I: 'Accende lumen sensibus'.

Belief in overcoming death and in a continued existence 'in eternity' (5) lay at the centre of Mahler's spiritual world throughout his life. A letter from Mahler to Bruno Walter demonstrates that the belief in the ascent of the soul towards immortality, presented allegorically at the end of *Faust*, was of the greatest personal relevance to him: 'I see everything in such a new light – am in such a state of flux, sometimes I should hardly be surprised suddenly to find myself in a new body. (Like Faust in the last scene.)'[27]

In Goethe's view the ascent of the soul to *höhern Sphären* (higher spheres) is an act of grace, and grace is finally granted to the *Unsterbliches* (immortal part) of Faust's soul. Mahler saw in this a further link to the hymn, which he made clear by making compositional references to Part I: compare Part I, bars 46–61 with Part II, bars 1213–227, and Part I, bars 108–22 and 479–88 with Part II, bars 1228–243. The textual content at these parallel points centres on ideas of divine grace – the principle that in Part I is solicited 'collectively' ('Imple superna gratia' ('Fill with divine grace')), and in Part II is initially imposed on Gretchen, the child murderer, to set an example, and is then actually embodied by her: 'Vergönne mir, ihn zu belehren' ('Grant me to instruct him'). She beseeches the Mater Gloriosa that she might assume the role of a psychagogue, a *dux animae* (spiritual guide) for Faust's soul, and finally his *Unsterbliches* (immortal part) is allowed to follow her into the *Höhen der ewigen Reiche* (heights of kingdoms eternal).

It was thereby possible for Mahler to return full circle to that emphatic invocation of the creator-spirit with which the hymn began. From the elemental formative power of nature through the creative power of the individual to the most fundamental, universally ensouling power of the spirit, the idea of 'creator-hood' finally achieves transcendence. The Eighth Symphony accordingly closes with the creator's invocation, an expanded version of the 'Veni creator spiritus' theme played by the additional brass ensemble.

Das Lied von der Erde

When listening to the music of *Das Lied von der Erde* immediately after this overwhelming final apotheosis of the Eighth Symphony, one would be inclined to agree with the astonished Bruno Walter, who posed the following question:

> Can the man who reared the structure of the Eighth 'in harmony with the Everlasting', be the same as the author of the *Trinklied vom Jammer der Erde* [Drinking Song of Earthly Woe] – the man . . . who seeks to forget in drink the senselessness of life and finally leaves it in deep melancholy? Is it the same master who, after his gigantic symphonies, constructs a new form of unity out of six songs? He is scarcely the same as a man or as a composer. All his previous work had grown out of his sense of life . . . *Das Lied von der Erde* is . . . written *sub specie mortis*. Earth is vanishing; he breathes in another air, a new light shines on him – and so it is a wholly new work that Mahler wrote: new in its style of composition, new in invention, in instrumentation, and in the structures of the various movements. It is more subjective than any of his previous works . . . Every note carries his individual voice; every word, though based on a poem a thousand years old, is his own, *Das Lied von der Erde* is Mahler's most personal utterance, perhaps the most personal utterance in music.[28]

Research was quick to look for reasons for this decisive change in Mahler's compositional style, and found them in his personal life. Alma described the year 1907 as 'heavily underlined in the calendar of our life',[29] and recounted its events under the title 'Suffering and Dread'. That summer the family had to come to terms with the death of their elder daughter Maria Anna from diphtheria, Mahler's diagnosed heart condition, and his resignation as director of the Vienna Hofoper, with its attendant press campaign.[30] The profound effect of these events can be gauged once again from the loving account by Bruno Walter, who noticed at that time a 'marked shift in his whole outlook. The mystery of death had always been in his mind and thoughts; now it was within

sight; his world, his life lay under the sombre shadow of its proximity ...
There was no mistaking the darkness that had descended upon his
being.'[31]

Origins

According to Alma Mahler, Mahler received Bethge's collection *Die
chinesische Flöte* from Theobald Pollak, a senior servant to the Court
and family friend.[32] She recounts:

> Now, after the loss of his child and the alarming verdict on his heart, exiled
> from his home and his workshop, these poems came back to his mind; and
> their infinite melancholy answered to his own. Before we left Schluderbach
> [the family's refuge in summer 1907 after Maria's death] he had sketched
> out, on long, lonely walks, those songs for orchestra which took final shape
> as *Das Lied von der Erde* a year later.[33]

Recent research has suggested, however, that Bethge's book did not
appear until 5 October 1907, that is after the end of their holiday that
year.[34] Most of the composition was therefore not done until summer
1908, the work being completed on 1 September, the day Mahler finished
the orchestral draft of the sixth (and last) movement.

The earliest known date is to be found in the manuscript of a version of
the eventual second movement for voice and piano, marked 'Toblach July
1908'.[35] Since this keyboard version has the appearance of a fair copy, it is
doubtful that the given date actually represents the earliest stage of work.
Contrary to expectations, this piano version, first published in 1989 as part of
the Supplement to the Complete Critical Edition, did not necessarily represent a first step towards the subsequent orchestral version. In the third and
fifth movements alone there is evidence that the piano adaptation was based
on the *completed* draft orchestral score. It was clearly Mahler's intention to
devise independent pianistic solutions, which prove it to be an entirely valid
alternative version.[36]

Symphony and song

The double conception of the work – as a song cycle with piano accompaniment and as a unified sequence of orchestral songs – is a crucial
indication of the complex blending of different forms and genres pursued
by Mahler as resolutely in this work as he had hitherto done only in the
Eighth Symphony. The contrasting poles of *Das Lied von der Erde* are Lied
and instrumental symphony, whose fusion marks the conclusion of a line
of development extending from the song quotations in the first two symphonies, through the Lied movements 'Urlicht' and 'Mitternachtslied' in the
Second and Third, to the purely vocal Finale of the Fourth.

This dualistic concept is a further indication of Mahler's universal understanding of the symphonic genre. The gradual process of moulding and concentrating the songs into a symphonic whole[37] should not be seen simply as a case of expanding the piano version into a larger-scale orchestral structure. The symphonic cohesion of the six movements owes much more to the overriding spiritual requirements and intellectual content of the cycle. *Das Lied von der Erde* is thus symphonic first and foremost, and its main title, together with movement headings such as 'Von der Jugend' and 'Von der Schönheit' apparently modelled on the chapter titles of Nietzsche's *Also sprach Zarathustra*, point to the universality of the work's artistic and idealistic message.

Position in Mahler's oeuvre, scoring and first performance
Although Mahler superstitiously neglected to accord *Das Lied von der Erde* a number as with his other symphonies, in truth, 'Fate' – and Mahler firmly believed in a higher predestination in his life and work[38] – had not been cheated at all by such numerical games. On the contrary, in a cruel twist, Mahler's early death seemed to mock his superstition by preventing him from both finishing his Tenth Symphony and hearing the first performances of the Ninth and *Das Lied von der Erde*.

Uncertainty surrounds the question of the use of the solo voices. In the short score and the piano version of the third Lied, Mahler considered an alternative setting with soprano instead of tenor, but a later instruction in the copyist's manuscript causes far more confusion; here, at the alto's entry in the second movement, he notes 'if need be, can also be sung by a baritone'. As in all available versions, the Complete Critical Edition has taken this to indicate a general freedom of choice between alto and baritone in performance. But it remains doubtful whether Mahler's comment regarding the second movement can be applied without hesitation to the fourth and sixth movements.

At the posthumous first performance on 20 November 1911 in Munich, Bruno Walter conducted the original version with the Munich Konzertverein using tenor (William Miller) and alto (Sarah Charles Cahier).[39] The success of the new work was less clear-cut, although a critique spoke of the work having been received with genuine approval.[40] Already full of anticipation, on 30 October 1911 Webern begged Berg to go to Munich with him: 'My dear friend, when you have read the last part of the enclosed poem from *Das Lied von der Erde*, will you not expect the most wondrous things that music can offer? Something so heavenly, the like of which has never been heard of . . . For heaven's sake, what kind of music must that be?'[41] Still obviously struggling to keep his composure after the dress rehearsal, he wrote to his teacher: 'I have just heard Mahler's *Lied von der Erde*. I cannot speak ... I rank the experience which I have just gone through alongside the things that were and are most precious to me ... This music ... my God, for this I would dearly like to pass away.'[42]

Structure and musical style

Table 8.1 provides a formal outline of the work.

There has been no lack of attempts to classify these six Lieder as movements of a conventional symphony. 'Das Trinklied' corresponds to a first movement (albeit concise by Mahler standards), whilst 'Der Abschied' functions as an extended final movement. 'Der Einsame im Herbst' represents the slow movement, followed by two shorter scherzos (third and fifth movements) which frame a more peaceful character piece (fourth movement).

Quite independently of this, there exist relationships between the subject matter of individual movements. For example, the first and fifth movements are both drinking songs and share a certain exuberance of musical expression, whereas the third and fourth movements are linked by the anaphora of Mahler's own titles: 'Von der Jugend' and 'Von der Schönheit'. Similarly there is a connection between the titles 'Der Einsame im Herbst' and 'Der Trunkene im Frühling'. In this case the order of the seasons is literally turned back to front. 'Der Abschied', Mahler's setting of two poems already interrelated in the original, not only introduces a profound change in the inner content of the whole work, but also seems to act as a complementary conclusion and counterbalance to all five preceding movements.

The cohesion of the work also depends on the subconscious unity of both melodic-thematic material and musical language. Both factors can be attributed to the central role played by exoticism in *Das Lied von der Erde*. No other work by Mahler is characterized to such an extent by pentatonic, modal and whole-tone scales and figures. Even the earliest analyses of the work regarded the sequence of notes A–G–E in bars 5–7 of 'Das Trinklied' as the central motive of the whole work. It recurs not only in transposed form at the beginning of the second and fifth movements, but also in inversion in the final moment of 'Der Abschied' – as a C major chord with added sixth. This sequence of notes is characteristic of the Aeolian mode, but its origins can also be traced back to the ancient Chinese scale *Gong*.[43]

The relationship between exotic colouring and poetic subject matter is immediately obvious, but this also reveals a certain affinity with contemporary tastes for the ornamental language of *Jugendstil* and for all things Japanese or Chinese – for porcelain and unusual chinoiserie. Mahler may well have also derived musical inspiration from Puccini's *Madame Butterfly* (1904) which he performed for the first time at the Vienna Opera on 31 October 1907 – the last significant new production of his period of office.[44]

Table 8.1 *Formal outline of* Das Lied von der Erde

Movement	Title	Author of poem	Basic key	Metre	Soloist
I	'Das Trinklied vom Jammer der Erde'	Li-Tai-Po	A minor	$\frac{3}{4}$	Tenor
II	'Der Einsame im Herbst' [Bethge: 'Die Einsame im Herbst']	Tschang-Tsi [Ch'ien-Ch'i]	D minor	$\frac{3}{2}$	Alto [or Baritone according to the *Stichvorlage*]
III	'Von der Jugend' [Bethge: 'Der Pavillon aus Porzellan']	Li-Tai-Po	B♭ major	$\frac{2}{2}$	Tenor [or soprano according to the keyboard version]
IV	'Von der Schönheit' [Bethge: 'Am Ufer']	Li-Tai-Po	G major	$\frac{3}{4}$ subsequently mainly $\frac{4}{4}$	Alto
V	'Der Trunkene im Frühling' [Bethge: 'Der Trinker im Frühling']	Li-Tai-Po	A major	$\frac{4}{4}$	Tenor
VI	'Der Abschied' [Bethge: 'In Erwartung des Freundes' and 'Der Abschied des Freundes']	Two poems: Mong-Kao-Jen and Wang-Wei, texts extensively re-worked by Mahler	C minor/ C major	$\frac{4}{4} - \frac{3}{4}$	Alto

Mahler absorbs all these 'exotic' influences completely into his late style, which first came to light in the solo scene with Pater Profundus in Part II of the Eighth Symphony (fig. 39), and whose most important characteristics include:

(1) The dominance of the purely linear.
(2) Increase in formal freedom and ambiguity akin to filmic sequences.
(3) More sparing chamber-like or soloistic use of orchestral resources.
(4) A preference for lyrical, melancholic, or resigned melodic and expressive moods.

If the Eighth Symphony involved an affirmatory commitment to ideological beliefs, then, in part due to the biographical background to its composition, *Das Lied von der Erde* addresses the equally ideologically rooted, yet openly subjective expression of inner experience.

The music: form and meaning
'Das Trinklied vom Jammer der Erde'
The first movement offers immediate evidence of Mahler's unique symbiosis of song and symphony.[45] The text, which Mahler shortened by

several lines,[46] is divided into three verses which correspond in unortho-
dox ways with the three main sections of first-movement sonata form: the
exposition embraces the first verse (bars 1–89) as well as a written-out
repeat of the exposition (bars 89–202) using the text of the second verse;
both sections finish with the sombre refrain: 'Dunkel ist das Leben, ist der
Tod' ('Dark is life, and so is death'); the development (bars 203–323) begins
at the exact mid-way point of the movement with a longer, purely instrumental interlude (bars 203–63) and subsequently includes the first five lines
of the third verse; finally the recapitulation (bars 325/326–405), greatly
varied as always with Mahler, brings the remaining seven lines of the third
verse to a dramatic climax (bar 361) and again fades away with the gloomy
refrain. A latent tripartite structure emerges, analogous to the three verses,
which at the same time recalls bar form with doubled *Stollen* and *Abgesang*.

The emotionally charged music implements the poem's classical idea
of *Vanitas* (empty boasting) in all its manifestations – disgust of life,
drunkenness through the loathing of one's existence and of the futility of
things earthly – with a fearless vulgarity and even ugliness rarely equalled
elsewhere, even in Mahler. The recurrent quieter passages in between
speak of the spirit of affirmation, that 'sweet fragrance of life' which
counteracts the fatalism and death cry of the ghostly ape. Rather than
the inescapable negativity of the refrain, it is this dualism between longing
for life and the warning *memento mori* which defines the message of 'Das
Trinklied' and indeed the whole of *Das Lied von der Erde*.

'Der Einsame im Herbst'

In the second movement Mahler may lay bare the feeling of existential
isolation and demoralization with an intensity near breaking-point, but
in the vision of sleep's consolation (bars 85–101) and in the hymnic
upsurge 'Sonne der Liebe' (Sun of Love; bars 127–35) – which significantly shares the key of E♭ major with the Eighth Symphony – he breaks
through the predominant tone of gloom and despair.

The structure reveals a paradoxical 'complex simplicity' through the
sequence of four distinctly differentiated verses (bars 25–49, 50–77, 78–101
and 102–37) framed by an introduction (bars 1–24) and postlude (138–54),
which are divided into increasingly divergent halves until by the end only a
distant structural relationship is discernible. With its largely autonomous
and more linearly than harmonically conceived part-writing and occasional
Lydian colouring,[47] the movement far surpasses earlier models of chamber-
like orchestration in the *Kindertotenlieder* and *Rückertlieder*.

'Von der Jugend'

The third movement functions as a cheerful contrast to what has gone
before, its image of the green and white porcelain pavilion evoking ideas

of poetic, unspoilt beauty and subsumed within a setting of extreme delicacy. The prevailing bright mood, subtly highlighted by the novel use of triangle and piccolo, is temporarily darkened by melancholy clouds (bars 70–96). Mahler makes use of a loose pentatonicism with hints of modality, a perfect example of which can be found in the twelve-bar introduction which establishes the stylistic parameters of the music.

'Von der Schönheit'

The third movement's impression of chinoiserie lightly dabbed onto silk or parchment is suggested again here in the unconventional mixture of pentatonic and diatonic scales, which assumes a folk-like simplicity akin to the 'Blumenstück' second movement of the Third Symphony.

Mahler's almost palpable musical portrayal in the middle section (bars 43–95) of the group of *junge Mädchen* (young girls) collecting *Lotusblumen* (lotus flowers) on the river bank being harassed by a gang of hot-headed youths on their *mut'gen Rossen* (spirited horses) was fittingly described by the work's first analyst, Joseph von Wöss, as the 'most realistic thing' that Mahler had ever written.[48] At the *Funkeln* (flashing) of one of the maiden's *heißen Blicks* (passionate eye) the music appears to pledge the fulfilment of her desire in the form of an undulating, wordless postlude of Schumannesque poetic eloquence (bars 124–44).

'Der Trunkene im Frühling'

The penultimate movement not only forms a companion piece to 'Von der Jugend' but also takes up the braggadocio of the opening movement, the protagonist now clearly giving in freely to intoxication and nonchalantly resigning himself to Fate.

Structurally, six widely differing verses can be identified (bars 1–14, 15–28, 29–44, 45–64, 65–71 and 72–87 plus the postlude) each of which, apart from the fifth, consists of two contrasting musical ideas. After the sparkling orchestration of bars 1–7 of the first verse the music slips unexpectedly into the submediant (F major), and, with the entry of the first violins, ushers in a contrasting lyric expressiveness which later develops into the music of the bird twittering in spring (compare bars 22–3 with 60–1). The singer resists its luring call (bars 65–72), whereupon the music becomes a riot of increasingly distant harmonies and vocal demands. The drinker's inebriation becomes sheer existential intoxication and complete loss of inhibition.

'Der Abschied'

By contrast, at the beginning of 'Der Abschied' weighty, oppressive sonorities outline the dirge-like mood of a movement which, at nearly half an hour, almost constitutes an independent second section to the first five Lieder. 'It is cruel ... that music should be so beautiful' said an enraptured Benjamin Britten,[49] and Shostakovich called the 'Abschied' simply 'the greatest piece of music that has ever been written'.[50]

Its secret can be glimpsed in the extreme contrast between a mood of profound lamentation and intense, quasi-religious ecstasy of affirmation. Mahler's setting leaves no doubt that the farewell between two friends, one of whom is disappointed in the world and is going to move for good *in die Berge* (into the mountains), is also a farewell to life. What may have been primarily a literary game of question and answer in the relationship between the two ancient Chinese poets Mong-Kao-Jen and Wang-Wei acquires in Mahler a symbolic, existential character.

Through radical changes and reworkings of the text, Mahler vividly brings to light the theme of death only hinted at in the original. Especially revealing is his transformation of the Wang-Wei poem from first person (*Ich stieg vom Pferd* (I dismounted from my horse)) to third person (*Er stieg* ... (He dismounted ...)), and the almost mythical depersonalization and neutralization of linguistic expression that result.

This alteration also stresses the analogies between the first and second parts of the movement (bars 1–302 and 303–508), whose opening vocal sections form parallel structures (compare bars 19–26 with 375–81). This large-scale formal duality, loosely linked with oriental constructs of *Yin* and *Yang*, is primarily the result of Mahler's combination of two complementary poems, but it could only be risked by a composer for whom the principle of developing variation had become second nature. This principle works supremely well at the end of the movement (from bar 460), where Mahler once again achieves an overwhelming level of intensity. 'Air from another planet' truly seems to be wafting in, as the text of Schoenberg's contemporaneous second string quartet puts it. In both cases the musical breakthrough is accompanied by a change of subject matter: in the added image of the *liebe Erde* (dear Earth) constantly blossoming anew, Mahler counteracts Death with the principle of eternal re-creation. The voice repeats the last word of the text *ewig* (for ever) seven times and the music glows in the brightest of colours while seeming melodically to circle within itself *ad infinitum*. Worlds away from the Eighth Symphony's spirit of collective upheaval and exaltation, the end of *Das Lied von der Erde* nevertheless proclaims the conviction shared by all of Mahler's works that death is followed by a transcendent form of new life.

9 The last works

JÖRG ROTHKAMM
(*translated by* JEREMY BARHAM)

'Farewells' and new beginnings in the Ninth Symphony

As noted in the previous chapter, Mahler was reported to have had a superstitious fear of completing a ninth symphony, believing that since Beethoven and Bruckner number nine had been the furthest that a symphonic composer could progress.[1] Mahler attempted to avoid this fate when he composed *Das Lied von der Erde*, his actual 'ninth'. Such arguments are supported by the fact that Mahler had been diagnosed with a serious heart problem in 1907 which made him aware of the limited time remaining to him. He also had had to cope with the death of his daughter Maria that year, and it is therefore not surprising that Mahler approached his Ninth in a particular frame of mind, denying himself from the start music of a celebratory nature. However, in view of the advanced stage of the sketches for the Tenth symphony, it is inappropriate to call the Ninth Mahler's final 'farewell' to the world, as did many reviewers of the posthumous first performance.[2] If anything, the Ninth, together with *Das Lied von der Erde* and the sketches for the Tenth, could be seen as a 'farewell' trilogy, particularly since all three works mark a clear break with the preceding Eighth Symphony and embody Mahler's late style.

Like its two companion works, the Ninth Symphony was written during Mahler's summer sojourns in Toblach, in the composing hut at the Altschluderbach villa. Sketches possibly date back as far as 1908. In August 1909 Mahler reported the completion of the orchestral draft to his friend and disciple Bruno Walter:

> I have been working very hard and am just putting the finishing touches to a new symphony ... The work itself ... is a very satisfactory addition to my little family. In it something is said that I have had on the tip of my tongue for some time – perhaps (as a whole) to be ranked beside the Fourth, if anything. (But quite different.)[3]

A fair copy of the score was ready on 1 April 1910. A manuscript prepared by a New York copyist and corrected for publication by Mahler also exists. However, Mahler neither survived to see the score published nor was able to test out the instrumentation through rehearsal. Bruno Walter had the honour of conducting the first performance on 26 June 1912 in Vienna.

Unlike his Fourth Symphony with which Mahler compared the Ninth, the latter is purely orchestral and is scored for larger forces, with mostly quadruple wind. Although they share a classical four-movement structure, the Ninth's outer movements are expansive and slow moving, and the middle movements shorter and faster.

Andante comodo

The opening movement does not conform to the traditional expectations of a symphonic first movement. Although its structure has been interpreted with some success as lying variously between first-movement sonata form and double-variation form, precise formal definitions have often been completely repudiated. In view of its stylization of the funeral procession, a musico-cultural phenomenon which defines not only individual passages of the movement but also its entire structural design,[4] there is much evidence to suggest that, unusually, this is a character movement in the tradition of the march, scherzo and minuet. Each of the six slow-moving and extended sections (beginning at bars 1, 47, 108, 246, 314/317 and, with some qualification, 416) can be regarded as a stylized funeral cortège. A series of more impassioned 'trios' (beginning at bars 29, 80, 174 and 372), form interpolations of equal importance rather than lightweight interludes. The tonal structure also suggests this formal division: the cortège sections are dominated by the main key of D major and its submediant B major, and the other sections often by the tonic minor and more distant keys.

The frequent return of a funereal, anacrustic main rhythm, even in the 'trio' sections (see Example 9.1), suggests that the whole movement could be regarded as a composition on the theme of 'cortège'. After all, the movement is almost continuously in a procession-like $\frac{4}{4}$ time. The tempo is also repeatedly slowed to the calm walking pace of a cortège.

Five motives, each with up to twenty-four variants, form the entire material of the movement. These one-and-a-half- to two-and-a-half-bar motivic building blocks are often broken down further into cells of between a half and a single bar. This process distinguishes the three main motives (a, b and c) from the less frequent d and e motives. The latter consist of material borrowed from *Das Lied von der Erde* and therefore are subject to minimal variation. However, it becomes clear that all the motives are amenable to mutual combination.

Motive a, with its distinctive rhythm, is the predominant cortège motive (Example 9.1). The opening minor third, the falling second and the alternating down beats and anacruses are all characteristic. This heavy, march-like gesture is mostly scored for harps, basses, timpani or bells.

Example 9.1 Ninth Symphony, first movement, harp, bars 3–4

Example 9.2 Ninth Symphony, first movement, first violin, bars 29–30

Example 9.3 Ninth Symphony, first movement, first horn, bars 43–4

Motive b, with its dotted rhythms, primarily appears in the impassioned 'trio' sections (Example 9.2). This motive is often given to the strings which can clearly articulate the rhythmic phrasing.

The fanfare-like motive c is frequently played by the brass (Example 9.3). It consists of a repeated three-note pattern of falling minor seconds, whose dotted rhythms are softened the first time by a quaver triplet. This motive is also predominant in the 'trio' sections.

The ornamental, quasi-transitional arpeggio of motive d (initially appearing in the third bassoon, bar 80) is mainly assigned to the woodwind. A figure consisting of semiquaver movement, it is possibly derived from the oboe part in the second half of bar 56 in the fifth movement of *Das Lied von der Erde*. Motive e (initially heard in first violins from bar 92) is a combination of a and c. It incorporates both the dotted and the cortège rhythms. The beginning of the motive seems to be a melodic borrowing from the tenor part of bars 295–7 in the first movement of *Das Lied von der Erde*, where the text runs 'Du aber, Mensch, [wie lang lebst denn du?]' ('But you, O man, [for how long do you live?]).

In the unusual structure of the movement's opening, individual ideas try to articulate themselves, giving the impression of the slow 'starting up' of a procession. Within an underlying rhythmic framework, longer melodies emerge only gradually from these fragmented motives. The section beginning at bar 108 is unmistakeably cortège-like with its subdued and pallid sonorities, and Mahler expressly writes over the passage from bar 327 *Wie ein schwerer Kondukt* (like a solemn cortège). In view of this, and the very restrained and delicate passages elsewhere in the movement

Example 9.4 Ninth Symphony, second movement, woodwind and viola, bars 1–4

Example 9.5 Ninth Symphony, second movement, first violin, bars 90–3

(marked, for example, *Schattenhaft* (shadow-like) and *Misterioso*), one does not really need to be aware of the quotations from *Das Lied von der Erde* and Beethoven's Piano Sonata *Les Adieux* op. 81a (bars 245–50) to understand that the meaning of this Symphony is related to concepts of farewell and death. Mahler's verbal annotations in the orchestral draft also suggest that he conceived at least the first movement of the Ninth in a mood of farewell: *Quasi niente* (as if nothing) (bar 208), 'O Jugendzeit! Entschwundene! O Liebe! Verwehte!' ('Oh youth! Vanished! Oh love! Lost!') (from bar 267), and *Leb' wol! Leb' wol!* (Farewell! Farewell!) (from bar 436).[5]

At the same time representatives of the Second Viennese School in particular have frequently cited this movement as a point of reference for modern music because of its occasional tonal uncertainty and the extreme complexity of its mosaic-like musical texture, developed from simple motives through intense polyphonic processes. Alban Berg, for example, described the Andante comodo as 'the most wonderful thing that Mahler has written'.[6]

Im Tempo eines gemächlichen Ländlers

The second movement is also elaborately structured, albeit in a different way. The four differently paced themes, or dance characters, are clearly identifiable,[7] but their combinations are unusually bold. The movement's heading, which continues 'Etwas täppisch und sehr derb' ('Somewhat clumsy and very coarse'), characterizes the first, strongly diatonic, theme in C major (Example 9.4). Although this *gemächlicher* Ländler is of ostensibly simple construction, a multi-voiced web of distinct contrapuntal voices soon develops.

The second dance theme, an Austro-German waltz in a tonally distant E major/minor, is presented from bar 90 in a slightly faster tempo (Example 9.5).

Example 9.6 Ninth Symphony, second movement, trombone followed by first violin, bars 147–54

Example 9.7 Ninth Symphony, second movement, first violin and oboe, bars 252–9

From bar 147 a second waltz in the style of a French *valse* follows, distinguished more by its melody, first presented in ironic manner in the lowest registers, than by its rhythm (Example 9.6).

The fourth dance, a much slower Ländler marked *ganz langsam* can be heard from bar 218 onwards in a suitably reduced tempo. Elements of the *gemächlichen* Ländler are nevertheless interpolated from the beginning of this dance (Example 9.7).

These four dances are combined with each other, montage-like, in a variety of ways throughout the movement.[8] In bar 261 the waltz is heard again, in bar 333 the much slower Ländler, in bar 369 the *gemächlicher* Ländler, in bar 404 the waltz, in bar 423 the French *valse*, in bar 486 the waltz, and in bar 523 the *gemächlicher* Ländler again. However, allusions to other dances can also be heard within these with resultant shifts in tempo relations.

It is interesting to compare the orchestral draft of the movement in which the individual sections were arranged in yet another way. The movement was also somewhat longer, and Mahler had considered titles such as 'Scherzo' and 'Menuetto infinito'.[9] Despite its populist elements, this movement, like the second movement of the Fourth Symphony, can be interpreted semantically as a 'dance of death'.[10] Bruno Walter suggested that the movement had a 'tragic undertone', giving the impression that 'the dance was over'.[11]

Rondo-Burleske

The title of the third movement is an indication of the music's ironic, grotesque and parodic character, and its structural realization of this in rondo form. In its gestures and its A minor tonality it is reminiscent of the second movement of the Fifth Symphony. The main theme (*Allegro assai. Sehr trotzig* (very defiant)) acts as a refrain and alternates twice with a subsidiary theme (*leggiero*) first heard in bar 109, and three fugati

Example 9.8 Ninth Symphony, third movement, first and second violins, bars 7–10

b.7-10 I,II.Vlns.

Example 9.9 Ninth Symphony, third movement, first violins, bars 109–16

b.109-16 I.Vln.

Example 9.10 Ninth Symphony, third movement, first trumpet, bars 352–9

b.352-9 1.Trp.

(bars 79–108, 209–61 and 311–46), which make partial use of material from the main theme.[12]

The first part of the movement is a three-part a–b–a^1 structure which begins with a six-bar introduction and later introduces a march-like second theme (from bar 64). The three fugati serve as developments of the principal material. According to Constantin Floros 'the fugal style of the 1920s is anticipated. The polyphonic sections involve the use of a sequential technique otherwise rejected by Mahler … In the brightly orchestrated first fugato, the equality of the voices has been carried to such an extent (mm. 79–108) that it is difficult to determine what is theme and what is counterpoint.'[13] (Example 9.8).

The subsidiary material is more simply structured. Its melody is reminiscent of popular operetta of the time; the rhythm is straightforward and the instrumentation at times like that of a salon orchestra. Mahler's intended parody of the trivial is also revealed here in the subtle differentiation of phrasing and articulation (Example 9.9).

Far removed from these sections of the movement is the more extended, dream-like episode (bars 347–521), an example of the Mahlerian category of 'Musik aus weitester Ferne' ('music from the furthest distance'),[14] interpreted by Floros as symbolic of that ideal world so lacking in the hectic, wild reality of the main sections of the movement and the trivial surroundings of the subsidiary material.[15] Here the melody, with its turn figure taken from the third fugato, unfolds quietly and in the nature of a hymn (Example 9.10).

Adagio
Also apparently far removed from 'reality', the long-drawn-out final Adagio resumes Mahler's custom established in the Third of ending a

Example 9.11 Ninth Symphony, fourth movement, first and second violins, bars 1–4

Example 9.12 Ninth Symphony, fourth movement, cello, bars 28–30

symphony in a hymnic and elegiac mode. The similarity of the opening violin turn figure with the Adagio of Bruckner's Ninth Symphony has often been mentioned, but the semitonal descent into the key of Db major indicates that here Mahler is operating on quite a different stylistic level. At the entry of the whole string section Mahler begins to extend the tonal framework through deceptive cadential shifts and distant scale degrees. The main theme complex unfolds in tripartite song form (with sections beginning in bars 3, 13 and 17) and is presented in a full-voiced texture and with warm sonorities (Example 9.11).

The considerably thinner and paler subsidiary theme is first heard in bar 11 and then more fully from bar 28 in the lowest registers of the cellos and contrabassoon. The counterpoint to this is scored in the highest register of the strings, but is instructed to be played *ohne Empfindung* (without feeling). This two-voiced writing is further defamiliarized by the Phrygian-coloured C♯ minor, the enharmonically altered sister key to Db major (Example 9.12).

While the subsequent variant of the subsidiary theme (bars 88–107) is similarly pallid, each of the numerous varied recurrences of the main theme (at bars 49, 107 and 126) marks an increase in intensity, particularly through richer instrumentation. A climax is reached in bars 118–22 when the brass intone the chromatic germ cell and turn motive *fortissimo* with bells in the air.

The final *adagissimo* section (from bar 159) brings the main thematic material to a point of increasing dissolution. One could even speak of 'dissociation'[16] or of a 'written out ... ritardando',[17] epitomized in the last bar by Mahler's annotation *ersterbend* (dying away). A further unmistakeable allusion appears in these last bars which is significant for the interpretation of the Symphony. From bar 163 in the violins Mahler quotes the passage 'Im Sonnenschein! Der Tag ist schön auf jenen Höh'n!' ('In the sunshine! The day is fine upon the hills!') from the fourth of his *Kindertotenlieder*.

The Tenth Symphony: analysis of its composition and 'performing versions'

The origins of Mahler's unfinished Tenth Symphony were closely linked with the profound personal crisis in the last year of his life. This is not only substantiated by his wife Alma, but also revealed by annotations in the manuscript of the work itself. Having once again moved to his summer residence near Toblach in the Dolomites, Mahler began composition in July 1910. His wife was taking a cure at this time, during which she began a relationship with the young architect Walter Gropius. Aware of her husband's extreme sensitivity, she attempted to hide the liaison from him, agreeing with her lover that they would only exchange letters under the strictest secrecy when she returned to Toblach. However, at the end of July Gropius addressed one of his letters directly to Mahler, who was deeply shaken by the brutal nature of the revelation and broke off the composition of the Tenth for over a week. During this time a discussion between the participants was arranged in order to resolve the situation. Although Alma made it clear that she would not leave her husband, at the same time she continued to pursue her relationship with Gropius. As Mahler carried on sketching the Symphony during August, he was therefore justifiably fearful of losing his wife and decided to seek the advice of Sigmund Freud, the founder of psychoanalysis. Mahler's condition improved as a result of their conversations, so that he was able to conclude his preliminary work on the Symphony by the beginning of September.

Of the five planned movements, most were only notated in a short score of between three and five staves containing the part-writing and occasional instrumental instructions. Only the first and second movements, and thirty bars of the third movement exist in orchestral draft. In total, including preliminary short score and sketch pages, 174 pages are known to exist, of which all but two have been published.[18] Facsimile editions appeared in 1924 and 1967; a further page was published partly in 1975 in an exhibition catalogue in Basle; five further pages appeared in Deryck Cooke's performing version of 1976; excerpts of another were included in an essay by Frans Bouwman in 2001; and six more were published in 2003 both in the comprehensive analysis of the work by the present author, and in a volume produced by the Bavarian State Library.[19] The only remaining entirely unpublished manuscript page, a short score sketch for the Adagio housed in the Österreichische Nationalbibliothek, is reproduced here, followed by the hitherto only partly published short score sketch page housed in the Paul Sacher Foundation (Plates 9.1 and 9.2).

In the following discussion bar numbers from Cooke's performing version – the most comprehensive transcription of the original material

Plate 9.1. Hitherto unpublished short-score sketch page of the opening of the Adagio of the Tenth Symphony (ÖNB Mus. Hs. 41.000/6 Bl. 6). Reproduced by kind permission of the Musiksammlung of the Österreichische Nationalbibliothek, Vienna.

to date – will be used. According to this the Symphony has 1,945 bars. The balanced proportions of the Symphony's cyclical movement plan is comparable to that of the Seventh Symphony: two extended, predominantly slow movements at the beginning and the end, two scherzi as second and fourth movements, and a short intermezzo entitled *Purgatorio* in the middle.

Adagio
Only the introductory Adagio in F♯ major has an orchestration complete enough to be performed in the concert hall without additions. Although Mahler would most probably still have made numerous changes, the music in the orchestral draft of the Adagio is nevertheless highly elaborate and sophisticated, not only revealing elements of Mahler's late style, but also at times pointing beyond this towards modernism.

Despite the continual variation of the material, two main recurring motive groups can be identified. The movement begins in Andante tempo with a variant of the first group, played by unaccompanied violas in quasi-recitative style (Example 9.13).

Plate 9.2. Hitherto partly unpublished short-score sketch page of the Adagio (bars 110–40) of the Tenth Symphony (PSF Sammlung Grumbacher Nr. 173). Reproduced by kind permission of the Paul Sacher Foundation, Basle.

Example 9.13 Tenth Symphony, first movement, viola, bars 1–4

A variant, clearly related to this motive in its diastematics, is heard ten times as the principal voice of the texture (first in bar 28) and forms its own subgroup. This first motive group assumes a variety of characters, from a melancholy quality reminiscent of the *traurige Weise* (sorrowful manner) of the third act of Wagner's *Tristan und Isolde* and in Franz Liszt's *Trauergondel No. 2*,[20] to a diabolical or burlesque scherzando character expressed through accompanying dance-like patterns in the strings, exaggerated articulation of paired semiquaver movement and the large number of leaps, mordents and trills.

The spacious cantilena of the second motive group, initially appearing in Adagio tempo from bar 16 and marked *sehr warm*, unfolds mostly over quiet, largely minim-beat movement in the lower strings and (at least) three low brass instruments, usually trombones (Example 9.14).

Example 9.14 Tenth Symphony, first movement, first violin, bars 16–19

b.16–19 I.Vln.

Each motivic appearance in the movement signals a change in tone colour, and these predominantly two- to four-bar statements suggest that Mahler built the movement according to the principles of classical periodic structure. The harmony confirms this, since only rarely do progressions occur that cannot be explained within the framework of traditional functional harmony.

Despite obvious features of double-variation form, it is sonata form that determines the structure even though this is a slow movement. As in classical practice, two clearly differentiated motive groups are presented from the outset: one in the major (group two) and the other in the minor (group one). A continually varied and expanded 'repeat' of the exposition then follows (from bar 40). The development begins in bar 104 with the last motive group to be heard (group one), and here the music deviates from the familiar harmonic patterns and moves far away from the initial key. Through frequent brief exchanges with the second motive, the two groups are brought ever closer together. Classical periodic structures now give way to a collage-like process (bars 120–8), before the reprise (bar 141), according to classical principles, returns to F♯ major and to harmonies familiar from the exposition, restating motive two but with greater harmonic freedom. After the climax of the movement at bars 194–212, the coda (from bar 213) re-establishes F♯ major in a process of structural, textural and motivic dissolution. This interpretation of the movement's form is supported by the positioning of four of the five unaccompanied or quasi-unaccompanied presentations of motive one. Leaving aside the climactic passage of the movement, bars 194–212, these occur at the beginnings of, respectively, the exposition, the exposition repeat, the development and the coda.

It is only this climax which does not seem to fit into the sonata-form scheme, and, as confirmed in a short-score page published in 2003,[21] this passage was actually a later addition. After the A♭ minor wind chorale, a more dissonant sonority is gradually built up in bars 203–8 containing nine different pitches, collapsing the world of traditional functional harmony. Mahler himself provided an explanation for it in a poem written to his wife on the return journey from his discussion with Freud: 'In one single chord my hesitant notions / Converge with the power of searing emotions'.[22] This allusion is surely too unusual to be

Example 9.15 Tenth Symphony, first movement, bars 203–12 in short score

b. 203-12

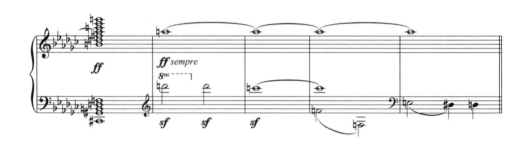

taken purely metaphorically, and indicates the enormous psychological tension through which Mahler was prompted to create a sound harmonically far in excess of anything he had previously dared to do.

It is also interesting that the starting point from which all the tension of the ensuing sonority grows is an unaccompanied A, two above middle C, in the first violins. The chord is built up in four stages with triads below and above, first *forte* and then *fortissimo*. The initial pitch, A, is then continued alone in the trumpets after the nine-note chord. The final condensed combination of the unaccompanied A and the abrupt tutti repetition of the nine-note chord suggests that the choice of this pitch, held for ten bars in all, is to be understood symbolically as the initial, and only 'playable', letter of the name Alma (Example 9.15).

Scherzo

The second movement in F♯ minor forms a stark contrast to the Adagio. It is structured in scherzo form with repeated trio plus coda built from scherzo and trio material. Structural points of articulation occur in bars 1, 165, 246, 300, 366 and 423. However, the special quality of the movement lies less in its formal design than in its rhythmic and metrical characterization. It is not simply the numerous time-signature changes in the scherzo sections of the movement that appear modern, but more importantly the shortening and lengthening of certain rhythmic components or

Example 9.16 Tenth Symphony, second movement, horns 'a2', bars 1–4

Example 9.17 Tenth Symphony, second movement, first, second and third oboes, bars 2–5

even whole phrases. Bound up with this is the principle of creating distinct motive groups in a way that differs from conventional notions of theme or motive: lacking a primary motivic identity, motivic shape instead emerges from the sum of all variants. Two different motive groups are only occasionally contrapuntally combined, the first of which is characterized rhythmically by frequent varied repetitions of the pattern minim followed by two to five crotchets (Example 9.16).

The most extraordinary aspect of the variation technique is the rhythmic and metrical shifting of the motive: the minim falls both on weaker down beats and unstressed beats (for example, bars 85–7, 112 and 125), and sometimes reduces to a crotchet (for example, bars 61, 124 and 151). This motive group is juxtaposed with a second whose *scherzando* character is clear not only from the rapid changes of melodic direction and register, but also from its extremely complex accentual changes (Example 9.17).

Its capricious rhythmic profile is very diverse, and the simultaneous appearance of the two motivic strands intensifies these unusual rhythmic qualities all the more. There is little regularity within the rhythmic profile of each voice, and large-scale repetitions are impossible because of the contrapuntally interdependent phrase alterations taking place within constantly shifting time signatures. Even before Stravinsky's *Rite of Spring* Mahler was thus producing avant-garde rhythmic ideas, and these examples are the most advanced of his entire output (compare the passage from bar 60 with three bars after fig. 121 in the *Rite*).

The rhythmic relationships are considerably simpler in the trio sections where motive groups three and four predominate. Group three is structured vocally and in the manner of a (round) dance (Example 9.18) while the fourth group is an eight-bar Ländler melody divided into question and answer phrases. The second half of the first phrase reveals that this $\frac{3}{4}$ motive is partly derived from motive two of the Adagio (Example 9.19).

Example 9.18 Tenth Symphony, second movement, second violins, bars 320–5

b.320-5 II.Vln.

Example 9.19 Tenth Symphony, second movement, first violin and viola, bars 167–70

b.167-70 I.Vln. + Vla.

Thus Mahler gives expression to various forms of dance in this movement: from the unrestrained, fugal music of the scherzo section to the quieter, folk-like trios. Similar approaches can be found in the scherzo of Mahler's Sixth Symphony (bars 5 onwards) or in that of Bruckner's Second Symphony (the opening and bars 164 onwards).

Purgatorio

At 170 bars (including the unwritten *da capo* of the A section) the B minor third movement is the shortest of Mahler's output. Structured according to a simple A–B–A scheme and in quite strict period form, the *Purgatorio* presents motivic material that will become important in the following movements: an anacrustic semiquaver figure (motive one, from bar 4), segments of a semi-quaver scale (motive two, from bar 9) and a figure lasting six quavers (motive three, from bar 30). The fourth motivic group, a falling, stepwise dotted idea in seconds first heard in bar 66, is particularly interesting (Example 9.20).

Mahler marked three of the extended and distinctively harmonized variants of this fourth motive group with verbal exclamations related to his personal crisis: 'Tod! Verk!' ('Death! Procl[amation]! / Transf[iguration]!'), 'Erbarmen!! / O Gott! O Gott! Warum hast du mich verlassen?' ('Have mercy! / O God! O God! Why have you forsaken me?') and 'Dein Wille geschehe!' ('Your will be done!'). A preliminary short-score page, published in 2003, reveals that the first abbreviation stands for 'Todesverkündigung' ('proclamation of death').[23] The third exclamation is a biblical quote but could also relate to Mahler's wife. It is highly probable that the fourth motive group also makes reference to Alma's song 'Erntelied' which Mahler encountered and was revising a few days before writing this movement. The variants in the Finale, which Mahler marked with his wife's pet name also support this hypothesis (see below). Such a quotation could be interpreted as a subtle personal declaration, since the subject matter of the song from which it is derived concerns the desire for love.

Example 9.20 Tenth Symphony, third movement, first violin, bars 84–5

The title of the movement, which Mahler alternatively intended to label 'Inferno', signifies purification or cleansing. Undoubtedly it is a reference to Siegfried Lipiner's 'Purgatorio' poems from his *Buch der Freude*, as well as to Dante's *Comedia*, the so-called *Divine Comedy*. Liszt had already 'set' the latter to music in his *Dante Symphony*, which bears some musical similarities. However, Mahler appeared to position the meaning of his movement somewhere between damnation and salvation. A note in a letter written during the composition of the Symphony corroborates this: 'silently I ask whether I may still hope for salvation, or whether I am to be damned'.[24]

[Scherzo]

The fourth movement which begins in E minor was originally entitled *Scherzo* by Mahler, but its title was later crossed out, possibly because the movement is structured more in sonata form. Despite this, the character of the second theme complex (from bar 123) which Mahler at one point expressly labelled as a 'dance', gives evidence of its original, trio-like function within the scherzo tradition. As with the Adagio, there is at the very least a superimposition of different generic forms at work here: traditional scherzo form is enriched by developmental sonata-form elements (from bar 166) thus allowing the distinctive qualities of a recapitulation to emerge clearly from bar 380; a coda follows at bar 518.

In contrast to previous movements, the fourth is structured around short one-to-two-bar motives (six in total). These are skilfully combined to generate ever-new thematic complexes (eight-bar themes being the norm) in accordance with periodic principles.

The movement was written soon after the personal crisis erupted, and the musical motto at the very opening (bars 1–4) could be interpreted as the musical expression of a comment written by Mahler on the title page: 'Wahnsinn, fass mich an, Verfluchten!' ('Madness, seize me, accursed one!'). This rapid succession of two seventh chords a semitone apart (*ff* in the brass) returns a further five times in varied form throughout the movement. Mahler's additional comment on the title page highlights the movement's frantic dance character: 'Der Teufel tanzt es mit mir' ('The devil dances it with me').

Notably, during the last thirty bars the motivic writing and instrumentation are drastically reduced until from bar 570 only percussion

('P[au]k[e]', 'Tr.[ommel] u.[nd] B.[ecken]') can be heard, ending with a single *forte* stroke on the *vollständig gedämpfte Trommel* (completely muted drum) in bar 578. Mahler wrote in the short score: 'Du allein weiss, was es bedeutet / Ach! Ach! Ach! / Leb' wol mein Saitenspiel! / Leb wol / Leb wol / Leb wol // Ach wol / Ach Ach.' ('You alone know what it means / Ah! Ah! Ah! / Farewell my lyre! / Farewell / Farewell / Farewell // Ah well / Ah Ah'). Mahler often referred to Alma as his 'Saitenspiel', a term used by Nietzsche and associated with his insanity. The closing muffled drum stroke symbolizes death, having been inspired by the drum beat of a funeral procession witnessed by Mahler in New York in 1908.

Finale

The fifth movement in D minor begins with the first of several similar drum strokes. Rather than introduce new thematic ideas, the movement uses mostly varied forms of nine motives heard earlier in the Symphony (two from the Adagio, four from the *Purgatorio* and three from the fourth movement). Of central importance is the descending scalic motive related to Alma that made several appearances in the *Purgatorio*, which is heard alternating many times with the cortège-like music of the opening. The 'Alma' motive is embedded by turns within a lyrical melody (from bar 30), an ominous chord progression (from bar 12), and a gesture of joyous exaltation (from bar 106). The movement closes with an impassioned, extended variant of this motive which Mahler annotated with: 'für dich leben! / für dich sterben! / Almschi!' ('to live for you! / to die for you! / Almschi!') (bar 395).

The movement is formally unconventional, and of particular note is the varied return of the passage with the nine-note chord from the Adagio (bars 275–83) which is further dramatized by the addition of a motive from the fourth movement. Once again this entire climactic passage arrives relatively unexpected, but it has important consequences for the music that follows which is heavily suffused with motive two from the Adagio. This leads into familiar tonal regions so that the Symphony travels full circle to end in F♯ major.

'Performing versions'

Despite its fragmentary notational state, the Tenth Symphony is characterized by fully developed symphonic thinking, and can be ranked equally alongside Mahler's previous symphonies. Reception history nevertheless shows that it took a long time before the public got to know and value Mahler's Tenth.[25]

After Mahler's death and the posthumous first performances of *Das Lied von der Erde* and the Ninth Symphony, the existence of a Tenth was at first just a rumour. However, as early as April 1920 Alma Mahler had two pages of the short score published. Then, in what was a period of economic inflation, she decided not only to publish his letters but also large sections of the manuscript of the Tenth in facsimile. The idea behind this was, amongst other things, to obtain additional royalties through performances of the work. But Alma would first have to produce, or have produced, a playable version of the Symphony. Several composers asked by her to do this are said to have turned it down. Her then prospective son-in-law, Ernst Krenek, agreed to prepare a fair copy of the introductory Adagio and to 'complete' the third movement *Purgatorio*. The resultant abbreviated draft symphony nevertheless met with little success at its first performance in 1924 at the Vienna Opera House under Franz Schalk. It renewed many of the doubts vociferously expressed prior to the performance regarding the validity of Krenek's 'reworking', which at the very least distorted the dramatic structure of the work. Because of this and the general waning of enthusiasm for Mahler in Europe, very few conductors took up the two movements. Only in the USA, Alma's later adopted home, were there a few isolated performances after 1933. In 1951 a New York publisher produced scores of the two movements at her request, and for the time being she gave up on her earlier attempts to restore the entire torso to life. Meanwhile the American Mahler expert Jack Diether had approached various composers with this in mind. In 1948 he managed to persuade Joseph H. Wheeler, a British musicology and composition student, to take on the project. Independently of this the American Clinton A. Carpenter also began work on an orchestration of the three unknown movements in 1949. However, despite repeated revisions neither 'arranger' was quick to achieve a public performance of the whole Symphony. A third person got there first: the British musicologist and writer Deryck Cooke. In 1959, in the light of Mahler's forthcoming centenary celebrations, he started work on the commentary for a BBC broadcast to include the two known movements and parts of the three unknown movements. From the outset he secured advice in particular on matters of instrumentation from the composer and conductor Berthold Goldschmidt who conducted the radio broadcast on 19 December 1960 – intended as the climax of the Mahler year – whilst Cooke commented on the individual musical examples.[26]

Having learnt of the scope of this programme, which had been conceived without her participation, Alma immediately forbade any further broadcast of the performing version, presumably furious that a work so closely linked to her personal fate had been brought to life by someone unknown to her. Cooke and Goldschmidt nevertheless continued to decipher and orchestrate the remaining missing passages. Only in 1963, with the help of German and American friends who played her a recording of the radio broadcast, was Alma persuaded of the validity and stylistic fidelity of the version. As a result, she made available further manuscript material that had not been included in the facsimile published in 1924. Thus it was that an orchestral version of the whole Symphony lasting some eighty minutes was performed for the first time in London on 13 August 1964 under Goldschmidt. After the performance Cooke undertook a thorough revision of his version assisted by the composers and musicologists Colin and David Matthews. The score of this revised performing version was published in 1976, and largely because of its thoroughly Mahlerian orchestration and the generally sparing and finely judged nature of its additional material it has since enjoyed far greater circulation than Wheeler's and Carpenter's independent versions premièred respectively in 1967 and 1983.

With knowledge of all three preceding versions, the American Remo Mazzetti prepared his own 'Performing edition' in 1985 which he has since revised many times. Aware in turn of Mazzetti's version, Rudolf Barshai conducted the first performance of his 'Performing version' of the Symphony in 2000. The 'reconstruction' by the Italians Nicola Samale and Giuseppe Mazzuca was premièred in 2001. All of these more recent editors have availed themselves of the transcription of the manuscript material included by Cooke in his published score.

Because the short score of all five movements is continuous, the six versions that have been performed to date are surprisingly similar. Listeners' inclinations depend ultimately on their expectations: do they want a close realization of Mahler's instructions or a reworking that corresponds with the level of completion of the other symphonies and is therefore necessarily freer? Whatever the case, any evaluation must take into account the degree to which the different editors have actually striven for 'completion' in the sense that Mahler would have understood it.

For example, Deryck Cooke and his team decided to present the work at 'the stage [it] had reached when Mahler died, in a practical performing version'.[27] Thus from the start they subjugated themselves, as it were, to the existing draft. Compared with Wheeler and Samale/Mazzuca, who are similarly cautious in making additions to the draft and, along with Mazzetti and Barshai, offer plausible alternatives for some passages, it seems that Cooke adopted the most professional approach, and moreover is the only one to have given detailed explanations for his decisions.

The other angle of approach can perhaps best be explained in terms of composers who have a close affinity with Mahler and are prepared as editors to submit completely to the Mahlerian style but to remain compositionally creative. For Cooke's inherently 'honest' approach always becomes problematic whenever structural simplicity or choice of instrumentation in the draft are the direct consequence of its unfinished state and therefore appear unconvincing in the context of Mahler's late works. This is particularly the case in the last two and a half movements which exist merely in short score. In the end only someone who considered the draft no more than a preliminary stage and was prepared to make changes to its very substance could come close to replicating the characteristics of Mahler's late works. In this respect Carpenter's version is the most daring attempt so far, for although he realized that a true Mahler completion was unattainable, he at least strove for the *degree* of completion of a Mahler symphony, viewing Mahler's draft text not as untouchable but as a model that could be developed. While no one would expect fidelity to the text in such circumstances, it is also true that Carpenter could have kept closer to the manuscript at several points without sacrificing his freedom.

Despite their supposed diversity, none of the reworkings, when considered in the light of the existing sketch material, is as developed as Mahler's previous scores. Even Carpenter's version resists rearranging or expanding entire passages as Mahler did, for example, *en route* from the draft orchestral score to the fair copy of the Ninth Symphony. In this respect even the most daring reworking remains heavily dependent upon the unfinished draft. The existing performing versions nevertheless allow the draft to emerge all the more clearly in its entirety, and considering the many compositional innovations that Mahler's Tenth exhibits even as a torso, this is an achievement of considerable value.

Mahler the re-creative musician

10 Mahler as conductor in the opera house and concert hall

HERTA BLAUKOPF
(*translated by* JEREMY BARHAM)

Mahler was taught piano, harmony and composition at the Vienna Conservatoire but did not study conducting, 'the hardest thing', as he later said.[1] He was simply thrown in at the deep end and left to sink or swim. The art of the conductor (at the time usually referred to as *Kapellmeister*) was still so inextricably linked with composition, that the introduction of conducting as a subject in its own right had for far too long been considered unnecessary, and was only introduced in Vienna in 1909, when the Conservatoire of the *Gesellschaft der Musikfreunde* was turned into a state academy.[2] After all, had not the great German conductors of the nineteenth century, Weber, Mendelssohn and Wagner, all been composers? Even the younger Hans von Bülow could lay claim to an extensive compositional output, albeit one which was scarcely acknowledged. Section nine of Mahler's 1883 contract as Musical and Choral Director in Kassel still specified the duty to supply musical arrangements and, at the request of the management, to 'provide compositions' for special occasions.[3] Even his *Kapellmeister* contract in Vienna of 15 April 1897 committed him to produce 'new compositions or orchestrations deemed necessary by the management'.[4]

The apprentice years

Mahler was indeed thrown in at the deep end when he took up his first engagements at small provincial theatres whose repertoire included operettas, operas and spoken plays. We do not know what he conducted during his few weeks at the spa town of Bad Hall in summer 1880. However, his second engagement at the *Landschaftlichen Theater* in Laibach (now Ljubljana) in 1881 seems to have been a truly valuable learning experience for the budding conductor. The orchestra consisted of eighteen musicians and the choir of seven men and seven women,[5] an easily manageable number of people; but he had to be imaginative when an instrument stipulated in a score was not available: we have no clear idea of what instrumentalists were at his disposal – perhaps nine string players, four woodwind, four brass and one percussionist. Although there is no evidence, we can assume that

Mahler conducted existing or improvised arrangements. However, it is known that Mahler presented Beethoven's *Egmont* Overture at the ceremonial opening of the 1881–2 theatre season, and was warmly mentioned in the local German-language newspaper. The first opera he rehearsed in Laibach was Verdi's *Il trovatore*, which presumably he only got to know during rehearsal. The evening passed off 'without any substantial hitches' and 'under Mahler's conductorship the orchestra put up a good show'.[6] Mahler certainly took greater care with his beloved *Magic Flute* which followed shortly after this, as was confirmed by its review. He went on to conduct Rossini's *The Barber of Seville*, Gounod's *Faust* and Weber's *Der Freischütz* among many other works, as well as a whole host of operettas.

The next post his Viennese agent found him came by chance. A conductor who had been working at the *Stadttheater* in Olmütz (Moravia) left in the middle of the season, and a replacement was urgently sought. In January 1883 Mahler set off in haste from Vienna to Olmütz only to find himself subject again to the most dreadful provincial conditions: 'I am paralysed, like one who has been cast forth from heaven', he wrote to a friend, 'So far – thank God – what I have been conducting is almost exclusively Meyerbeer and Verdi. By dogged scheming I have succeeded in getting Wagner and Mozart out of the repertory; – for I could not endure rattling off, say, *Lohengrin* or *Don Giovanni*.'[7] 'Meyerbeer' meant *Les Huguenots*, which Mahler had never heard prior to taking up his engagement. He probably got to know Verdi's *Un Ballo in maschera* and Bizet's *Carmen* in a similar way, in other words by conducting them.

The singers did not have an easy time with this inexperienced conductor. After the first act of *Les Huguenots* the singer playing Marcel rushed into wardrobe and shouted 'I can't sing with this man. He holds his baton in his right hand, then in his left, and keeps on passing his free hand over his face, so that I can't see any of his cues.'[8] The reason for this unprofessional behaviour was the pince-nez worn by the short-sighted Mahler which kept slipping down his nose. Because of this he got some tape from a dresser to fix it in place, which then looked so comical that the actors on the stage began to laugh.

Sometimes the players and singers sympathized with this ridiculous 'idealist' and rehearsed with greater care than usual for his sake. This happened to such an extent that a stage manager from Dresden, who attended several performances, saw in him a 'young Conductor . . . who is quite outstanding',[9] and recommended him to Kassel where the post of Royal Choral and Musical Director had become available. Mahler went there and conducted an overture and various choruses as well as the dress rehearsal of Marschner's *Hans Heiling* (an opera which in fact was just as unfamiliar to him as *Les Huguenots* had been). He received a contract, and now for the first time was connected not to a poor provincial theatre but to a proper establishment, managed with paternalistic severity by a former Prussian officer. Although this was a step up socially, it was a step down in terms of repertoire, for Mahler was only second in rank at this theatre, and it was the *Hofkapellmeister* – with whom the young and ambitious Choral and Musical Director immediately came into conflict – who had an 'option' on the classics.[10] His repertoire in Kassel consisted of operas by Meyerbeer, Maillart, Flotow, Rossini and Donizetti, along with Weber's *Der Freischütz*, probably the only work he liked.[11] In the two seasons that Mahler served in Kassel, he conducted about sixty evenings of opera, while the *Hofkapellmeister* conducted about 165. Although we do not have direct evidence, Mahler presumably conducted operettas and incidental music on top of this. A newspaper review does tell us that in February 1885 Mahler conducted Karl Goldmark's *Sakuntala* overture as an introduction to a play, and this can scarcely be the only duty he carried out in the spoken theatre.[12]

The first concerts

Mahler was unhappy because he did not have enough to do, and the little that he did do was not artistically interesting to him. He wanted to leave Kassel as soon as possible. When Hans von Bülow conducted two concerts there in January 1884, Mahler wrote him an enthusiastic letter, imploring: 'take me along in any capacity you like'.[13] Bülow gave this handwritten cry of pain to the Kassel Theatre, where it remains today. In the following season another way opened up of escaping, at least temporarily, from the conditions at Kassel. With the permission of his *Intendant*, Mahler took on the directorship of a choral society in Hannoversch-Münden. This transported him once a week to another world – the world of the concert. As early as 13 February 1885, Mahler was in a position to perform what he had been rehearsing with his choir. He conducted Haydn's oratorio *The Seasons* with players and soloists from Kassel. The review in the *Hessische Morgenzeitung* praised Mahler as follows: 'A proficiency of this kind, such deep understanding of the work performed, such indefatigability and charm are things we seldom find all together'.[14]

Not content with a mere concert, Mahler decided to put on a music festival, and together with a colleague from Marbach he made preparations for a three-day event. A number of choral societies, amongst them of course Mahler's choir from Münden, an eighty-strong orchestra made up of several Court Orchestras and a military band, as well as distinguished vocal soloists took part. Even before the festival began Mahler was vehemently attacked, and also subjected to anti-Semitic abuse. One obstacle after another was put in his way, but he overcame them and for the first time proved himself as an organizer. The music festival took place and was a success, in particular Mendelssohn's oratorio *St Paul*, which he himself conducted. The performances of *The Seasons* and *St Paul* were the first concerts given by Mahler the Theatre Director.

Mahler belonged to that class of artists who never stop learning. Even in his later years in New York he enjoyed rehearsing a work that he had not given before.[15] He never remained satisfied with what he had achieved, and never conducted a work in exactly the same way twice. But the period of his true apprenticeship finished after Kassel, which he left a year before his contract ended. In Prague, where he worked for the next season (1885–6), he was regarded as a first-rate Musical Director who even had the right to conduct the 'classics', by which he meant Mozart, Beethoven and Wagner. As early as September he conducted *Don Juan* (as *Don Giovanni* was called at that time) which he regarded as a particular honour since Mozart had composed the opera for Prague. In December he prepared *Das Rheingold* and *Die Walküre* in their original Bayreuth production. On the anniversary of Wagner's death, 23 February, he conducted Beethoven's Ninth Symphony – from memory – for the first time in his young life, and to finish the season he gave his first performance of *Fidelio*.

Music and gesture

As a confirmed Wagnerian it was not enough for Mahler that a singer perform their part with musical accuracy. He demanded dramatic expression in their voice and gestures as well. This required a special study of the parts, and close interaction with details of the production. How Mahler dealt with this in Laibach is not known. In Olmütz he was already acting as stage director. The aforementioned observer also described rehearsals for Méhul's opera *Joseph*: 'Mahler jumped from the podium, across the double-bass players, on to the stage, produced, stage-managed and conducted'.[16] Here we can already see Mahler as an interpreter of *Gesamtkunstwerke* in the Wagnerian sense, and this would later contribute to his brilliance and reputation in Vienna. Of course such interference with the stage action would not have been tolerated in Kassel, and even in Prague where Angelo Neumann the Director of the German Theatre reigned supreme, he could hardly have leaped up on to the stage during rehearsals. However, rehearsing parts was different. Mahler shared an apartment in Prague with the bass Johannes Elmblad.[17] The young son of the landlady, who was a good pianist, often acted as repetiteur, and reported that Mahler drew the singer's attention to elements in the staging even while he was just beginning to memorize the part. By doing this Mahler wanted to ensure that musical phrase and expressive interpretation were unified. So it was, for example, that he performed every gesture – fear, doubt, joy – bar by bar during the singer's preparation of the role of Daland in *The Flying Dutchman* 'in order that the whole character of the money-grabbing sailor was brought vividly to life'.[18]

Some ten years later we observe Anna von Mildenburg studying a role with Mahler in Hamburg: 'Accuracy [*Korrektheit*] is the soul of an artistic performance' said Mahler in the first piano rehearsal for *Die Walküre*. Urged to keep to the correct note values, she succeeded in giving them the right stress, shape and appropriate expression: 'Through him the smallest note attained importance and became a powerful aid in my difficult task. Similarly he taught me to attach just as much importance to each rest as to the sung notes'; and of course he told her about Wagner during these rehearsals and advised her to read the prose works.[19] Bruno Walter also remembers Mahler's activities in Hamburg (1891–7):

> I can see him now, at an orchestral rehearsal of *Götterdämmerung*, stepping down from the conductor's desk and hurrying to the trumpets and trombones to examine a particular passage in the funeral music with them, or borrowing the stool of a double-bass player to get up on to the stage in order to deliver instructions.[20]

Certainly when he was conductor at the Stadttheater in Leipzig (1886–8), and even more so as Director of the Budapest Opera House (1888–91), Mahler exerted influence upon staging and production, even though, as before, there were limits. By contrast, during his directorship of the Hofoper in Vienna (1897–1907), he was all-powerful both in the orchestral pit and on the stage: 'However engrossed he was in the musical work with singers and players during a stage rehearsal with orchestra, the eagle-eyed dramatist in him was watching: nothing escaped him on the stage, in interpretation, lights, costume – everything was under his watchful eye'.[21] To be sure, there were in-house stage-managers who helped him, but Director Mahler was the one true ringmaster. In her memoirs the distinguished soprano Marie Gutheil-Schoder, who later tried her own hand at producing, described very graphically Mahler's manner of working at the Hofoper:

> First of all he liked to watch a scene performed as we imagined it, as it emerged naturally from the scenic construction. Then he began to correct it. He never used a director's book, but corrected what he saw with a completely free mind. His influence on the shaping of a role was uncanny. If he was pleased by a particular interpretation, he quietly let it continue, then came a small correction, a new thought and he would incorporate it, subtly

but with demonic persistence, until suddenly something quite different had grown from the scene.[22]

The operatic repertoire

As Director in Vienna, Mahler was relatively free to decide on the repertoire, and what he would either conduct himself or hand over to others. Thus one can see which operatic works he preferred and those that interested him less. Above all he was ambitious and hard-working, and during his time in Vienna he stood on the conductor's rostrum 639 times (almost twice as often in the early years compared with later years).[23] The Mozart, Beethoven and Wagner repertoire which he had mastered in Prague was favoured again in Vienna. In the ten years of his directorship he conducted *The Marriage of Figaro* forty-nine times and *The Magic Flute* thirty-eight times. These were closely followed by thirty-seven performances of *Tristan and Isolde* – twenty-one of them in the famous new production of 1903 with Alfred Roller's stage designs. By 1900, a prominent Viennese critic already recognized in *Figaro* and *Tristan* the twin poles of Mahler's interpretative genius:

> Perhaps even greater than his energy are the versatility and flexibility of his mind, which allow him to move from one work and from one composer to another in such a way that he can represent work and composer with the most refined characteristics of period and style . . . Thus at the extreme ends of his talent lie on the one hand Wagner's *Tristan and Isolde* and on the other Mozart's *Marriage of Figaro* . . . These two works, which never before sounded so perfect at the Vienna Opera House, seem to me to encapsulate the depths and heights of Mahler's nature.[24]

What was there in between these extremes? As early as 1897 Mahler staged Smetana's opera *Dalibor*, conducting nearly all of the performances himself as was the case with Tchaikovsky's *Eugene Onegin* and Bizet's *Djamileh*. However, the new production of *The Flying Dutchman*, along with *Tannhäuser*, *Die Meistersinger*, *The Tales of Hoffmann*, *Aida* and *Carmen*, were handed over to other conductors after a few performances. It clearly suited him to rehearse these works carefully himself and then consolidate what had been rehearsed in a few performances, before entrusting them to the repertoire. In contrast, of the twenty-four performances of *Cosi fan tutte* given during his directorship, he conducted twenty-one. The fact that, leaving aside ballets, Mahler also directed nearly every new production, does not mean that he considered them all significant. But he felt a duty to give his contemporaries a chance, and the choice at that time was neither very great nor very appealing. None of the newer operas prepared by Mahler was able to maintain a lasting place in the repertoire. Of Puccini's manifestly popular works, Mahler conducted only *Madame Butterfly*, the last new production of his time in office. Richard Strauss's *Salome*, which he admired and wanted to perform, was forbidden him by *Hoftheater* censorship. The few months that Mahler spent at the Metropolitan Opera in New York (1908 and 1908–9) can be regarded as a continuation of his work in Vienna. He made his debut with *Tristan*, followed this with Mozart's *Don Giovanni* and *Die Walküre*, and closed the season with *Fidelio* using reconstructions of Alfred Roller's Viennese stage sets. Although, for example in *Don Giovanni*, he considered that the singing 'was almost unsurpassable', Mahler pined after his Viennese performance, which he believed 'Mozart too ... would have liked better'.[25] In the following season at the Metropolitan Opera Mahler conducted *The Marriage of Figaro* and Smetana's *The Bartered Bride* in German, and in the spring of 1910 some further performances of Tchaikovsky's *The Queen of Spades*.

The concert repertoire

In autumn 1898 the Vienna Philharmonic, which consisted exclusively of members of the opera orchestra, approached the Director with a request to lead their subscription concerts – nine per season. Their collaboration was a short one. He conducted twenty-seven concerts in all, but, primarily through annoyance at the orchestra's behaviour, resigned in spring 1901.[26] If we compare his programmes with those of his predecessor Hans Richter, it is immediately apparent that Mahler put far fewer soloists on the platform. Apart from the singers in Beethoven's Ninth Symphony and Mahler's own Second Symphony we find only six soloists in the twenty-seven concerts. As for the programmes, there were few surprises: he conducted much Beethoven, along with Haydn, Mozart, Schubert, Brahms, some Mendelssohn, Berlioz and Smetana, as well as the first performance of Bruckner's Sixth Symphony. Of course he also included some of his own works in his programmes: the Second Symphony and some songs as well as the First Symphony, whose failure triggered the grave crisis between him and the Philharmonic players.

Mahler only became a true concert conductor when he was working for the New York Philharmonic Society (1909–11). This fulfilled a lifelong ambition of his:

> I am glad to be able to enjoy this for once in my life (apart from the fact that
> I keep on finding it *very instructive*, for the technique of the theatre is totally
> different, and I am convinced that many of my previous inadequacies in

instrumentation arose from my being accustomed to hearing music in the totally different acoustic conditions of the theatre). Why did neither Germany nor Austria offer me this?[27]

In spring 1909 a committee of sponsors appointed Mahler Director of the Philharmonic Society. He immediately began by reorganizing the orchestra, dismissing and engaging musicians, ordering new timpani and planning the repertoire for the following season.

Fortunately for Mahler it was not a matter of presenting a different programme for each of the forty-six concerts. Some were simply repeated, and others assembled from the repertoire of earlier concerts. Thus Mahler was able to perform the suite he had arranged from works by J. S. Bach not only in November 1909 as part of the so-called 'Historical Cycle', but also in this and the following season a further twenty times. The programmes for the different cycles did not in any case correspond exactly to the title under which they were advertised, for the 'Historical Cycle' also included Wagner and Liszt. The Beethoven Cycle was, however, true to its name, although this did not preclude Mahler from conducting Beethoven symphonies or overtures in other subscription concerts. A special feature were the Wagner Concerts, in which preludes and scenes from Wagner's music dramas were brought to the concert platform. Those who found Wagner too heavy going could relax in a Tchaikovsky programme.

Unlike his concerts in Vienna in which he had seldom used soloists, the large number of violinists, pianists and singers appearing in Mahler's American concerts was striking. Perhaps his views on concert soloists had changed or perhaps he was just complying with public demand. As at the Vienna Opera, in his New York concerts he strove to present his listeners with new works – and not just his own such as the First Symphony or the *Kindertotenlieder*, both of which met with little appreciation. Among contemporary composers, he performed works by Elgar, Dukas, Debussy, Enescu, Rachmaninov, and of course Richard Strauss, whose *Till Eulenspiegel* he included more than ten times in his programmes.

In the 1910–11 New York season Mahler conducted as many as forty-nine concerts. These contained ninety-four different works by thirty-eight different composers,[28] and he did this despite being stricken in February with what would be his final illness and therefore being unable to conduct the later planned programmes. Meanwhile the cycles had been dropped and the number of concerts outside New York had been increased: between 5 and 10 December 1910 Mahler and his orchestra performed in Pittsburgh, Cleveland, Buffalo, Rochester, Syracuse and Utica – an immense mental and physical strain – and in January 1911 they gave a Wagner programme in Philadelphia and Washington. The make-up of the programmes had scarcely changed since the previous season. Of particular note was the 'All-Modern Programme' of the 17 and 20 January 1911 which included an overture by Hans Pfitzner and Strauss's *Ein Heldenleben*. Sandwiched between these two compositions was Mahler's Fourth Symphony, the last of his own works that he conducted. His final concert on 21 February was an Italian evening including works by Busoni and Martucci, as well as Mendelssohn's Fourth Symphony, the 'Italian'.[29]

Conducting technique and tempi

Mahler was perhaps the greatest, but not the only great, conductor of his time. In Leipzig he was engaged alongside Arthur Nikisch. In Hamburg he personally got to know the revered Hans von Bülow. Meanwhile his friend and rival, Richard Strauss, worked in Meiningen, Weimar, Munich and Berlin. In Vienna Mahler met Hans Richter to whom Wagner had entrusted the first performance of the *Ring* cycle. He himself engaged Bruno Walter and Franz Schalk at the Vienna Opera House, and in New York he met Arturo Toscanini, from whose clutches he jealously guarded the *Tristan* he had rehearsed. Mahler worked during a time when the recently invented recording process was not yet adequate for orchestral reproduction. So a picture of Mahler the conductor can only be reconstructed through his own statements and the judgements of his friends and opponents. What seems above all to have differentiated Mahler from his contemporaries was his tempi. He said to Natalie Bauer-Lechner: 'You should hear me conduct Weber's *Freischütz* once; you wouldn't recognise it, simply because I take quite different tempi – and the right ones! – in which you hear what you've never heard before. For example, the second Finale is always played loud and fast, whereas I take it quite slowly and softly; this has a magnificent effect.'[30] It seems that he also took the overture to *Der Freischütz* more quietly, for the Hamburg critic Ferdinand Pfohl asked him to explain why he had specified mutes for the first pair of horns. Mahler evidently defended himself as follows: 'I believe I can answer to this alteration to the horn sound with reference to Weber himself, because it is entirely compatible with the fantastic and the romantic, and thus with Weber's sense of nature'.[31] Mahler took the overture to *The Magic Flute* slower than usual, and yet according to him it sounded faster because one could follow the quaver figures exactly.[32] When conducting, it appears to have been important to him not studiously to beat time but to bring out with his gestures only 'the significant melodic and rhythmic content at any one moment'.[33]

It is no surprise that particularly detailed descriptions of Mahler's conducting were to emerge after his Vienna debut (*Lohengrin* on 11 May 1897). It was unanimously reported that he conducted the overture more slowly than was usual, and that afterwards he was showered with applause:

> Mr Mahler is a small, slender, energetic figure, with intelligent, sharply chiselled features . . . The way he looks is the way he conducts: full of energy and subtle understanding. He belongs to that younger school of conductors, which, in contrast to the statuesque posture of the older Kapellmeisters, has developed more vivid use of expressive gesture. These younger ones speak with their arms and hands, with movements of the whole body.[34]

This description matches exactly the well-known silhouettes of Otto Böhler, which portray Mahler in a variety of conducting poses.[35] Another critic recognized from this *Lohengrin* performance that Mahler had 'the theatre in his blood': 'His interest does not end at the footlights, but only really begins there. He demonstrates the beat for the choir and soloists, the *correct* beat, and thereby secures a convincing performance.'[36]

The animated, almost frenzied gesticulation described above was typical of Mahler's early and middle years. According to contemporary reports his baton painted every nuance in the air. However, over time his gestures did decrease, and in later years his movements were described as balanced and economical. The young Otto Klemperer, who observed Mahler many times and was close to giving up his own conducting career in the face of Mahler's ability (he considered Mahler 'a hundred times greater' than Toscanini), only remembered this frugal use of gesture, and described Mahler's tempi as follows:

> His tempi – one felt they could not have been otherwise . . . I can only repeat: everything was absolutely natural. It had to be like that . . . I still remember the opening of the second movement of Beethoven's Seventh Symphony: it sounded quite different, but I could absolutely say 'yes' to it. When he conducted, you felt it couldn't be better and it couldn't be otherwise.[37]

It cannot have been coincidental that Klemperer mentioned this particular symphony, for Mahler conducted it many times (in thirteen concerts), and the second movement must surely have sounded like a Mahler movement *avant la lettre*.

Comments of orchestral players

The musicians who worked under Mahler did not have an easy time. There was scarcely an orchestra that did not rebel against him and his artistic demands. He so infuriated the Kassel orchestra by his endless rehearsals that musicians and members of the chorus threatened to come armed with sticks and thrash him (though the threat was not carried out).[38] The orchestra of the Leipzig Stadttheater complained about Mahler to the Leipzig town council: '[he] not infrequently demands what is absolutely impossible. When this cannot be done, the member of the Orchestra involved is accused of malice and stubbornness.'[39] Even the Hamburg orchestra, with few exceptions, detested him. Mahler's suspicion was that for most of them art was simply a 'cow which they milk' in order to live as comfortable a life as possible:

> And yet, there are some amongst them who are more willing and better than the rest; one ought to have more patience with them than I am able to manage. For if one of them doesn't immediately give me what is on the page, I could kill him on the spot; I come down on him, and upset him so much that he really hates me.[40]

The Vienna orchestra ought to have truly loved and honoured him, for shortly after taking up his post he secured a raise in their salaries which until then had been shamefully low. But the majority of musicians did not love him. He was too brusque towards them, too demanding, too obsessed with detail – and moreover he was a Jew, albeit one baptized as a Catholic. Because of this people held many things against him which they would have accepted from someone else. Even Mahler's relationship with his orchestra in New York was very strained, at least in the second season. One observer described the situation: 'You see, Mahler had a peculiarity, a special characteristic – he listened to the gossip and intrigues of the orchestra men. It was so in Vienna, and it was so here in New York, too. In every orchestra there is at least one musician who lives on such plots, and Mahler would listen to him and become upset.'[41]

The 'Retuschen'

The two brief quotations given earlier illustrate that Mahler thought he knew how Weber or Mozart would have judged his interpretations. This self-confidence gave him the necessary encouragement to alter the scores of some of the works of the masters. He introduced cuts, sometimes radical, and more frequently made changes to instrumentation, so-called *Retuschen* (retouchings). His excision of the entire last act of Meyerbeer's *Les Huguenots* caused astonishment; that he never performed a Bruckner symphony without cuts met with annoyance in Vienna. His retouchings – the doubling, adding or leaving out of orchestral parts, or the performance of string quartets using string orchestra – were the object of bitter opposition. True, Wagner had conducted Beethoven's symphonies with his own retouchings, but that had been considerably earlier, and at the beginning of the twentieth century the concept of *Werktreue* (being faithful to the original) was becoming established. On the other hand, as Kurt Blaukopf writes: 'The concept of *Werktreue* is questionable. Its implementation tacitly presupposes that the true sound of an art work may be derived from the written notation with which the composer signifies his intentions.'[42] As a practitioner Mahler of course knew that the score alone does not constitute the work, and that the large modern concert hall may demand a different instrumentation from that notated by the old masters, and he took this into account in his own way. Nevertheless, as David Pickett observes: 'In the light of these creative efforts [by Wagner, Bülow or Nikisch] Mahler's Retuschen in the works of Beethoven, Schubert and Schumann may seem tame; and indeed they are in the main sober, well-considered attempts to come to terms with problems set either by the composers, or by the different circumstances under which Mahler worked.'[43] Nowhere did Mahler make such radical changes as in the scores of his own works. Even after these had long been published, from one performance to the next Mahler found new and, he was convinced, clearer solutions. Clarity of musical expression was indeed his overriding aim, and he once wrote with some self-mockery to Bruno Walter that 'I should like to publish revisions of my scores every five years'.[44]

Mahler as conductor of his own works

Mahler himself gave the first performances of all his compositions from *Das klagende Lied* to the Eighth Symphony. In Europe, as in America, his works gained little sympathy, and at times were met with hostility. Even when the public declared their allegiance to him, as at the première of the Eighth, dreadful reviews appeared the following day. He conducted his own symphonies to show supporters and opponents alike what he was driving at in his music. But this was only one of his motives. His main aim was to hear in full what he had put down on paper, or at best tried out on the piano, thereby verifying his own aural imagination. With some symphonies such as the Second, Fourth, Fifth and Sixth, he had particular movements played by his current orchestra prior to their first performance. The initial instrumental *Retuschen* arose from this (he hardly ever interfered with the compositional structure of a work). Of course, the results of rehearsing for first performances and of the first performances themselves, were reflected even more in Mahler's scores. Almost every subsequent performance under his directorship led to new changes, for as we have already seen, he was a lifelong learner, even in matters of orchestral technique. His concert hall experiences did not just lead him to remove or emphasize individual voices; he learnt much else from the players' reactions to his music. An instinctive *ritardando* from the orchestra would often be countered by the instruction *nicht schleppen* ('do not drag'), and bars that were taken too fast by *nicht eilen* ('do not rush'). Mahler conducted his first five Symphonies relatively frequently, the Sixth and Seventh just three times each, and the Eighth only once. Thus the definitive version of the symphonies, particularly those he conducted many times, was arrived at through continual monitoring. But just how truly 'definitive' was this? We can assume that Mahler's symphonies would have developed alongside him, had he lived longer. They would probably have forged yet further ahead into the twentieth century whilst not denying the time of their origin.

11 Arrangements and *Retuschen*: Mahler and *Werktreue*

DAVID PICKETT

To most of his contemporaries Mahler was known first and foremost as an operatic conductor. He was active in this sphere from 1880 to 1910, reaching the heights of the profession. That he always wanted to be free of the routine of the theatre and to conduct concerts is perhaps not surprising, given that all his mature compositions involve concert orchestras; but, since there were few independent concert orchestras, like most conductors in Germany and Austria Mahler was obliged to earn his living mainly in the opera house.

Mahler's model for the concert conductor was exceptional in all senses: Hans von Bülow, who had not held a regular operatic appointment since he left Hannover in 1880. Bülow was a fine pianist who championed the late Beethoven sonatas and gave the first performance of Tchaikovsky's First Piano Concerto, was Wagner's chosen conductor for the premières of *Tristan* and *Die Meistersinger*, and later a friend of Brahms. Mahler wrote to Bülow after one of the latter's concerts with the Meiningen Orchestra when it visited Kassel in January 1884, asking to be taken on as an apprentice; but Bülow replied curtly and coldly and when choosing a replacement assistant in Meiningen in 1885 preferred to recommend his inexperienced protégé, Richard Strauss, over either Mahler or Felix von Weingartner. Later, in Hamburg, Bülow would recognize Mahler's gifts as a conductor, though not as a composer and, apart from the occasional performances he gave in Prague and Budapest, Mahler's first real opportunities as a conductor of the symphonic repertoire presented themselves in Hamburg when he deputized for Bülow in December 1892 and took over the 'Bülow concerts' with the Hamburg Philharmonic after his death in February 1894.

At the same time, the Musical Directorship of the Hamburg Philharmonic was about to become vacant due to the imminent retirement of Julius von Bernuth, and Mahler pressed his friend Ferdinand Pfohl to intercede on his behalf with those responsible for appointing Bernuth's successor, saying:

> You must understand, dear friend, that an activity such as that which
> the opera demands of its conductors has an intolerable, even fatal effect

in the long run. Out of instincts of self-preservation and self-respect I
must conduct concerts, refresh myself in the concert hall, recreate,
complement the one-sidedness of opera conducting through the activity of
symphonic conducting . . . In short, I must also some time be able to
conduct a symphony by Beethoven and Mozart. I want to save myself in this
way, and in the circumstances I can do so only through your support and
your help.[1]

Pfohl duly spoke on Mahler's behalf to a certain Senator Schemmann,
earnestly mentioning all Mahler's good points and praising his work in
the Hamburg Opera, only to receive the response:

My dear young friend, what you say is completely true, as far as it concerns
an operatic conductor; but how can you believe that Mahler, who up to now
has only worked as an operatic conductor, could be capable of conducting
concerts? Opera and concerts are two such very different things, that can
never be associated. Mahler is indeed a good opera conductor, but believe
me he can quite definitely never conduct concerts.[2]

Mahler conducted the eight 'Bülow concerts' with the Hamburg
Philharmonic during the 1894–5 season but, according to Foerster: 'The
critics mainly agreed that Mahler was an outstanding interpreter only in the
theatre. Without the stage and the artificial light he felt out of his element. So
again the unexpected came to pass: after a single season Mahler was succeeded at the conducting desk of the Hamburg Philharmonic by Felix
Weingartner.'[3]

In March 1897 Mahler conducted Beethoven's Fifth Symphony in a
trial engagement with the Kaim Orchestra in Munich. The critic of the
Allgemeine Zeitung wrote of this concert that:

On the basis of this first appearance, we are far from giving an opinion on
the conducting talent of the guest. According to what we saw and heard we
have a mind to class him rather with the new-fangled virtuosi than in the
higher category of well promising conductors . . . Mahler appears to be . . .
the right conductor for modern works, and we are perhaps faced with a time
when an impresario must engage two conductors, one classical and one
modern.[4]

The 'modern' work referred to was Berlioz's *Symphonie fantastique*, of
which Mahler conducted the second and third movements. When
Weingartner was selected as the conductor of the Kaim Orchestra,
Natalie Bauer-Lechner reported that 'Mahler said irritably: "I could
have done what they wanted – played Beethoven in their soulless and
senseless way, and spared myself a lot of effort in the process. But in music
at least I will maintain my standards even if my life is a struggle in other
respects." '[5]

Mahler's concert orchestras

Mahler was thirty-eight-years old when at precisely 12:30 on Sunday 6 November 1898 he stood for the first time before the Vienna Philharmonic Orchestra in the Goldener Saal of the Musikverein to conduct the first of the eight subscription concerts which formed their annual series. He was at the full height of his powers, having assumed the direction of the Vienna Court Opera the preceding year. The orchestra was composed of the same players who depended upon him for their positions in the Opera Orchestra, though they all had a say in the running of the Philharmonic Orchestra. Six months earlier, Mahler had negotiated a new contract for the opera players involving a 20 per cent increase in pay and other improvements in employment conditions,[6] and this, together with his other improvements to the musical standards in the Opera, must have increased his popularity with the players. Hans Richter, who had conducted the orchestra for the 1875–82 and 1883–97 seasons had been unanimously re-elected by the players for the 1898–9 season, but had withdrawn in September 1898, citing pains in his right arm and the fact that he would be retiring from the Opera in the near future.[7] Mahler was the obvious candidate to fill the gap which had so suddenly opened up, though there were already signs of the discontent among players and singers at the Opera that was to drive him from the Philharmonic after less than three seasons and eventually from Vienna.[8]

Mahler's first programme with the Vienna Philharmonic was:

Beethoven: Coriolan Overture
Mozart: Symphony No. 40 in G Minor
Beethoven: Symphony No. 3 in E♭ ('Eroica')

Richter had conducted the same Beethoven Symphony at his first and final concerts with the orchestra, and Mahler's programming can be seen as symbolic: he wanted to parade his interpretation of the work in the same concert hall where he had most probably stood as a student to hear Richter's first concert in 1875. This interpretation had already been developed in three widely separated performances in Hamburg, including his farewell benefit performance at the Hamburg Opera, and he had also conducted the symphony at the memorial concert for Bülow in Hamburg. The 'Eroica' would later be the main work on his first programme as Music Director of the New York Philharmonic. Mahler's juxtaposition of his 'Eroica' performance with that of Richter was duly noted by the Viennese critics, who later in the season also took exception to his performance of Beethoven's op. 95 Quartet with full strings, though eventually the focus of adverse criticism of Mahler's concert conducting in Vienna, and later in New York, centred on his manifold changes to the instrumentation of earlier composers.

Mahler was conductor of the Vienna Philharmonic until February 1901, when an illness provided an excuse for his resignation, and conducted the New York Philharmonic Orchestra from November 1909 until February 1911. If we add the 'Bülow concerts' that he conducted in Hamburg, we see that he had his own concert orchestra for a period of only five seasons. There was also guest conducting, most of which involved his own symphonies; but that he acquired a reputation as a concert conductor comparable to that of Toscanini, Furtwängler, Mengelberg or Boulez in such a short period is remarkable.

Instrumental changes, rearrangements, *Werktreue* and the critics

Mahler was neither the first nor the last conductor to 'touch up' the music of Beethoven and other composers, though he was the one who was most pilloried for it. The practice derives from an earlier and perhaps less honourable era, when Bach arranged the works of Vivaldi for organ and Handel plagiarized Kerll in tacitly adapting that composer's Fourth Canzona as the chorus 'Egypt was glad when they departed' in his own *Israel in Egypt*. In a pre-copyright age this recycling of the works of otherwise dead and unperformed composers was considered fair game; and it was a way of at least keeping their music, if not their names, before the public. Not much later, in 1789, Mozart adapted Handel's *Messiah* to the spirit of his own time for the concert series of Baron van Swieten, with his own harmonizations and counterpoints, and adding horn, trumpet and trombone parts in contemporary style. Half a century later, Liszt appropriated and adapted Mozart's *Ave Verum Corpus* for his own *Evocation à la chapelle sixtine*, and this was in its turn freely arranged for orchestra by Tchaikovsky as the third movement of his *Mozartiana Suite*.

Although much of the primary evidence has been destroyed, we know that Mahler followed the tradition of opera performance in adapting stage works for the production at hand. Well-documented examples of this are his addition of the court scene to the third act of *Figaro*, his revision of the libretto of *Euryanthe*, and his use of Beethoven's Third *Leonore* Overture to sustain the tension and cover up the noise of the scene change in the second act of *Fidelio*; but there were others. The purpose of these changes was to make the staging of the operas theatrically more effective, and thus better appreciated and understood by the public, and a similar purpose might be said, *grosso modo*, to be the motivation for his changes to concert works.

Justification of this is provided by Busoni when he wrote in 1902 to the Belgian critic, Marcel Rémy. Rémy had evidently criticized Busoni's 'alterations' in the *Prélude, Chorale et Fugue* of César Franck, and Busoni replied: 'You start from false premises in thinking that it is my intention to "modernize" the works. On the contrary, by cleaning them of the dust of tradition, I try to restore their youth, to present them as they sounded to people at the moment when they first sprang from the head and pen of the composer.'[9]

Busoni explained further in 1907 when he wrote:

> What the composer's inspiration necessarily loses through notation, his interpreter should restore by his own ... Every notation is in itself the transcription of an abstract idea. The instant the pen seizes it, the idea loses its original form ... The performance of a work is also a transcription, and still, whatever liberties it may take, it can never annihilate the original.[10]

According to this philosophy, Wagner's original intention of remedying 'defects' in instrumentation[11] has been supplemented by an obligation placed upon the interpreter to divine the intentions of the composer and, if necessary, to modify the text so as to be truthful to these original intentions. When used in this, its widest sense, the concept of *Werktreue* implies a consideration of each individual work, rather than a generic approach towards the oeuvre of any one composer, style or period.

But the prime influence on Mahler was Wagner, whose proposed changes to Beethoven's Ninth Symphony are well known.[12] Less well known is Wagner's edition of Palestrina's *Stabat Mater*, with redistributed voices, antiphonal choirs and fully supplied dynamics; and even more relevant is his edition for the Dresden Opera in 1847 of Gluck's *Iphigénie en Aulide*, and the concert ending to that opera's overture which he subsequently provided. When Wagner's essay 'On Conducting' is read in the light of what we know about Mahler, it becomes clear that Mahler took to heart nearly every one of Wagner's suggestions, and developed them further.[13]

Wagner's disciples, Bülow, Nikisch and Richter, certainly made changes to Beethoven's scoring along the lines suggested by Wagner, and the first two occasionally even made major changes to the structure of Beethoven's works, as when Nikisch used the coda of the Third *Leonora* Overture to conclude the Second Overture.[14] Although not all Bülow's Beethoven *Retuschen* are known, it is clear that in his later years he often took a more arbitrary position than Mahler. For instance, he 'solved' the well-known balance problem of bar 190 of the first movement of Beethoven's Eighth Symphony by introducing the timpani in unison with the double basses.[15] According to Weingartner, in bar 470 of the

Trio of the Ninth Symphony, Bülow changed the c′ of the second bassoon to b.[16] It was also Bülow's practice in later years to perform the Ninth Symphony without its Finale.

We do not know what Mahler thought of Weingartner's books on performing the symphonies of Beethoven, Mozart, Schumann and Schubert, or even whether he read them, but Pfohl describes his reaction to Weingartner's earlier pamphlet on conducting.[17] The highly polemical essay concerns itself mainly with a description of Bülow's conducting career, leading to a discussion of his later style and waywardness, and a description of how Wagner's advice in his essays on conducting had been taken to excess by the younger generation of conductors. Several instances of this are given but, except for his hyperactive podium style, none could be unequivocally ascribed to Mahler. Pfohl reports:

> In September 1896, Weingartner's book had hardly appeared than Mahler
> broke into my studio with the violence and tumult of a storm. He ran about
> the room forwards and backwards like an irritated tiger in a cage. He
> escaped it to avail himself of the stool offered him, stamped, and screamed:
> 'Have you read Weingartner's book yet? What a 4th former [*Quartaner*],
> what a cretin [*Trottel*]!'[18]

When Mahler's younger contemporaries, Weingartner and Strauss, made changes to the instrumentation of Beethoven, Schubert and Schumann it was on a limited basis, and they were not criticized for it: Mahler's 'crime' was that he did this in a wholesale manner. He ran into trouble with the critics over his changes to Beethoven, particularly to the Ninth Symphony, and in response to these criticisms wrote a manifesto and distributed it at a performance of the symphony with the Vienna Philharmonic Orchestra in February 1901. In his brief essay, Mahler claimed not to have exceeded Wagner's recommendations, that he was merely making clear Beethoven's intentions, which had been compromised by the primitive instruments of his time, by his defective physical hearing, and rendered less transparent by the increase in the number of string instruments employed in the larger concert halls of Mahler's day.[19]

Distinguished musicians like Schoenberg, Zemlinsky, Gabrilowitsch and Wellesz fully approved of Mahler's actions. All had his changes to the Ninth Symphony in their own scores and all but Wellesz employed them in concert. In his autobiography, Wellesz wrote:

> The study of this score arranged by Mahler is still for me today a model of
> brilliant interpretation of the idea of the work. The changes show the way in
> which Mahler understood how to lend Beethoven's inner inspiration its
> intended sound, even in such places where the latter's genius was far ahead
> of the instrumental possibilities of his time.[20]

Mahler's *Retuschen*

It is interesting to compare Mahler's extant conducting scores with those of other conductors. Some conductors use an intricate system of hieroglyphics to indicate which instruments are playing, others amplify dynamics by writing them in large letters, or write brief memos to remind them about tempi and other practical matters. Fritz Busch wrote bowings on almost every page, Mengelberg wrote metronome marks every few bars, Klemperer indicated the periodic metre, Bruno Walter wrote remarks to help him with the expressive content of the music, and Scherchen wrote so many marks of all kinds that the original printed notes often became illegible. Mahler's scores do not resemble the scores of any of these conductors: there is not a single metronome mark, bowings are indicated only sporadically, periodic metre is indicated only in a few places in the first movement of Beethoven's Fourth Symphony, there are no poetic remarks dealing with expressive content, and only rarely does he make a mark to remind himself of dynamics, tempi or the entry of instruments. Instead of all these possibilities, we find in Mahler's extensively annotated scores changes of dynamics and instrumentation known collectively by the term *Retuschen*, which mostly aim to ensure the instrumental balance that he expected. Often a change of dynamics was sufficient to achieve this, but if not, Mahler changed the scoring. So extensive are Mahler's *Retuschen* that for the majority of the works in his repertoire he was obliged to enter his changes into a set of orchestral parts in advance of the rehearsals. Many conductors have their own orchestral materials with their preferred bowings, with instructions as to repeats, and other valuable markings. Mahler's orchestral parts have all these, plus his *Retuschen*, and often have many extra orientation numbers in addition to the standard rehearsal letters to enable him to rehearse in minute detail without wasting time. In Beethoven's Seventh Symphony there are no less than 147 of these. In the absence of bar numbers in the orchestral parts and scores of the day, this highly characteristic feature of Mahler's materials allowed him to stop and start with the minimum of trouble in rehearsal.

If Mahler's care in preparing to the utmost were not obvious from a perusal of the sources, we have the witness of Foerster who knew Mahler well in Hamburg:

> In those days I found Mahler always at the writing desk. He was never satisfied with the score, perfecting it to the last detail with regard to dynamics and execution; he also transferred every one of his rigorously measured signs to the individual orchestral parts. One can imagine how much time this preparatory work devoured. "There are only a few

rehearsals," he said more than once, "therefore everything must be prepared in advance." ... Mahler's enemies – what great man has none? – knew no better than to speak of unusual tempi, of arbitrary modifications, of straining after effect. None of them surmised with what feeling of responsibility Mahler approached his task, with what pedantic strictness and exactitude he reflected on every nuance, even on the most trifling of the marks which he copied into the score and parts.[21]

Mahler usually provided his sets of parts with string desks of 9, 9, 6, 5, 5. This agrees with the playing strength of 17, 17, 11, 10, 10 that we know from Vienna Philharmonic programme booklets of 1898.[22] When he totally overhauled the personnel of the New York Philharmonic a decade later, Mahler effectively established for the string complement the present-day norm of 16, 14, 12, 10, 8, arranged with first violins to his left, cellos and violas centre left and right respectively, second violins on his right and double basses either central behind the woodwinds or to the left behind the cellos. Sometimes he would reduce the complement, even for short sections of a work. In Beethoven's Ninth and Mozart's 41st Symphonies this is even minutely specified, as in bars 768–71 of the Scherzo of his own Fifth Symphony.[23] In some passages he would have all the violins play the first violin part, either omitting the original second violin part, or dividing the viola section to cover both this and the original viola part. Cellos were sometimes also used to strengthen important viola parts. In the main, Mahler accepted the bowings that were printed in the parts or supplied by the leaders. He discussed these in rehearsal, in order to get the effect he considered necessary, and from time to time insisted on bowings that were not comfortable for the players, including repeated downbows and places where the players were instructed to change bow many times on a single note.

In the woodwinds, apart from carefully worked-out doubling, Mahler's most common change was to raise the clarinets by an octave, or to add them if they were not playing, in order to bring out what he considered important. In rare cases where strengthening of dynamics, doublings and reinforcements were not sufficient, he instructed the oboes and clarinets to raise their bells. When he was unable to obtain a delicate enough sound from the oboe, Mahler substituted the softer-toned flute or clarinet, as in bars 12–15 and 62–4 of the second movement of Beethoven's Fifth Symphony, where the second flute sometimes played the first oboe part. When necessary, Mahler was quite prepared to remove woodwind instruments; for instance, the oboes were initially marked *ppp* in bar 340 of the first movement of Beethoven's Third Symphony, and subsequently removed altogether from bars 342–3, 346–7 and 350–1 to clarify Beethoven's busy texture. Whereas in Vienna Mahler could call on as many players as he needed, in Hamburg he was limited to roughly the resources of Wagner's *Lohengrin*, with only triple woodwind. This probably explains the more frequent use of the E♭ clarinet in his Hamburg *Retuschen*. In general, Mahler mostly used this instrument to reinforce the flutes, though sometimes also the oboes. Even when Mahler had access to full doubling, he sometimes later retained the E♭ clarinet, though rewriting the part, as for instance in Beethoven's Third and Fifth Symphonies and the *Weihe des Hauses* and *Meistersinger* overtures. In sections of *Coriolan* Overture Mahler's third bassoon in Hamburg was also employed on the contrabassoon.

In addition to the moderation of dynamics, the filling-in of missing melodic notes which the natural horns and trumpets could not play in classical works, and their removal to clarify the texture, Mahler used brass instruments to reinforce the winds and sometimes the strings. Where the original instruments cannot be spared from the duties assigned by the composer, Mahler used his supplementary brass players, giving them an additional and different role in the music from the original parts with which they coexisted. Apart from changing pitches to fit the harmonies, Mahler's altered timpani parts do not generally draw attention to themselves. Critics, however, frequently pointed out that Mahler required the timpanist to play very loudly in certain passages.[24]

Mahler's repertoire

Beethoven

The works of Beethoven were central to Mahler's repertoire. He conducted most frequently the Third, Fifth, Sixth, Seventh and Ninth Symphonies and the *Coriolan* and *Leonore* No. 3 overtures. Extant scores and orchestral parts give us a good idea of his interpretation of these works.

We do not have the set of orchestral parts which Mahler used in Hamburg for his 'Eroica' performances, but a score has survived from those times. In it we find indications of wind doublings, participation of the E♭ clarinet, modification of dynamics for balance, and changes of articulation. For example, in the second subject of the first movement, Mahler changed Beethoven's *portato* indications (see Example 11.1).

He reduced the strings to half the number of desks in some *pianissimo* passages of the first movement (for example bars 99–110, 382–95 and 502–11) and the Finale (bars 277–302) and changed notes where he perceived that Beethoven's choice was compromised by the instruments of the time, as for instance in the reinforcement of the first violins an octave higher by the first flute in bars 316–18 of the first movement, and

Example 11.1 Beethoven, Third Symphony, first movement, bars 83–6

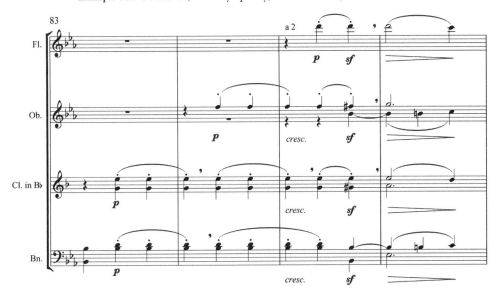

extending the range of the flute to b³ elsewhere. Though this was not a Mahler invention, the trumpets participate fully in the theme of bars 655–64 of the first movement, and the horn and oboe parts of bars 113–16 and 516–19 are changed to participate fully in the wind theme that is only incompletely realized in Beethoven's text.

The revisions read like a sketch for the later version that Mahler prepared in Vienna, where he copied and extended his changes into a new score. A copyist entered these into a set of printed parts, making manuscript parts for the extra players. All the woodwinds were selectively doubled, with an additional part for the E♭ clarinet which Mahler wrote out himself. The three extra horns did not have much to play, though they doubled the entries in the Trio of the Scherzo, and since Mahler marked the beginning of the Trio *piano*, they were there by reason of colour rather than for balance.[25] The third and fourth trumpet players only participated in nine bars of the second movement (bars 160–8) and three notes of the Finale (bars 419–20, where they reinforce Beethoven's parts for Oboe 1 and Clarinet 2). It is also interesting to note that, while Mahler introduces his extra horns and marks all participants *fff* in bars 276–9 of the first movement, the woodwinds, some of which had been doubled in bars 243–8, were single from the second beat of bar 248 onwards.

But Mahler did go further than Wagner, both in letter and in spirit. His experiment with the Hamburg Philharmonic orchestra on 11 March

1895 using an off-stage band instead of the orchestral wind players in Beethoven's Ninth Symphony was documented by Bruno Walter:

> He had the B-flat march in the finale played by an off-stage orchestra, while the tenor and the male chorus sang on the podium, the main orchestra re-entering with the start of the subsequent fugato. This was no mere whim. He thought he had discovered by a glance into Beethoven's workshop his intention as pre-figured in Schiller's text: namely, that the winged progress of the young men should, from the hesitant pianissimo of its start, through the crescendo to the ultimate fortissimo, make its way as though from a vast distance into a victorious presence. To this effect he employed means which Beethoven, hampered by the restrictions of his time, would not have dared to use.[26]

It would appear from Mahler's score that the players he used for this experiment were those who had time to get off and on stage: 2nd piccolo, two E♭ clarinets, two horns, two trumpets, trombone and tuba. Walter concluded: 'Naturally, in his audacious interference with the score, Mahler was on the wrong track, and he never repeated the experiment'.[27] On the mistaken assumption that Beethoven would have preferred it so, Mahler also habitually made a significant change to the Scherzo, by omitting the first eight bars after the Trio, and beginning the recapitulation from the entry of the second violins.[28]

Mahler's changes to Beethoven's Fifth and Seventh Symphonies were no less extreme, and beyond those amendments which definitely bring clarity to the texture when performed with a large body of strings in a reverberant hall, can be cited the interchanging of trumpets and horns in bars 89–100 of the first movement of the Seventh Symphony (which actually does not sound as radical as it looks on paper) and the muted horns reinforcing the clarinets in bars 38–9 and elsewhere in the Scherzo of the Fifth Symphony, about which the critic of the *New York Daily Tribune* wrote: 'Into the cadence of the second subject of the third movement Mr. Mahler injected a bit of un-Beethovenian color by changing the horn parts so that listeners familiar with their Wagner were startled by hearing something very like Hagen's call from *Götterdämmerung* from the instruments which in the score simply sustain a harmony voice in octaves'.[29]

Mozart

Mahler's main contact with Mozart was in the opera house, though before his move to Vienna in 1897 he also conducted Mozart's *Requiem* four times, always on Good Friday when opera performances were banned. In Hamburg he conducted *Figaro* fourteen times, *Die Zauberflöte* twenty-nine times and *Don Giovanni* twenty-eight times,[30] and in Budapest *Figaro* (four times) and *Don Giovanni* (six times, in a new production which gained the enthusiastic approval of Brahms).[31] In Vienna Mahler added *Così fan tutte* to his repertoire and by 1906 he was able to celebrate the 150th anniversary of Mozart's birth in Vienna by producing these four works there, together with *Die Entführung aus dem Serail*, and *Zaïde*.[32]

In his Mozart performances we find Mahler reacting against nineteenth-century performance style, at least from the time of his arrival in Vienna. We hear from Bauer-Lechner that already in 1897 he dismissed half the then-normal complement of strings from a rehearsal of *Die Zauberflöte*.[33] He also used a harpsichord or spinet for the secco recitatives that formerly had been spoken at the Vienna Court Opera.[34] His restudying of *Figaro* in 1906 caused him to clarify the libretto by the addition of a short scene from Beaumarchais's original, set in recitative, partly secco and partly accompanied by divided strings, though admittedly including divisi chords for cellos reminiscent more of *Die Walküre* than anything Mozart wrote.[35] Erwin Stein reported that Mahler 'abolished the extra top notes and cadenzas which singers used to insert, but he maintained those *appoggiaturas* which he felt to be in the style of the music'.[36]

Mahler also tried to clarify Mozart in the concert hall, when he conducted Symphonies 40 and 41. He treated these two works differently: the *Jupiter* Symphony was played with selectively doubled woodwind and with a full complement of strings, reduced in places in the first movement; and, at least in New York, where the critics commented approvingly on it, Mahler conducted the G minor Symphony with a reduced body of strings throughout, and doubled the flute.[37] He also prescribed carefully worked-out and detailed supplementary dynamics to enliven the bare instructions provided by Mozart. Here again, Mahler took his cue from Wagner, who wrote of the Andante of the G minor Symphony 'If expression-marks are lacking, the marvellous lilt of the movement takes their place and tells our imagination how it should be performed. Perhaps Mozart left so few expression-marks in order that we should do just this.'[38] Mahler's supplementary dynamics include and go beyond Wagner's: what Wagner prescribed for the imagination, for instance the crescendo in bar 53, Mahler made an acoustic reality. In the *Jupiter* Symphony Mahler divided the first violins in bars 34–6 of the slow movement, realizing Mozart's implied dialogue (see Example 11.2); and in bars 397–403 of the last movement the final appearances of the headmotif of the movement were made audible by the reinforcement of the horns and trumpets respectively.[39]

Schubert

Mahler conducted two symphonies by Schubert: the *Unfinished* in B minor, D. 759 and the 'Great C major', D. 944. Mahler's own score of the *Unfinished* has disappeared, but a score and set of parts in the New

Example 11.2 Mozart, Symphony No. 41, second movement, bars 34–6

York Philharmonic Archive contain evidence that they may have been used by him. Like the materials in the opera houses where Mahler worked, other people have used them and much of what may have been Mahler's conception has been obscured. There are many doublings that are more characteristic of Mahler than Weingartner, but nothing exceptional. The case of the 'Great C Major' Symphony is different. There exist a score from Mahler's Hamburg performance in 1894 and a score and set of parts that he used in Vienna in April 1900, and also in New York in November 1910. The significant differences between the two scores reflect both a development of Mahler's ideas and the difference in his available forces. Since the Hamburg score of the Symphony does not have any doubled wind parts, the E♭ clarinet is kept very busy, but it is omitted from the later score, which calls for selective doubling of all the woodwind and brass.

Some of Mahler's changes here (and elsewhere) may have been copied from other conductors. Although unlikely to have heard Mahler conduct the work, Tovey mentions 'the horrible marine-parade custom of giving the tune to the trumpet' at the end of the first movement, and excoriates 'a very eminent conductor [who] once made one of the leading London orchestras play the string parts pizzicato [in the Trio to the Scherzo]: a brilliant but thoroughly debased remedy, of which he had the good grace to be ashamed'.[40] Both of these changes feature in Mahler's score and parts.

Mahler frequently used his second pair of horns to reinforce the bassoons when these play inner voices rather than the bass line, for example in bars 288–325 of the first movement. Another common device of Mahler's was to remove trumpets where he felt that they obscure the thematic material, as in the first seventeen bars of the Allegro of the first movement. In his later score he also removed the timpani from these bars, and omitted the strings from bars 676–7 of the movement, allowing the wind alone to answer the string statement of the first four bars of the main theme. In both scores, the beginning of the Finale was similarly thinned

Example 11.3 Schubert, Symphony in C, Finale, bars 1–8

out: woodwind, horns and trumpets were all doubled, with trombones marked down to *mf*, and answered by the strings. The changed
dynamics of the strings and the fermatas respond both to the rhetorical
implications of the music and to the demands of the acoustics (see
Example 11.3).[41]

Mahler's cuts in the second and last movements of the 'Great' C major
Symphony appear to have been introduced only in America. Perhaps he
thought the work was too long for his audience, or made excessive
demands on the stamina of his orchestra. The cuts are very skilfully
made and were only detected in part by the critics. Mahler removed
what might in any case have been cut in performance, had Schubert
notated it by repeat signs. When Schubert repeated a passage and varied
the instrumentation or extended its development, Mahler chose between
the two versions and excised one. Sometimes he made a cut from within a
section to the later repeat of the section which is differently scored, but
never in such a way that it was obvious.[42]

Schumann

Until recently most conductors made changes to the instrumentation of
Schumann's symphonies, often following Weingartner's recommendations. Many conductors, including Toscanini and Giulini, have used
Mahler's 'editions' in preference to the originals. Frederick Stock, the
long-time conductor of the Chicago Symphony Orchestra, went even
further than Weingartner or Mahler by including piccolo, cor anglais,
two extra trumpets, tuba, triangle, snare drum, tambourine, cymbals and
bass drum in his version of Schumann's Third Symphony, and also made
substantial changes to the actual notes.[43]

It is doubtful whether anyone today would argue seriously in favour of
the cymbal crash with which Mahler opened Schumann's *Manfred* Overture
in November 1910.[44] But the rest of Mahler's revisions are of great interest.
Apart from the low E♭s for the third trumpet in bars 287–93, which are out

of range for the modern instrument, the overture can be played successfully without intervention, and usually is; but Mahler's revisions demonstrate his profound understanding of, and empathy with, Schumann's sound-world, which benefits from his superior mastery of the orchestra. Accepted as a realization and interpretation of Schumann by Mahler, it is hard to find fault with it. Mahler clarifies and makes Schumann's music more easily realizable, makes the bowing more practical, and greatly intensifies the expression by means of supplementary dynamics and reinstrumentation.

Mahler's *Retuschen* in Schumann's symphonies have been discussed many times, notably by Erwin Stein and Mosco Carner.[45] However, it has rarely been pointed out that his experience with the Second and Third was limited to two performances of each in New York in October 1910 and January/February 1911 respectively. In less hectic times and with performances extended over more of his lifetime Mahler might well have revisited some of his *Retuschen*, as he did in the case of Beethoven.

'Contemporary' music

In that their creative lives overlapped with Mahler's, Brahms, Bruckner, Tchaikovsky, Smetana, Dvořák and Wagner were his contemporaries, and he conducted premières of the music of some of them. Strauss, Busoni, Pfitzner, Rachmaninov, Rimsky-Korsakov, Debussy and Stanford were among more direct contemporaries whose music he also conducted. In the case of Brahms, after Mahler's performance of the Third Symphony with the Vienna Philharmonic in 1899, Bauer-Lechner reported:

> Mahler is delighted with the Brahms Symphony, which was wonderfully played. Its one failing, he feels, is a lack of brilliance in the instrumental setting; but this might easily be taken care of with a few changes in the scoring. 'Also I felt the greatest desire to make a few cuts here and there but was prevented from doing so by my inner reluctance to tamper with the work of one who was so recently alive – not to mention my fear of how the critics and public would attack me.'[46]

Mahler had included his heavily retouched version of Beethoven's *Weihe des Hauses* Overture at the same concert, and from the set of parts of the Brahms symphony that he used in New York we see that he dared to make changes to the scoring at a later time and out of earshot of the Viennese critics, when he added a couple of small reinforcements in the wind parts. In the case of other recently deceased composers, Mahler was less afraid. His *Retuschen* in the overture to Smetana's *Bartered Bride* are extremely far-reaching, and there are many changes in the score and parts of Dvořák's *Scherzo Capriccioso*, op. 66, used by Mahler. Unfortunately, materials of Tchaikovsky works that Mahler may have used in New York bear scant evidence of what he might have done, but the little that remains of his Wagner materials indicates that he was not averse to making small but telling changes to the instrumentation, including the addition of the Eb clarinet to the Prelude to *Die Meistersinger*.

(a) Bruckner

Mahler's connection with Bruckner was loose; they met infrequently from Mahler's time as a student onwards, and Mahler helped make the published piano-duet arrangement of the older master's Third Symphony. In Hamburg Mahler conducted the first concert performance of Bruckner's D minor Mass, and later in Vienna the first complete performance of his Sixth Symphony. Mahler's repertoire also included Bruckner's *Te Deum* and Fourth and Fifth Symphonies. The critic Theodor Helm pointed out at the time that Mahler made cuts in the three symphonies, and these have been documented by Ernst Hilmar.[47] One would like to be able to suggest that Mahler was actually improving the discredited early published versions, but the matter is more complicated when Mahler makes cuts in an edition which is already shorter than Bruckner's original, as in the Fourth and Fifth Symphonies.[48] As in the case of Schubert, Mahler removed what he regarded as repetitive material, even though Bruckner's repetitions are more varied than Schubert's. Thus in the slow movement of the Fourth Symphony, Mahler omitted the first sixty-four bars of the recapitulation, which include the only return of the second subject (viola tune) and moved directly to the Coda. Radical though this was, given the state of Bruckner's reputation as a master of symphonic form during Mahler's lifetime, it is unlikely that Mahler damaged it further with his few performances of Bruckner's symphonies incorporating *Retuschen* by no means as extensive or radical as those he applied to Beethoven or Schubert.

(b) Other contemporaries

In New York, Mahler conducted a lot of contemporary music, including Elgar's *Enigma Variations*. The set of parts appears not to have been used much since Mahler and indicates that Elgar's scoring passed muster. But this was not the case with Loeffler's *La Villanelle du diable*, op. 9, or Pfitzner's *Christelflein* Overture, op. 20, both of which received Mahler's emendations; and Georges Enesco was probably not at all happy to find changes and cuts in his *Suite d'orchestre*, op. 9, when he conducted the work from the same materials in 1938. To achieve an even greater sense of strain in the high notes in Strauss's *Till Eulenspiegel*, Mahler replaced the D clarinet by the Bb instrument in the passage that begins seventeen bars before the Epilogue.[49]

String quartet arrangements

Mahler conducted three string quartets in arrangements which he made for string orchestra with double basses. In Hamburg on 19 November 1894 he conducted the variation movement from Schubert's *Death and the Maiden* Quartet, D. 810, and in Vienna the variations from Haydn's *Emperor* Quartet, op. 76, no. 3, on 4 December 1898, and Beethoven's Quartet in F minor, op. 95, on 15 January 1899.

The journal *Die Wage* reported an interview with Mahler a week before the January 1899 concert:

> A quartet for string orchestra! That sounds odd to you. I already know all the objections which one will raise: the destruction of intimacy, of individuality. But one is mistaken. What I am proposing is but an ideal performance of the quartet. Chamber music is fundamentally written for a small room. It is really only enjoyed properly by the performers. The four people who sit at their music desks are also the public to whom this music applies. When chamber music is transferred to the concert hall this intimacy is already lost. And still more is lost: in the large room the four voices disperse, they do not speak to the listeners with the power which the composer wanted to give them. I give you this power, because I reinforce the voices. I release the expansion which lies dormant in the parts and give the notes wings. Indeed, we also strengthen an orchestral piece by Haydn, an overture by Mozart. Do we alter thereby the character of their works? Certainly not. The volume of sound which we give a work depends upon the room in which we perform it. I should have to perform the Nibelung Ring with a different, reduced orchestra in a small house, as opposed to an immense auditorium, in which I should even have to reinforce the orchestra. I am not acting against the composer's intentions, but according to his wishes. Beethoven, in his last quartets, certainly did not think of the restricted little instruments ... He realised a mighty idea in four voices. This idea must be recognized, must really stand out. But the voice of one violin in a small room equals as much as twenty violins in a hall. And twenty violins in the large hall can produce a piano, a pianissimo still much more tender, more delicate, indeed let's say more intimate, than one violin – which one would hear either not at all or too loud ... The truly appreciative listener ... will not think of the number of the performers, but listen to the singing of the four voices.[50]

Mahler's friend, Natalie Bauer-Lechner, herself a professional quartet player of distinction, comments about Mahler's concert and the disturbance it created:

> From the very first bars, the quartet sounded so tempestuous that one couldn't doubt that [the opening] could not be played by 'four miserable fiddlers' [*von vier armseligen Manderln*], as Mahler put it. Then the tender

cantilenas and solo parts were played so discreetly, softly, and with such magical sounds, that a single violinist could not have rendered them more beautifully. This finally refuted the opponents' fears that this important aspect of quartet playing would suffer from the weight of numbers. I have never heard, nor would I have thought it possible, such powerful tone, without any roughness or coarseness.[51]

The critics disapproved of Mahler's experiment largely on the grounds that the works were originally written for an intimate setting of four solo players who did not need to be conducted, and Mahler never returned to it. Mahler made more changes to Schubert's quartet than to Beethoven's, by means of reassigning voices and divisi, and the selective addition of double basses, and these can today be studied in published scores and recordings.[52] Questions of copyright aside, it might reasonably be asked whether what Mahler did constitutes as much of an arrangement as Schoenberg's reworking of *Verklärte Nacht*; certainly the significance of the Schubert arrangement is lessened by the fact that Mahler never conducted more than the slow movement.[53]

The Bach Suite

Unlike the Schubert and Beethoven string quartets, as the only one of his arrangements that was published in his lifetime, the *Suite aus der Orchesterwerken von Joh. Seb. Bach mit ausgeführtem Continuo zum Konzertvortrage bearbeitet von Gustav Mahler* must be regarded as a finished work. It would not be fair to claim that Bach's B minor and D major Orchestral Overtures, BWV1067/8, were unknown in the concert hall in Mahler's time. Indeed, Bülow conducted the latter in Hamburg on 3 November 1890 and the former on 21 March 1892, and we know that Mahler was a frequent and prominent audience member at Bülow's concerts. Unlike Bülow, who used an edition by Mendelssohn and David,[54] Mahler worked from the Bach Gesellschaft Edition to prepare his suite, which was the first work on his Wednesday series of eight concerts, described as an 'Historical Cycle', with the New York Philharmonic on 10 November 1909, when it was announced only as 'Bach: Suite for Orchestra'.

Mahler showed again that he was ahead of his time by playing continuo in this concert, not only in the Suite but also in Bach's E major Violin Concerto, and arias by Handel and Grétry, as he had previously done in Mozart opera performances, seated centre stage with his back to the audience and picking up his baton from time to time. The so-called 'Bach Klavier' that Mahler used was a Steinway grand piano, probably a 'model A' of modest dimensions. It had something like metal tacks affixed to the hammers to approximate the more metallic sound of a harpsichord, while at the same time being loud enough to be heard in Carnegie Hall and capable of producing dynamic changes.

Mahler's decision to combine selected movements of the B minor and D major Suites was explained by critics at the time as a need to avoid the monotony of key that either of the suites would produce. The movements are:

  I Ouverture (B minor)
  II Rondeau and Badinerie (B minor)
  III Air (D major)
  IV Gavotte Nos. 1 and 2 (D major)

Mahler suppresses Bach's repeats in the opening movement, though not elsewhere. The *Rondeau* leads *attacca* to the *Badinerie*, in which pizzicato and arco alternate. The first twenty-eight bars of the *Rondeau* are then reprised. The only advantage Mahler takes of the repeats in the *Air* is to substitute a long diminuendo in the last two and a half bars. The fourth movement begins with Bach's *Gavott I*, with the clavicembalo participating only in the written-out repeats, as at the beginning of the *Rondeau*, probably implying that Mahler conducted the start of the movements. *Gavott II* follows with written-out repeats of each section in which the clavicembalo figures prominently. The first *Gavott* returns without repeats.

Volker Scherliess suggests that Mahler's choice of material may be viewed as a Scherzo and slow movement enclosed by opening and closing movements, thus reminiscent of a classical symphony.[55] But it is stretching credulity to describe the *Rondeau* as scherzo-like, and the assertion that Mahler's juxtaposition of Bach's movements bestows on them even a 'schema of quasi symphonic form' must be rejected. Gennady Rozhdestvensky is nearer the mark when he refers to the Suite's form as 'proportional and symmetrical – two three-movement structures [movements II and IV] preceded by solemn preambles'.[56]

The instrumentation largely follows Bach's original which means that flutes are used only in the B minor movements, and three trumpets and timpani introduced only for the Finale. Mahler's printed 'clavicembalo' part is not what we would today understand as a continuo part,[57] in that the left hand frequently abandons the bass line to play chords that accompany flourishes, added counterpoints and spiced-up harmonies in the right hand. Alma Mahler tells us that Mahler frequently improvised variants, as one might reasonably expect by the time he arrived at the twentieth performance little more than a year later.[58] The organ

Example 11.4 (a) Bach Suite, Gavotte 2, trumpet in D, bars 40–2 (cf. Bach's bars 24–6); (b) Bach Suite, Gavotte 2, violins, violas and harpsichord, bars 16–20 (= repeat of bars 1–4)

participates only in the first movement, throughout the *Grave* and *Lentement* sections and at climaxes in the middle section. It dominates the opening chord and is clearly intended to be a large instrument. The direction in the score to reinforce the flutes ('in *forte* with additional flutes, reinforced by a clarinet if needed') points to the expectation of a large body of strings, and details in the writing for the clavicembalo imply that Mahler expected this to be heard clearly through the texture.[59] Mahler treats the text freely, applying varied and detailed articulations, and realizing a few counterpoints that Bach had omitted. Striking examples of this are Mahler's exact imitation of the first violin's first bar of the *Lentement* in the right hand of the clavicembalo a bar later, which thus anticipates the basses (plus clavicembalo and organ pedals) in the following bar, and the anticipation of Bach's trumpet parts in bars 25–7 of *Gavott II* by the clavicembalo in the written-out repeat of bars 1–3 (See Example 11.4).[60]

Unlike many other conductors, who unashamedly changed things simply to make them 'more effective' and attract applause, Mahler used his extensive *Retuschen* to interpret what he felt to be the intentions of the composers behind the notes they wrote. In Bach and Mozart his approach was more modern than that of his contemporaries; Beethoven was allowed to benefit from the greater perfection of instrumentation since his time; and Mahler also gratuitously put his superior knowledge of instrumentation at the service of contemporary composers. When he avoided repeats, including those written out by Schubert and Bruckner, Mahler was a man of his time, though it is interesting to note that he appears to have observed the exposition repeats in the first movements of both the Mozart symphonies. It would also be unfair to criticize in hindsight Mahler's incomplete awareness of historical style in Bach or Mozart without acknowledging that he made what improvements he could given the state of scholarship at the time, and was far in advance of the majority of his colleagues who kept nineteenth-century practice alive for a further fifty years.

Of course, the realization of Mahler's aims was a dangerous process and there is no wonder that others did not agree with his conclusions. But those who protested loudest during his lifetime were critics and not other composers or performers, most of whom were happy to hear Mahler's interpretations of the works he conducted. Julius Bittner claimed that 'not only I, no, many others have had ... the impression that they had heard the Ninth correctly for the first time'.[61] Ernst Decsey reported that, during a performance of *Tristan* in December 1906, he

> had the distinct impression that Mahler changed the instrumentation while he conducted, he rebalanced the orchestra, he improvised, that is, he sometimes waved off two desks of first violins in order to let the seconds come through, then he called them back into action ... in short it was music-making from the nerves.[62]

The critic of the *New York Evening Post* explained the eloquence of Mahler's Beethoven readings, writing that 'he does not hesitate to retouch the score in accordance with the methods which Beethoven himself would certainly have approved had he written for a modern orchestra. The audience is not conscious of these changes, except that because of them many places become clearer and more melodious.'[63]

The experience of hearing Mahler's *Retuschen* in the flesh has convinced me of the truth of these and other similar statements – testimony that leads to the conclusion that many critics knew of the details of the admittedly extensive changes not from the evidence of their own ears, but from the tales told by the orchestra members, or from the look of Mahler's changes in the score. But Mahler knew intimately the exact and subtle effects to be had from mixing orchestral colours, a good example of which is given in bars 41–52 of the *Weihe des Hauses* Overture. In Mahler's version, the two bassoons (Tovey's inaudible 'hurrying footsteps'[64]) are doubled and also reinforced by the cellos, for the first six bars playing pizzicato. Though this looks like a radical change, the aural impression is not that the cellos have been added, but simply that the bassoons' semiquavers stand out as if in relief without compromising the colour of the bassoons or obliging the trumpets or drums to play softer, and the unprejudiced listener is engaged more with Beethoven's music than the means employed by Mahler to make it audible.

But at this remove in time, the question of the objectivity of Mahler's interventions – whether there can really be 'no talk of a reinstrumentation, alteration, or even of an *improvement*' of the works, as Mahler claimed in his 1901 manifesto of his far-reaching changes to Beethoven's Ninth Symphony – is irrelevant, for each generation forges its own definition of *Werktreue*. At present the pendulum of dominant performance practice has swung to the opposite extreme from Mahler's habits; but despite this, occasional performances in recent years utilizing his *Retuschen* have shown that they can have the same positive effect on an audience that they had when Mahler himself used them.

PART FOUR

Reception and performance

12 Issues in Mahler reception: historicism and misreadings after 1960

CHRISTOPH METZGER
(*translated by* JEREMY BARHAM)

Methodological considerations

The reception history of a composer comprises the sum of inherited accounts, condensed over time into a reflection of that person and his or her work. It is defined by all existing sources and testimonies, some of which are handed down without question while others are critically scrutinized. Changes in historically recorded contexts and revisions of aesthetic judgements are rare. In such cases reception history can have a corrective function and can uncover and identify processes of evaluation. Up to the early 1990s, research in reception history was developed in German-speaking musicology with the aim of describing anew the interplay between author, text and reader, or between composer, work and listener. At the heart of this lay questions involving aesthetic expectations and their fulfilment.[1] Whilst at the beginning of the 1990s such research was still seen as a forward-looking model for new academic practice, it has not yet established itself accordingly. In this context Mahler reception history offers a prototype for investigations which reveal a dramatic picture of scholarly history over long stretches of time. Indeed Carl Dahlhaus refers to the special status of research into Mahler reception as a 'history of events'.[2]

Through this, the interplay between institutions and individuals responsible for handing down traditions can be clarified. Preconditions for this type of almost Foucauldian archaeological investigation are the comprehensive research, analysis and evaluation of source materials from different institutions. For example, it has been possible to reconstruct from these the course of almost one hundred years in the performance history of the Third Symphony. The evidence thus discovered could ultimately be seen as a potential archive that may be consulted for the purposes of legitimation and the forming of a tradition. It emerges that the works themselves by no means governed the way they were handed down, but rather the official directives of institutions together with their publications ultimately determined historical classifications. Analyses, commentaries, reviews and so on, originally secondary literature produced in the context of the concert hall and the festival, peripheral to performances by various orchestras, and mostly forgotten, turn out to be central material. It often found its way from programmes into music criticism, even forming part of the promotional activity of publishing houses, but it is seldom archived. By contrast, the most enduring impression stems from musicology itself and accompanying literature, which reinforced certain words and expressions over the decades, as composers were accepted into specialist dictionaries. Texts duly arose from this process which defined and consolidated aesthetic and musico-political viewpoints at the initial stage of important first and early performances, but whose complex interrelationships can only be analysed through studying the sources from a detached perspective. New data have recently drawn attention on several levels to accusations of historicism in reception, as well as to practices of misreading, and this has led to minor corrections within the history of Mahler reception.[3]

Inherited misreadings

The misjudgements found in various musical dictionaries and reference works from the early years still define the image of Mahler's performance history today. The importance and success that he demonstrably achieved as a composer after 1903 are seldom quantified in the literature, and are regularly suppressed. The measure of success or failure in these and later years is surely to be found in the frequency and locations of performances. At times, regular concerts and high levels of acceptance of new composers put even the musicological world under a certain commercial pressure. Here is one example: as early as 1903 Mahler managed to negotiate with the Peters publishing house an all-inclusive fee for the publication rights to his Fifth Symphony – a fee that was almost equivalent to the salary he received as Director of the Vienna *Hofoper*.[4] Whatever one may think of this arrangement, it demonstrates the high regard in which the composer was held even before the Symphony was performed. Another example: in order to get an idea of the extent to which Mahler himself disseminated his work, consider the fact that up to 1911 Mahler had conducted a total of seventy concerts of his own symphonies, while between 1902 and 1950, shortly before his death, the Dutch conductor Willem Mengelberg far exceeded this with the substantial figure of at least 375 proven performances of the symphonies. Mengelberg's quantity of performances is by far the largest but he is only just being discovered as a significant conductor whose interpretations were very close to Mahler's own.[5] Several important festivals and cycles were organized between 1911 and 1923, long before the two big centenary festivals in 1960 in New York and Vienna.

The earliest of these was the Mahler commemoration on 19 October, 1911. Then in the Viennese winter season of 1918 all the symphonies were performed for the first time, under various conductors. In 1918 Bruno Walter organized a cycle of six different Mahler symphonies, and in 1920 the Amsterdam Mahler Festival was celebrated as an international event. The first German Mahler Festival took place in Wiesbaden in the following year, after attempts to hold the event in Berlin had failed. In 1921 Hermann Scherchen conducted a Mahler cycle in Leipzig; in 1922 Anton Webern conducted several symphonies as part of the popular Arbeiter-Sinfonie-Konzerte; in 1923, Klaus Pringsheim, the brother-in-law of Thomas Mann, directed the first Mahler cycle in Berlin. The first radio broadcast (of excerpts from various symphonies) was given by Erno Rapee in 1942 in the USA. This laid the ground for the American Mahler renaissance, bolstered by media support but unnoticed in Europe.

The authority of the music dictionary

Given such a successful performance history, and one which was also reported widely in the daily press, some astonishing things are to be found within the ranks of German-language musicology. With Hugo Riemann, 'the greatest European musicologist of his generation',[6] one can immediately see a clear canonization of the academic opinion of Mahler, which defined the composer's public image for generations between 1905 and at least 1960 in the most widely circulated music dictionary.[7] Aesthetic judgements never have more far-reaching consequences than when made in a dictionary with encyclopaedic aspirations. Significantly, Riemann's negative attitude towards the composer intensified as the latter's success grew. Aesthetic and political criteria became intertwined. His influential judgements, typically ambivalent from the outset in 1905, finally turned into a blatant, even aesthetically grounded, anti-Semitism.[8] The sixth edition of his music dictionary stated: 'At present Mahler is generally known as one of the foremost opera conductors; he has awakened interest with his compositions, but these lack a strong sense of individuality and are merely the results of a skilled eclecticism'.[9] In the tenth edition (1922), now also edited by Alfred Einstein, which appeared just two years after the 1920 Amsterdam Mahler Festival and three years after Riemann's death (1919), the tone becomes more severe:

> Mahler's symphonic writing, which initially grew out of his Lied compositions,
> is so indifferent to so-called originality of feeling or refinement of
> themes that one may believe it possible – even on racial grounds (Mahler
> was a Jew) – to exclude him completely from the ranks of creative

musicians. In reality Mahler is both simplistic and complex at one and the same time; his music is a confessional art, which aims to address universal concerns directly whilst inevitably acknowledging the ruptured nature of one born at the latter end of a cultural epoch. The attempt to overcome this dualism explains the tension of this music, in which Romanticism is finally subverted.[10]

It was not until 1961 that a heavily reworked twelfth edition of the dictionary appeared. Its editor, Wilibald Gurlitt, excised the politically and aesthetically questionable passages and alluded with some surprise to the widely divergent nature of opinions on Mahler. Unlike Riemann, he did not distinguish positively and negatively between conductor and composer, and this had important aesthetic implications which are still evident in the literature, for most ambivalent aesthetic judgements have invoked such a polarization. Nevertheless, Gurlitt laid the foundations – no doubt unwittingly – for the stock theme of Mahler's 'problematic', 'puzzling' and 'remarkable' popularity, which since the 1970s has been held up as a manifestation of more recent historicism. In the 1960s this popularity topos had already involved the seemingly unjustified admission of the conductor-composer into the ranks of true composers. Allied with this was the accusation that through his influential post of Director of the Vienna *Hofoper*, Mahler saw to it that there was an unwarranted number of performances of his symphonies – an accusation that in reality was refuted by the large quantity of performances given by other conductors. From these few examples it is clear that Mahler's reception history was closely linked to the history of musicology itself.[11]

Significance within academia

What qualitative and quantitative methods are available to sift through and categorize the extensive range of sources for reception study?

In principle the presentation and examination of sources is organized chronologically (the rule of succession, according to Dahlhaus), only part of which can be outlined here. What stance did musicology adopt towards Mahler after 1960? From lists of lectures it is possible to verify that, with few exceptions, specific discussion of Mahler in the German-speaking world only began in 1978. Before then, according to reliable sources, Guido Adler, Professor of Musicology in Vienna from 1898 to 1927, had introduced his students to Mahler's work, one of the best known results of which was Egon Wellesz's 1928 book *Die neue Instrumentation*, which dealt with new instruments and their use by Mahler.[12] Apart from this, only Hans Heinrich Stuckenschmidt's 1954 class at the Technische

Universität, Berlin and a lecture by Rudolf Stephan in the winter semester of 1969–70 at the Freie Universität in Berlin are known to have taken place. At the invitation of Stephan, Otto Kolleritsch gave a guest lecture in 1973 with the pioneering title 'Historical Investigation of Mahler's Current Importance' ('Historischer Versuch über Mahlers Aktualität'). In the same year Hans Heinrich Eggebrecht, Professor at Freiburg, at long last gave a lecture on Mahler. The *Österreichische Musikzeitschrift* and the *Neue Musikzeitschrift* had published special Mahler volumes as part of the centenary, but this did not lead to a revival in musicological terms until 1972 with the journal *Musik und Bildung*, published in Mainz. A similar picture is painted by the only five dissertations to have appeared by 1952 in Vienna, Bonn and Hamburg, by Fritz Egon Pamer, Heinrich Schmidt, Anton Schaefers, Hans Tischler and Helmut Storjohann. Given the composer's marginal significance in the history of scholarship up to the mid-1970s, one wonders what factors would have been necessary to bring about a change in this situation. Although discussions of the composer were initially limited to general topics, his significance would soon become apparent and he was quickly fashioned into a typical *fin-de-siècle* figure.

American readings from the 1930s

While after 1930 Mahler's historiography came to a standstill, there were indications of increasing interest in the USA, sparked by a variety of factors. At the root of this American preoccupation lay a combination of several different events which had begun, significantly, in the year that Mahler achieved his greatest number of performances, including the première of the Third Symphony in Krefeld (1902). Given this series of performances and a vigorous publication programme it is justifiable to speak of a reception which extended from East Coast cities such as New York, Boston and Philadelphia to places in the Mid-West such as Minneapolis and Cleveland. With regard to these American performances, one of the leading music critics of the 1930s, Warren Storey Smith, claimed that for many years Brahms had been considered Bruckner's 'worst enemy' and Strauss had 'impeded' Mahler's 'cause'.[13] In addition to the performance situation, Smith is alluding here above all to the criteria of assessment which were ranged against Mahler and Bruckner into the 1930s as a consequence of Brahms reception, with its lingering echoes of that of Beethoven.[14] If one can speak of an American reception, it should be emphasized that this was cultivated in only one journal. Between 1932 and 1963 this journal, *Chord and Discord* (the official journal of the Bruckner Society of America), published two volumes of ten issues. Hermann Danuser has pointed out that the declared aim of the journal was to promote not just the music of Bruckner but also that of Mahler: 'From the fourth issue onwards, the journal bore the subtitle: "A Journal of Modern Musical Progress". This refers to the background against which Bruckner and Mahler were to succeed in the USA: the perceived conservative symphonic tradition of Brahms.'[15]

What is unique about the journal was that it claimed to report as comprehensively as possible on performances, press reviews and radio broadcasts.[16] The imparting of such information would place Bruckner and Mahler within the contextual intricacies of reception history for the first time. These reports, alongside clearly focused essays, provided the objective facts necessary to establish an overall view. The very first articles by Gabriel Engel discussed typical assumptions made in 1930s music criticism. The ambitious project of *Chord and Discord* was introduced by Engel as follows:

> That distinguished sage among American critics, Mr W. J. Henderson, can perhaps still remember the gloomy day more than forty-five years ago, when the New York Philharmonic, under Theodore Thomas, first played Bruckner's Seventh Symphony. Concerning that occasion, Mr Krehbiel, young Henderson's senior colleague and the acknowledged head of the critical profession, perceiving the opposing fury with which the press greeted the gigantic work, rose ... and said in mingled admonition and prophecy: 'It is neither wise nor just to pronounce condemnation on an artwork in so superficial and flippant a manner as nearly all the New York newspapers did on this occasion; but bearing in mind a score of marvelous things in the symphony, notably several moments that approach grandeur in the slow movement, and remembering that that is not always the highest type of beauty which is obvious at a glance, we are yet constrained to say that for the present the work is a failure. It may be beautiful in twenty-five years; it is not beautiful now.'[17]

Engel then charts a period of twenty years in order to review the extent to which American music criticism managed to change over that time. He came to the sobering conclusion: 'In short, the "twenty-five-year" period Mr Krehbiel had mentioned in that early review of Bruckner's Seventh, was over; but American musical criticism was still "tradition-bound". It seemed unable to listen to a new work of art without holding it up to the light of Beethoven, Wagner, Brahms and others during the initial hearing.'[18]

Under the banner of a critique of tradition, parallels emerged between American and Austro-German music criticism, although in the USA these revealed connections with musicology. In the USA criteria for assessing value such as the predominance of tradition were openly identified with composers as well as music critics. In the jostling for position within America it was precisely the younger generation of music critics who emphasized the break with the older generation. The name of Henry Krehbiel repeatedly crops up in this context. In his first few years at the *New York Herald Tribune* he reported on police matters and baseball – not unusual in a journalistic career – but came to dominate music criticism in New York into the 1920s. Other important writers, including, for example, W. J. Henderson, had also written adventure stories or books on completely different topics such as marine navigation before working as music critics.[19] It was characteristic of American music criticism in the 1930s that younger authors also followed developments in Europe. For example, a report in *Chord and Discord* acknowledged the journal *23* as 'the most progressive monthly musical magazine published in Europe'.[20] There were at least five factors which together made American music criticism of the 1930s an influential leader in its field:

(1) A general scepticism towards traditional norms extending to the complete rejection of musicological practices, as in the case of Henderson, who, as Krehbiel's successor at the *New York Herald Tribune*, condemned the working processes of musicology and the *Grove Dictionary of Music and Musicians*.

(2) Most authors expressly rejected methods of analysis which relied on tonal criteria from the field of Beethoven reception. Instead, parallels were drawn with literary forms. Hans Tischler, who gained his doctorate in Vienna with a dissertation on Mahler under Schiedermair (1937), summarized his findings, after detailed harmonic investigations, as follows: 'Each of Mahler's symphonies is a drama of general ideas or principles, not of describable actions'.[21]

(3) The 1930s were a period when music criticism was finding its bearings and when its defining problem, according to Oscar Thompson, was one of self-discovery. For their want of method, Thompson also polemicized against 'Papa' (the context indicates that this refers to the Viennese music critic Julius Korngold) and 'Mother Europe'.[22] His critique of Viennese music criticism – further hints were unnecessary – was intended to induce stylistic change and establish a style of his own.

(4) Thompson saw the advantage of the 'directness' in American criticism that was qualitatively different from that in Vienna which he accused of vain self-absorption.[23] Consequently writers such as Grant and others avoided musical analysis which was dependent on musicological techniques. Instead the word 'expression' was frequently used.

(5) Aesthetic value judgements from Austro-German music criticism in the form of words like 'trivial', 'banal', 'deep', 'sublime' or 'popular' transferred from melodic characteristics to works (and their composers), were considered at the time by the writers of *Chord and Discord* to be historical opinions and were avoided.

If one looks at the extremely diverse reception profile cited above, it can be seen that American articles such as those in *Chord and Discord* adopted critical positions towards most assessments of Mahler. Thus

American criticism tried to outdo even the most captious voices from Vienna, and yet no alternative terms of reference were established in these articles. Criticism in America stressed aspects of nature (with reference to performance instructions such as *wie ein Naturlaut*), and these were placed in opposition to art (and existing opinion). At the same time parallels were drawn with literary genres in order to describe works with new metaphorical imagery.[24] By the beginning of the 1960s, the journal's original aim – to promote the achievements of Bruckner and Mahler – had clearly been achieved, and a few years after the New York Mahler Festival of 1960 the journal ceased publication.[25]

Adorno and after

Theodor W. Adorno's Mahler monograph can be considered representative of a burgeoning change in attitude which was also linked to the Mahler centenary. Interestingly, his study combines the most important themes from Guido Adler and various Viennese music commentators such as Max Graf, Julius Korngold, Paul Stefan, Hans Tischler and the renowned musical literary figure Paul Bekker, who barely forty years earlier had published the first study of Mahler's entire symphonic output. Bekker's book, which had a single print run of 1,000 copies, provided Adorno with the basic material for his musical analyses, which for the most part confine themselves to precisely the same passages previously discussed by Specht, Kretzschmar, Adler as well as Bekker and others.[26] Adorno's analytical process leaps between separate, widely scattered sections of music and in many cases is not fully understandable because he subsumes all of Mahler's works under one topic. Because of this the temporal unfolding of works is broken up and individual passages are mostly snatched out of context and viewed in isolation. Surprisingly Adorno's book, like Bekker's in the 1920s, gained initial recognition outside the sphere of musicology, and, like Bekker's which was reprinted in 1969, did not attain its present leading position in musicology until the mid-1970s when its rediscovery began. It has the status of a work of cultural history which, through the experience of anti-Semitism, draws attention to aesthetically rooted dogmas and the ways in which these were disseminated by leading musicologists: 'the judgment on Gustav Mahler passed not only by the Hitler regime but by the history of music in the fifty years since the composer's death exceeds that which music generally presents to thought and even to philosophical thought'.[27] Adorno focused on a period that was defined by European reception up to the 1930s and subsequent reception in America. In order to understand this focus, one must take into account Adorno's philosophical and cultural-critical disposition, clues to which are evident from the following passage: 'Mahler can only be seen in perspective by moving still closer to him, by entering into the music and confronting the incommensurable presence that defies the stylistic categories of program and absolute music no less than the bald historical derivation from Bruckner'.[28] Or: 'Mahler's atmosphere is the illusion of familiarity in which the Other is clothed. Timidly, with obsolete means, he anticipates what is to come.'[29] Many passages attest to Adorno's celebrated attempt to draw parallels with the model of the novel as a formal type: 'Mahler's relation to the novel as a form can be demonstrated, for example, by his inclination to introduce new themes, or at least to disguise thematic material so that in the course of the movements it appears quite new'.[30]

Viewed more closely, the methodology of Adorno's book also reveals, alongside the findings of the European writers mentioned above, themes applied to Mahler by progressive American music journalists such as Gabriel Engel, William Parks Grant and Warren Storey Smith in *Chord and Discord*. These writers can be classified into three groups: forward-looking music critics such as Shanet, Smith, Lert, Grant, Diether and Engel; émigrés from the Viennese locale such as Graf, Tischler, Stein and Bekker; and contemporary witnesses, conductors or writers close to Mahler such as Walter, Pringsheim, Werfel and Newlin. Adorno's method was strikingly different from earlier work on Mahler in the way that it interwove cultural-political themes from critical theory with the works and their general reception. The approach was at the same time pioneering and problematic because Adorno's thought processes were expressed in vague formulations. He divided the book into the following sections: 'Curtain and Fanfare' (*Vorhang und Fanfare*), 'Tone' (*Ton*), 'Characters' (*Charaktere*), 'Novel' (*Roman*), 'Variant-Form' (*Variante-Form*), 'Dimensions of Technique' (*Dimensionen der Technik*), 'Decay and Affirmation' (*Zerfall und Affirmation*) and 'The Long Gaze' (*Der lange Blick*). The metaphorical nature of these titles clearly betrayed Adorno's attempt to gather distinct topics together to form the blueprint for a unique terminology. Adorno deals with all the symphonies: the Ninth Symphony is the most frequently discussed, with forty-three citations; next come the Third, Fourth and Sixth Symphonies, each with twenty-four or twenty-five references. The Third Symphony is dealt with in the chapter entitled 'Novel', which, together with the final chapter, has received particular attention because of its inter-generic account of the musical process. Adorno deserves recognition for attempting in part to establish a new conceptual approach expressly related to handed-down formal schemata, the expansion of which is discerned in processes of breakthrough (*Durchbruch*), suspension (*Suspension*), and fields of dissolution (*Auflösungsfeld*).

Adorno, Mahler and Lachenmann reception

The end of the 1970s saw renewed developments in Mahler reception through the slowly increasing number of performances worldwide. For example, between 1955 and 1975 the Third Symphony was performed on average no more than five times a year. After 1978 the frequency at times increased to over fifteen performances, and radio broadcasts meant that the Symphony could be heard every two weeks.[31] Mahler's techniques, which thanks to Adorno are now recognized as involving the breakdown of formal schemata and an often pointillist soundscape, were of particular interest to younger composers from the mid-1970s to the end of the 1980s. Adorno writes: 'Mahler's progressiveness does not reside in tangible innovations and advanced material. Opposed to formalism, he prefers what is actually composed to the means of composition and so follows no straight historical path.'[32] This and other similarly broad formulations offered the best preconditions for the aesthetic referencing subsequently admitted by composers such as Hans Zender, Helmut Lachenmann, Peter Ruzicka and Dieter Schnebel, and later by Michael Denhoff, Detlev Glanert, Hans-Joachim Hespos and Walter Zimmermann. During the Hamburg Mahler Festival the music theorist Heinz-Klaus Metzger described how young composers' initial interests in Webern were shifting towards Mahler, and how between these twin poles an 'affinity' for the latter had emerged.[33] Without exception Mahler's music was approached with a fundamentally philosophical attitude. The influence of Adorno, for whose arguments American reception had prepared the way, was focused on his distinctive method. All traditional analytical techniques were called into question so that the pregnant symbol of *Naturlaut* (sound of nature) could be shifted to the centre of attention. The clearest expression of this was to be found in Helmut Lachenmann's response to the following question posed by Peter Ruzicka: 'Mahler reception, particularly in German-speaking countries, has been particularly inspired by Theodor W. Adorno's exegesis. The idea of aesthetic negation is especially persistent in his analytical vision. Do you see this approach as having a decisive impact that might conceivably bring further repercussions for the reception of New Music?' Lachenmann replied: 'This very stance towards New Music can be demonstrated by the credibility of present Mahler disciples. Whether or not the meaning of New Music is grasped, in truth the attitude of our public towards it is characterised by aesthetic negation.'[34]

When asked about the compositional inspiration he had gained from Mahler's work, Lachenmann answered:

> The *Naturlaut* in Mahler's music seems to me a remarkable phenomenon, and one which I have examined in other connections and contexts . . . The

emancipation of sound en route towards the serialists or the Cage school
was purely the result of relatively abstract constructive, or to be precise,
deconstructive organisational principles: on the one hand total serialism,
on the other hand total chance. At 'corresponding' moments, so to speak, in
Mahler's creative process, his inventiveness gives rise to a conscious
artlessness for art's sake ... My music avoids the emphatic gesture, is
integrated with its operational mechanics, makes its dynamic condition
known, and releases the expression locked within.[35]

Lachenmann's comment thus reorientates Mahler's work within a musical practice which reflects the position of the early 1970s. Instead of serial
processes and the chance functions developed by John Cage, Mahler
offered an alternative approach which was held up as a unique compositional technique: nature phenomena as *musique concrète*.[36]

Adorno's historicism

Adorno exerted significant influence on Mahler reception in terms of
research interests and writing styles. His familiar, at times bewitching,
manner is found in countless articles that make reference to him. As
Eggebrecht remarked: 'The current understanding of Mahler is utterly
preoccupied with Adorno, and any alternative understanding is immediately confronted with the task of dealing with this preoccupation'.[37]
There is a problem of content here since, as mentioned, Adorno derived
his source material almost exclusively from study of the scores and from
1920s publications. His technique involves comparing Mahler's characteristic formal schemata – and their dissolutions – with the figure of the
composer himself, an approach that had already been adopted by
Riemann and other conservative musicologists. Adorno employs this
technique to produce precisely that kind of biographically motivated
literature which the philosopher Nietzsche and the musicologists Adler
and Bekker had previously emphatically rejected because they recognized
in it the stamp of historicism.[38] In view of this, there is little to distinguish
Adorno's book methodologically from those types of composer mono-
graphs published in comparatively high print runs by the Schlesischen
Verlagsanstalt in Berlin during the 1910s and 1920s in the series
'Berühmter Musiker Lebens- und Charakterbilder nebst einer Einführung
in die Werke der Meister' which, for example, between 1900 and 1922
published a total of 32,000 copies of the book on Beethoven by the cultural
historian Theodor von Frimmel. Adorno similarly makes no reference to
source material from the field of music criticism. Clearly, but no doubt
unintentionally, he was in accord with the spurious, one-sided, belated and

misguided canon of historicism. He also neglected to mention the frequent performances of the symphonies up to the 1930s in Europe (particularly in the Netherlands), even ignoring the well-documented Mahler Festival in Amsterdam. Mengelberg's influence went unrecognized. One searches in vain for references to Mahler's reception in American exile. Adorno essentially recycled those insights into the significance of music-theoretical concepts that had already been noted in progressive Viennese music criticism: 'Song and symphony meet in the mimetic sphere that exists prior to neatly separated genres ... All categories are eroded in Mahler, none is established within unproblematic limits.'[39] As yet Adorno's legacy within the reception of the composer has seldom been given critical consideration, but it was probably through him that a typically 1960s historicism established itself, thus posing considerable problems for research into Mahler reception.

All the objective and formal judgements that have formed the basis of Mahler reception to date are consistent with a resolute historicism whose harmful consequences can only be unravelled through detailed study of institutions and their publishing outlets. A combining of the primary sources of music criticism with the kind of philosophy of history described by Herbert Schnädelbach in his critique of historicism would offer an entirely appropriate means of addressing the current situation: '[Historicism] is a thought process best characterised as the opposite of a "systematic" mode of thinking. Appealing to the historical variability and interconnection of all ideas and norms, it refuses to recognise a universal and eternally valid system in the scientific or philosophical interpretation of the world.'[40]

The methodological starting point had always been a concert praxis in which composers' works were presented under variable conditions. From this emerged a reception history pieced together from performances and what they revealed. Written evidence from concert programmes, newspaper discussions and literary or academic publications, determined the historical status of a work at a specific period of time. If musicological reception studies are to be defined as a multivalent method of historically analysing questions of verbal exegesis and interpretation, then it is imperative that in the future we take into account the institutional contexts from which texts have emerged and which shaped the characteristics of musical works.[41]

Historicism in Mahler reception after 1960

Different approaches from music criticism and musicology have been cited above which reveal a completely inadequate knowledge of the reality of performance history. This was the prevailing theme of reception studies up to the end of the 1980s. Two main topic areas still characterized Mahler literature: musical analysis fuelled by the critical apparatus of the nineteenth and early twentieth century, and biographically orientated literature. Well-trodden formal schemes and personal testimony together constituted the material that ultimately fashioned Mahler as a figure of the late nineteenth century. Virtually no evidence existed of research into the history of performance or interpretation. In fact, inaccurate information about performances was promulgated. Prior to 1975 Mahler was not treated as a subject suitable for scholarly activity. The American reception of Mahler was only discussed for the first time in 1991 by Danuser.

In view of all this, it appears that musicology itself has become a principal problem in reception study: a complex historicist approach has developed towards Mahler that is hard to disentangle and has settled over his work like a veil of mist. The forces of conservatism centring around Riemann have ultimately prevailed, and methodological alternatives such as those offered by Adler and Bekker, such as the latter's model of historical form-types as temporary ideal types, have not managed to gain acceptance.[42] Carl Dahlhaus has pointed out that within Mahler reception there was a distinct refusal to admit the composer into the canon of music history: 'The reception of Mahler is different again. Here the contrasting judgments associated with the recurrent clichés not only accentuated the moral, religious or aesthetic significance of his symphonies, whether positively or negatively; they also touched upon their historical stature – which not even detractors as vituperative as Hanslick or Kalbeck dared to question in the case of Wagner's music dramas.'[43] At the same time the performance history of musical works is also a history of interpretation, and this is linked to orchestras and their conductors.

Revisions

A change of direction could be detected, albeit tentatively, following the Hamburg Gustav Mahler Festival in 1989. The accompanying conference included an extensive programme of critical-historical papers, whose sharply defined questions disentangled larger issues in unprecedented detail. The papers were divided into five groups: Trends in Mahler Interpretation; Historical Significance I – Stages of Development; Historical Significance II – International Reception; Historical Significance III – Influences; Music and Text – Directions and Methods of Mahler Research.

The leading Czech musicologist Jiri Fukac discussed the significance that Mahler held for new developments in music aesthetics during the

1920s such as energetics, Gestalt theory, phenomenology and musical hermeneutics. In the section entitled 'Mahler: too complex for music aesthetics?' he writes the following: 'My painstaking, largely inconclusive reconstruction has shown that during the period of conflict-ridden, mass-media-provoking Mahler reception, both historically and systematically conceived tracts on music aesthetics, and even some of the more daring and innovative specialist trends that were just emerging, either hardly ever or only minimally – and certainly never more than partially – recognized Mahler's unique musical characteristics.'[44]

With a view to the critical rehabilitation of historical reception, those writers collected together in the section on international reception dealt with regional phases of dissemination. For example, Helmut Kirchmeyer reported on an interesting project: 'For some time now at the Robert Schumann Hochschule in Düsseldorf, field studies have been undertaken into the critical standing of individual composers within narrowly defined temporal and geographical limits, in order to contextualize positive and negative opinion, and to counter the practice of imposing on another century meanings that have arisen in this century'.[45] These conditions encourage the hope that the subdivision of the field of study reflects awareness of its problems, and that this in turn may lead to a re-formation of research activity. A three-fold division of Mahler's historical significance should distinguish between stages of development during his life, international performance history, and the compositional influences that shaped him and were exerted by him. Generally speaking, even the most widely divergent studies prove that through the investigation of historical reception a body of source material is allowed to develop which can indeed be placed in ever-changing contexts. Even so it is clear that the relational principles inherited from the past are best defined in terms of their consequences. The new Mahler reception will be measured by the degree to which it critically re-evaluates musicological principles so as to eradicate instances of historicism once and for all.

13 The history of the International Gustav Mahler Society in Vienna and the Complete Critical Edition

REINHOLD KUBIK
(*translated by* JEREMY BARHAM)

The foundation years

The history of the International Gustav Mahler Society in Vienna (henceforth IGMG) is of general interest because the organization both exemplifies, and was exemplary in, the struggles surrounding Mahler's work. It was founded on 11 November 1955, ten years after the end of the holocaust. Today Mahler has reached Olympian heights of recognition, even adoration, but at that time his work was as controversial as it had been during his lifetime. The catastrophic Nazi reign, with its ideological antecedents stretching back to the nineteenth century, contributed its share to this in Germany and Austria. However, to blame the neglect of Mahler's music on this alone would not represent the whole truth. There were only a few musicians throughout the world who believed in Mahler at that time and who occasionally performed a small number of his works in England, Scandinavia, the Soviet Union and the USA. The collection of concert programmes in the IGMG archive offers convincing proof that the much-discussed, surprisingly rapid 'Mahler boom' did not come into full effect until the 1970s.

The initiative for the founding of the IGMG came from the Vienna Philharmonic Orchestra. Its stance towards Mahler had always been ambivalent: affection and disapproval had played equal parts in their work with him during his appointment as Director of the Vienna Opera.[1] Although the orchestra had dishonoured itself because of the way it treated Jewish members during the time of the Third Reich,[2] it did perform Mahler's First Symphony again on 3 June 1945, a few weeks after the end of the war, and it took over the costs of maintaining Mahler's grave in the cemetery at Grinzing. On 4 May 1954 the orchestra asked Bruno Walter to take on the office of President of the soon-to-be-founded Mahler Society. Walter replied on 16 May: 'I am of course prepared with heartfelt willingness to take on the post of President of the Mahler Society which is to be founded ... For now I should like to suggest that you get in touch with Mrs Alma Mahler-Werfel. Your idea will certainly resonate with her.'[3] However, this was not the case. In October 1954 Alma wrote the following to the Board of Directors of the Philharmonic: 'I must say in all honesty that I have no interest in your establishing a society, at least for the time being. Given the way in which the Austrian state and the Vienna Philharmonic have behaved and still behave towards Mahler's work and particularly towards me, you will understand this' – a letter which contained some completely unfounded accusations. Despite this the Philharmonic did not give up, and continued to underline forcefully the need for such a society, if for no other reason than the urgent requirement to preserve and maintain existing memorials. Caring for Mahler's music was certainly the most important thing, but, as Alma Mahler noted, one could not 'ignore the fact that there are many people for whom appearances are important. The proof of this is that all year long so many people come from England, America etc. to see the "Mahler Häuschen" on the Attersee; these are Mahler enthusiasts who then have to learn that this "Mahler Häuschen" has been empty for years and is being used as a *laundry room*!!' In the end Alma did change her mind, and lent extensive support to the work of the IGMG until her death, amongst other things giving permission for all the manuscripts in her possession to be microfilmed and used in the preparation of the Complete Critical Edition.

On 11 November 1955 the constituent general assembly took place in the conference hall of the Vienna Philharmonic. Names such as Helene Berg, Emilie Bittner, Josef Polnauer, Otto Erich Deutsch, Emanuela Krenek, Harold Byrns, Heinrich Kralik and Elisabeth Wellesz were on the list of attendees. Erwin Ratz was elected President, Bruno Walter as Honorary President and Alma Mahler as Honorary Member. The first executive committee included, among others, Theodor W. Adorno, Ernst Krenek, Rafael Kubelik, Rudolf Mengelberg, Donald Mitchell, Eduard Reeser, Alfred Rosé and George Solti, as well as the leading officials of the Philharmonic at that time, Hermann Obermeyer and Helmut Wobisch. The orchestra donated a considerable amount of money towards the founding of the IGMG, and also advertised it assiduously by putting inserts into their concert programmes stating 'to affirm your wish to be a member please go to the office of the Vienna Philharmonic'.

The aims of the IGMG were laid down in its statutes:

(1) To promote Gustav Mahler's work through performances, the production of records and other sound media, the encouragement and support of academic work, making initial contacts with radio stations, and lectures.
(2) To set up a Gustav Mahler archive for which photocopies of complete manuscripts, sketches, letters and other documents are to be produced and made available for academic research.
(3) To set up a library which is to encompass all writings about Gustav Mahler.

(4) To prepare and publish a Complete Critical Edition of Gustav Mahler's works.
(5) To produce a series of publications in which the results of Mahler research may from time to time be disseminated.
(6) To maintain the memorials which are associated with his work.

It was not easy to implement all this. For example, the owners of source material relating to Mahler were largely unknown and had to be painstakingly sought out. Also, 'photocopying' meant at that time 'photographing' – a relatively expensive and lengthy process. Radio broadcasters mostly adopted an attitude of 'wait and see', and some of the publishing houses were cautious. Erwin Ratz had to rely to a large extent on his own resources, running the IGMG from his home which in practice consisted of a library and a work room only.[4] Without the active help of Emmy Hauswirth, who worked without payment for the IGMG until her death in 2000, this would all have been impossible. A moving letter from Erwin Ratz to Egon Wellesz, dated 2 October 1956, reveals how great the burden must have been for this unassuming academic:

> A year ago I was approached and asked to take on the leadership role. *I refused.* I hate any contact with the public, and am neither vain nor ambitious . . . With a heavy heart I agreed to it, and have bitterly regretted it. *My life is destroyed* and I have but one wish, to resign as soon as possible . . . the President is indeed the 'maid-of-all-work'. Not only does he have to have ideas, but he also has to execute them, dictate all the letters etc., and do all this in an honorary capacity . . . but where am I to find someone who will do this work?

Between 1956 and 1959 branches were set up in the Netherlands, the USA, Sweden, Japan and Germany. In 1958 commemorative plaques were put up in Toblach and the first 'Gold Medal for Special Services to Mahler's Work' was awarded (to Carl Schuricht). The gold medal is still awarded today at intermittent intervals at the discretion of the executive committee. Recipients have included orchestras such as the Concertgebouw, the Dresden Philharmonic, the Vienna Philharmonic and the Vienna Symphony, the conductors Eduard van Beinum, Rafael Kubelik, Dimitri Mitropoulos, Leonard Bernstein, Bernard Haitink, Josef Krips, Hans Swarowsky, Carlo Maria Giulini, Vaclav Neumann and Claudio Abbado, singers including Christa Ludwig, Dietrich Fischer-Dieskau, Marjana Lipovsek and Thomas Hampson, as well the musicologists Donald Mitchell and Edward Reilly. In 1959 a memorial plaque was unveiled in Steinbach am Attersee.

In the centenary year 1960, the Seventh Symphony appeared as the first volume of the Complete Critical Edition. But even the events of the anniversary year did not ensure the continued growth of Mahler's public profile. A letter from Erwin Ratz to Jascha Horenstein reveals the reservations felt towards Mahler. The Ninth Symphony had been chosen for a celebratory concert in Vienna, although Ratz had repeatedly argued for the Seventh:

> It is infuriating that it is always just the First, Second, Fourth and *Das Lied von der Erde* that are performed, and that no one knows the great works like the Sixth and the Seventh. I don't know whether you have ever studied the Seventh or whether you want to conduct it at all. But if the work does mean something to you, you must write a letter to Dr Seefehlner [the Director of the *Gesellschaft der Musikfreunde* at the time] and tell him that, because of its extraordinarily pessimistic and sombre character, the Ninth is not suitable for a celebratory concert. I am making this suggestion to you because I can already predict how people will react to the Ninth. To my great dismay I have had to experience this not only in Vienna but also in Amsterdam and other places. It is above all the ironic and bitter nature of the middle movements in which people see their own reflection and to which they then react so bitterly.

However, only a few years later in 1967 the complete symphonies were recorded for the first time by Leonard Bernstein. In 1969 Kurt Blaukopf's highly influential book *Mahler oder der Zeitgenosse der Zukunft* (*Mahler or the Contemporary of the Future*)[5] appeared. The future, in which the IGMG was to play a considerable role, had begun.

The period after Ratz

Erwin Ratz died in 1973 and Gottfried von Einem became the new President. Karl Heinz Füssl took over the Complete Critical Edition and Kurt Blaukopf the archive. In 1975 the IGMG moved to its current premises at Wiedner Gürtel 6. In 1976 the first issue of *News about Mahler Research* (*Nachrichten zur Mahler-Forschung*) appeared, followed in 1978 by the first publication in the series 'Bibliothek der IGMG', Edward R. Reilly's book *Gustav Mahler und Guido Adler*,[6] and in 1980 by the correspondence between Mahler and Richard Strauss, edited by Herta Blaukopf.[7] In 1979 the IGMG acted as co-organizers of a Mahler Colloquium in Vienna, mounting a photographic exhibition first seen in the Vienna Opera House and after that as a temporary exhibition in thirty-four countries until 1990. In 1981 a memorial plaque was put up on Mahler's long-time Vienna home, Auenbruggergasse 2. 1982 saw the publication of Mahler's letters and 1983 that of the 'unknown letters', both again edited by Herta Blaukopf.[8] In 1985, after long and difficult negotiations which protected it from demolition, the composing house on the Attersee was opened, having been moved about twenty metres and completely renovated. The IGMG installed cabinets displaying information as they had done in the composing hut at Maiernigg on the Wörthersee which opened to the public in 1986.

In 1991 Gottfried von Einem handed over the Presidency to Rainer Bischof, Secretary General of the Vienna Symphonic Orchestra and a successful composer in his own right. In 1992 after the sudden and untimely death of Karl Heinz Füssl, Reinhold Kubik was appointed the new Chief Editor of the Complete Critical Edition. In the same year the composing hut in Toblach was opened to the public. In 1994 the IGMG entered the electronic age, beginning with the data-processed inventory of the contents of the library and the archives. The American pianist Frank Fanning, who lives in Vienna, created the homepage and has managed the Society's internet site since 2001 (www.gustav-mahler.org). The biannual *News about Mahler Research* has developed into an internationally recognized specialist journal under Erich Wolfgang Partsch's leadership. Meanwhile the archive has become vast: at present it contains hundreds of books, catalogues, conference reports, doctoral and other theses; about 2,000 articles from specialist journals and papers (including reviews from Mahler's time); programmes, programme booklets and posters (with some originals); photocopies or transcripts of more than 1,500 letters from, to and about Mahler; a large visual archive (photographs of Mahler, his family, his circle of friends, his places of work, innumerable cartoons of Mahler, the signed portrait by Fritz Erler and Benno Mahler's silhouettes); nearly all known Mahler autographs either copied or on microfilm, first editions, scores with Mahler's markings (full scores, piano reductions, song editions, complete orchestral parts, engravers plates and brush proofs), new editions and compositions dedicated to Mahler by various composers; sound recordings (amongst them early shellac records and live recordings from early radio broadcasts) and electronic imaging; and other memorabilia (including cuff-links). Not to be forgotten are the documents from the history of the IGMG itself, including correspondence to and from Alma, Anna and Fritz Mahler, Bruno Walter, Rafael Kubelik, Theodor W Adorno, Ernst Krenek, Egon Wellesz, Leonard Bernstein, Luigi Dallapiccola, H. C. Robbins Landon, Györgi Ligeti, Charles Mackerras, Klaus Pringsheim, Willi Reich, Hans Rosbaud, Georg Solti and many others. In all the IGMG archive is a significant centre for Mahler documentation which is consulted by many researchers, students and interested parties.

The Complete Critical Edition

In a letter of 6 February 1956 to Erwin Ratz, Kurt Radecke of the publishers Bote and Bock stated:

> I must still seriously question your optimism that there would be no
> difficulty in making Mahler's music as popular as Bruckner symphonies. It

may be that in Austria, the composer's homeland, a special fondness exists
or rather could be re-awakened, but in Germany the occasional performances
of Mahler's symphonies have proved that the outcome would not be the same
as in Austria . . . If we nonetheless decide to become a full member of your
Society, we will do so because we do not wish to boycott the endeavours of the
IGMG, and wish to show you that for our part we would like to contribute,
even if we are in no way convinced of a successful outcome.

These sentences highlight the immense difficulties with which the
Complete Critical Edition initially struggled. Ratz had gone to Bote and
Bock because of the number of mistakes in the old edition of the Seventh
Symphony. The plan to produce a new version within the context of a
Complete Critical Edition developed gradually and not unproblemati-
cally from this contact. On 13 November 1956 Radecke wrote to Ratz again:
'It was never a question of you producing a revised edition for us . . . The
results of your revision of course remain the property of your Society for the
time being, unless we come to another agreement with you.' This raised
another important problem: Mahler's music was under copyright in Europe
until 1981. This was why it was decided that the planned volumes of the
Complete Critical Edition would be produced by whichever publisher
owned the copyright.

The poor economic situation of the time combined with the fact that
Mahler's music was performed only sporadically, thereby leading to the
belief that little money was to be made from it, unfortunately meant that
editions appeared which from today's standpoint do not bear comparison
with other complete critical editions such as those of Bach, Mozart or
Schubert. On the 12 March 1960 Ratz wrote to Josef Rufer:

Dear friend, I have just had a letter from Bote and Bock which made me feel
most bitter. Bote and Bock are asking me to agree that there should be no
critical commentary. That is absolutely out of the question . . . Everybody
familiar with my critical commentaries knows that unlike all other publishers,
I keep these extremely succinct . . . In my critical commentary not a single one
of the First edition's c. 500 printing errors is recorded . . . for any intelligent
person can recognise an obvious printing error when they see one.

This reveals two things: the attempt by the publisher to economize on the
edition's already modest amount of written commentary, and Ratz's
misunderstanding of the content and function of a critical report. The
report that was eventually included in the edition took only four pages to
deal with the whole of the Symphony. In order to save on expense, the
scores were not newly set but the print layout of the old plates was
preserved with added corrections. The sceptical attitude of publishing
houses is also evident in a letter from Peters in Leipzig dated 7 August

1968: 'Of course the project as you have proposed it (new edition of score and parts [of the Fifth Symphony]) presents not inconsiderable financial problems for us, particularly since, however confident one is in Mahler's future development, repayment of the necessary investments may take an inordinately long period of time'.

Moreover, Erwin Ratz was no trained philologist, nor did his interests constitute those of a historian concerned, for example, with biography; rather he was a 'structural analyst schooled in the Schoenberg circle'.[9] It was therefore not his intention to produce a Critical Edition in the strict sense of the term. First of all he wanted to provide usable performance material for practical musical purposes as quickly as possible, and secondly he wanted to publish 'Fassungen letzter Hand'.[10] The different stages in the genesis of a work – sketches, short score, fair copy, engraver's plates, corrections, first edition and subsequent revisions – did not interest him as such. This meant that at most he only compared the first published edition with the last stage of revisions and scarcely referred to any other sources that came before or between. For him it was not the process that mattered but solely the result, the 'final version'. This stance became increasingly entrenched as the Complete Critical Edition began to appear. At a time when so many publishers were likely to have accepted a substantial critical report, Ratz restrained himself: the critical report of his last publication, that of the Third Symphony (1972), took up no more half a page.

Although he had a series of advisors, including Josef Polnauer, Erwin Stein, Friedrich Wildgans and Karl Heinz Füssl, Ratz wanted to make all final publishing decisions himself. This was not always to the edition's advantage, as demonstrated, for example, by the history of the ordering of the middle movements of the Sixth Symphony. Ratz's claim that Mahler would have revoked the change in the order of movements made at the time of the first performance was not supported by credible documentary sources but made because he thought he could prove on purely analytical grounds that this was the only order appropriate to the structure of the work.[11] Ratz's arbitrary decision provoked a discussion which lacked any objective foundation, and, more importantly, influenced the perception of a whole generation of musicians and listeners.

When Deryck Cooke's new performing version of the Tenth Symphony appeared, Ratz went on the warpath. He vehemently rejected all attempts to complete the work and only approved of the edition of the Adagio and surviving sketch materials. This duly appeared in 1967, co-produced by the publishers Ricke (Munich) and Laurin (Meran).

Despite all the genuine objections that one might have to Ratz's work, his courageous and tireless pioneering efforts should be acknowledged.

To be sure, his successor Karl Heinz Füssl immediately had to correct some of the early editions and provide rather more extensive critical reports, but he did this without fundamentally deviating from Ratz's programme. At first Füssl called in other editors such as Zoltan Roman, Peter Revers, Stephen Hefling, Sander Wilkens and Renate Hilmar-Voit. The volumes that appeared under Füssl's aegis comply much more closely with the demands of a critical edition. However, assigning the new edition of the First Symphony to Sander Wilkens unfortunately proved to be a mistake. His confused arguments in support of the claim that the famous double-bass solo at the beginning of the third movement was a solo for the whole group rather than for a single player contradicted the sources and surviving reports of performances under Mahler's direction, and exposed the Critical Edition to ridicule from all Mahler researchers. The first Critical Edition worthy of the name was that of the piano versions of the *Wunderhornlieder* edited by Renate Hilmar-Voit. At the beginning of the process, the orchestral and piano versions were still being compared in order to iron out any differences. When I took over the editorship of the Complete Edition in 1992 after the untimely death of Karl Heinz Füssl, I put an immediate stop to this and gave the go-ahead for further extensive research, generously supported by Thomas Hampson, which highlighted the independent status of the piano versions. Furthermore, this edition was the first to contain an authoritative and appropriately wide-ranging critical commentary documenting the comparison of sources and substantiating the choice of readings.

In contrast to my predecessors I am a historian and philologist with editorial experience gained mostly from the Tübingen School which, represented by Georg von Dadelsen, Walther Dürr, Thomas Kohlhase and others, has played a part in important editions such as 'Das Erbe deutscher Musik', the 'Neue Bach-Ausgabe' and the 'Neue Schubert-Ausgabe'. The individual stages in a work's development not only constitute for me an important technical foundation for editorial practice, but also convey 'aesthetic' insights into the creative process which we would not otherwise have. It is my conviction that many of Mahler's early versions which he later reworked (or even rejected) have the right to exist, as long as the primary position of the 'Fassungen letzter Hand' is not infringed as a result. Many of Mahler's comments reveal that this was an absolute, undisputed priority for him. While his rejection of earlier stages of work may have been entirely a matter for him alone, for subsequent generations these early versions are not only considerably informative but also have their own independent aesthetic appeal. Mahler's instrumental technique gradually became more and more refined, matching his later stylistic development. However, he applied this technique indiscriminately to early works, thereby increasing their refinement whilst arguably diminishing the freshness and naturalness of the first versions. Mahler's comment in 1911 regarding his Fifth Symphony that he could not understand how he 'still had to make such mistakes' in the orchestration 'like the merest beginner',[12] makes me curious about these 'beginner's mistakes'. Studying his music is something I consider to be just as important and enriching as enabling his music to be heard. I also believe that it is not only the academic world that has gained from the publication of, for example, the early three-movement version of *Das Klagende Lied*. I am convinced that this version has just as much value for us musically – quite apart from the fact that we now know as a result of the source study required for the preparation of the edition, that Mahler only removed 'Waldmärchen' after the three-movement version of the work had been rejected by the publishers Schott.[13] I also intend to publish the 1893 five-movement Hamburg version of the First Symphony, the only one that may justifiably use the title 'Titan'. Having had experience of dealing with different versions of works, I believe very strongly that hybrid editions should be avoided at all costs. Thus on no account should either the 'Blumine' movement be included in the 'Letztfassung' (final, authoritative edition) of the First Symphony, or 'Waldmärchen' be combined with the two-movement version of *Das Klagende Lied* which was published in 1898.

The aim of the coming years will be to republish all previous volumes in accordance with the standards of a true critical edition. A start has been made with the new editions of the Fifth and Second Symphonies. 'Titan', and volumes containing Mahler's poetry and his *Retuschen* (including those to Beethoven's Third, Fifth and Ninth Symphonies) are to appear in the Supplement. A final, comprehensive work list is planned, somewhat fittingly since it was a 'small' work list that marked the beginning of the IGMG's publishing activities in 1958.

14 Musical languages of love and death: Mahler's compositional legacy

STEPHEN DOWNES

Introduction

Mahler's posthumous image is resolutely ambiguous. Appropriated as 'emblematic artist of modernity' or revered as a 'prophet of modernism' he has also, by contrast, been viewed as a 'model of the postmodern', and thus 'emblematic of the emancipation from modernism'. To others he is a relic of a romantic aesthetic, to be eschewed or disavowed. Adorno was an outspoken advocate of the need for progressive, advanced material, but his Mahler writings suggest an alternative, coexistent modernist practice in which manifold layers of meaning and structure are created by the combination of esoteric, immanent configurations with exoteric objects that invite intertextual associations.[1] For Donald Mitchell, similarly to Adorno, Mahler's 'radical modernity' is located in the 'multilayered, multi-dimensional character of the symphonies'. Against charges of Mahler's tendency to nostalgia, Mitchell argues that 'the great debate with the past was built into the very fabric of Mahler's symphonies and forms an inescapable part of his modernity'.[2] This complex relationship with cultural precedents is strikingly characterized in Adorno's image of Mahler's music as ghostly *reveille* in which shadowy, old materials reawake into new life and meaning. The range cast by Mahler's own shadow over the century which followed him is vast.[3] I will consider four areas: musical developments in Vienna, songs and operas of love and the night, aspects of symphonic syntax, and compositional reactions to his last completed work, the Ninth Symphony.

Musical 'Viennese'

Schoenberg's relationship to Mahler was ambivalent. He once confessed that between 1925 and 1935 he 'did not dare to study Mahler' for fear that his early aversion might return. His enthusiasm for Mahler's Third Symphony, declared in 1904, lay more on metaphysical rather than technical, compositional grounds, and his later characterization of Mahler as progressive was part of a search for his own legitimization through the construction of an ancestral lineage.[4] In 1949 he stated that he only came to understand Mahler after his 'symphonic style' could no longer influence him, but admitted that Mahler's 'strongly tonal structure' and 'more sustained harmony' may be reflected in works such as the Orchestral Songs op. 8 (1906). In this set, however, it is only 'Sehnsucht' – a *Das Knaben Wunderhorn* setting whose affective quality is based largely on bittersweet, modally mixed mediant relationships – which is close to a Mahlerian style. Schoenberg, as he declared, had already embarked on the 'rapid advance in the direction of extended tonality', exemplified by *Pelléas and Mélisande* op. 5 (1902–3).[5]

In the 1912 'Gustav Mahler' essay, which is arguably more a self-portrait than one of Mahler,[6] Schoenberg speaks of the overwhelming physical impact made on him by the Second Symphony.[7] On hearing the Seventh in 1909 he found, by contrast with a 'sensational intensity' which might too quickly fade, a more 'permanent impression' and 'perfect repose based on artistic harmony'.[8] This seemed to chime more closely with Schoenberg's own aims, reflected for example, in the 'warmth' turned to 'extreme of coolness', in a move towards a negation of hyper-expressive post-romanticism, that Adorno described in the Chamber Symphony op. 9.[9] Mahler's sustained applause in the face of a hostile audience at op. 9's first performance (1907) exemplified his public support for the struggling Schoenberg. At the time this was a risky stance to take, and one especially notable as he confessed to finding Schoenberg's new direction perplexing. When Mahler left Vienna for New York in December 1907 Schoenberg experienced something of an emotional crisis.[10] Only days later he composed 'Ich darf nicht dankend . . .' op. 14 no. 1, a setting of Stefan George's confessions to his muse, Ida Coblenz, which Schoenberg may have read as a poetic parallel to his sense of indebtedness to Mahler. The song's opening chords, harmonic relatives of the fourths in op. 9, are the source of material for an organic developmental process. In his *Harmonielehre* – the first edition (1911) was dedicated to the memory of Mahler the 'martyr' – Schoenberg cites 'certain quartal progressions' in Mahler, and the 'peculiar freshness that emanates from these chords', through which 'the future of our music speaks'.[11] The passages of fourth chords and thinner textures in 'Ich darf . . .' foreshadow the last of Schoenberg's *Six Little Piano Pieces* op. 19 (1911). According to Egon Wellesz, this piece was Schoenberg's response to Mahler's funeral, but its aphoristic abstraction marks Schoenberg's distance at this time from a Mahlerian style and aesthetic.[12]

In Schoenberg's Chamber Symphony formal compression and Mahlerian clarity in soloistic instrumentation provided a deliberate move away from the length of the First String Quartet op. 7 and the monumentalism of

Pelléas and Mélisande. By contrast with the grandiloquent proportions of the late romantic symphony Schoenberg sought new formal solutions through principles of economy and concentration, in a reconciliation of symphonic process and chamber dimensions.[13] *Die glückliche Hand* (1913), the incomplete *Séraphita* and symphonic project of 1914–15, however, mark a re-engagement with grandiose, metaphysical religiosity which is notably post-Mahlerian. The six-movement plan of the symphony is, in programme and form, comparable to Mahler's Second and Eighth Symphonies.[14] The sketches for the symphony also mark a return to more traditional formal and thematic processes (as well as an anticipation of certain twelve-note techniques). Stylistically much closer to Mahler are parts of the *Serenade* op. 24 (1920–3), which builds on the compositional methods that Schoenberg had developed since the abortive symphony, but whose irony and parodic mix of styles 'seem to collide with [Schoenberg's] long-standing aesthetic principles'.[15] Passages of the March and Dance movements are akin to the Mahlerian fractured musical language in which, as Adorno says, 'musical immediacy and naturalness are in doubt'.[16] They are therefore comparable with the March from Berg's *Wozzeck* (1917–22), a 'combination of Mahler and Schoenberg' which in 1924 was Adorno's 'ideal of genuine new music'.

Berg's significance for Adorno lies in his 'art of mediation' which is 'tested against what cannot be mediated' through a coexistence of the static and kinetic, of juxtaposition and dialectic. In the *Three Orchestral Pieces* op. 6 (1914–15) which he considered to be Berg's 'most Mahlerian score', Adorno describes how 'fragments awake to a second and catastrophic significance' in 'montage, allegory and terror', in a pursuit of the implications of the broken, allegorical quality of Mahler's symphonic style. Berg's 'panic-stricken amalgamation of Schoenberg and Mahler' is manifest in the construction of form from motivic processes operating within 'structural ruins'.[17] The March may be modelled on the 'apocalyptic' Finale of Mahler's Sixth, but there is also, as Derrick Puffett notes, an 'aesthetic of compression'. 'Reigen' is closely related to the Scherzo of Mahler's Seventh, as gestures generate a 'parodistic nightmare' incorporating 'banal dance elements' and 'grotesquerie'.[18] Berg uses similar techniques in the Tavern scene (Act 2 scene iv) from *Wozzeck* in the 'realism' of the alcohol-fuelled Ländler, the superimposition of duple and triple dance patterns which become 'grotesque and obsessive', and the 'nightmarish distortion' of the waltz.[19] *Wozzeck*'s Symphonic Epilogue is often cited as especially Mahlerian. Allen Forte's view, that the surface of post-Mahlerian appoggiatural style masks deeper, motivic, linear and set organizations,[20] is a useful caution to a one-dimensional hearing of the music's style and structural processes. The epilogue's source, an early sketch for a piano sonata written while Berg was still a pupil of Schoenberg, is a reminder, however, that the pupil's enthusiasm for Mahler was a decidedly more straightforward position than that held by his teacher.

A crucial 'link between the Schoenberg school and Mahler' for Adorno is the Viennese 'voluptuousness' and 'rapture' in Berg's music.[21] Some of the most striking examples of this post-Mahlerian affect are found in *Lulu* (1929–35). For Judy Lochhead, Berg's appropriation of a 'gorgeously beautiful' Mahlerian style (for example in the 'Freedom' music from Act 2 scene ii, and the 'coda' music from the sonata in Act 1 scene ii) and its juxtaposition with the 'predominant "sound" of the opera' is a strategy which reveals this 'Mahlerian' music as parodic. This style, she asserts, is not an 'authentic' one for Berg by the *Lulu* period. In Act 2 scene ii Lulu's alluring 'performance' of the borrowed Mahlerian style seduces Alwa, but the listener is not fooled, Lochhead argues, because in the context of the opera it is heard as 'exaggerated' romantic sound. In the final scene Lulu's Mahlerian performance fails, to powerfully 'tragic' effect.[22] The 'Mahlerian' is typically saturated with the possibilities of double meaning. The 'Death' chord at Lulu's *Todesschrei* in the final scene (bar 1294 ff.), built up to by the return of the 'rich Mahlerian coda theme',[23] is in its pungent layered dissonances a relative of the climactic chord from the Adagio of Mahler's Tenth, which Berg knew in detail from checking Krenek's version in 1924. In *Lulu* Berg is 'authentically' Mahlerian because of the eclectic mix of sound-worlds and the proliferation of possible meanings which results.

For Webern, by contrast, Mahler's deformations of the sounds of nature suggested the possibility of rising from depictive content to abstract structure. As Julian Johnson has demonstrated, the transformation of musical constructions of nature (especially, of course, the Austrian landscape), loss and memory lie at the heart of Webern's move from romanticism to modernism. Mahlerian gestures, overt in the massive *Passacaglia* (1908) and the funereal Orchestral Piece op. 6 no. 4 (1909) are more subtly mediated in Webern's response to Mahler's late style, for example, in the opening horn calls of the Symphony op. 21 (1928) which suggest a 'distant echo' of the opening of Mahler's Ninth. In Webern's utopian project, juxtapositions of dynamic and static, and qualities of space and distance, become part of a move towards 'higher' synthesis, which sought to exorcize Mahlerian heterogeneity.[24] This highlights Mahler's second role in Webern's mapping of the path to the new, in the 'desire for maximum unity'. He particularly admired Mahler's 'polyphony', created by secondary voices which were no longer mere accompanimental figures.[25] Webern's 'Classicist' preoccupation with unity and connection should not, however, mask the elements of polarity, fragmentation and symbiosis in Webern's atonal and serial works.[26] The continuing tension between these tendencies sustains a Mahlerian dialectic between singular particulars and the demands of formal wholeness.

Zemlinsky's links to Mahler, according to Adorno, lay in his eclecticism and, particularly in the op. 13 Maeterlinck Songs (1913), a 'folk-song tone which has become darkened, enigmatic in its own eyes'.[27] Puffett's impression is that, on listening to the last of the orchestral version of these songs, we 'seem to be hearing all the *Songs of a Wayfarer*, indeed all the Mahler symphonies, rolled into one, a lifetime's experience collapsed into a few minutes of music'.[28] The opposite of this compression can be heard in the 'infinite moment' of the final song of the *Lyric Symphony* op. 18 (1922–3).[29] After a long passage of *molto adagio* string and horn polyphony, expressive dissonances in fourths (recalling perhaps both Schoenberg's 'Ich darf . . .' and parts of Mahler's Seventh) resolve to the *Augenblik* (Example 14.1). This stretching or slowing turns to apparent endlessness when fourth chords return as part of a final cadence onto a 'pan-diatonic chord with a Lydian G♯'. In the 'endless' quality, the prominent celeste, and an unresolved upper-voice sixth, lie the case for calling this Zemlinsky's response to *Das Lied von der Erde*. But there are also striking differences from Mahler. Zemlinsky's Symphony is circular and through-composed, whereas *Das Lied* is linear with separate movements, and the lush, luxuriant orchestral sonority contrasts with Mahlerian clarity.[30] Closer to the Mahlerian 'ewig' than Zemlinsky's slow closing of the eyes in an attempt to preserve a moment of rapture, is the end of Berg's Violin Concerto (1935). Here the 'tonic' B♭ 'added sixth' is, for Robert Morgan, 'almost certainly a quote' from *Das Lied*, and also a musical evocation of Nietzschean eternal return, where, in the 'moment of dying' is also the 'moment of initiation'.[31]

Nachtstücke and *Liebeslieder*

In Berg's Violin Concerto the intrusion and mediation (or otherwise) of unexpected materials (Bach chorale and Carinthian folk melody) is a direct challenge to Viennese traditions of musical connection and unity. In the apparently 'neo-classical' first movement of Mahler's Fourth Symphony the expectations of symphonic form and development are invoked only to be seriously questioned, especially by the succession of shock events from the climax of the development to the recapitulation. The effect approaches the montages of nightmare, with the recapitulation a neurotic return or awakening. In 1930 Adorno described Mahler's

Example 14.1 Zemlinsky, *Lyric Symphony*, final movement, figs. 113–16

music as that which 'rouses itself from the disintegrating dream'. He was convinced that 'all contemporary compositional technique lies ready in Mahler's work'; in Mahler's 'murky, dimly lit tone' are the seeds, for example, of both Berg's *Wozzeck* and Kurt Weill's *Aufstieg und Fall der Stadt Mahagonny* (1930).[32]

The importance of Mahler for Weill is profound, and pre-dates the collaborations with Brecht. Of the Violin Concerto (1924), whose formal scheme can be compared with Mahler's Seventh Symphony, Adorno noted the 'remarkable ... Mahlerian quality, at times garishly expressive and painfully laughing ... a dangerous, surrealistic realm'.[33]

In *Der neue Orpheus* (1925) as Orpheus conducts Mahler to challenge the ears of the bourgeois concert audience, Weill offers a parody of a Mahlerian *Totentanz*. The work's opening, a juxtaposition of hyper-expressive gestures with mechanically repeated musical objects, may be compared with the 'Schattenhaft' scherzo of Mahler's Seventh, where brutal distortions, shrieks and rude arrestings of organic, developmental process lead to superimpositions and montage. Latent in these effects are the possibilities of both expressionist and surrealist techniques. They are suggestive of highly charged, disruptive moments of hysteria or of crazy, hallucinatory montages. Weill's extension of Mahlerian possibilities are comparable not only with the opening of Schoenberg's Variations For Orchestra op. 31 (1928), whose machine effects and expressionist outbursts evoke a Mahlerian dialectic of order and disruption,[34] but also with surrealist juxtapositions related to Stravinsky's *L'Histoire du soldat* (1918) which Weill greatly admired, where shock effects reinvigorate dead forms.

Adorno's admiration for *Die Dreigroschenoper* and *Mahagonny* – which he called the 'first surrealist opera' – is based on the fact that the music's turn to the 'debris of the past' is not heard as regressive or restorative. In *Mahagonny* the epic montage of the final scenes moves from spare, skeletal expressive counterpoint (No. 19) redolent of the opening of *Kindertotenlieder*, through grotesque distortions of popular dance forms (No. 20) in the manner of the shadowy scherzo in Mahler's Seventh, and finally (in the closing Largo) summons up the ghosts of Mahler's 'soldiers' tales' of the *Wunderhorn* songs (see Example 14.2). In Weill's post-Mahlerian language old tonal forms, which have lost their original aura, gain new meanings in ironic allusions, the play of intertextual reference, and dream-like recollections and juxtapositions.

Benjamin Britten's Mahlerian awakening at hearing the Fourth Symphony in 1930 while at the Royal College of Music led him to remark that this music was 'a mix of everything that one has ever heard, but it is

Example 14.2 Excerpts from Weill, *Mahagonny*, Act 3

Example 14.2 (cont).

definitely Mahler'.[35] Christopher Mark suggests that the 'luminous diatonic passages' of the final movement of Mahler's Fourth 'may well have
contributed towards Britten's heavy investment in diatonicism', thus
partly fulfilling a 'need to distance himself' from the influence of Frank
Bridge.[36] In early works such as *Our Hunting Fathers* (1936) Mahlerian
aspects of Britten's idiom are often noted (for example, the 'Messalina'
section as 'Mahlerian Nachtmusik',[37] or the virtuosic orchestral development in the Dance of Death).[38] When he showed the poems chosen for

Example 14.2 (cont).

this work to Bridge their discussion appears to have included disagreement over the significance of Mahler.[39] Certain Mahlerian aspects of Britten's *Variations on a Theme of Frank Bridge* (1937) are therefore of special interest. A 'Mahlerian declamatory rhetoric and bittersweet harmonic pathos' has been noted in the first variation, and Mahler's influence discerned in the 'expressive pattern' of the funeral march variation,[40] but the work's last section is perhaps more telling. In his sketch Britten assigned an aspect of Bridge's personality to each variation, and with the Finale's title, 'Our affection', a relationship between composer and teacher is evoked.[41] It has been described as a 'consummatory D major', an 'incandescent' Adagio in which the influence of Mahler's 'slow symphonic perorations' may already be discerned.[42] The predominantly slow harmonic pace combines with chromatic voice-leading, and an initial melodic emphasis on the ninth expands into more passionate rhetorical arcs (see Example 14.3). A chromatic sequence then leads to piquant, hushed major–minor ambiguity. It is a highpoint, expressive of 'what love tells me'. As Britten's musical language developed, Mahler's influence mixes with that of Stravinsky, Purcell and Mozart, generating a controlling, neo-classical element which meant that 'Britten was never in any danger of attempting to out-do the late romantic Mahler in emotional extravagance'.[43]

The sense of distance, melancholy and loss in Britten's mature song cycles with orchestral accompaniment continues to echo Mahler's broken

Example 14.3 Britten, *Variations on a Theme of Frank Bridge*, figs. 40–41 + 1

or darkened pastoral idiom. The horn-led major–minor expressive signature of the setting of Blake's 'Elegy' in the *Serenade* (1943) is evocative
of this tone, and the bassoon's B♭ minor obbligato in Tennyson's 'The
Kraken' from the *Nocturne* (1958) is, in harmony and gesture, reminiscent of passages in the first movement of Mahler's Ninth (for example
twelve bars after fig. 5). The last song of *Nocturne* inhabits another
'Mahlerian mood',[44] particularly at the impassioned climax (fig. 38)
and contributes to the cycle's combination of song with the symphonic.
Mahlerian symphonism is evident in the *Sinfonia da Requiem* (1940) with
its gestures of modal juxtaposition, ironic and banal tones, and dualism
between demands of 'abstract' form and programme. Similarly
Mahlerian issues inform the *Spring Symphony* (1949) and the *Cello
Symphony* (1963). Arved Ashby has proposed that Britten's indebtedness

to Mahler may lie most profoundly in the 'conciliation of a symphonic posture with an operatic inclusiveness'.[45] The *War Requiem* (1961) suggests a Mahlerian 'embracing of the world', and the treatment of climax in the 'Libera me' has been compared with Mahler's apocalyptic visions in the Sixth and Ninth Symphonies.[46] In Britten's operas the Mahler legacy goes beyond occasional thematic likeness (often noted in *Peter Grimes*[47]) to more profound and pervasive aspects. For example, the end of *Death in Venice* (1973) may be compared with the close of the first movement of Mahler's Ninth, and beyond this the overall 'tonal effect' of the opera closely parallels the structural and expressive ambiguity underpinning Mahler's movement.[48]

In 1936 Britten remarked that the Adagietto of Mahler's Fifth left a 'nice (if erotic) taste in my mouth'.[49] Of all Mahler's symphonic movements this, of course, has achieved a popularity which threatens to fade its charms. A creative, and eroticized, relationship with the movement, however, seems to inform Hans Werner Henze's 1963 setting of 'Being Beauteous' from Rimbaud's *Illuminations*. The work is a product of Henze's move away from Darmstadt asceticism and abstraction. He was driven by a feeling of alienation and an urge to find a language of direct expressive communication. On his move to Italy in 1953 Henze sensed the freedom to discover new concepts of beauty. Mahler's music now enabled Henze 'to find a wholly personal approach to the music of the present and of the past, the trivial and the ritual music of all periods'; he was then 'able to pursue this personal path outside the "acceptable" aesthetic course of the mainstream of self-styled modern music'.[50] His music of the early 1960s resonates most powerfully with this Mahlerian aesthetic. Stylistic contradictions, garish colours, allusions to tonal formulae, the old and the banal are all employed to express obsessions with love, death and renewal at the individual and social level. Parts of the opera *The Bassarids* (1965) are infused with the spirit and material of Mahler's Fifth. In the slow third 'movement', when Pentheus, the King of Thebes, is erotically charmed by Dionysus, Henze turns to a pervasively Mahlerian expressive melody and polyphony, and allusions to the second movement of Mahler's Fifth act as signposts or landmarks, invoking 'Mahler' for psychological effects.[51] Quotations function within a heavily coded syntax in which symphonic developmental process is broken or interrupted to dramatic effect.

Symphonic syntax

The parallels between the Mahlerian enthusiasms of Britten and Shostakovich are well documented. Shostakovich's differences from Britten lie in the importance of a 'socio-political dimension' and the 'epic/heroic', both of which in part stemmed from the ideas of Iwan Sollertinsky, who knew Shostakovich from 1927.[52] Sollertinsky wrote the first book on Mahler in Russian (1932) and was a crucial figure in Shostakovich's appreciation of Mahler's music.[53] In his first three symphonies, Shostakovich deliberately distanced himself from the romantic symphonic tradition, but the closer engagement with this in the Fourth (1934) is manifest in passages of what Richard Taruskin calls 'psychological prose' and 'individual subjectivity'. There is, then, a dualism which leads to 'extremes of inwardness and extroversion, and the manifestly ironic way in which these extremes are juxtaposed and even interchanged'.[54] The symphony's 'constructivist, mechanical effect' is Mahlerian after the manner of Sollertinsky, for whom the third movement of Mahler's Ninth was evocative of 'city clangour'. An anti-human element coexists with a paradoxical move to the 'threshold of admitting neo-romantic mellowness'.[55] Mahlerian allusions are especially potent in the character of the climactic passages (figs. 31, 48): the brass build-up to the recapitulation suggests the similar structural feature in the first movement of Mahler's Second, and also the climax to the Adagio of the Tenth, which Shostakovich had transcribed for two pianos in the late 1920s. Perhaps most Mahlerian of all is the Finale's gargantuan scope and breadth of allusion – funeral march, scherzo and dance medley are all combined in one vast structure. The long fade-out coda – with celeste adding an unresolved sixth and ninth in the last bars – recalls and transforms the mechanical wind-down of the second movement into a 'muted, drawn-out whimper' which Taruskin suggests is an intentional allusion to Mahler.[56]

For Sollertinsky everything in Mahler was 'compulsive, paradoxical, nervous', 'the lyric, darkened by the grotesque, the lyric made eccentric, a profoundly humane feeling disguised by the self-protective mask of buffoonery'. He called this last effect 'Chaplinesque'.[57] The first movement of the Fifteenth Symphony (1971) evokes conflicts and contradictions with similarly Mahlerian symbolic resonances in collisions of humour and pathos, quotation and inward subjective expression, mechanical and organic, human and inhuman. In the last movement death and sex jostle together in Wagner quotations of Fate (*The Ring*) and Eros (*Tristan*), an enigmatic succession of masks and allusions.

The crisis of faith, and cultural heterogeneity celebrated in an age of anxiety underpins Leonard Bernstein's early 'Jeremiah' Symphony (1942) and Third Symphony, 'Kaddish' (1963), both of which are Mahlerian in ambition. 'Torn between romanticism and modernism', challenged by the attempt at assimilation in the face of exclusion, Bernstein created music of multiple stylistic allusions which shifts between synthesis and discontinuity.[58] His inclusive aesthetic strains to embrace the Stravinskian, the post-romantic and popular Americana. Bernstein's universalism and pluralism occasionally call to mind the oft-noted parallels between the stylistic disjunctions and intrusions in Mahler and Charles Ives.[59] But Bernstein's symphonism lacks the pervasively discomforting quality caused by the defamiliarizing distortions which Ives may have heard in Mahler's music around 1910 and, 'unnerved and perhaps inspired' by Mahler's music, pursued further in his subsequent orchestral works.[60] Mahler and Ives were identified by Alfred Schnittke as the first twentieth-century composers to use techniques of 'polystylistics'.[61] Typical of Schnittke's exploration of this technique is the 'defamiliarization' and 'estrangement' of an early Mahler scherzo fragment in the second movement of the Piano Quartet (1988), later arranged for large orchestra as part of the Fifth Symphony. Fragmentation, superimposition and diffusion lead to a final quotation of the Mahler which may be heard as a 'moment of epiphany'.[62] But the end is incomplete and inconclusive, an unanswered question reflecting Schnittke's interest in the 'open and irrational' and 'scepticism towards structural guarantees'. As Alexander Ivashkin says, Schnittke's intensification of Mahlerian contrasts and ambivalence moves towards abstraction but nonetheless remains 'enigmatic' and 'hieroglyphic' in a post-Mahlerian sense, invoking a 'polyvalent encoding and subjectivity'.[63] Schnittke extended Mahler's musical heterogeneity (the coexistence of low and high idioms) and the 'nightmarish' or 'surreal' defamiliarizations in, for example, the scherzos of Mahler's Seventh and Ninth, while also intensifying the compulsion to 'keep going' in the face of nihilism and the 'immanent collapse of progressiveness'.[64] Schnittke's music evokes 'shadows' and 'brokenness' (for example, the open-ended, 'sad and macabre waltz' in the last movement of his Seventh Symphony[65]) and the ascetic or skeletal. A reviewer of the Sixth Symphony (1992) wrote: 'When the last notes evaporated, I had the queasy feeling of having heard a Mahler symphony with most of its musical flesh torn away, leaving a gruesome skeleton dangling forlornly in a black space'.[66] Even when Schnittke alludes to Mahlerian universality, as in the First Symphony (1972), it is 'not a loving embrace', for the 'Schnittkean Tower of Babel' speaks of 'cultural alienation', of 'negative dialectics', of 'freedom-against-tyranny, and ... I-against-the-world'.[67]

Schnittke greatly admired the third movement of Berio's *Sinfonia* (1968), which is famously based on the scherzo of Mahler's Second Symphony. He heard the movement as an 'experiment designed to generate and bring about the premature destruction of the new polystylistic form'.[68] Berio was attracted by Mahler's 'vivid but ironic eclecticism' and the fact that 'Mahler's music seems to bear the weight of the entire history of music'. *Sinfonia*'s third movement is based on processes of reduction, distortion and plethoric quotation, links between Mahler and superimpositions and interpolations, and periodic saturation in chromatic clusters.[69] It resembles a musical stream of consciousness, with abundant free associations tumbling in a hallucinatory whirlwind. As David Metzer says, the 'proliferation' of Berio's 'commentary' risks rupturing 'creative continuity between past and present' and 'threatens to obliterate' the Mahlerian source.[70] *Sinfonia* is just one of many 'symphonic' works of the 1960s and 1970s which engage overtly with Mahlerian style, technique or aesthetics. The significance of Mahler for György Ligeti is evident from lectures given in the 1960s and publications of the 1970s.[71] The Mahlerian spatial aspects of *Lontano* (1967) are further developed in *Melodien* (1971).[72] Furthermore, Ligeti's symphonic procedures often bear comparison with Adorno's Mahlerian categories of 'breakthrough' and 'disintegration'.[73] Alastair Williams has shown how Wolfgang Rihm's *Dis-Kontur* (1974) and *Sub-Kontur* (1975) demonstrate a 'Mahlerian' discovery of 'new latencies in old material', a 'symphonic afterlife' is gained in an aesthetic context of 'freedom', 'inclusivity' and evocations of the 'sublime'. The 1974 work includes a Mahlerian march, intense hammer blows and a 'transcendent' adagio, aspects of which may be attributed not only to the Mahler revival but also the legacy of Stockhausen.[74]

In 1972 Stockhausen wrote that 'Mahler is a universal being within whom all threads converge': in Mahler's music 'past, present and future merge'.[75] This utopian inclusivity is found in Stockhausen's *Hymnen* (1967). Here, through techniques of 'intermodulation', the musical work seeks to contain the whole world, a *Weltmusik* in which the 'familiar' and the 'abstract', materials with a past and those with no past (the new and the now) coexist.[76] Pierre Boulez, by contrast, in his desire to purge the past and extol cultural 'amnesia', famously condemned quotation as a 'shrunken and accepted form of death'.[77] Yet, writing in 1979 Boulez believed that Mahler's time had come: 'incongruities . . . quotation and parody' lead to listening in a 'richer', more 'varied' way. Nostalgia, far from being a fatal condition, is productively joined with a 'critical attitude', and 'banal' gestures 'mask paroxysms of insecurity'. He saw that 'contemporary music had finished its ascetic period' and had moved 'towards the luxuriant', a search for 'richness', 'proliferation' and 'ambiguity'.[78] At the height of 'Darmstadtian' modernism, in which Mahler's historical significance and contemporary relevance were largely dismissed, Dieter Schnebel wrote that the consequence of Mahler's layered orchestral textures was that 'traditional modes of thought like melody, accompaniment, theme, etc. lose their meaning' and are replaced by a 'tendency toward spatial division of sound bodies – space music'.[79] In the late 1960s

Schnebel's own music exhibited a break in style, towards Mahlerian expressivity, as personal, social and artistic motivations urged him to find a more directly communicative idiom, for example in a series of works entitled *Re-Visionen* (1970–89), including *Mahler-Moment* for strings (1985).

Remembering/dismembering the Ninth

Kurt Weill commented in 1926 that Mahler's Ninth 'already anticipated most of what the musical development of recent years has achieved'.[80] The Ninth has a rich 'posthumous' life either as inspirational spectre or disinterred fragment, in technical compositional process, emotive affect and spiritual renewal. It has been a focus for late twentieth-century reinterpretations of Mahler's metaphysics and symphonism, and a recurrent incentive to compositional exploration of their conjunction. Comparisons have been made between the thematic transformations, consonance–dissonance relationships and teleology of the first movement of Mahler's Ninth and Peter Maxwell Davies's *Second Taverner Fantasia* (1964). The *Fantasia* is especially Mahlerian in its tense, ironic relationship between surface sound and gesture and deep, hidden meaning generated by 'tragic contradictions, grotesque distortions and illusions'.[81] The 'cryptic coda' to a 'luminous Mahlerian Adagio', it has been suggested, 'opened up further symphonic possibilities' for Maxwell Davies.[82] In the First Symphony (1976) he engaged with the symphonic legacies of Beethoven and Sibelius, and in the Third (1984) explicitly turned to Mahler's Ninth. This is reflected in its structural plan, such as the 'window' in the third movement which offers a glimpse of the slow Finale, and the ending of the first movement.[83] Arnold Whittall has noted conflicts between 'rooted' and 'floating' textures which underpin Maxwell Davies's 'modernist doubt' about the 'capacity to ensure stability' through structural closure in D. This contrasts with Mahler's first movement, in which the goal of D is questioned but finally achieved, not destroyed. The more radical interrogation and conflict in Maxwell Davies's symphony confirms, as the composer himself famously said, that there can be no 'easy return to old tonality'.[84]

Interruptions, moments of crisis and the problem of closure and resolution are generated by the Mahler fragments in George Rochberg's *Music for the Magic Theater* (1965). In the montage of the first movement, intertextual references to the first and fourth movements of Mahler's Ninth can be heard to lie between music of the diatonic past (Mozart) and that of the dissonant present (Varèse). In Rochberg's 'ars combinatoria', links are sought between collage and continuity, the past and present, the nostalgic and the advanced, as the concept of linear time collapses.[85] The 'idea of history as "progress" was no longer viable' for Rochberg, and the 'radical avant-garde' was now 'bankrupt'.[86] In the Third String Quartet (1972) the 'aesthetics of survival' work against time and death in which allusive references to the music of the past are 'distant visions of sorrow and love'.[87] The evocation of a Mahlerian style in the quartet's fifth movement is clearly derived from the Finale of the Ninth Symphony. Rochberg's allusions reflect his belief in Mahler's continuing contemporary relevance, and his shared preoccupation with loss, nostalgia and the desire for renewal.[88]

Mahler's Ninth is also a model of spiritual and creative renewal for Jonathan Harvey. In the first movement of Mahler's Ninth, he hears the 'musical subject' being 'led out of shadows' in a 'utopian attempt to create order'. Harvey views the compositional process as the assembling of 'dark conflicts and contradictions in an intuitive drive toward the promised land of unity' and Mahler, a self-confessed kind of vessel or medium, is raised as a model example of this creativity. In the 3–2 motive of the Ninth and its recurrence in the oriental temporalities and symmetrical pentatonicism of *Das Lied von de Erde* he perceives the vision of a 'rebirth and a dissolution into wholeness' after the 'horrific death of the subject'. This compares with both the spiritual trajectory and the musical materials of Harvey's *Madonna of Winter and Spring* for orchestra and live electronics (1986), or the *Song Offerings* (1985), a setting of divine love poems by Tagore.[89] Roger Smalley's Symphony (1981–2) evokes a redemptive journey through funereal depths and a demonic scherzo in music suggestive of a post-Mahlerian semantic world. This is overt in *Konzertstücke* (1980) which, like the symphony, is a continuous multi-movement design. In the opening 'Romanze' (variations 1–4) slow, lyrical material on strings and harp distantly recall the Adagietto of Mahler's Fifth. In the expressive content of both the second trio of the Scherzo (variation 8), marked 'vulgar and brutal' and the third section, titled 'Nachtmusik', the Mahlerian associations become more overt (variation 11 is marked 'Schattenhaft'). In the fourth section 'Cadenza' (variation 13, bars 284–6) there is a quotation of an important brass figure from the first movement of Mahler's Ninth (fig. 13), here transfigured by the whole-tone harmony which surrounds it.[90] The quotation functions as a kind of signpost, a window into the music's dark soul. It is a symbolic moment, comparable with the Mahler allusion in Henze's *The Bassarids*, part of a coded musical syntax. Material from Mahler's Ninth plays a more thorough structural as well as expressive-symbolic role in Michael Finnissy's String Trio (1986). A pitch sequence extracted from the motives of the opening of the Symphony, transposed up a minor third, becomes the 'generating interval' employed as drones and pedal points and a 'broken cantus firmus'.[91] The minor-third motive from the opening of the Ninth is a 'structural determinant' in the Trio, part of 'one huge parody' as the work quotes Mahler's tempo instructions and 'takes as its framework the psychological programme of the first movement of Mahler's Ninth', generating an 'intimate and expressive world'.[92] It is yet another example of old materials resurrected in new complexity, one of a legion contributing to the picture of Mahler's posthumous identity as both oracle and sphinx. The legacy remains as fascinating, yet as puzzling as the inscrutable expression on his death mask which so enthralled Adorno.

15 Mahler conducted and recorded: from the concert hall to DVD

LEWIS M. SMOLEY

If the number of recordings and concert performances is any indication, the post-1960s Mahler boom was not just a passing fancy. Rather, the public has taken Mahler to their collective hearts, assigning him a stature virtually equal to that of the idolized masters of the symphony, Beethoven and Brahms, as their successor. During Mahler's lifetime few but he would have dreamed that his works would achieve such stature. It has been less than a full century since he died, and we are now witnessing what Mahler predicted: that his time has surely come.

Performances by Mahler and his followers

But it was not so when Mahler lived. Despite his celebrity as a conductor, when he tried to foster his own music the results were far from consistently successful. He did have the early encouragement and support of Richard Strauss, who was the first conductor other than Mahler to perform one of the symphonies, giving the First in Weimar in 1894 and the Second in Berlin in 1895.

Mahler premièred all of his orchestral works except the last three (*Das Lied von der Erde*, the Ninth and the unfinished Tenth) to mixed reactions. As an operatic conductor he had no equal, but as a conductor of symphonic music it would appear that critical and public acclaim was more dearly sought and not always found. In the period *c.* 1890–1910, continental European audiences and critics measured every new symphonic work against their heroes, Beethoven and Brahms. By comparison, Mahler's symphonies, although conducted by the composer, were often received with confusion and even disdain because of their erratic structural complications, extreme length, difficult, banal and sometimes ugly tunes, commonplace marches and waltzes that seemed out of place in a symphony, and incomprehensible disorienting interjections.[1] Just when Mahler's audiences seemed to adjust after a few hearings of his early symphonies, he would put them off with the next one. But the lyrical beauty of, for example, *II (ii)* and *III (ii)*,[2] was undeniable. With the advent of the Third Symphony, the public seemed to come round despite its enormous length – the première being a resounding, and for Mahler unprecedented, success.[3] But the Fourth, so very different, enraged the Viennese public, who thought its stylistic references to their beloved Haydn, Mozart and Schubert a virtual insult. Viennese critics took the Symphony to task as a pastiche of 'contrived naïvetés' and impertinent quotations.[4] Premières of the abstract, morose and structurally complex middle symphonies were received with mixed reviews.[5] Only that of the Eighth, in Munich the year before Mahler died, was an unmitigated success. Yet Mahler instinctively knew that greater familiarity and the passage of time would work to the advantage of his music, and he was undoubtedly right.

Fried, Mengelberg and Walter

Mahler's extraordinarily detailed score notations revealed his concern about entrusting the performance of his works to others. Besides Richard Strauss, he worked closely with two contemporary conductors who championed his music: Oskar Fried and Willem Mengelberg. Mahler laboured over lengthy notes that he sent to Fried advising him on details for a performance of the Second Symphony. We are fortunate that a performance of that symphony conducted by Fried in Berlin in 1924 was recorded, the very first Mahler symphony recording, which introduced untold numbers of new listeners to Mahler's music. Mengelberg, perhaps Mahler's closest colleague, with whose interpretations he seemed quite satisfied, was entrusted by the composer with a substantial number of performances of his symphonies.[6] This might seem rather startling, given the wayward, indulgent manner of Mengelberg's performance of the Fourth, recorded many years later (9 November 1939) with the RCO[7] at a performance in Amsterdam. It is difficult to tell whether this recorded Fourth is a true example of how Mengelberg conducted Mahler's music when the composer was present (as he was for most of Mengelberg's Mahler performances). In 1920, Mengelberg also organized the first Mahler Festival, a series of concerts with the RCO in Amsterdam, the one city that embraced his music without reservation.

Mahler also shared his music and musical philosophy with Bruno Walter, a rising young conductor whom he met in Hamburg in 1894 and immediately recognized as a kindred spirit as well as an enormously talented musician. His first-hand exposure to Mahler's rehearsal and performance practices and his many conversations with the composer deepened his understanding of Mahler's works. Walter conducted the Third Symphony, a work that Mahler discussed with him on several occasions, in Vienna and Munich during the composer's lifetime (1909). Walter's interpretative orientation reflected his gentle nature, quite different from the composer's erratic, highly intense and occasionally insensitive manner. His Mahler performances were therefore sometimes criticized for toning down the demonic side of Mahler's musical persona – although one experiences none of this in his scathing performances of 'Das Trinklied' from *Das Lied von der Erde* – or for tempering the modernistic effects and dynamic extremes of the later symphonies.[8] Unmitigated tragedy was also alien to Walter's sensibilities. Consequently, he distanced himself from (and never performed) the Sixth Symphony; for him it was 'bleakly pessimistic' and 'reeks of the bitter taste of the cup of life'.[9]

Walter demanded complete faithfulness to every detail of a score. His performances in Europe and the United States set the standard for Mahler interpretation for an entire generation, although it was a standard formed from Walter's essential conservatism and spiritual orientation which imbued the music with majestic power and transcendent beauty. Richard Specht suggested that 'Walter was more romantic, more dreamy, more exuberant ... not so fierce in the execution of climaxes, and often had for all that something wavering, irregular, since he gave himself up extemporaneously to his sudden inspirations'.[10] Walter was entrusted with conducting the posthumous premières of *Das Lied von der Erde* (Munich, 20 November 1911, strangely coupled with the Second Symphony) and the Ninth (Vienna, 26 June 1912), works to which he was especially devoted throughout his brilliant conducting career.

After 1945, when Mahler's popularity began to revive, a myth developed that his music had rarely been performed following his death. The facts speak otherwise: several conductors, including Walter, Fried and Mengelberg, programmed Mahler's works throughout Europe during the first two decades after his death. Following closely upon Mahler's own performances of the First and Second Symphonies (and *Kindertotenlieder*) in America, Walter performed the Fourth, Fifth, and Ninth Symphonies and *Das Lied von der Erde*. He must have overcome the rebuff a New York audience gave him when he conducted the First Symphony there in 1917 for the very first time,[11] since he chose that very work for his final concert with the NBC Symphony in 1951.

Zemlinsky, Webern and Klemperer

Zemlinsky and Webern are rarely mentioned as interpreters of Mahler's music. Both knew Mahler intimately: the former not only preceded Mahler in the affections of Alma, but had one of his operas presented during Mahler's tenure at the Vienna Opera; the latter, as a principal member of the Schoenberg circle, came into frequent contact with Mahler and, like his colleagues, idolized the older composer.

Zemlinsky gave the third and fourth performances of the Eighth (28–30 March 1912) during his first season as music director of the CPO (his final performance in Prague (1 June 1927) was also of the Eighth). A year later (3 March 1913), he also introduced *Das Lied von der Erde*, 'a hallmark of his concert repertoire',[12] to Prague audiences who were much more accepting of Mahler's works than those of the more conservative Vienna and Berlin. His first five seasons with the CPO saw him conduct performances of Symphonies 1, 2, 3, 4, 7, 8, 9, *Kindertotenlieder*, *Das Klagende Lied* and *Das Lied von der Erde*. He also gave the first performance of the Adagio and 'Purgatorio' movements from the unfinished Tenth in Prague, only two months after their world première in Vienna. During the 1930s, before the Nazi ban, Zemlinsky continued to programme Mahler's music unstintingly, completing the symphonic cycle with a performance of the Fifth on 25 April 1934. During the 1935–6 season, he participated in the first Mahler Festival given in Prague. Radio broadcasts – an important means of disseminating Mahler's works – were aired in Berlin (RAVAG) of the Second, Eighth and *Das Lied von der Erde*, but transcriptions of these performances have yet to be discovered.

Webern's efforts to promote appreciation of Mahler's music in the composer's 'adopted city' and elsewhere were extraordinary. As early as 1911, he conducted *Kindertotenlieder* in Danzig, and again in Stettin on 31 March 1913. On 11 December of that year, he gave the Fourth in Vienna, making a positive impression despite the animus felt by the Viennese after its première there.[13] During the 1920s he conducted the VSO to great acclaim at the Worker's Symphonic Concerts, founded in 1905 by David Josef Bach, including performances of two orchestral songs (9 November 1921), *Das Klagende Lied* (November 1926) and two performances of the Eighth (18 and 19 April 1926).[14] A review of the Second on 21 June 1932, stated:

> The conductor's extraordinary musicality, his talent as a leader, his interpretive
> strength, which grew in the Mahler symphony to giant dimensions, resulted
> in an exceptional achievement. He imbued the work with his intensity and
> led the chorus, soloists, and orchestra out of the depths of combat and
> struggle up to the pure height of a common affirmation of unshakeable
> faith in a spiritual resurrection. The listeners, who filled the hall to the last
> seat ... were spellbound, deeply moved and elevated.[15]

After the thunderous ovations, Webern raised the huge, heavy score above his head, to imply that it was the work and not himself that deserved such praise. Insightful readings of the Sixth in 1930, 1932 and 1933 resulted from deep immersion in this difficult score, and, not unaware of the trouble brewing in Europe at this time, during a rehearsal of the Symphony he made the orchestra hold a particularly interesting chord for an excessively long time, remarking that 'we simply must revel in this sonority for a little while. Who knows when we shall hear this work again.'[16] In contrast to his compositional style, Webern generated electrifying performances of Mahler, and it is both unfortunate and surprising that no air checks of his highly acclaimed Mahler interpretations remain.

In 1905 another important early Mahler devotee, Otto Klemperer, was engaged to conduct the off-stage band in a performance of the Second Symphony under Oskar Fried. Klemperer met the composer during rehearsals, and was so impressed with the Symphony that he made a piano reduction of it, later playing the scherzo movement to Mahler from memory. Mahler was sufficiently pleased with this that he recommended Klemperer for a position at Prague's German Opera House.

In January, 1929, Klemperer replaced Mengelberg in performances of the Second Symphony and *Das Lied von der Erde* with the RCO. Although the performances were a resounding success, some critics complained that the tempi were generally faster than those they were used to with Mengelberg.[17] Nevertheless, after the final performance of the Second on 13 April, the reviewer for *De Courant Nieuws van der Dag* remarked that while Klemperer's tempi may be faster than Mengelberg's (87 as against 110 minutes), they were closer to those of the composer.[18]

Unlike Walter, Klemperer was not an uncritical worshipper of Mahler. While identifying closely with the Second, Fourth and Ninth (his favourite), *Das Lied von der Erde, Kindertotenlieder* and the *Gesellen* Lieder, he found the Third unimpressive, the Fifth overblown and structurally flawed, the Sixth's Finale incomprehensible, the Seventh troublesome and unconvincing, and the Eighth admirable but not the equal of the Ninth.[19] Although he never conducted the First, Third, Fifth, Sixth or Eighth Symphonies, Klemperer still ranks with the handful of conductors with personal ties to Mahler who are considered his greatest interpreters. Recordings of his personal favourites abound, including six of the Second, five of the Fourth, and three of the Ninth. His approach to Mahler's music was practically the polar opposite of Walter's. Where Walter was romantic and tender, exuding warmth and charm, Klemperer was more objective, cooler, as well as more intense and agitated, with fiery whirlwind climaxes. His sense of structural cohesiveness is particularly apparent in his many recordings of the Second and Ninth Symphonies. But his 1960s recorded performances of the Second, Fourth, *Das Lied* and the Ninth, also bear witness to his dynamic treatment of Mahler's idiom, in which he was not content to drain the music of its fiery

passion in order to achieve immaculate playing. In his last years, his tempi
became substantially slower, causing the music to drag mercilessly, as for
example in *VII (i)* with the NPO recorded for EMI in 1968, although even
as late as his 1971 performance of the Second Symphony, Klemperer still
manages to produce some thrilling moments – particularly the climax
towards the end of the first movement and the terrifying grave-opening
segment in the Finale.

Later conductors: Scherchen, Stokowski, Furtwängler and Mitropolous

Hermann Scherchen, another important but too-often overlooked
Mahler conductor, first came to know the composer's music as early as
1906 while studying the newly published Sixth Symphony. Having witnessed performances of the Second and Seventh in 1910 in Berlin under
Oskar Fried, he took up the cause, conducting a substantial number of
performances throughout the world after Mahler's death. He was also a
gifted intellectual and philosopher of music. In 1919 he wrote an article
on the Third Symphony for *Freie Deutsche Bühne* in which he described
his view of Mahler as musician-philosopher:

> Mahler, as a musician, is led at all times by his vision of the world. He is torn by
> the prophetic drive which his music shall communicate to all men ... His
> humanity was filled with the deepest love for all living beings: his music was
> to tell this to the whole world trying to reach everyone, to be understood even
> by the simplest people ... thus, his music includes everything making up
> humanity, from the sound of nature to the coarsest folksong, from the most
> intimate song of the soul to the most grotesque farce ... And quite truly here it
> is his soul, the artist's vision of the world that ennobles his work ... the ear
> slowly ... begins to comprehend and to love whereas before it shrank back in
> fear, because at the same time it senses the embrace of the deepest flame of the
> soul. This is what makes the art of Mahler the Art of our time.[20]

While Scherchen's Mahler interpretations focused on expressionistic
characteristics, emphasizing dissonances and grotesqueries, and eliciting
a chamber-like transparency, he did not shrink from the monumental
dimensions of more opulent sections or moments of devastating crisis.
His readings occasionally gave the impression of an improvisatory and
intuitive naturalness. While Klemperer's tension was always goal-driven,
with Scherchen it was part and parcel of the music's expressionistic
character. He had his eccentricities: tempi were often shockingly fast, as
in his rapid pace for the march theme in *VI (i)*, the trio section of *V (i)*,
and the principal theme of *VII (i)* which is so fast that Scherchen has

virtually to stop for breath before the second theme enters; yet his fifteen-minute reading of the Fifth's Adagietto is the slowest on record; *rubato* and *rallentando* could stretch out a phrase- or section-ending to the limit (though not nearly as much as with Mengelberg), for example *II (i)* at 4:35, and during the approach to the final climax of the Finale; relative rather than absolute, his tempi were nevertheless for the most part even, although tempo contrasts could be extreme (most disturbingly in *V (v)*). Substantial cuts were sometimes made, allegedly the result of insufficient rehearsal time. Most egregiously he cut almost half of *V (iii)* and substantial portions from the Sixth. Fortunately Scherchen did record complete versions of both these symphonies for Westminster.

Of his 1950s symphonic recordings with the VSOO, the Seventh (1953), is still considered one of the most interesting of the early recordings of this provocative symphony.[21] His Ninth with the VSO (19 June 1950) provided an excellent example of his *rasenische* (delirious) approach. As I said in my review of the recording: 'When intensity increases, the music behaves like a wild beast'.[22] Though unpredictable and occasionally wayward, Scherchen was a thoroughly knowledgeable and perceptive Mahler interpreter.

Although Stokowski and Furtwängler were not renowned as Mahler conductors, the former gave the American première of the Eighth and produced one of its most significant recordings (London, 1950), while the latter gave numerous Mahler performances between 1912 and 1932, including *Kindertotenlieder*, *Das Lied von der Erde* and the First, Second, Third and Fourth Symphonies. Several of these performances were with the BPO, and it may come as something of a surprise to contemporary Mahler devotees that this orchestra frequently performed Mahler's music before the advent of the Nazi regime. Between 1915 and 1924, it performed all of the nine completed symphonies, as well as *Das Lied von der Erde* and *Das Klagende Lied*, the total number of performances of these works exceeding fifty during this period.[23] Without the Nazi proscription, Mahler would certainly have been accepted as a major composer in Europe long before his 1960s renaissance.

In America that renaissance was largely initiated during the post-World-War-II period by the then conductor of the NYPO, Dimitri Mitropoulos. A dedicated Mahlerian, Mitropoulos was responsible for programming several of Mahler's more difficult works in New York for audiences that had little familiarity with them. For Mitropoulos, Mahler's music was the connecting musical and philosophical link between the nineteenth and twentieth centuries. In 1956 he conducted the Third Symphony in New York (the first performance there since Mengelberg's in 1922), a work with which he had an especially personal affinity.

Mitropoulos's exhilarating reading of the Sixth Symphony in its American première at Carnegie Hall in 1947,[24] his conducting of the first cycle in New York and his release of the first commercial recording of the First Symphony in 1940 helped overcome early antagonism to Mahler's music in America and virtually laid the foundation for the Mahler renaissance.

The history and significance of the recorded legacy

After Oscar Fried's 1925 recording of the Second Symphony Polydor recorded *Kindertotenlieder* in 1928 with a fledgling Jascha Horenstein. The first electronic recording of the Fourth Symphony appeared in Japan in 1930 on the Parlophone label. Western training is evident in Konoye's noticeable efforts to elicit the Viennese *Gemütlichkeit* of the first movement. Although the orchestra sounds stiff, the woodwind timbres are nasal, and brass slips give a wince, linear clarity and attention to detail make this performance surprisingly impressive for its time and place.

Another Second arrived in 1936 (released by RCA Victor) with the MSO under Eugene Ormandy, finally reissued on CD a few years ago. Walter's monumental performance of *Das Lied von der Erde*, with Kerstin Thorborg, Charles Kullman and the VPO appeared in 1937 on the Columbia label, and was to undergo numerous reissues. The next year Walter and the VPO collaborated again on a benchmark recording of the Ninth for Victor. Nonetheless, when World War II began only seven recordings of five of Mahler's works had been released.

Immediately after the war ended Walter recorded the Fourth Symphony for Columbia with the NYPO and soloist Desi Halban (daughter of Selma Kurz whom Mahler had engaged at the Vienna Opera). But despite a generally idiomatic reading with some powerful climaxes, Walter seems surprisingly uninspired, tempi are hasty and passages sink into routine. Though possessing a sweet and gentle vocal quality, Halban is hardly an ideal soloist. In 1947, Walter and Columbia broke ground again with the first Western recording of the Fifth Symphony, also with the NYPO. Here Walter's profound understanding of the composer's dramatic sensibilities comes through more convincingly than in his Fourth, although a measure of intensity remains in reserve. His Adagietto is paced rather quickly (7:37), anticipating the current fashion. The Finale is full of life, moving inexorably to an uplifting return of the chorale passage from the second movement.

Although two recordings of *Lieder eines fahrenden Gesellen* appeared in the late 1940s (Fritz Reiner, 1946, and Eduard van Beinum, 1948), by the end of the decade huge gaps in the Mahler repertoire remained to be filled. During the 1950s previously unrecorded works in the Mahler canon were issued on disc. The introduction of the $33\frac{1}{3}$ rpm long-playing record enabled Mahler's huge symphonies to be transcribed on to one or two discs, replacing the cumbersome 78 that required as many as a dozen. Improved sonic techniques made the wealth of inner details in Mahler's complex scores audible for the first time. *Des Knaben Wunderhorn* and the *Rückertlieder* (complete) entered the record catalogue in 1951 on Vanguard and Mercury respectively, and Vanguard released the latter the following year with the same forces as for the *Wunderhorn* recording. The revised two-part version of *Das Klagende Lied* also appeared on record in 1951.

As for the completion of the Mahler symphonies on disc, the Third first appeared in 1952 conducted by Adler in what is still considered one of the finest recorded performances, whose enthusiastic reception secured Adler the opportunity to première the Sixth Symphony with the VPO the very next year.[25] Unfortunately both Adler recordings were issued on an obscure label (SPA) of limited distribution. Years later these important performances became better known through various reissues. Columbia records released a Vienna performance of the Eighth under the able direction of Hermann Scherchen in 1952. Scherchen's reading of Part I is forceful and dramatic, and his remarkably goal-oriented sense of pacing in Part II has rarely been equalled in later recorded performances. But sonic quality was still far from adequate for such massive forces. The last remaining unrecorded Symphony, the Seventh, appeared in 1953 under Hans Rosbaud for Urania, and Hermann Scherchen for Westminster – the latter full of intensity despite the deliberate tempo of the first movement, and possibly his best Mahler recording. Particularly noteworthy are a lively, engaging waltz in the third movement, with old-style string portamenti (not as exaggerated as Mengelberg's) in the second *Nachtmusik*, and the stirring conclusion to the Finale. Scherchen's recording serves this often misunderstood work better than the Rosbaud, which suffers from inferior sound quality.

Horenstein and Barbirolli

During the 1950s and 1960s, two major Mahler conductors came into their own through both the frequency of their performances and the significance of their recordings: Jascha Horenstein and Sir John Barbirolli. Horenstein had a long history of interest in Mahler's music having conducted the First Symphony on his debut with the VSO in 1924. But it was his monumental 1959 performance of the Eighth at the Royal Albert Hall in London that solidified his fame as one of the most important Mahler interpreters of his age. Fortunately that performance (long circulating underground) has been issued by the BBC as part of its Legendary Performances series. A few years earlier Horenstein conducted the First Symphony in two recordings that assured his international reputation for a thorough understanding of Mahler's idiom. Although the first of these recordings, released by Vox in 1956, with the VPMO (another name for the VSO) was not the most technically proficient, Horenstein's reading was so brilliantly conceived that it became a bench-mark against which interpretations were to be judged, until his recording of the First with the more polished LSO was issued by HMV some years later. One of the more memorable details in both recordings is the way Horenstein wilfully enforces the *pesante* marking at fig. 56 at the section of the Finale also marked 'Triumphal', indicating that he viewed this section as the real climax of the entire work. Most Mahler conductors (including Walter and Leonard Bernstein) did not follow his lead here, yet by this tempo adjustment Horenstein measurably enhances the dramatic impact of the closing section.

Although Horenstein performed but never recorded the Second and Fifth Symphonies, his recordings of the Third, Fourth, Seventh and Ninth Symphonies and *Das Lied von der Erde*, were and remain among the best of these works. Only the Sixth had the drawback of an orchestra (the SPO) unfamiliar with the work and Mahler's idiom in general. Horenstein manages to overcome the lack of energy and overabundant caution surely rooted in the players' discomfort with a difficult work requiring all of their powers of concentration and precision.

Horenstein's stylistic orientation was very different from that of Walter, Klemperer, Mengelberg and Scherchen, the leading Mahler inter-preters by reputation during the 1950s. Although he instinctively under-stood Mahler's idiom better than most, he also refused to allow his personality to dominate his readings. In a perspective that combined Walter's charm with Klemperer's objectivity, climaxes were perfectly timed but not excessively overbearing. His sense of proportion and organization was extraordinary, resulting from diligent preparation and analysis, yet his readings have a natural flow that makes Mahler's Vien-nese idiom so thoroughly alluring.

England's greatest Mahler advocate and interpreter, Sir John Barbirolli, programmed all of Mahler's symphonies and song cycles except the Eighth during the period 1954–70. He gave his first perfor-mance of a Mahler work as early as 1931 when he conducted *Kindertotenlieder* at a Royal Philharmonic Society concert with contralto Elena Gerhardt. Although he was 'extremely disappointed' when he attended a rehearsal of the Fourth under Oskar Fried a few months previously, Barbirolli was soon converted to unstinting advocacy,[26] once advising:

> If you want to conduct Mahler well, his music must be under your skin and in your bones ... you must know exactly where the musical ideas begin and where they end, and how each fits into the pattern of the whole. In Mahler's symphonies, there are many highlights, but only one real climax, which one must discover. To do so needs less a simple study of the score than an all-embracing aesthetic reflection.[27]

He studied each score meticulously, taking care to comprehend the composer's intention in the minutest details. As Charles Reid so aptly puts it in his biography, '[w]hen Barbirolli embraced Mahler's music, what happened, or what developed, amounted to an act of adhesion, almost of fealty, as well as of implicit defiance.'[28] He was not to be distracted or deterred by the anti-Mahler sentiments that had been *au courant* before he came upon the scene.

Yet Barbirolli's interpretative temperament enabled him to balance clear-headed intelligence with emotive fervour: 'You have to keep an icy cool head to conduct *Tristan* and Mahler's Ninth, whatever is going on in your heart,' he was heard to say. While Barbirolli's lyricism was impassioned, he instinctively knew how to shape a phrase without succumbing to affectation. His affinity for Mahler's grotesqueries enhanced the demonic aspect of Mahler's music: witness the growlings in the low brass during the Scherzo in his 1969 recording of the Sixth Symphony with the NPO. Despite the clarity resulting from deep immersion in the score, Barbirolli was not unwilling to chance an enlightening characterization or to indulge in unmitigated brashness when called for (for example, in VI (i) (1966)). During the 1990s, when increased interest in recordings of historic concert performances reached a peak, Barbirolli's small Mahler discography was enhanced by recordings of the Second, Third, Fourth, Sixth and Ninth Symphonies. Of these, his performance of the Third won the Toblach Prize for best Mahler recording of the year in 1999. But his most universally touted recording of a Mahler work is his 1969 Fifth Symphony with the NPO. The kind of vehemence that Barbirolli elicited in the slower-than-usual scherzo is of a different order – more demonstrative, fraught with frustration and weighted with profound anger. It was a revelation to hear the second movement given such an unusual characterization. Like Klemperer, Barbirolli probably liked the Ninth best of all Mahler symphonies. His profound reading with the BPO (EMI, 1963) became an instant success. His broad tempi in the first movement convey a sense of world-weariness essential to an understanding of that movement. During the development section, Barbirolli gradually increases the tempo to fever-pitch (sometimes interrupted with minor affectations), bursting its seams with the shattering explosion of the Fate motto. After a performance of the Ninth a year earlier in New York, Barbirolli received a letter from conductor William Steinberg, another great Mahlerian interpreter, who had been present, complimenting Barbirolli for what Steinberg thought was the most breath-taking and moving performance of the Ninth he had ever heard.

It is a pity that William Steinberg left us only one commercial Mahler recording, a First Symphony with the PSO released in 1953. Recently, Steinberg's live performance of *Lieder eines fahrenden Gesellen*, with Dietrich Fischer-Dieskau and the NYPO, was made available as part of that orchestra's limited edition release of *The Mahler Broadcasts 1948–1982*. It is a meagre legacy for a major Mahler conductor whose dynamic performances of the Sixth Symphony and *Das Lied von der Erde* with the BSO in the early 1970s were a crowning achievement. A performance of the latter with the BSO (2 January 1970) and two great singers at their very best, Jon Vickers and Maureen Forrester, has been preserved and deserves an appearance on disc. Vickers gave a much better reading of his three songs for Steinberg than he did in his only other recording of the work under Colin Davis released in 1984. His *Heldentenor* voice is perfect for 'Das Trinklied', matching Steinberg's fiery reading. Yet he also had greater control to sing softly and with lilting simplicity when called for in 'Der Trunkene im Frühling' than he would have later under Davis.

The 1960s to 1980s: Bernstein, Solti, Kubelik, Haitink and Tennstedt

The turbulent and politicized 1960s were perfectly suited to ignite passionate interest in Mahler's music. His soul-searching symphonic dramas seemed to new audiences to be a quintessential expression of their world-view that sought redemption from tyranny, bigotry, pseudo-sophistication and corrupt hedonism. One ardent Mahler advocate emerged to cultivate awareness of the significance of Mahler's music for that troubled time: Leonard Bernstein. Stirred by the enthusiasm of his predecessor at the NYPO, Dimitri Mitropoulos, Bernstein introduced the music of Gustav Mahler to American audiences, both young and old, through a Young Persons Concert in 1960 entitled 'Who was Gustav Mahler?'[29] Millions listened and watched in awe as Bernstein described the composer as the musical hero of our age, a prophet who predicted that his time would come. With the NYPO Bernstein performed the entire Mahler oeuvre (except *Das Klagende Lied*) to audiences around the world that were at last becoming attuned to their universalistic message of worldly redemption. He is the only conductor who could boast of having recorded three complete Mahler symphony cycles (one issued in video format). His fervent advocacy of Mahler also resulted in several lectures released on video tape: 'The Little Drummer Boy' (exploring Mahler's Jewish background);[30] 'Four Ways to Say Farewell' (an analysis of the Ninth Symphony);[31] and a significant part of his ground-breaking Norton Lecture Series given at Harvard College, the fifth of which, 'The Twentieth-Century Crisis', discusses *IX (iv)* as evidence of Mahler's anticipation of the modern crisis in tonality.[32] No other performer has done as much to enhance his audiences' understanding of Mahler's music.

Bernstein's unique approach emphasized the music's schizoid character and effusive romantic lyricism. His early performances came under severe criticism for their controversially flamboyant mannerisms and apparent self-indulgence compared with the more tempered performances of Walter, Klemperer and Horenstein, or the unostentatious readings of Barbirolli and Mitropoulos. A good example of the extraordinary pains he took to underline or emphasize an especially beautiful phrase occurs in his first recording of the First Symphony, in which he outdoes Mahler's own directions to wrench as much feeling as possible out of the Finale's second theme. Even in that early recording, Bernstein shows his genius for intuitively enhancing a phrase usually ignored by his colleagues. Towards the end of the second-theme section treated so garishly by Bernstein, appears a two-and-a-half-bar phrase marked *rubato*, a direction that rarely appears in Mahler's scores, despite the free-style conducting indulged in by many conductors of his age. Most conductors ignore it and continue to follow the *accel.* marking of the previous bar. Bernstein instead takes the marking seriously, and creates a captivatingly flowing phrase by following the rise and fall of the musical line. Bernstein's recordings are replete with such special touches, and the recordings of the Third, Seventh and Eighth from the first cycle are among the greatest issued. In later years his presumed self-indulgences began to disappear, but not his unequalled ability to generate thrilling performances. His second cycle on CD includes excellent readings of the First, Third, Fifth and Sixth Symphonies, while it is his video-taped performance of the Second that I believe is the best he ever presented. Early criticism rapidly turned to praise as Bernstein's energy and intuitive grasp of Mahler's powerful musical personality became irresistible. He became the premier Mahler interpreter of his age, recognized for the significance and profundity of his understanding of Mahler's art and the message of redemption it should bring to a befuddled and dangerously nihilistic world.[33]

A spate of new Mahler recordings beginning in the 1960s enhanced the composer's reputation immensely. Entire symphony cycles soon appeared, the first completed in 1974 by Maurice Abravanel with the USO. A new generation of conductors began to perform and record

Mahler's work, including Claudio Abbado, Georg Solti, Rafael Kubelik, Bernard Haitink and Klaus Tennstedt. Their advocacy of Mahler as a rediscovered classical composer whose music spoke profoundly to the current age widened audiences' experience of his music, its breadth of expression and aesthetic diversity leading each conductor to develop somewhat different perspectives.

Solti's approach to Mahler has all the dramatic power of his Wagner interpretations. His Mahler recordings – particularly those of the Fifth and Sixth Symphonies with the CSO – are powerhouses, full of confidence and bravado. His recordings of the Second and Eighth Symphonies appeared soon after Bernstein's first recordings and became their major competitors primarily because of high-powered sonics. Although his readings are well-conceived for the most part, they tend to highlight (some would say overplay) the powerful moments at the expense of what happens in between. A sharp-edged, brassy sound quality pervades his later CSO recordings. Occasionally Solti seems too intent on moving quickly through lyrical passages, as if bent upon getting to the high points, giving the impression of being too calculated in design and phrase shaping. His readings contain a few moments where attention is paid to important, but often unnoticed, details. For example, during the long crescendi that lead to major climaxes in *I (i)* and *(iv)* Mahler directs that the tempo be held back (*zurückhalten*) as the rhythmic underpinning becomes more and more agitated (at figs. 25 and 51 respectively). This nuance is very difficult to achieve given the players' natural tendency to speed up as rhythmic figuration becomes more rapid, but Solti makes a valiant effort to produce the overwhelming effect of apparently pressing forward while at the same time holding back. The awkward moments and lack of cohesion in his LSO Third are vastly improved on in his reading with the CSO, although the Finale ends at too brisk a pace to project the majesty of the closing moments. His Fourth with the RCO is similarly too hurried to be effective, a problem that he overcomes to some extent in the CSO version, while his initially highly praised Seventh (1972) now seems to understate the grotesqueries and to ride rough-shod over the Finale. An prevailing agitation that made the Ninth seem uncomfortably driving in the recording with the LSO is mostly abated in the CSO recording, whose timpani and brass are uncharacteristically suppressed.

Czech conductor Rafael Kubelik was also one of the first to record a complete Mahler symphony cycle. As a native Bohemian, he brought an inherent understanding of the Slavonic character of some of Mahler's lighter musical material, particular his use of native dances with obsessive dotted rhythms. Affectations do occur more frequently than with others, but usually their expressivity enhances a lyrical phrase or rhythmic detail without seriously impeding the flow of the musical line. An instructive example is Kubelík's freely flexible and characterful treatment of the main theme of *I (i)*. His sense of structural cohesion is usually flawless, as in the Seventh, and his best recording from the complete symphony cycle is undoubtedly his Second, given more dramatic weight and depth than most subsequent recordings. But his penchant for rapid tempi and propulsive agitation works better in the Fifth Symphony than in the Fourth, where it results in an unidiomatic coldness, and the performance of the Third hangs together only if one accepts the swift *allegro* in the first movement. The drawbacks of, for example, a pervasive objectivity in the Ninth, which seems far removed from the soulful qualities of the outer movements, are nevertheless generally far outweighed by the many positive aspects of his first-rate cycle.

Given the fact that the orchestra with which Haitink recorded his first complete traversal of the symphonies was Amsterdam's RCO, known for its long association with Mahler's music during Mengelberg's director-ship, it might be presumed that he would have an edge in creating characterful readings. But although his recordings are thoughtful and deeply felt, a predominant sense of restraint and sometimes stiff and inflexible rhythm temper their power. That said, and despite the heavi-ness of approach and darkness of atmosphere in several of his recordings, *Das Lied von der Erde*, the Ninth Symphony, and the Adagio from the incomplete Tenth are still considered among the best available.[34]

Haitink's as-yet incomplete second cycle with the BPO, begun in the late 1980s, is generally more polished, if less dramatic. The Fifth and Sixth frequently leave the impression of detachment from the emotive core of the music, while the Seventh is often too dour and severe. The mysterious atmosphere that opens *VI (iv)* and the easy-going lyricism of *IV (i)* nevertheless offer captivating detail, and Sylvia McNair is one of the most enchanting sopranos to record the Fourth.

Like Haitink, Tennstedt's concert performances often fared far better than his recordings.[35] Sometimes he reveals a profound understanding of Mahler's dark images, and this is particularly noticeable in his recordings of the Fifth and Sixth Symphonies. His readings often sound sponta-neous, and his treatment of lyrical melodies, as in the second theme from *II (i)*, is expansive and heavily underscored. Occasionally, he seems to wallow in the emotional effusiveness of the music, taking us to levels of expression rarely experienced in other performances (for example, at about five minutes into the movement, during the closing section of the first subject before the march tread leads back to the return of the second theme). Such indulgences of tempo inflection sometimes excessively contort linear flow, as in the frequent *luftpausen* and long *ritardandi* in both of his recordings of *V (ii)* with the LPO. Elsewhere, his romantic approach results in climaxes of enormous power, generated from an intuitive sense of drama (for example, the chorale in the V (*ii*)) and bitter poignancy (the principal climax of VI (*ii*) (Andante)). His most consistently successful recorded performance is undoubtedly the Eighth Symphony (1987), which is less frenetic than Bernstein's and Solti's, and builds patiently to its uplifting conclusion.

Notwithstanding frequent affectations (particularly disturbing in his early recording of the Second Symphony with the CSO), Abbado's florid treatment of lyrical passages can be quite moving, and his performances of the Third and Seventh – two of the most problematic of Mahler symphonies for their broad scope, variegated content and integration of contrasting subjects – stand out as excellent examples of his grasp of Mahler's idiom. His later live recordings of the Third (1999) and Seventh with the BPO (2002) show that his approach to these works remains consistent and assured.

Other Mahler symphony cycles were released during the 1980s conducted by Maurice Abravanel, Eliahu Inbal, Seiji Ozawa, Lorin Maazel, Vaclav Neumann, Gary Bertini, Hiroshi Wagasugi and Giuseppe Sinopoli. They vary in style from the objective approach of Abravanel and Inbal, the highly polished performances under Ozawa, the analytical yet thoughtful readings of Sinopoli, to the highly mannered sensibilities of Maazel. Prominent conductors who chose to record several but not all of Mahler's symphonies include Herbert von Karajan (his two recordings of the Ninth, the first to be issued on compact disc, are still among the best), James Levine (who has recorded all the symphonies except the Eighth) and Zubin Mehta (whose several recordings of the Second show a particular affinity for this work). The advent of digital technology enabled release of high-resolution, almost distortion-free performances of numerous historical performances previously thought too encumbered with sonic disturbances. Many of these performances were by conductors who made no commercial recordings of Mahler's music, such as Carl Schuricht, Bruno Maderna and Benjamin Britten, but a host of recorded performances by the great Mahler conductors, particularly Bruno Walter, Otto Klemperer, Jascha Horenstein and Sir John Barbirolli were also released.

Early works, lost works and transcriptions

Given the relatively meagre number of Mahler's works and the unabated increase in his popularity, recordings of esoteric compositions, such as early versions of completed compositions, incomplete works and arrangements of other composers' music have begun to appear. The discovery of the long-lost

'Blumine' movement from the original version of the First Symphony resulted in its first recording in 1968, by the New Haven Symphony under Frank Brieff. But as with most of the subsequent recordings of the First that included 'Blumine', the other four movements were played using the final published version. The early version of the five-movement 'symphonic poem' performed in Budapest in 1889 was recorded in 1989 in Suntory Hall, Tokyo, with the TSO under the direction of Hiroshi Wakasugi, and appeared on disc in 1992. Only one other recording of the Budapest version has appeared since,[36] and a recent Hungaroton disc claims to be of the 1893 Weimar version of the five-movement symphonic poem 'Titan'.[37]

Totenfeier was recorded several times during the early 1990s. Both new and historical recordings of the Sixth Symphony with the order of the middle movements reversed to Andante–Scherzo, also appeared, thus making public the controversy over which order represents Mahler's final intentions. Various attempts at completion of the Tenth Symphony have been recorded, beginning with the first version by Deryck Cooke, given its première recording in 1966 with the PO under Eugene Ormandy. Subsequently, other completed editions by Joseph Wheeler, Clinton Carpenter and Remo Mazzetti, as well as revised versions of the Cooke edition, were released during the 1990s. In 1973 Mahler's earliest surviving composition, a movement from a projected Piano Quartet in A minor, was recorded by the Amsterdam Concertgebouw Piano Quartet; several recordings of this student work appeared thereafter. Piano-duet transcriptions of the Sixth Symphony by Alexander Zemlinsky and the Seventh by Alfredo Casella, were recorded in the early 1990s by the duo Silvia Zenker and Eveline Trenkner. Recently, an organ transcription of the Fifth by David Briggs and a piano reduction by Chitose Okashiro of Bruno Walter's arrangement of the First Symphony for piano duet have been released. Orchestrations of Mahler's early songs by Luciano Berio and Harold Burns, and chamber-orchestra versions of the Fourth Symphony by Erwin Stein, the *Gesellen* Lieder and *Das Lied von der Erde*, both arranged by Arnold Schoenberg, have also appeared.

Arrangements or completions of other composers' music by Mahler have been recorded, such as Weber's opera, *Die Drei Pintos*,[38] works by Bach and Schubert, and *Retuschen* of symphonies and other orchestral works by Beethoven, Schubert and Schumann.

The 1990s: Rattle, Boulez and beyond

During the late 1980s and early 1990s a new crop of Mahler specialists entered the field, most of them intent on recording complete symphony cycles. Sir Simon Rattle began his traversal of the Mahler symphonies with a highly praised recording of Deryck Cooke's revised edition of his 'Performing Version' of the Tenth with the BoSO.[39] Rattle's Mahler performances are often highly individualized, such as his intensely dramatic Second Symphony, dividing critics who find his recordings uneven, brilliant (as with the Second), unduly wayward or too controlled.[40] Recently, his appointment as music director of the BPO has resulted in a new recording of the Fifth Symphony and the revised Cooke Tenth, both highly praised: Richard Osborne says of the former that 'it can safely be ranked among the half-dozen or so finest performances on record'; David Gutman considers Rattle's Tenth 'the strongest possible case for an astonishing piece of revivification that only the most die-hard purists will resist'.[41]

Pierre Boulez has also recently taken to recording Mahler's symphonies, and when compared with his 1960s performances of the Second, Third, Fifth, Sixth, Eighth and Ninth Symphonies with the BBCSO, a substantial development in his understanding of Mahler's idiom becomes evident. Boulez is a master of the delineation of detail and balancing of principal and inner voices so essential to the successful performance of Mahler's complex music. His nearly complete DG cycle contains several examples of his ability to bring important hidden details to the surface without over-emphasis: each appearance of the multi-faceted grotesque motivic figures in the dark first subject group of *III (i)* comes through despite occasionally dense counterpoint which is often a blur in other recordings. Equally notable are the brilliant sheen of the strings and the clarity of the complex polyphony during the climactic section of *VI (ii)* (Andante).

The force of Mahler's popularity has even produced a phenomenon new to the classical music world: a successful businessman fulfilling a lifelong dream of performing Mahler's Second Symphony. Gilbert Kaplan's recording with the LSO was highly acclaimed for its depth of understanding and attention to detail.[42] He has gone on to conduct the Symphony with orchestras around the world. Most recently his scholarly collaboration with Renate Stark-Voit has resulted in a new critical edition, used for his recording with the VPO and to be issued by the Mahler Gesellschaft.[43]

By the 1990s, virtually every conductor wanting to make a name for himself with the listening public has been drawn to perform Mahler's symphonies. Numerous symphony cycles are being added to the recorded repertoire by conductors such as Riccardo Chailly (RCO), Edo De Waart (NRSO), Christoph von Dohnanyi (CO), Michael Gielen (SWGRO), Yoel Levi (ASO), Andrew Litton (DSO), Leif Segerstam

(DNRS), Yevgeny Svetlanov (RSSO), Emil Tabakov (SPO) and Michael Tilson Thomas (SFSO).

Unusually, Benjamin Zander has released the Fourth, Fifth, Sixth and Ninth Symphonies for Teldec with accompanying commentaries. With the advent of the DVD format, untold possibilities might be considered beyond the video recording of Mahler performances, such as thorough analysis of the scores using recorded performances with running commentary, a format that has been employed for other composers' music in recent times, and has already taken place in varied ways with the Third and Ninth Symphonies.[44] Another example of how DVD can extend the recorded repertoire into unexplored areas is a release of *Das Lied von der Erde* in a staged version directed by Georges Bessonnet. In this unusual and highly provocative scenario the singers take on the roles of Gustav and Alma, giving the work an entirely new orientation. Visual references to a young girl (presumably an evocation of the memory of the Mahlers' lost child Maria) during the fourth song, 'Von der Schönheit', might substantially revise one's understanding of the work as a whole.

The inception of the new millennium brings with it not the slightest indication that Mahler's popularity will diminish. His music is regularly included in the programming of every major orchestra around the globe and recordings continue to appear. The eleven symphonies alone (including *Das Lied von der Erde*) have been commercially recorded more than 1,100 times, reaching, if not exceeding, the number for Beethoven symphonies. Mahler has certainly taken his place beside the giants of symphonic literature, as he well knew he would and should.

16 New research paths in criticism, analysis and interpretation

JOHN WILLIAMSON

This composer, then, was really two composers, one romantic, the other modern.[1]

Among composers of comparable reputation, Mahler's output is quite concise in quantity and limited as to type. Its inverse proportion to commentary is correspondingly striking. In recent years, more than with most composers, literature about literature has become an increasingly pressing concern in specialist publications on Mahler. Partly this is because of the peculiarly intense relationship between the composer's music and certain commentators. Deryck Cooke's views have acquired for many an added interest in that he is also the best-known and most widely accepted of those who have 'finished' the Tenth Symphony. Henry-Louis de La Grange has worked a sea-change in the way that Mahler has been perceived in France. Adorno's interpretation has steadily acquired an interest in its own right: his Mahler is virtually a separate entity from the composer Mahler, a forerunner and commentator who illuminates the world-view that is expounded systematically and cumulatively from *Dialektik der Aufklärung* to *Negative Dialektik*.

None of these can unequivocally be called an analyst. Cooke perhaps comes closest to the popular image in that he comments directly on specific works, and makes some effort to link discussion with formal categories that for concert-goers are staples of old-fashioned programme notes. La Grange behaves in a similar fashion on a grander scale. His sections on works, however, tend to be a special case of the massive documentation of reception history that is a key feature of his biography. With Adorno, there is a case for saying that he is in many ways a deeper analyst than virtually any other commentator but that his approach transcends 'purely' musical and traditional analysis in its aims while remaining rather primitive in method, committed to 'reductive, formal and motivic' techniques that are informally and implicitly presented.[2] Max Paddison has noted that these methods, where they can be precisely documented, derive from ideas suggested by Schoenberg and remain subservient to Adorno's over-arching view of Mahler's music as ideologically modernist, albeit 'through the debris of an essentially traditional tonal material'.[3] Such a viewpoint is itself ferociously ideological, and to challenge Adorno on matters of detail is almost bound to shrink before his current historical status, which for many is almost beyond question. Yet analysis need not be committed solely to grand theory, and the current state of consideration of Mahler's music is curiously subservient to the spell that such theories cast.

Mahler himself contributed more than a little confusion to the picture by the terms in which he spoke about his music, by the manner in which he entrusted these thoughts to companions and disciples, and by the contradictory positions that he seems to adopt. His comments on the Symphony in E of Hans Rott – 'the founder of the New Symphony as I understand it', a fellow pioneer in the 'new age that was then dawning in music' – imply a progressive 'modernist' view of the symphony in which radical experiments with form may be an important constituent.[4] Yet the means through which this might be documented, close reading of formal categories, shrivels in the lack of enthusiasm with which Mahler viewed 'analysis', if his withering comment on the unfortunate Nodnagel's 'ghastly analysis' is to be taken as more than an exasperated snarl at a lesser intelligence.[5] There is little encouragement among Mahler's initial followers to write formal analysis without hermeneutics, though whether the latter are to illuminate intuitively or critically is in many ways a key question of Mahler studies. That analysis has to document a process of generic transformation of the symphony seems certain, but the complexity of the Mahlerian symphony encourages many different ways of 'reading' it, if the standard late twentieth-century view of music as a species of text is to be followed. Thus analysis of notes and explication of text war over the Mahlerian symphony in ways that are as yet not mutually enlightening.[6]

Mahler as late romantic, Mahler as early modernist

The problem of locating Mahler in the categories of critical discourse about modernism is as good a way of raising analytical issues as any. Two commonly encountered issues help to frame the problem: the idea of the 'emancipation of the dissonance' and the breakdown of the autonomous artwork and its subsequent reconstitution from the resulting fragments of a vanished experience. The shadows of Schoenberg and Adorno lie particularly heavy here. In earlier Mahler literature, particularly in writers like Hans Tischler, the technical dimensions of Mahler's harmony and its relation to the Schoenbergian tradition loomed large (Tischler, as a scholar of early music, knew that dissonance treatment was an important constituent of style).[7] Since Adorno, it has become more usual to define Mahler's modernity not with tonal adventures and harmonic surprises but in relation to the breakdown of the idea of the autonomous artwork into those avant-garde manifestations that, according to Peter Bürger, deny 'the category of individual creation'.[8] The unified work that art has failed to deliver is located beyond art in life, defined almost as that idea of a 'progressive universal poetry . . . not as harmonious and identical work, but as a project exceeding the limits of genre and style'.[9]

This is the avant-garde that 'rebels' with Adorno's Mahler 'against the illusion of the successful work'.[10] Adorno's Mahler picture is not merely a reflection of an obsession with avant-gardes but an attempt to infiltrate the latter into an image of musical romanticism that had lost its capacity to shock. His argument, however, is essentially with an idea of romanticism that is challenged by many aspects of romantic music itself, not least in those moments where 'saturation of expression' threatens continuity from Schubert to Wolf. That is why he reduces romanticism to topoi in Mahler as Peter Franklin notes.[11] Romanticism as topos is thus only one of a number of contending signifiers in Mahler that might combine to bring the music to speech (as Adorno wished), and the successors of Adorno have concentrated in varying proportions on how that might be brought about and what the music might be saying rather than the niceties of what Kofi Agawu would term introversive semiosis.[12]

Perhaps surprisingly, much of this continuing argument has taken Mahler back to early romantic roots. Investigation has followed a number of paths. At its most straightforward, there is Stephen Hefling's understandable desire to compare the ironist in Mahler with specifically romantic forms of irony.[13] That such investigation may begin with Friedrich Schlegel and Heine is entirely appropriate. Most of the contributors to the symposium on irony of which Hefling's paper is a part are committed to a historical view of the phenomenon (only Hefling attempts deep analysis) and see it in relatively discrete and well-documented packages. Writers of a more theoretical orientation, however, have arrived at a similar point of view to Hefling. Thus in Hans Heinrich Eggebrecht's book on Mahler, early literary romanticism flavours his critique of Adorno:

> What Mahler presents as essence of his comments about the concept 'world', appears – at first glance – fundamentally not to be distinguished from the tone in which to a large extent 'world' has been described since Wackenroder and Schopenhauer, Friedrich Schlegel and Novalis, E. T. A. Hoffmann and Jean Paul in the nineteenth century.[14]

The concept 'world' in such contexts is a radical alternative to the concept 'art', and the irony resides in their mutual regard:

> Mahler's interpretation expresses that 'Romantic' concept of art in which the poetic world of the limitless is opposed to the real limited world – or even to that specific aesthetic idea of art in which it is intended to be a

'world in itself' – or even, from the viewpoint of social history, to that 'bourgeois' concept of art in which it functions as counterpoise to social reality.[15]

Martin Geck, on the other hand, is a commentator who claims for Mahler romantic attributes expressed as a state of mind rather than tangible qualities. In Mahler,

> The differentiation of the language of forms remains preserved while the elementary mimetic power of the music is freed from its fetters and that all happens not with the illusory idea that the artistic subject can master this contradiction but in resignation at this historically evolved contradiction. To such a way of thinking belongs a monstrous courage – it is the courage of the radical early Romantic, who in opposition to the idealistic main stream holds unity to be unobtainable and seeks the infinite in forms that bear the visible sign of finiteness.[16]

Geck's 'radical early Romantic' returns the attention to Friedrich Schlegel. To some extent Geck reflects the argument waged between Eggebrecht's and Adorno's Mahler books over the conflicting ideas of *Gebrochenheit*, autonomy, and romanticism. Eggebrecht and Geck are talking about much the same thing, though one looks at it from the standpoint of romanticism, the other from the side of idealism. Both are agreed that Mahler's music is in some way not fractured as in Adorno's interpretation but rather fractures 'not only pure music and the fine appearance of purity but also the ideology of autonomy'; the central idea of romanticism, absolute music, is opposed by Mahler's music, which 'in its empirical tone appears as not "born from the spirit"'.[17] They qualify and go beyond Adorno by relegating real 'unbroken' and 'autonomous' music to the sphere of the commentator's imagination.

Theoretical study of Mahler has pursued an essentially historical course. Analytical systems have tended to remain on the margins of Mahler discourse (which renders all the more delightful the Adorno faction's belief that it stands for the outsider, for the insulted and the injured, and for the downtrodden). The signs of an analysis that has absorbed and gone beyond Adorno are not promising. Hermeneutics in recent years have partly contracted to the decoding of hidden programmes rather than criticism. At best, these have generated interesting if inconclusive perspectives on well-trodden areas such as the huntsman's funeral of the First Symphony.[18] One of the largest conferences on Mahler in recent years, the Bonn Symposium of 2000, dutifully attempted to embrace Eggebrecht's ideas, but shied away from extensive discussion of their mechanics and turned instead to familiar categories: *Autonomie, Immanenz* and *Bruch*. In these, the potential for analysis is regularly overwhelmed by their implications for Mahler's historical status. When one writer proclaims that 'the symphony's autonomy is its history', the triumph of Adorno the aphorist over Adorno the systematic thinker seems close to completion.[19] Equally the historicizing tendency in theory has demonstrated the ease with which it has survived all flirtations with analytical systems.

Originality

In contrast to the decoding of programmes, critical hermeneutics has mostly aimed at unlocking the agendas in aesthetic categories. In the same symposium, Eckhard Roch considered how far Eggebrecht's category of *Naturlaut* in Mahler was part of a 'jargon of inauthenticity'. On close inspection, this turns out to be a reconsideration of old friends: Mahler's 'banality', his lack of originality and his colloquial tone. These affect thematic characters to such a degree that they point to a besetting problem of Mahler studies since Adorno and Floros, the concentration on the semantic level of topics at the expense of those that aid formal cohesion. Roch is explicit on what he regards as the problem of listening to and commenting on Mahler:

> It is less the symphonic form than the motivic-thematic material, the lack of musical substance of his ideas, which sparks off conflict. Mahler's themes and motives speak – as Eggebrecht put it – a 'colloquial tone', as it were; they lack the thematic originality that the nineteenth century valued as the supreme criterion for the quality of higher art music. But in Mahler the weight of originality of ideas is transferred to originality of procedure (from the intellectual creation, if you like, to the intellectual labour).[20]

At which point Roch turns to his main theme, the bond that links preformed sounds of nature in Mahler to his techniques of alienation, irony and parody. Eggebrecht's *Naturlaut* is quickly exposed as undermined by rhetoric. The cumulative effect of Mahler's reduction to absurdity of authentic experience is to devalue; Mahler no longer criticizes, he destroys aesthetic categories in preparation for his successors.

It is difficult in such writing, which has been present in much German characterization of nineteenth- and twentieth-century music for several decades, to discern any fundamental shift away from the paradigms that Adorno established, and it is all too obvious that such efforts as have been supplied by Eggebrecht to make new beginnings can be steered back to Mahler's historical position before the Second Viennese School. If the unoriginality of Mahler's thematic material is taken as demonstrated, then everything seems to follow. His symphonies represent the crisis of the old rather than the new symphony that he discerned in Rott and himself. What is seldom undertaken in analysis of Mahler is systematic demonstration of the specifics of his unoriginality. Simply to point to topoi will not do; they have been musical constants from the Baroque onwards, subject to variations of procedure (or reinvention) long before Mahler; and that new topoi can be created or unearthed seems a logical extension of some thoughts by Raymond Monelle.[21] Analysts have on the whole taken procedural innovation too much for granted while accepting the old theme of Mahler's banality in disguise as irony or parody.

This situation has not been helped by the distinctive and sometimes distinguished musicological genre of 'Mahler and his predecessors'.[22] The question of categorizing seeming quotations from other composers is central to discussion of Mahler. Because the charge of banality was countered among the composer's earlier admirers with concepts such as irony and parody, analysts have tended to point to supposed allusions with a degree of pride, though in many ways they demonstrate the continuing belief in Mahler's lack of thematic originality. One of the most important acts of analysis in recent years has been La Grange's placing of such activity in historical context in an essay that did not gainsay Mahler's capacity to refer to other music but reminded us of the 'spontaneity and freshness' that contemporaries had detected in his *Wunderhorn* songs.[23] That they had been disturbed by this seems now a passing phenomenon, infected with late nineteenth-century nationalism and anti-Semitism. In spite of the sanity with which La Grange surveys this field, the debatable nature of many of the extracts considered adds to the feeling that Mahler studies have overemphasized an area that is not without precedent in earlier composers. The prevalence of the view that this is of greater moment in Mahler than in Schumann may simply have something to do with the accumulated and insistent weight of the past in an era of regular concerts and mass audiences. In a systematic look at quotation in the nineteenth-century symphony, the greater prevalence of the phenomenon in Bruckner, Mahler and Strauss in comparison with the generation of Mendelssohn and Berlioz is striking.[24]

Another factor concerns the nature of the various allusions and quotations themselves. When Bruckner quotes a motive from *Tristan und Isolde* in the 1873 version of the Third Symphony, he reveals by a subtle reworking the continuing presence of tags from species counterpoint underlying even Wagner's melodic structures.[25] Much of the doubt that greeted Mahler in his own time probably stemmed from the fact that his kind of allusion to the past failed to display in a clear and obvious manner that foundation in traditional forms of contrapuntal prolongation that had still been manifest in the generation of Bruckner and Brahms. Kofi Agawu has demonstrated that such prolongations may still be present in

Mahler, an exercise that suggests an interesting clash between traditional technical correlatives and the ongoing rush to reveal tonal breakdowns that increasingly look less convincing as predictors of the future.[26]

Processes

Early writers on form and process in Mahler evaluated the composer against the yardsticks of traditional theory of form in a rough and ready way. In Paul Bekker's treatment of the first movement of the Sixth Symphony, the presence of first and second themes, of development, recapitulation and coda are noted and taken to some degree for granted:

> With the repeat of the exposition, the precisely shaped development, the carefully worked-out reprise, and the grandly laid-out coda, it could serve as a pedagogical model for the construction of the symphonic sonata form. Admittedly these formal relationships to the old style of symphony are mainly of a superficial kind. The position of the sections in relation to one another, their importance for the progress of the symphonic action, the uninterrupted rising line of the chain of ideas are distinguished from the conception of the older symphony, which rises only to the development and is mostly recapitulatory in the second part.[27]

Among those who have followed, Del Mar has noted its 'strict sonata form' and La Grange has re-emphasized Bekker's picture while noting Bernd Sponheuer's view that the orthodoxy of the movement is an essential part of building the negative structure of the whole work that is confirmed in the Finale.[28]

Yet the qualifications that Bekker added to his description of a textbook sonata form have been brought increasingly into the centre of the picture in the form of the small but increasingly important departures from conventional structure that Mahler allows himself: the extended episode in the development, the beginning of the reprise (with its violently 'forced' interpolation of the major mode), the 'fantasy' recapitulation of the second subject, and Bekker's sense of a continuous rising line, which, however, is surely present in many of Mahler's predecessors from Beethoven onward; what he presumably means is the final transformation of minor to major, an act generally more typical of a finale than a first movement. Such departures are dutifully recorded by commentators whose point is that they represent a form of conceptual reorientation within traditional form.[29] Adorno's notion of the variant replaces the idea of 'integrative' thematic and motivic working, leading to a turning from architectonic to logical form. That the 'architectonic' form was always essentially a metaphor weakens much of this chain of thought, without dispelling the widely accepted view that Mahler's technique of motivic working is different in kind from that of his most distinguished predecessors.

In such a conceptual rethinking of sonata form, it is the episode that has generated most interest. Geck has pointed out that it is only where the main themes are 'peacefully' handled 'and to a certain degree brought into line with each other' that the principle of unity achieves an idealistic harmoniousness.[30] A similar note is sounded by Robert Samuels when he comments: 'Freedom and reconciliation are the signifieds of the thematic working here, too; in addition to being given in inversion, the first subject is combined melodically with motivic material from the second subject, for the only time in the whole movement'.[31] A music in which reconciliation of thematic opposites is achieved only in episodic sections implies neither an architectonic metaphor nor logical form (in Jülg's sense), but may be better handled in narrative codes, an idea that has invaded Mahler studies in the last decade in various forms.

That processes in Mahler are narratives may be viewed in two ways. The first assumes there is an underlying world-view that the music in some degree expresses, of which the most sustained example may well be that of Eveline Nikkels, who views Mahler's music as a kind of sympathetic response to the influence of Nietzsche.[32] This hovers once more on the verge of the decoding of secret programmes, though not of the autobiographical kind familiar from Berg studies but rather related to that variety of rhetorical decoding that has attained prominence in Bach studies.[33] A second and more influential approach has been to trace the analogies between narrative modes and musical processes. This too, however much it has come to inhabit a semiotic world, has its roots in Adorno, most obviously in the chapter of his book simply entitled 'Roman'.[34] There narrative in Mahler is both epic in manner and as plain in its material as Madame Bovary's circumstances. What Adorno described was a mode of constructing music out of narrative curves that rose to climaxes and collapsed like Dostoevsky or Balzac.[35] That the examples chosen are fundamentally modelled upon the unities of the theatre (most obviously the episode of Natasha and the bonfire of the banknotes in *The Idiot*) reveals the degree to which the 'novelistic' in Adorno's account can almost always be replaced by the word 'dramatic'. He gives as much away when he writes that 'passages of fulfilment such as are found in his works are better known to opera and the novel than to otherwise absolute music', though it is arguable that such an idea would only occur to an analyst immured in the German musical tradition.

In parenthesis, it might be noted that of all the areas of the theory of form that apply to sonata and symphony, the idea of episode is probably the least clearly defined (the latest *Grove* considers an episode entirely in relation to fugue). That it may be either a fresh theme or a novel variant of existing themes is not the least of its problems. Most listeners would recognize an episode before defining exactly what makes it episodic. It is the nature of the episode in Mahler that it seldom introduces specifically new themes in a developmental context but that it gives a radically new turn to existing material. When Eggebrecht speaks of the 'posthorn episode' in the third movement of the Third Symphony, he is using the term very loosely for what other analysts might well call a trio section.[36] This is part of the problem of identifying forms in Mahler. The proliferation of sections in the longer movements leads to a difficulty in discerning what is episodic and what part of the expected structure. The need for narrative explanations in Mahler is underpinned by this mutability of the traditional formal categories, though it was not unknown to Beethoven and Schubert.

The nature of the episode that occurs in the Sixth Symphony's opening movement is defined initially in terms of movement, an instruction to gradually hold back the tempo that few conductors read as anything other than a sudden slowing down. Almost at once the second principal change in the music's motion occurs. The regularity of the development is largely defined in terms of a limited range of tonalities. A minor, E minor, A minor and D minor in succession define the music's range strictly, while the bass moves largely by linear progression. The episode immediately establishes the importance of the pedal point, which had been more of an incidental feature of earlier development. From there it moves into a different tonal orbit in which G major, E♭ major, and B♭ major are three strikingly alien areas that have little contact with the main key. These fundamental changes force a reorientation upon the thematic material, revealing the motivic links that had existed subcutaneously between the two main subjects of the movement. As a result, a further dimension to the interpolation arises. To departures from the movement's norm in tempo and tonality can be added not divergence of theme or motive but of characteristics. It is no accident that commentators turn to images of the pastoral here, nor that Mahler encouraged them with the sounds of cowbells.

In raising this issue, Adorno was fully aware of that curious *fin-de-siècle* phenomenon whereby the musicality of literature and the narrativity of music exerted a mutual fascination. How to describe the process of famous moments in Proust without knowledge of music drama is a familiar case. What is the entry of the phrase from Vinteuil's sonata at the Marquise de Saint-Euverte's soiree but an analogy to moments of unexpected re-encounter in opera? The literary leitmotif is (like) a musical phrase. It is understandable that musicologists have turned to the rich field of the novel and narrative in general to test the possibility that, just as the novel may borrow the musical motive, the symphony might have sought to emulate the tone and indirections of the novel, reinforced in this by the breadth of Mahler's own reading. Other writers have been less convinced and broadly speaking, recent analysts have tended to read formal traces in Mahler's symphonic movements either as parts of a narrative or in the light of genre.

The question of how generic factors affect the Mahlerian symphony tends to be answered in at least three ways. There is an approach that in essence resembles the notion of a ruling topic, exemplified at its most sweeping in Jörg Rothkamm's essay on the first movement of the Ninth Symphony.[37] In this, the characteristics associated with the term 'Kondukt' are elevated to the status of ruling topic of the movement, which to be sure does not exclude others. Eggebrecht's idea of a 'Vokabel' is invoked here in terms that embrace both motive and topos (Eggebrecht combines in the word character, substance and ability to be designated).[38] From motives with funerary associations, a list that goes beyond the specific example invoked by Eggebrecht (the descending major second), Rothkamm takes the plunge into the much-debated world of the formal structure of the movement. Where others have read sonata or variation (or a mixture of the two), he sees marches and trios, Mahler's simile of the 'Kondukt' elaborated into an appropriate formal scheme. The points of division chosen work quite well, though they also earn a similar degree of polite applause when they designate other theories in other writers: quite simply, they are obvious points of division, only one of which Mahler chose to designate 'Kondukt'.[39] However we define the latter (and Rothkamm's definitions seem sensible), there remains the problem that the section isolated by Mahler has specific funerary associations (the tolling bell in particular, the relentless drums, the fanfares of the trumpets) that are not uniformly present elsewhere in 'march' sections. Whereas Rothkamm sees new kinds of form concept, it is difficult not to feel that the move from generic characteristic to formal type lacks truly rigorous preparation.

Set against such a view is the notion of symphonic form as generic conflict, or perhaps more precisely as a genre in conflict. When applied to the Finale of the Sixth Symphony, this can seem all too like Adorno's position, especially when his followers take up the idea of the shattering of positives as a form of triumph of the coming modernism. This area is dealt with by Siegfried Oechsle in an article that is perhaps more likely to be read for its questioning of Adorno's position than for any startling moments of insight. But like so many other treatments of generic conflict (in this case between thematic and pre-thematic, in essence non-symphonic, material), it collapses powerless before the firm belief that Mahler made the Second Viennese School and twelve-note writing – inevitable? Oechsle does not quite say this but the implication is strong.

From such relentless historicism it is a relief to return to the third possibility, genuinely tough (and pugnaciously opinionated) analysis. That musical genres and form are reinterpretable and capable of reformulation in terms that provoke insight into the music is the message of Warren Darcy's study of the Sixth Symphony's Andante.[40] His resistance to the normalization of form that he sees as prevalent in studies of this movement leads to a series of new concepts that acknowledge the movement's rather odd genuflection to rondo (a term that Mahler used with such nonchalance in the scores of the Fifth and Seventh Symphonies as to seem in retrospect breathtaking). In the idea of rotation – the 'recycling' and 'reworking' of referential statements – lies an acknowledgment of a basic procedure in Mahler that has resisted precise delineation in traditional theory of form. That it could be applied to movements that Darcy does not consider in their entirety is part of its seductive power. The thought of a reading of the opening movement of the Second Symphony as rotational structure is compelling precisely because the categories of the sonata exposition (which Darcy considers), the differentiated subject groups, are so precisely preserved in the development (which he does not), and also because the coda so carefully recycles the basic statement of the first theme, possibly even as a 'Kondukt' in Rothkamm's sense. The idea of sonata deformations, of which rotation is a prominent part, is perhaps the most vigorous recent attempt to propose a new theory of form, not merely for Mahler but for the symphonic tradition. As such it does not scruple to integrate techniques from an eclectic range of sources.

Its rival in Mahler studies has been narrative theory, which has taken several forms depending on how closely it has adopted semiotic approaches. If Vera Micznik has tended to concentrate on reconciling biography with symphonic narrative, and if Anthony Newcomb has pioneered a method that is broadly analogous to literary form, then Robert Samuels has made the most direct reference to semiotic theory.[41] This is not, however, a semiotics that adheres to a single viewpoint that can be referred to one of the founding fathers of the discipline, to Saussure, Peirce or Morris. Nor does he attempt to disprove the probability that more specifically musical forms of semiotics such as that of Nattiez are currently lacking in the techniques to cope with a Mahler symphony, though they may have something to say about a melody such as the main theme of the Andante of the Sixth Symphony. Instead ideas of code derived from Barthes and to a lesser extent Eco dominate his approach that leads directly from consideration of motive to form. The motive, however, operates on several levels, and it is hard at moments to separate his technique from the Schenkerian approach typified by Allen Forte in a provocative essay on the Adagietto of the Fifth Symphony.[42] Semiotics of this kind is as pluralistic as theories of deformation.

Samuels's book stands so well on its own as a penetrating view of the Sixth Symphony and as a suggestion of how a semiotic approach might evolve that it is pointless to attempt a summary here. Two features require some attention, however, the approach to form and the ultimate signification. Darcy is correct to stress the problems generated analytically by a normative approach to form when the proportions of the rondo are distorted so radically, a problem that affects the Finale of the Seventh Symphony in even greater measure.[43] By remaining largely at the level of motivic activity, Samuels explicitly comes to view tonal activity as 'a kind of motivic reference', which is faintly reminiscent of earlier Mahlerians like Tischler who argued at length over the symbolism of keys as though they were abstract entities rather than part of a musical process in which contrapuntal norms were continuously being tested.[44] The problem of how to deal with Mahler's rich synthesis of diatonic simplicity and chromatically enriched counterpoint is deferred by Samuels to his treatment of the Finale. There it still takes a secondary role to considerations of form and to such widespread and (to judge by Darcy) continuing strategies as the invention of formal categories to explain what might be termed the 'suicide of the symphony'. This 'glib aphorism', as Samuels puts it, does not really convince me in the context of such a dazzling array of codes and formal contexts as he provides.[45] More decisively, it does not convince him either: a solution is set up as a target then knocked down with the frank admission that Mahler's refusal to 'destroy the form' (Samuels's quotation marks) renders closure 'problematic'.[46] Far from presenting the simplified picture that his chapter title seems to promise and that the various analogies with nineteenth-century literature suggest, Samuels ends with the teasing possibility of ambiguity and asserts not an interpretation of Mahler at the close but the value of the semiotic method. The book may stand on its own, but the method, like so much that follows a semiotic path, remains open-ended. We remember Barthes's words, that 'connotators are always in the last analysis discontinuous and scattered signs, naturalized by the denoted language that carries them. As for the signified of connotation, its character is at once general, global and diffuse.'[47]

Reading and re-reading the recent analytical literature on Mahler, I am struck by how seldom writers achieve or even attempt a convincing closure; in particular German writers on Mahler seem paralyzed by the need to conclude formal and analytical discussion with historicist assertions.

Declarations of worth or even value judgements on the works have long since ceased to be the coin of Mahler scholarship, and when Allen Forte attempts one at the close of his article on the Adagietto, the effect is oddly abrupt in comparison to the level of detail that has preceded it.[48] The last truly convincing Mahlerian finale is that of Adorno (which may be why so many writers – as here – invoke them in their final remarks). However ambiguous my feelings about his writings, whatever his reputation as a difficult writer, the final paragraph of his book has the impact not of analysis but of a great work of art. The final sentence falls into place like Palestrina's last stone. It is only in retrospect that one worries about that reference to the 'script of truth': where is the scholar that would dare to write that nowadays?[49] Whose truth is being described, Mahler's or Adorno's, and if the former, can we be certain that it is really Mahler's voice or that of Monelle's fictional Gustav?[50] On such unanswerable questions theories of narrative and semiotics may well ponder in vain. Mahler's music belongs unequivocally to the world of artworks, whether by himself or the likes of Visconti, and for all the disintegrative forces that analysis and criticism have revealed, his works leave an impression of finality and increasingly high craftsmanship. The investigation of the latter remains an honourable profession for musicians.

Appendix: selected discography

LEWIS M. SMOLEY

The following discography refers to those recordings mentioned or alluded to in the text of Chapter 15, and a few others selected for their importance in the recorded repertoire. For a more complete listing, see Péter Fülöp (ed.), *Mahler Discography* (New York: The Kaplan Foundation, 1995), and Lewis M. Smoley, *Gustav Mahler's Symphonies. Critical Commentary on Recordings Since 1986* (New York: Greenwood Press, 1996). Only those recordings generally available on compact disc are listed, unless otherwise indicated.

The symphonies and *Das Lied von der Erde* (alphabetical listing by last name of conductor)

Complete cycles

ABBADO, CLAUDIO: Carol Neblett; Marilyn Horne; Jessye Norman; Frederica von Stade; Cheryl Studer; Sylvia McNair; Andrea Rost; Anne Sofie Von Otter; Rosemarie Lang; Peter Seiffert; Bryn Terfel; Jan-Hendrik Rootering; Rundfunkchor Berlin; Prague Philharmonic Chorus; Tolzer Knabenchor Wiener Sangerkirschen; Konzertvereinigung Wiener Staatsopernchor; Chicago Symphony Orchestra and Chorus; Vienna Philharmonic; Berlin Philharmonic – 12-DG 4470232 (rec. 1976–95)

ABRAVANEL, MAURICE: Beverly Sills; Florence Kopleff; Christina Krooskos; Netania Davrath; Jeannine Crader; Lynn Owen; Blanche Christiansen; Nancy Williams; Marlena Kleinman; Stanley Kolk; David Clayworthy; Malcolm Smith; University of Utah Civic Chorale and Combined Choruses; Salt Lake City Children's Chorus; Utah Symphony Orchestra – 11-Vanguard Classics 2030 (rec. 1963–74)

BERNSTEIN, LEONARD: Janet Baker; Sheila Armstrong; Martha Lipton; Reri Grist; Erna Spoorenberg; Gwyneth Jones; Gwyneth Annear; Anna Reynolds; Norma Procter; John Mitchinson; Vladimir Ruzdiak; Donald McIntyre; London Symphony Orchestra Chorus & Boys Choir; Schola Cantorum Women's Chorus; Boys' Choir of Church of Transfiguration; Edinburgh Festival Chorus; London Symphony Orchestra; New York Philharmonic – 12-Sony 89499 (rec. 1960–75)

BERNSTEIN, LEONARD: Barbara Hendricks; Christa Ludwig; Helmut Wittek; Margaret Price; Judith Blegen; Gerti Zeumer; Trudeliese Schmidt; Agnes Baltsa; Kenneth Riegel; Hermann Prey; Jose Van Dam; Vienna Singverein & Sangerknaben Konzertvereinigung; Vienna State Opera Chorus; Westminster Choir; New York Choral Artists; Brooklyn Boys Chorus; New York Philharmonic; Vienna Philharmonic; Concertgebouw Orchestra – 16-DG 459080 (rec. 1975–88)

BERNSTEIN, LEONARD: Janet Baker; Sheila Armstrong; Christa Ludwig; Edith Mathis; Edda Moser; Judith Blegen; Gerti Zeumer; Ingrid Mayr; Agnes Baltsa; Kenneth Riegel; Hermann Prey; Jose Van Dam; Vienna St. Opera Chorus; Wiener

Singverein; Konzertvereinigung; Vienna Boys Choir; Edinburgh Festival Chorus; London Symphony; Vienna Philharmonic – 9-DG Video 072 223; 072 200; 072 515; 072 225; 072 226; 072 227; 072 216; 072 229; 072 515 (rec. 1972–77)

BERTINI, GARY: Krisztina Laki; Florence Quivar; Gwendolyn Killebrew; Lucia Popp;Vardy; Hagganer; Venuti; Howells; Quivar; Frey; Titus; Vogel; Cologne Radio Choir; Prague Philharmonic Choir; Sudfunkchor Stuttgart; Little Singers of Tokyo; Knabenchor Collegium Josephinum Bonn; Frauenchor des BR und des WDR; Kolner Rundfunkchor & Sudfunk-Chor Stuttgart; Cologne Radio Symphony Orchestra – 13-EMI CDC 7 54907; CDS 7 54384; CDS 7 47568; EMI CDC 7 54178; EMI CDC 7 54179; CDS 7 47592; CDC 7 54184; CDC 7 54846; CDS 7 54387 (rec. 1984–95)

CHAILLY, RICCARDO: Melanie Diener; Petra Lang; Barbara Bonney; Jane Eaglen; Anne Schwanewilms; Ruth Ziesak; Sara Fulgoni; Anna Larsson; Ben Heppner; Peter Mattei; Jan-Hendrik Rootering; Prague Philharmonic Choir; Netherlands Radio Choir; Netherlands Children's Choir; Royal Concertgebouw Orchestra – 12-Decca 475 6686 (rec. 1987–2004)

DEWAART, EDO: Charlotte Margiono; Birgit Remmert; Larissa Diadkova; Alessandra Marc; Gwynne Geyer; Regina Nathan; Doris Soffel; Nancy Maultsby; Vinxon Cole; David Wilson-Johnson; Andrea Silvestrelli; City Boys Choir Elburg; Netherlands Radio Choir; Leipzig Opera Choir; Netherlands Radio Choir; Netherlands Radio Philharmonic – 14-RCA BMG 74321 276012 (rec. 1995–96)

GIELEN, MICHAEL: Juliane Banse; Christiane Boesinger; Alessandra Marc; Christine Whittlesey; Margaret Jane Wray; Cornelia Kallisch; Eugenie Grunewald; Dagmar Peckova; Glenn Winslade; Anthony Michaels-Moore; Peter Lika; EuropaChorAkademie; Freiburger Domsingknaben; Aurelius-Sängerknaben Calw; SWR Symphony Orchestra of Baden-Baden and Freiburg – 13-Hänssler Classic CD 93.130 (rec. 1980–2004)

HAITINK, BERNARD: Elly Ameling; Ileana Cotrubas; Heather Harper; Hanneke van Bork; Maureen Forrester; Aafje Heynis; Birgit Finnilä; Marianne Dieleman; William Cochran; Hermann Prey; Hans Sotin; Children's Choir of the Churches of St. Willibrord and St. Pius X, Amsterdam; Toonkunstkoor Amsterdam; De Stem des Volks, Amsterdam; Collegium Musicum Amstelodamense; Netherlands Radio Chorus; Royal Concertgebouw Orchestra – 10-Philips 442 050 (rec. 1962–72)

INBAL, ELIAHU: Helen Donath; Doris Soffel; Faye Robinson; Teresa Cahill; Hildegard Heichele; Livia Budai; Jane Henschel; Kenneth Riegel; Hermann Prey; Harald Stamm; Limburger Domsingknaben; Dale Warland Singers; Women's Chorus of Frankfurter Kantorei; Chorus of North German Radio, Hamburg; Bavarian Radio Chorus, Munich; Südfunkchor Stuttgart; Chorus of West German Radio, Cologne; RIAS Chamber Chorus, Berlin; Children's Chorus of Hessian Radio; Frankfurt Radio Symphony – 15-Brilliant Classics BLC 92005 (originally recorded on the Denon label) (rec. 1985–86)

KUBELIK, RAFAEL: Martina Arroyo; Edith Mathis; Elsie Morison; Erna Spoorenberg; Julia Hamari; Norma Procter; Marjorie Thomas; Donald Grobe; Dietrich Fischer-Dieskau; Franz Crass; Bavarian Radio Chorus; Tölzer Boys' Choir; North German Radio (NDR) Chorus, Hamburg; West German Radio (WDR) Chorus, Cologne; Regensburg Cathedral Boys Choir; Munich Motet

Choir; Bavarian Radio Symphony Orchestra – 10-DG 429 042; 10-Polygram 29042 (rec. 1967–71)

MAAZEL, LORIN: Eva Marton; Jessye Norman; Agnes Baltsa; Kathleen Battle; Sharon Sweet; P. Coburn; Florence Quivar; Brigitte FassBaender; Richard Leech; S. Nimsgern; Simon Estes; Vienna State Opera Chorus; Schönberg Choir; ORF Choir; Vienna Boys' Choir; Vienna Philharmonic Orchestra – 14-Sony SX14K48198 (rec. 1982–89)

NEUMANN, VACLAV: Gabriela Benacková; Eva Randová; Christa Ludwig; Inga Nielsen; Daniela Šounová; Vera Soukupová; Libuše Márová; Thomas Moser; Wolfgang Schöne; Richard Novák; Magdaléna Hajóssyová; Kühn Children's Chorus; Prague Radio Chorus; Czech Philharmonic Chorus and Orchestra – 11-Supraphon 111860 (rec. 1976–82)

OZAWA, SEIJI: Kiri TeKanawa; Marilyn Horne; Jessye Norman; Faye Robinson; Judith Blegen; Florence Quivar; L. Myers; Kenneth Riegel; Benjamin Luxon; G. Howell; Boston Boys Choir Tanglewood Festival Chorus; Boston Symphony Orchestra – 14-Philips 4388742 (rec. 1980–93)

SEGERSTAM, LEIF: Tina Kiberg; Kirsten Dolberg; Anne Gjevang; Eva Johansson; Inge Nielsen; Majken Bjerno; Henriette Bonde-Hansen; Raimo Sirkiä; Jorma Hynninen; Carsten Stabell; Copenhagen Boys' Choir; Danish National Radio Choir; Danish National Radio Symphony Orchestra – 13-Chandos 9572 (rec. 1991–97)

SINOPOLI, GIUSEPPE: Rosalind Plowright; Brigitte Fassbaender; Hanna Schwarz; Edita Gruberova; Cheryl Studer; Angela Maria Blasi; Sumi Jo; Waltraud Meier; Kazuko Nagai; Keith Lewis; Thomas Allen; Hans Sotin; New London Children's Chorus; The Southend Boys' Choir; Philharmonia Chorus and Orchestra – 15-DG 4714512 (rec. 1985–95)

SOLTI, GEORGE: Kiri Te Kanawa; Heather Harper; Lucia Popp; Arleen Auger; Isobel Buchanan; Helga Dernesch; Mira Zakai; Yvonne Minton; Helen Watts; René Kollo; John Shirley-Quirk; Martti Talvela; Chicago Symphony Chorus; Glen Ellyn Children's Chorus; Vienna State Opera Chorus; Wiener Singverein; Vienna Boys' Choir; Chicago Symphony Orchestra; London Symphony Orchestra – 10-London:Decca 430 804 (rec. 1970–84)

SVETLANOV, EVGENY: Natalia Guerassimova; Olga Alexandrova; Galina Boiko; Galina Borissova; Alexei Martynov; Dimitri Trapeznikov; Anatoly Safiouline; Russian Academic Choir of TV 'Ostankino' Moscow Boys Choir; Children's Choir and Double Mixed Choir of the Moscow Academy of Choral Singing; Russian State Symphony Orchestra – 13-Russian Season RUS 288 123; 288 136:7; 288 111:12; 288 133; 288 134; 288 135; 288 117:18; 288 151:52; 288 132 (rec. 1990–96)

TABAKOV, EMIL: Tiha Genova, soprano; Vessela Zorova, alto; Bulgarian National Choir; Brigitte Pretschner, alto; Bulgarian National Choir; Kinderchor 'Bodra Smyana'; Lyudmila Hadzhieva, soprano; Maria Temeschi,Darina Takova, sopranos; Tamara Takac, Boryana Tabakova, altos; Janos Bandi, tenor; Pal Kovacs, baritone; Tamash Syule, bass; Bulgarian National Chorus; Children's Chorus of Bulgarian Radio; Sofia Philharmonic – 15-Capriccio 49 044-62 (rec. 1987–93)

TENNSTEDT, KLAUS: Edith Mathis; Doris Soffel; Ortrun Wenkel; Lucia Popp; Elizabeth Connell; Edith Wiens; Felicity Lott; Trudeliese Schmidt; Nadine Denize;

Richard Versalle; Jorma Hynninen; Hans Sotin; Southend Boys' Choir; Tiffin School Boys' Choir; London Philharmonic Choir; London Philharmonic – 11-EMI 72941 (rec. 1977–87)

WAKASUGI, HIROSHI: Shinobu Satoh; Naoko Ihara; Kiyomi Toyoda; Misako Watanabe; Yukie Ohkura; Yuri Oh-Hashi; Makoto Hayashi; Futoru Katsube; Keizoh Takahashi; Shin-yukai Chorus; Tokyo College of Music Female Chorus; Tokyo Broadcasting Children's Chorus Group; Tokyo Metropolitan Symphony Orchestra – 15-Fontec FOCD 3274; 2705:06; 9018:19; 9020; 9021; 9022:23; 9024:5; 9026:27; 9028:29 (rec. 1988–91)

Individual recordings
Symphony No.1

BARBIROLLI, JOHN: Halle Orchestra – Barbirolli Soc. CDSJB 1015; Dutton Laboratories 1015 (rec. 1957)

BARBIROLLI, JOHN: New York Philharmonic – 12-New York Philharmonic NYP 9801:12 (rec. 1959)

BOULEZ, PIERRE: Chicago Symphony – DG 289 459 610 (rec. 1999)

BRIEFF, FRANK: New Haven Symphony (with Blumine added to 1898 version) – Odyssey 32160286 (LP) (oop) (rec. 1968)

HAITINK, BERNARD: Berlin Philharmonic – Philips CD 420 936 (rec. 1987)

HAMAR, ZSOLT: Pannon Philharmonic Orchestra (Pécs, Hungary) (1893 Weimar version) Hungaroton Classic HCD 32338) (rec. 2005)

HORENSTEIN, JASCHA: Vienna Symphony Orchestra – 2-Vox 5508 (rec. 1953)

HORENSTEIN, JASCHA: Vienna Symphony Orchestra – Tuxedo 1048 (rec. 1958)

HORENSTEIN, JASCHA: London Symphony Orchestra – Unicorn UKCD 2012 (rec. 1969)

LEVI, YOEL: Atlanta Symphony Orchestra – Telarc CD-80545 (rec. 2000)

LEVINE, JAMES: London Symphony Orchestra – RCA RCD1 80894 (rec. 1974)

LITTON, ANDREW: Royal Philharmonic – Virgin Classics VC 7 90703

MEHTA, ZUBIN: Israel Philharmonic – 2-London 443032 (rec. 1974)

MEHTA, ZUBIN: New York Philharmonic – Sony SBK 53259 (rec. 1980)

MEHTA, ZUBIN: Israel Philharmonic – Angel CDC 49044 (rec. 1986)

MITROPOULOS, DIMITRI: Minneapolis Symphony Orchestra – Sony 62342 (rec. 1940)

MITROPOULOS, DIMITRI: New York Philharmonic – Italian Disc Instit. IDA 6358; 8-Fonit Cetra DOC 43 (rec. 1951)

MITROPOULOS, DIMITRI: New York Philharmonic – Hunt CD 556 (rec. 1960)

RATTLE, SIR SIMON: City of Birmingham Symphony Orchestra – EMI CDC 7 54647

RUUD, OLE KRISTIAN: Norrköping Symphony (1889 Budapest version) – Simax PSC 1150 (rec. 1999)

SCHERCHEN, HERMANN: London Philharmonic Orchestra – Palladio PD 4180 (rec. 1954)

STEINBERG, WILLIAM: Pittsburgh Symphony Orchestra – Angel 66555 (rec. 1953)

TENNSTEDT, KLAUS: Chicago Symphony Orchestra – Angel CDC7 54217 (rec. 1991)

WAKASUGI, HIROSHI: Dresden Staatskapelle – Eterna 3 29 119 (rec. 1986)

WALTER, BRUNO: NBC Symphony – Cedar AB 78595; Classica D'Oro 1033 (rec. 1939)

WALTER, BRUNO: New York Philharmonic – Legend LGD 106 (rec. 1950)

WALTER, BRUNO: New York Philharmonic – Sony 63328 (rec. 1954)

WALTER, BRUNO: Columbia Symphony Orchestra – 2-Sony 45674 (rec. 1961)

Symphony No. 2

BOULEZ, PIERRE: Felicity Palmer; Tatiana Troyanos; London Philharmonic Choir; BBC Choral Society; BBC Symphony Orchestra – 2-Documents LV 915:16 (rec. 1973)

FRIED, OSCAR: Gertrud Bindernagel, soprano; Emmi Leisner, contralto; Berlin Cathedral Choir; Berlin State Opera Orchestra – 2-Pearl GEMM CDS 9929 (rec. 1924)

HAITINK, BERNARD: Charlotte Margiono, soprano; Jard van Nes, contralto; Netherlands Radio Chorus; Rotterdam Philharmonic – 2-Rotterdam Philharmonic STB 91011 (rec. 1990)

HAITINK, BERNARD: Sylvia McNair, soprano; Jard van Nes, contralto; Ernst-Senff Chor Berlin Philharmonic – 2-Philips 438 935 (rec. 1994)

KAPLAN, GILBERT: Maureen Forrester; Benita Valente; London Symphony Chorus; Ardwyn Singers; BBC Welsh Chorus; Cardiff Polyphonic Choir; Dyfed Choir; London Symphony Orchestra – 2-MCA 110011 (rec. 1989)

KAPLAN, GILBERT: Latonia Moore; Madja Michael; Vienna Singverein; Vienna Philharmonic – 2-DG B000989 (rec. 2003)

KLEMPERER, OTTO: Valda Bagnall, soprano; Florence Taylor, contralto; Hurlstone Choral Society; Sydney Symphony Orchestra – Doremi 7759 (rec. 1950)

KLEMPERER, OTTO: Ilona Steingruber, soprano; Hilde Rössl-Majden, contralto; Vienna Academy Chamber Choir and Singverein der Gesellschaft der Musikfreunde; Vienna Symphony Orchestra – Vox Classics 5521 (rec. 1951)

KLEMPERER, OTTO: Jo Vincent, soprano; Kathleen Ferrier, contralto; Concertgebouw Orchestra and Chorus of Amsterdam – 2-Verona 27062 (rec. 1951)

KLEMPERER, OTTO: Elisabeth Schwarzkopf, soprano; Hilde Rössl-Majden, contralto; Philharmonia Chorus and Orchestra – EMI Classics 67255 (rec. 1961–2; rel. 1963)

KLEMPERER, OTTO: Galina Vishnevskaya, soprano; Hilde Rössl-Majden, contralto; Vienna Singverein; Vienna Philharmonic Orchestra – Music & Arts 881 (rec. 1963)

KLEMPERER, OTTO: Heather Harper, soprano; Dame Janet Baker, mezzo-soprano; Bavarian Radio Chorus and Orchestra – Angel 66867; Enterprise 937 (rec. 1965)

KLEMPERER, OTTO: Heather Harper, soprano; Dame Janet Baker, mezzo-soprano; Philharmonia Orchestra & Chorus – 2-Nuova Era 6714 (rec. 1965)

KLEMPERER, OTTO: Anne Finley, soprano; Alfreda Hodgson, contralto; New Philharmonia Chorus and Orchestra – 2-Arkadia CDHP 590 (rec. 1971)

LEVI, YOEL: Barbara Bonney; Mary Phillips; Atlanta Symphony Orchestra and Chorus – 2-Telarc 2CD-80548 (rec. 2002)

LITTON, ANDREW: Heidi Grant Murphy; Petra Lang; Dallas Symphony Orchestra & Chorus – 2-Delos DE 3237 (rec. 1999)

MEHTA, ZUBIN: Ileana Cotrubas, soprano; Christa Ludwig, contralto; Vienna State Opera Chorus; Vienna Philharmonic – 2-Decca 4406152 (rec. 1975)

MEHTA, ZUBIN: Kathleen Battle, soprano; Maureen Forrester, contralto; New York Philharmonic Chorus; New York Philharmonic – 12-New York Philharmonic NYP 9801:12 (rec. 1982)

MEHTA, ZUBIN: Sylvia Greenberg, soprano; Florence Quivar, contralto; Rinat National Choir; Tel Aviv Philharmonic Choir; Ihud Choir; Israel Philharmonic – Pickwick 1136 (rec. 1988)

MEHTA, ZUBIN: Nancy Gustafson, soprano; Florence Quivar, contralto; Prague Philharmonic Choir; Israel Philharmonic – Teldec 4509945452 (rec. 1994)

MEYROWITZ, SELMAR: Sara Jane Charles-Cahier; Berlin State Opera Orchestra: 'Urlicht' – Symposium 1337 (rec. 1930)

NEUMANN, VACLAV: Gabriela Benackova-Capova; Irina Arkhipova; Prague Philharmonic Chorus; Czech Philharmonic – Canyon Classics PCCL 00190 (rec. 1992)

ORMANDY, EUGENE: Corinne Frank Bowen; Ann O'Malley Gallogly; Twin City Symphony Chorus; Minneapolis Symphony – Biddulph WHL 032 (rec. 1935)

RATTLE, SIR SIMON: Arleen Auger; Janet Baker; City of Birmingham Symphony & Chorus – 2-EMI ZDCB 7 47962 (rec. 1987)

SCHERCHEN, HERMANN: Mimi Coertse, soprano; Lucretia West, contralto; Vienna Academy Chamber Choir; Vienna State Opera Orchestra – Paladio PD 4180 (rec. 1958)

SCHURICHT, CARL: Edith Selig, soprano; Eugenia Zarenska, mezzo-soprano; Paris National Choir and Orchestra – 2-Melodram 27504 (rec. 1958)

SCHURICHT, CARL: Ruth Margret Puetz, soprano; Marga Hoffgen, alto; Chor der Frankfurter Singakademie; Hessian Radio Chorus & Orchestra – 2-Originals SH 819:20 (1960)

WALTER, BRUNO: Maria Cebotari; Rosette Anday; Vienna State Opera Chorus; Vienna Philharmonic Orchestra – 2-Nuova Era 22314-5; 2-Archipel 82 (rec. 1948)

WALTER, BRUNO: Nadine Conner; Joan Watson; Westminster Choir; New York Philharmonic (sung in English) – 2-Bruno Walter Society 1067–8 (LP) (rec. 1948)

WALTER, BRUNO: Emilia Cundari; Maureen Forrester; Westminster Choir; New York Philharmonic – 2-Sony 45674 (rec. 1957)

Symphony No. 3

ADLER, F. CHARLES: Hilde Rössl-Majden, contralto; Vienna State Opera Chorus; Vienna Boys' Choir; Vienna Philharmonic – 2-Harmonia Mundi 43501 (rec. 1952)

BARBIROLLI, JOHN: Lucretia West, contralto; St. Hedwig Cathedral Choir and Children's Choir; Berlin Philharmonic – 3-Hunt CD 719 (rec. 1969)

BARBIROLLI, JOHN: Kerstin Meyer, contralto; Ladies of the Halle Orchestra; Boys of Manchester Grammar School; Halle Orchestra – 2-BBC Legends BBCL 4004-7 (rec. 1969)

BOULEZ, PIERRE: Yvonne Minton, mezzo-soprano; BBC Singers; BBC Choral Society (Women's Voices); Hertfordshire County Youth Choir; West London Youth Choir; BBC Symphony – 2-Artists FED 024-25 (rec. 1974)

BOULEZ, PIERRE: Yvonne Minton, mezzo-soprano; Camerata Singers; Boys' Choir from The Little Church Around The Corner; Trinity Church Boys' Choir; Brooklyn Boys' Choir; New York Philharmonic – 12-New York Philharmonic NYP 9801:12 (rec. 1976)

BOULEZ, PIERRE: Anne Sofie von Otter, mezzo-soprano; Frauenchor des Wiener Singverein; Wiener Sängerknaben; Vienna Philharmonic – 2-DG 289 474 038 (rec. 2003)

HAITINK, BERNARD: Jard Van Nes, contralto; Ernst Senff Women's Choir; Tölzer Boys' Choir; Berlin Philharmonic – 2-Philips 432 162 (rec. 1990)

HORENSTEIN, JASCHA: Lucretia West, contralto; Bergamo Chorus; Turin Radio Symphony – Rococo RR 2083 (LP) (oop) (rec. 1960)

HORENSTEIN, JASCHA: Norma Proctor, mezzo-soprano; Ambrosian Singers; Wandsworth School Boys Choir; London Symphony Orchestra – 2-Unicorn UKCD 2006 (rec. 1970)

LEVINE, JAMES: Marilyn Horne, contralto; Chicago Symphony Chorus; Glen Ellyn Children's Chorus; Chicago Symphony Orchestra – [2-RCA RCD2 1757] (rec. 1975)

LITTON, ANDREW: Nathalie Stutzman; Women of the Dallas Symphony Chorus; Texas Boys Choir; Dallas Symphony Orchestra – 2-Delos DE 3248 (rec. 2000)

MADERNA, BRUNO: Ursula Boese, contralto; Bergamo Children's Choir; Milan RAI Choir and Symphony Orchestra – 4-Arcadia CDMAD 0284 (rec. 1973)

MEHTA, ZUBIN: Maureen Forrester; Los Angeles Master Chorale; California Boys' Choir; Los Angeles Philharmonic – 2-London 443032 (rec. 1978)

MEHTA, ZUBIN: Florence Quivar, contralto; Israel Kibbutz Choir; Rinat National Choir; Ankor Children's Choir; Israel Philharmonic – 2-London 443032 (rec. 1992)

MITROPOULOS, DIMITRI: Beatrice Krebs, contralto; Westminster Choir; New York Philharmonic (sung in English) – 2-Hunt CD 557 (rec. 1956)

MITROPOULOS, DIMITRI: Lucretia West, contralto; Cologne Radio Chorus; Cologne School Boys' Choir; Cologne Radio Symphony Orchestra – 2-Tahra 209 (rec. 1960)

SCHERCHEN, HERMANN: Hilde Rössl-Majdan, contralto; Vienna State Opera Chorus; Vienna Symphony Orchestra – Paragon LBI 53014 (oop) (rec. 1950)

RATTLE, SIR SIMON: Birgit Remmert, contralto; City of Birmingham Symphony Youth Chorus; Ladies of the City of Birmingham Symphony Chorus; City of Birmingham Symphony – 2-EMI 5 56657 (rec. 1998)

SCHERCHEN HERMANN: Sona Cervena, contralto; Leipzig Radio Choir, Children's Choir and Orchestra – 2-Tahra TAH 101; 2-Tahra 147 (rec. 1960)

SCHURICHT, CARL: Ruth Siewert, contralto; Eberhard Ludwig Gymnasium Children's Choir; South German Radio Choir and Orchestra – 2-Living Stage LSY035161 (rec. 1960)

ZANDER, BENJAMIN: Lilli Paasikivi; Ladies of the London Philharmonic Choir; Tiffin Boys' Choir; Philharmonia Orchestra – 3-Telarc 80599 (rec. 2004) (with discussion disc)

Symphony No. 4

BARBIROLLI, JOHN: Heather Harper, soprano; BBC Symphony Orchestra – BBC Legends 4004 (rec. 1967)

BOULEZ, PIERRE: Juliane Banse, soprano; Cleveland Orchestra – DG 289 463 257 (rec. 2000)

BRITTEN, BENJAMIN: Joan Carlyle, soprano; London Symphony Orchestra – BBC Legends BBCB 8004 (rec. 1961)

HAITINK, BERNARD: Roberta Alexander, soprano; Royal Concertgebouw Orchestra – Philips 412 119 (rec. 1983)

HAITINK, BERNARD: Sylvia McNair, soprano; Berlin Philharmonic – Philips 434 123 (rec. 1992)

HORENSTEIN, JASCHA: Margaret Price, soprano; London Philharmonic Orchestra – EMI 8 26146 (rec. 1970)

KARAJAN, HERBERT VON: Edith Mathis, soprano; Berlin Philharmonic – DG 419 863 (rec. 1979)

KLEMPERER, OTTO: Elfriede Trötschel, soprano; Cologne Radio Symphony Orchestra – Frequenz 991 005 (rec. 1954)

KLEMPERER, OTTO: Elfriede Trötschel, soprano; Berlin Radio Symphony Orchestra – 2-Melodrama (LP) 215 (rec. 1956)

KLEMPERER, OTTO: Elisabeth Lindermeier, soprano; Bavarian Radio Symphony Orchestra – Melodram 40057 (rec. 1956)

KLEMPERER, OTTO: Elisabeth Schwarzkopf, soprano; Philharmonia Orchestra – EMI 567035 (rec. 1961; rel. 1962)

KONOYE, HIDEMARO: Eiko Kitazawa, soprano; Tokyo New Symphony Orchestra – Denon CO 2111 (rec. 1930)

LEVI, YOEL: Frederica Von Stade; Atlanta Symphony Orchestra – Telarc CD-80499 (rec. 1999)

LEVINE, JAMES: Judith Blegen, soprano; Chicago Symphony Orchestra – RCA RCD1 0895 (rec. 1974)

LITTON, ANDREW: Heidi Grant Murphy; Dallas Symphony Orchestra – Delos DE 3261 (rec. 2003)

MAAZEL, LORIN: Heather Harper; Berlin Radio Symphony Orchestra – Via Classics 642 314 (rec. 1969)

MEHTA, ZUBIN: Barbara Hendricks, soprano; Israel Philharmonic – Decca 4488972 (rec. 1979)

MENGELBERG, WILLEM: Jo Vincent, soprano; Concertgebouw Orchestra of Amsterdam – Iron Needle IN 1386 (perf. 1939).

RATTLE, SIR SIMON: Amanda Roocroft, soprano; City of Birmingham Symphony – EMI 5 56563 (rec. 1998)

SOLTI, GEORGE: Irmgard Seefried, soprano; New York Philharmonic – 12-New York Philharmonic NYP 9801:12 (rec. 1962)

WALTER, BRUNO: Desi Halban, soprano; New York Philharmonic – Sony 64450 (rec. 1945)

WALTER, BRUNO: Irmgard Seefried, soprano; Vienna Philharmonic – Urania 158 (rec. 1950)

WALTER, BRUNO: Irmgard Seefried, soprano; New York Philharmonic – Music & Arts CD 656 (rec. 1953)

WALTER, BRUNO: Maria Stader, soprano; French National Radio Orchestra – Classica D = Oro 1050; Nuova Era 2233 (rec. 1955)

WALTER, BRUNO: Hilde Güden, soprano; Vienna Philharmonic – DG 435 334; 4-Andante 4973 (rec. 1955)

WALTER, BRUNO: Elisabeth Schwarzkopf, soprano; Royal Concertgebouw Orchestra –
14-Royal Concertgebouw Orchestra MCCL 97018 (rec. 1952)

WALTER, BRUNO: Elisabeth Schwarzkopf, soprano; Vienna Philharmonic –
2-Arkadia CD 767 (rec. 1960)

ZANDER, BENJAMIN: Camilla Tilling; Philharmonia Orchestra – 2-Telarc 80555
(with discussion disc)

Symphony No. 5

BARBIROLLI, JOHN: New Philharmonia Orchestra – Angel 66962 and 64749
(rec. 1969)

BOULEZ, PIERRE: BBC Symphony Orchestra – 2-Arkadia CDGI 754.2) (rec. 1968)

BOULEZ, PIERRE: BBC Symphony Orchestra – Hunt CD 718 (rec. 1970)

BOULEZ, PIERRE: BBC Symphony Orchestra – Arkadia CDGI 718.1) (rec. 1970)

BOULEZ, PIERRE: Vienna Philharmonic – DG 453 416 (rec. 1997)

HAITINK, BERNARD: Berlin Philharmonic – Philips 422 355 (rec. 1988)

KARAJAN, HERBERT VON: Berlin Philharmonic – 2-DG 415 096 (rec. 1973)

LEVI, YOEL: Atlanta Symphony Orchestra – Telarc CD-80394 (rec. 1995)

LEVINE, JAMES: Philadelphia Orchestra – RCA RCD1 5453 (rec. 1977)

LITTON, ANDREW: Dallas Symphony Orchestra – Delos DOR 90193 (rec. 1993)

MADERNA, BRUNO: Milan RAI Symphony Orchestra – 4-Arcadia CDMAD 0284
(rec. 1973)

MEHTA, ZUBIN: Los Angeles Philharmonic – London 433 877 (rec. 1976)

MEHTA, ZUBIN: New York Philharmonic – Teldec 4509974412 (rec. 1989)

MITROPOULOS, DIMITRI: New York Philharmonic – Hunt CD 523; 6-Tahra 1021
(rec. 1960)

NEUMANN, VACLAV: Leipzig Gewandhaus Orchestra – Philips 426 638 (rec. 1966)

RATTLE, SIR SIMON: Berlin Philharmonic – EMI 7243 5 57385 (rec. 1998)

SCHERCHEN, HERMANN: Vienna State Opera Orchestra – DG 471268 (rec. 1952)

SCHERCHEN, HERMANN: Milan Radio Orchestra – Stradivarius STR 13600 (rec. 1962)

SCHERCHEN, HERMANN: French National Orchestra – Harmonia Mundi 1955179
(rec. 1965)

TENNSTEDT, KLAUS: New York Philharmonic – 12-New York Philharmonic NYP
9801:12 (rec. 1980)

TENNSTEDT, KLAUS: London Philharmonic – Angel EMI CDC 7 49888 (rec. 1990)

WALTER, BRUNO: New York Philharmonic – Sony 64451 (rec. 1947)

ZANDER, BENJAMIN: New England Conservatory Youth Philharmonic Orchestra –
CPI 329407 (rec. 1997)

ZANDER, BENJAMIN: Philharmonia Orchestra – 2-Telarc 80569 (rec. 2001) (with
discussion disc)

Symphony No. 6

ADLER, F. CHARLES: Vienna Philharmonic – 2-S.P.A. 59:60 (LP) (oop) (rec. 1953)

BARBIROLLI, JOHN: Berlin Philharmonic Orchestra – Testament SBT 1342 (rec. 1966)

BARBIROLLI, JOHN: New Philharmonia Orchestra – Angel 69349 (rec. 1967)

BARBIROLLI, JOHN: New Philharmonia Orchestra – Hunt CD 726 (rec. 1969)

BOULEZ, PIERRE: BBC Symphony – Artists FED 032 (rec. 1973)

BOULEZ, PIERRE: Vienna Philharmonic – DG 445 835 (rec. 1995)

HAITINK, BERNARD: Berlin Philharmonic – 2-Philips 426 257 (rec. 1989)

HORENSTEIN, JASCHA: Stockholm Philharmonic Orchestra – 4-Music & Arts CD 785 (rec. 1966)

KARAJAN, HERBERT VON: Berlin Philharmonic – 2-DG 415 099 (rec. 1977)

LEVI, YOEL: Atlanta Symphony Orchestra – Telarc CD-80444 (rec. 1998)

LEVINE, JAMES: London Symphony Orchestra – 2-RCA RCD2 3213 (rec. 1978)

MEHTA, ZUBIN: Israel Philharmonic – Teldec 4509-98423 (rec. 1996)

MITROPOULOS, DIMITRI: New York Philharmonic – 12-New York Philharmonic 9801 (rec. 1955)

MITROPOULOS, DIMITRI: Cologne Radio Symphony Orchestra – 6-Tahra TAH 1021(rec. 1959)

NEUMANN, VACLAV: Leipzig Gewandhaus Orchestra – 2-Berlin Classics 0090452 (rec. 1966)

RATTLE, SIR SIMON: City of Birmingham Symphony – 2-EMI CDS 7 54047 (rec. 1990)

SCHERCHEN, HERMANN: Leipzig Radio Orchestra – 2-Tahra 147 (rec. 1960)

ZANDER, BENJAMIN: Boston Philharmonic Orchestra – 2-IMP DMCD 93 (rec. 1995)

ZANDER, BENJAMIN: Philharmonia Orchestra – 3-Telarc 80586 (rec. 2002) (with discussion disc)

Symphony No. 7

BARBIROLLI, JOHN: BBC Northern Symphony Orchestra and The Halle Orchestra – 2-BBC Legends BBCL 4034 (rec. 1960)

BOULEZ, PIERRE: Cleveland Orchestra – DG 447 756 (rec. 1996)

HAITINK, BERNARD: Royal Concertgebouw Orchestra – 2-Philips 410 398 (rec. 1982)

HORENSTEIN, JASCHA: New Philharmonia Orchestra – BBC Legends 4051; Music & Arts 727 (rec. 1969)

KUBELIK, RAFAEL: New York Philharmonic – 12-New York Philharmonic NYP 9801:12 (rec. 1981)

LEVI, YOEL: Atlanta Symphony Orchestra – 2-Telarc 2CD-80514 (rec. 1999)

LEVINE, JAMES: Chicago Symphony Orchestra – 2-RCA RCD2 4581 (rec. 1980)

MADERNA, BRUNO: Vienna Symphony – Hunt CD 547 (rec. 1967)

MADERNA, BRUNO: Milan RAI Symphony Orchestra – 4-Arcadia CDMAD 0284 (rec. 1971)

NEUMANN, VACLAV: Leipzig Gewandhaus Orchestra – Berlin Classics 0090462 (rec. 1968)

RATTLE, SIR SIMON: City of Birmingham Symphony Orchestra – EMI CDC 7 54344 (rec. 1992)

SCHERCHEN, HERMANN: Vienna Symphony Orchestra – Orfeo C 279 921; Enterprise 4133 (rec. 1950)

SCHERCHEN, HERMANN: Vienna State Opera Orchestra – DG 471263; Legend 13 (rec. 1953)

SCHERCHEN, HERMANN: Vienna Symphony Orchestra – Notes PGP 11022 (rec. 1960)

SCHERCHEN, HERMANN: Toronto Symphony – Music & Arts CD 695 (rec. 1965)

Symphony No. 8

BOULEZ, PIERRE: Edda Moser; Linda Esther Gray; Wendi Eathrone; Elizabeth
Connell; Bernadette Greevy; Alberto Remedios; Siegmund Nimsgern; Marius
Rintzler; BBC Singers; BBC Choral Society; Scottish National Orchestra Chorus;
Wandsworth Boys Choir; BBC Symphony – 2-Artists FED 041-42 (rec. 1975)

HORENSTEIN, JASCHA: Joyce Barker; Beryl Hatt; Agnes Giebel; Kerstin Meyer; Helen
Watts; Kenneth Neate; Alfred Orda; Arnold Van Mill; BBC Chorus & Choral
Society; Goldsmith's Choral Union; Hampstead Choral Society; Emanuel School
Boys' Choir; Orpington Junior Singers; London Symphony – 2-BBC Legends 4001
(rec. 1959)

LEVINE, JAMES: Carol Neblett; Judith Blegen; Jann Jaffe; Isola Jones; Birgit Finnilä;
Kenneth Riegel; Ryan Edwards; John Cheek; Glen Ellyn Children's Chorus;
Chicago Symphony Chorus and Orchestra (first movement only) – 12-Chicago
Symphony CSO CD90 (rec. 1979)

MITROPOULOS, DIMITRI: Mimi Coertse; Hilde Zadek; Lucretia West; Ira Malaniuk;
Giuseppe Zampieri; Hermann Prey; Otto Edelmann; Vienna State Opera Chorus;
Vienna Singverein; Vienna Boys' Choir; Vienna Philharmonic Orchestra – Orfeo
D'Or 519992; 6-Tahra 1021 (rec. 1960)

SCHERCHEN, HERMANN: Elsa Maria Matheis; Daniza Ilitsch; Rosette Anday; Erich
Majkut; Georgina von Milinkovic; Georg Oeggl; Hugo Wiener; Vienna Academy
Chamber Choir; Vienna Singakademie Chorus; Vienna Boys' Choir; Vienna
Symphony Orchestra – 2-Tahra TAH 120 (rec. 1951)

SCHERCHEN, HERMANN: Rita Meinl-Weise; Sigrid Ekkehard; Anneliese Müller;
Gertraud Prenzlow; Herbert Reinhold; Kurt Rehm; Willi Heyer-Krämer; Berlin State
Opera Choir; Berlin Staatskapelle – Tahra TAH 110 (Part I only; rec. 1951)

STOKOWSKI, LEOPOLD: Frances Yeend; Uta Graf; Camilla Williams; Martha Lipton;
Louise Bernhardt; Eugene Conley; Carlos Alexander; George London; Schola
Cantorum; Westminster Choir; Boys' Chorus from Public School No. 12,
Manhattan; New York Philharmonic – 12-New York Philharmonic NYP 9801:12
(rec. 1950)

Das Lied von der Erde

BOULEZ, PIERRE: Violeta Urmana, mezzo-soprano; Michael Schade, tenor; Vienna
Philharmonic – DG 289 469 526 (rec. 2001)

HAITINK, BERNARD: Janet Baker, contralto; James King, tenor; Royal
Concertgebouw Orchestra – Philips 432 279 (rec. 1975)

HORENSTEIN, JASCHA: Alfreda Hodgson, contralto; John Mitchinson, tenor; BBC
Northern Orchestra – BBC Legends 4042 (rec. 1972)

KARAJAN, HERBERT VON: Christa Ludwig, contralto; Ludovic Spiess and Horst
Laubenthal, tenors; Berlin Philharmonic – Hunt CD 739 (rec. 1970)

KARAJAN, HERBERT VON: Christa Ludwig, contralto; Rene Kollo, tenor; Berlin
Philharmonic – Foyer CF 2056 (rec. 1972)

KARAJAN, HERBERT VON: Christa Ludwig, contralto; Rene Kollo, tenor; Berlin
Philharmonic – DG 419 058 (rec. 1973–74)

KLEMPERER, OTTO: Elsa Cavelti, contralto; Anton Dermota, tenor; Vienna
Symphony Orchestra – Tuxedo 1036

KLEMPERER, OTTO: Christa Ludwig, contralto; Fritz Wunderlich, tenor;
Philharmonia and New Philharmonia Orchestras – EMI: Angel 47231
(rec. 1964, 1966)

LEVINE, JAMES: Jessye Norman, mezzo-soprano; Siegfried Jerusalem, tenor; Berlin
Philharmonic – DG 439 948 (rec. 1998)

NEUMANN, VACLAV: Christa Ludwig; Thomas Moser; Czech Philharmonic – Praga
PR 254 052 (rec. 1983)

SCHURICHT, CARL: Kerstin Thorborg, mezzo-soprano; Carl Martin Ohmann, tenor;
Royal Concertgebouw Orchestra – Archiphon ARCH-3.1; 13-RCO 97017
(rec. 1939)

SINOPOLI, GIUSEPPE: Iris Vermillion; Keith Lewis; Staatskapelle Dresden – DG 453
437(rec. 1997)

WAKASUGI, HIROSHI: Naoko Ihara; Makoto Tashiro; Tokyo Metropolitan
Symphony Orchestra – Fontec FOCD 9030 (rec. 1991)

WALTER, BRUNO: Kerstin Thorborg; Charles Kullman; Vienna Philharmonic –
Dutton Laboratories 9722; Enterprise 4172 (rec. 1936)

WALTER, BRUNO: Kathleen Ferrier; Julius Patzak; Vienna Philharmonic – Decca
Legends 289 466576 (rec. 1952)

WALTER, BRUNO: Elena Nicolaidi; Set Svanholm; New York Philharmonic –
Archipel ARPCD 0139; Music & Arts 950 (rec. 1953)

WALTER, BRUNO: Maureen Forrester; Richard Lewis; New York Philharmonic –
Curtain Call 206 (rec. 1960)

WALTER, BRUNO: Kathleen Ferrier; Set Svanholm; New York Philharmonic –
12-New York Philharmonic NYP 9801:12 (rec. 1948)

WALTER, BRUNO: Mildred Miller; Ernst Haeflinger; New York Philharmonic – Sony
42034 and 64455 (rec. 1960)

Symphony No. 9

BARBIROLLI, JOHN: Turin Radio Symphony Orchestra – Arkadia CDMP 403.1
(rec. 1960)

BARBIROLLI, JOHN: New York Philharmonic – 12-New York Philharmonic NYP
9801:12 (rec. 1962)

BARBIROLLI, JOHN: Berlin Philharmonic – EMI Classics 67926 (rec. 1964)

BERNSTEIN, LEONARD: Berlin Philharmonic – 2-DG 435 378

BOULEZ, PIERRE: BBC Symphony Orchestra – 2-Arkadia CDGI 754.2 (rec. 1971)

BOULEZ, PIERRE: BBC Symphony Orchestra – 2-Memories HR 4493:4 (rec. 1972)

BOULEZ, PIERRE: Chicago Symphony Orchestra – DG 289 457 581 (rec. 1998)

HAITINK, BERNARD: European Community Youth Orchestra – 2-Philips 438 943
(rec. 1993)

HORENSTEIN, JASCHA: Vienna Symphony Orchestra – 2-Vox Classics 5509 (rec. 1952)

HORENSTEIN, JASCHA: London Symphony Orchestra – 2-BBC Legends 4075
(rec. 1966)

HORENSTEIN, JASCHA: French National Orchestra – 2-Disques Montaigne WM 362
(rec. 1967)

HORENSTEIN, JASCHA: American Symphony Orchestra – 4-Music & Arts CD 785
(rec. 1969)

KARAJAN, HERBERT VON: Berlin Philharmonic – 2-Japanese DG 2258-9
  (rec. 1979–80)
KARAJAN, HERBERT VON: Berlin Philharmonic – 2-DG 410 726 (rec. 1982)
KLEMPERER, OTTO: New Philharmonia Orchestra – 2-Angel 67036 (rec. 1967)
KLEMPERER, OTTO: Vienna Philharmonic Orchestra – 2-Living Stage 34705
  (rec. 1968)
LEVINE, JAMES: Philadelphia Orchestra – RCA CD 84553 (rec. 1979)
LEVINE, JAMES: Munich Philharmonic Orchestra – 2-Oehms OC 503 (rec. 1999)
MADERNA, BRUNO: BBC Symphony Orchestra – Arkadia CDMAD 0161
  (rec. 1971)
MADERNA, BRUNO: Turin RAI Symphony Orchestra – Arkadia CDMAD 0284
  (rec. 1972)
MITROPOULOS, DIMITRI: New York Philharmonic – 6-Tahra 1021 (rec. 1960)
MITROPOULOS, DIMITRI: Vienna Philharmonic Orchestra – 4-Andante 4996
  (rec. 1960)
NEUMANN, VACLAV: Leipzig Gewandhaus Orchestra – Berlin Classics 0021872
  (rec. 1968)
RATTLE, SIR SIMON: Vienna Philharmonic – 2-EMI 56580 (rec. 1998)
SCHERCHEN, HERMANN: Vienna Symphony Orchestra – Orfeo D'Or C228901
  (rec. 1950)
WALTER, BRUNO: Vienna Philharmonic – Dutton Laboratories 9708 and 5005; EMI:
  Angel 63029 (rec. 1938)
WALTER, BRUNO: Columbia Symphony Orchestra – 2-Sony 64452 (rec. 1961)
ZANDER, BENJAMIN: Philharmonia Orchestra – 3-Etlarc 80527 (rec. 1999) (with
  discussion disc)

Symphony No. 10
Performing Version by Deryck Cooke (1964, final rev. 1972)
INBAL, ELIAHU: Frankfurt Radio Radio Symphony (first version) – Denon CO-
  75129 (rec. 1992)
LEVINE, JAMES: Philadelphia Orchestra – 2-RCA RCD2 4533 (rec. 1978/80)
ORMANDY, EUGENE: Philadelphia Orchestra (first version) – Columbia MPK 45882
  (rec. 1965)
RATTLE, SIMON: Bournemouth Symphony Orchestra (revisions by Rattle to final
  Cooke revision) – 2-EMI CDC7 54406 (rec. 1980)
RATTLE, SIMON: Berlin Philharmonic (revisions by Rattle to final Cooke revision) –
  EMI 5 56972 (rec. 2000)

Performing version by Joe Wheeler (1966)
OLSON, ROBERT: Mahler Fest Orchestra (ed. Olson) – MahlerFest 10 (rec. 1998)
OLSON, ROBERT: Polish National Radio Symphony (ed. Olson) – Naxos 8.554811
  (rec. 2000)

Performing version by Clinton Carpenter (1966, rev. 1982)
FARBERMAN, HAROLD: Philharmonia Hungarica – Golden String GSCD 024
  (rec. 1995)
LITTON, ANDREW: Dallas Symphony – Delos DE 3295 (rec. 2002)

Performing version by Remo Mazzetti, Jr. (1989, rev. 1992–3; 1997)

SLATKIN, LEONARD: St. Louis Symphony – RCA 09026–68190 (rec. 1995)

LOPEZ-COBOS, JESUS: Cincinnati Symphony (rev. 1997) – Telarc CD-80565 (rec. 1997)

Performing version by Nicola Samale and Giuseppe Mazzuca (1999)

SIEGHART, MARTIN: Vienna Symphony Orchestra – private issue (rec. 22 Sept. 2001)

Performing version by Rudolf Barshai (2000)

BARSHAI, RUDOLF: Junge Deutsche Philharmonie – 2-Brilliant 92205 (rec. 2004)

First movement only

BOULEZ, PIERRE: London Symphony Orchestra – 3-Columbia (Japan) 75DC 959–61 (rec. 1970)

MEHTA, ZUBIN: Los Angeles Philharmonic – 2-London CSA 2248 (rec. 1976)

MEHTA, ZUBIN: Israel Philharmonic – 2-Sony Classicla S2 K 52579 (1992)

MITROPOULOS, DIMITRI: New York Philharmonic – Movimento Musica 02005 (oop) (rec. 1955)

MITROPOULOS, DIMITRI: New York Philharmonic – 6-Tahra 1021; 12-New York Philharmonic NYP 9801:12 (rec. 1960)

SCHERCHEN, HERMANN: Vienna State Opera Orchestra – DG 471246 (rec. 1952)

SCHERCHEN, HERMANN: Leipzig Radio Symphony Orchestra – 2-Enterprise 4133; 2-Tahra TAH 147 (rec. 1960)

First and third movements only

MITROPOULOS, DIMITRI: New York Philharmonic – 12-New York Philharmonic NYP 9801 (rec. 1960)

Miscellaneous orchestral-choral works

Das Klagende Lied

Original Part I and revised Parts II and III

BOULEZ, PIERRE: Stuart Burrows; Evelyn Lear; Ernst Haeflinger; Gerd Nienstedt; Grace Hoffman; Elisabeth Söderström; [chorus]; London Symphony Orchestra – Sony SK 45841 (rec. 1969)

CHAILLY, RICCARDO: Susan Dunn; Brigitte Fassbaender; Markus Baur; Werner Hollweg; Andreas Schmidt; Düsseldorf Musikverein Choir; Berlin Radio Symphony Orchestra – London 425 719 (rec. 1992)

HICKOX, RICHARD: Joan Rodgers, soprano; Linda Finnie, alto; Hans Peter Blochwitz, tenor; Robert Hayward, baritone; Bath Festival Chorus; Waynflete Singers Bournemouth Symphony Orchestra – Chandos CHAN 9247 (rec. 1993)

RATTLE, SIMON: Alfreda Hodgson; Helena Döse; Robert Tear; Sean Rae; City of Birmingham Orch. & Chorus – EMI:Angel CDC 747 089 (rec. 1983–84)

SINOPOLI, GIUSEPPE: Cheryl Studer; Waltraud Meier; Reiner Goldberg; Thomas Allen; Shin-Yuh Kai Chorus; Philharmonia Orchestra – DG 435 382 (rec. 1993)

THOMAS, MICHAEL TILSON: Marina Shaguch, soprano; Michelle DeYoung, mezzo-soprano; Thomas Moser, tenor; Sergei Leiferkus, baritone; San Francisco Symphony and Chorus – RCA BMG 09026-68599 (rec. 1997)

Original three-movement version

NAGANO, KENT: Eva Urbanova; Jadwiga Rappe; Hans Peter Blochwitz; Hakan
  Hagegard; Halle Choir & Orchestra – Erato 3984-21664 (rec. 1998)

Revised version (Parts II and III only)

FEKETE, ZOLTAN: Ilona Steingruber; Sieglinde Wagner; Erich Majkut; Vienna
  Chamber Choir; Vienna State Opera Orchestra – Lyrichord LL 69 (LP) (oop)
  (rec. 1951)

HAITINK, BERNARD: Heather Harper; Norma Proctor; Werner Hollweg; The
  Netherlands Radio Chorus; Amsterdam Concertgebouw Orchestra – 2-Philips 434
  053 (rec. 1973)

MAHLER, FRITZ: Margaret Hoswell; Lili Chookasian; Rudolf Petrak; Hartford
  Chorale and Symphony Orchestra – Vanguard VRS 1048:VSD 2044 (LP) (oop)

MORRIS, WYN: Anna Reynolds, mezzo-soprano; Andor Kaposy, tenor; Teresa Zylis-
  Gara, soprano; Ambrosian Singers; New Philharmonia Orchestra – Angel 36504
  (rec. 1967)

ROZHDESTVENSKY, GENNADY: Teresa Cahill; Janet Baker; Robert Tear; Gwynne
  Howell; BBC Singers; BBC Symphony Chorus; BBC Symphony Orchestra – BBC
  Radio Classics 15656 91412 (rec. 1996)

Songs and song cycles
Lieder und Gesänge

Baker, Dame Janet, mezzo-soprano; Geoffrey Parsons, piano – Hyperion CDA
  66100 (rec. 1983)

Fischer-Dieskau, Dietrich, baritone; Gerald Moore, piano – 3-Angel CDMC 63167
  (rec. 1962)

Fischer-Dieskau, Dietrich, baritone; Leonard Bernstein, piano – 2-Sony SM2 K 47170
  (rec. 1968)

Fischer-Dieskau, Dietrich, baritone; Wolfgang Sawallisch, piano – Orfeo C 333 931
  (rec. 1978)

Fischer-Dieskau, Dietrich, baritone; Daniel Barenboim, piano – 2-EMI TOCE
  6679-80 (rec. 1978)

Halban, Desi, soprano; Bruno Walter, piano – Sony Classical CD 46450 (rec. 1947)

Hampson, Thomas, baritone; Luciano Berion, conductor; Philharmonia Orchestra
  (orchestral arrangement by Luciano Berio) – Teldec 9031 74002 (rec. 1992)

Ludwig, Christa, mezzo-soprano; Gerald Moore, piano – Seraphim S 60070 (rec. 1960s)

Stückgold, Grete (with unidentified orchestra): 'Ich ging mit Lust' – Symposium
  1337 (rec. 1921)

Des Knaben Wunderhorn

Bernstein, Leonard: Christa Ludwig; Walter Berry; New York Philharmonic – 2-Sony
  Classical SM2K 48590 (rec. 1969)

Fischer-Dieskau, Dietrich, baritone; Wolfgang Sawallisch, piano – Orfeo C 333 931
  (rec. 1976)

Fischer-Dieskau, Dietrich, baritone; Daniel Barenboim, piano – Sony SK 44935
  (rec. 1989)

Hampson, Thomas, baritone; Geoffrey Parsons, piano – Teldec 9031 74726 (rec. 1993)

Ludwig, Christa, mezzo-soprano; Walter Berry, baritone; Leonard Bernstein, piano – 2-Sony Classical SM2K 47170 (rec. 1968)

Morris, Wyn: Janet Baker; Geraint Evans; London Philharmonic – Nimbus NI 5084 (rec. 1966)

Prohaska, Felix: Maureen Forrester; Heinz Rehfuss; Vienna State Opera Orchestra – Vanguard OVC 4045 (rec. 1963)

Stückgold, Grete (with unidentified orchestra): 'Wer hat dies Liedlein erdacht?' – Symposium 1337 (rec. 1921)

Szell, George: Elisabeth Schwarzkopf; Dietrich Fischer-Dieskau; London Symphony Orchestra – Angel CDC7 47277 (rec. 1968)

Weigert, Hermann: Heinrich Schlusnus; Berlin State Opera Orchestra: 'Rheinlegendchen' and 'Der Tamoursg'sell' – Symposium 1337 (rec. 1931)

Lieder eines Fahrenden Gesellen

Baker, Janet, mezzo-soprano; Sir John Barbirolli; Halle Orchestra – Angel CDC 747793 (rec. 1967)

Brice, Carol, contralto; Fritz Reiner; Pittsburgh Symphony Orchestra – Columbia ML 4108 (LP) (oop) (rec. 1946)

Fischer-Dieskau, Dietrich, baritone; Wilhelm Furtwängler Vienna Philharmonic – Orfeo C 336 931 (rec. 1951)

Fischer-Dieskau, Dietrich, baritone; Wilhelm Furtwängler; Philharmonia Orchestra – Angel CDC7 47657 (rec. 1952)

Fischer-Dieskau, Dietrich, baritone; Leonard Bernstein, piano – 2-Sony Classical MCD 89008 (rec. 1968)

Fischer-Dieskau, Dietrich, baritone; Rafael Kubelik; Bavarian Radio Symphony Orchestra – DG 429 157 (rec. 1968)

Fischer-Dieskau, Dietrich, baritone; Daniel Barenboim, piano – 2-EMI TOCE 6679–80 (rec. 1978)

Fischer-Dieskau, Dietrich, baritone; Daniel Barenboim; Berlin Philharmonic – Sony Classical SK 44935 (rec. 1989)

Flagstad, Kirsten, soprano; Sir Adrian Boult; Vienna Philharmonic – London 414 624 (rec. 1957)

Hampson, Thomas, baritone; Leonard Bernstein; Vienna Philharmonic – DG 431 682 and DG Video 072 280 (rec. 1990)

Hampson, Thomas, baritone; David Lutz, piano – Teldec 9031 74002 (rec. 1992)

Horne, Marilyn, mezzo-soprano; Zubin Mehta; Los Angeles Philharmonic – London 430 135 (rec. 1978)

Ludwig, Christa, mezzo-soprano; Sir Adrian Boult; Philharmonia Orchestra – Angel CDM 69499 (rec. 1958)

Miller, Mildred, mezzo-soprano; Bruno Walter; Columbia Symphony Orchestra – Sony MK 42025 (rec. 1960)

Schey, Hermann, baritone; Willem Mengelberg; Amsterdam Concertgebouw Orchestra – Music & Arts KICC 2063 (rec. 1939)

Zareska, Eugenia, mezzo-soprano; Eduard van Beinum; London Philharmonic Orchestra – Symposium 1337 (rec. 1946)

Kindertotenlieder

Baker, Dame Janet, mezzo-soprano; Sir John Barbirolli; Halle Orchestra – Angel CDC 747793 (rec. 1967)

Baker, Dame Janet, mezzo-soprano; Leonard Bernstein; Israel Philharmonic – 2-Columbia M2 K 42195 (rec. 1974)

Ferrier, Kathleen, contralto; Bruno Walter; Vienna Philharmonic – Gala 307 (rec. 1949)

Fischer-Dieskau, Dietrich, baritone; Karl Böhm; Berlin Philharmonic – 2-DG 416 631 (rec. 1963)

Forrester, Maureen, contralto; Charles Munch; Boston Symphony Orchestra – RCA AGL1 1338 (oop) (rec. 1958)

Hampson, Thomas, baritone; Leonard Bernstein; Vienna Philharmonic – DG 431 682 (rec. 1988) and DG Video 072 280 (1989)

Horne, Marilyn, mezzo-soprano; Henry Lewis; Royal Philharmonic – London OS 26147 (LP) (oop) (rec. 1968)

Ludwig, Christa, mezzo-soprano; Andre Vandernoot; Philharmonic Orchestra – Angel CDM 69499 (rec. 1958)

Ludwig, Christa, mezzo-soprano; Herbert von Karajan; Berlin Philharmonic – 2-DG 415 096 (rec. 1974)

Prey, Hermann, baritone; Bernard Haitink; Amsterdam Concertgebouw Orchestra – Philips 434 053 (rec. 1970)

Rehkemper, Heinrich, baritone; Jascha Horenstein; Berlin State Opera Orchestra – 2-Pearl CDS 9929 (rec. 1928)

Tourel, Jennie, mezzo-soprano; Leonard Bernstein; New York Philharmonic – 2-Sony Classical SM2K 47576 (rec. 1960)

Rückert Lieder

Baker, Janet, mezzo-soprano; Michael Tilson Thomas, conductor; London Symphony Orchestra – 2-Columbia M2K 44553 (rec. 1987)

Charles-Cahier, Sara, contralto; Selmar Meyerowitz, conductor; Berlin Symphony Orchestra – 2-Pearl CDS 9929 (rec. 1930)

Ferrier, Kathleen, contralto; Bruno Walter, conductor; Vienna Philharmonic – London 433 802 (rec. 1952)

Fischer-Dieskau, Dietrich, baritone; Leonard Bernstein, piano – 2-Sony SM2 K 47170 (rec. 1968)

Fischer-Dieskau, Dietrich, baritone; Daniel Barenboim, piano – Angel CDC7 47657 (rec. 1978)

Forrester, Maureen, contralto; Ferenc Fricsay, conductor; Berlin Radio Symphony Orchestra – DG LPE 17199 (LP) (oop) (rec. 1959)

Hampson, Thomas, baritone; Leonard Bernstein, conductor; Vienna Philharmonic – DG 431 682 (rec. 1990) and DG Video 072 280 (rec. 1991)

Horne, Marilyn, mezzo-soprano; Zubin Mehta, conductor; Los Angeles Philharmonic – London 26578 (LP) (oop) (rec. 1978)

Kullman, Charles; Malcolm Sargent, conductor (unidentified orchestra): 'Ich atmet einen Lindenduft' (in English) – Symposium 1337 (rec. 1938)

Ludwig, Christa, mezzo-soprano; Herbert von Karajan, conductor; Berlin Philharmonic – 2-DG 415 099 (rec. 1974)

Thorborg, Kerstin, contralto; Bruno Walter, conductor; Vienna Philharmonic –
Music & Arts CD 749 (rec. 1936)

Weber's *Die Drei Pintos*
BERTINI, GARY: Lucia Popp; Werner Hollweg; Hermann Prey; Kurt Moll; Heinz
Fruse; Franz Grundheber; Netherlands Vocal Ensemble; Munich Philharmonic –
3-RCA PRL3–9063 (LP) (oop)
ARRIVABENI, PAOLO: Robert Helzer; Peter Furlong; Barbara Zechmeister; Sophie
Marilley; Eric Shaw; Alessandro Svab; Stewart Kempster; Sinead Campbell; Ales
Jenis; Wexford Festival Opera Chorus; National Philharmonic Orchestra of
Belarus – 2-Naxos 8.660142:43

The Welte-Mignon piano rolls (Mahler, piano)
SYMPHONY NO. 4: Fourth Movement; Symphony No. 5: First Movement; 'Ging
heut' morgens übers Feld' (from *Lieder eines fahrenden Gesellen*); 'Ich ging mit
Lust durch einen grünen Wald' (from *Lieder und Gesänge*) – Golden Legacy
(GLRS 101)

Transcriptions
Symphony No. 1 (4-hand piano version by Bruno Walter)
Hrsel, Zdenka and Martin, piano duet – Praga PRD:DSD 250 197 Okashiro, Chitose;
piano (transcribed for one piano by Chitose Okashiro) – Chateau C10001
(rec. 2002)

Symphony No. 5
David Briggs, organ of Gloucester Cathedral (transcribed by David Briggs) – Priory
PRCD 649 (rec. 1998)

Symphony No. 6 (arr. Zemlinsky)
Zenker, Silvia and Evelinde Trenker, pianists – MD & G L3400 (rec. 1991)

Symphony No. 7 (arr. Casella)
Zenker, Silvia and Evelinde Trenkner, duo pianists – D&G MD&G L 3445 (rec. 1992)

Retouchings
Bach Suite
CHAILLY, RICCARDO: Royal Amsterdam Concertgebouw Orchestra – 2-Decca
B0002336 (rec. 2004)
LOPEZ-COBOS, JESUS: Berlin Radio Symphony Orchestra – Schwann CD1 1637
(rec. 1975)
MENGELBERG, WILLEM: New York Philharmonic – Camden CAE 387 (LP) (oop)

Beethoven symphonies: Nos. 5, 6, 7 and 9
TIBORIS, PETER: Leah Anne Myers; Ilene Sameth; James Clark; Richard Conant;
Janacek Opera Chorus; Brno Philharmonic; Warsaw Philharmonic – 5-Albany
TROY 110 (rec. 1994)

Schubert quartet 'Death and the Maiden'
TURUVSKY, YULI: I Musici de Montreal – Chandos CHAN 8928 (rec. 1990)

Schubert Symphony No. 9
TIBORIS, PETER: Warsaw Philharmonic – Albany TROY 89 (rec. 1993)

Schumann symphonies
CECCATO, ALDO: Bergen Philharmonic – 2-BIS CD 361, 364 (rec. 1987–88)

Notes

Introduction: marginalia on Mahler today
1. See Theodor Adorno, *Mahler. A Musical Physiognomy*, trans. Edmund Jephcott, University of Chicago Press, 1992, p. 46, and Carl Dahlhaus, *Realism in Nineteenth-Century Music*, trans. Mary Whittall, Cambridge University Press, 1985, pp. 113–14.
2. Gerhard Scheit and Wilhelm Svoboda, *Feindbild Gustav Mahler. Zur antisemitischen Abwehr der Moderne in Österreich*, Vienna, Sonderzahl, 2002, p. 268.
3. See Theodor Adorno, 'Mahler Today', trans. Susan Gillespie in Richard Leppert (ed.), *Essays on Music. Theodor W. Adorno*, Berkeley and Los Angeles, University of California Press, 2002, pp. 603–11, esp. pp. 604 and 609.
4. Luciano Berio, citing the Italian poet Leopardi, in *Gustav Mahler. L'Attrazione d'Amore/Luciano Berio. Voyage to Cythera*, DVD, dir. Frank Scheffer, Allegri Film BV 1998/1999.
5. See Riccardo Chailly on his collecting of early recordings and his use of Willem Mengelberg's personally annotated score of Mahler's Fifth Symphony in performance, in *L'Attrazione d'Amore*.
6. Henry-Louis de La Grange, in *What the Universe Tells Me. Unraveling the Mysteries of Mahler's Third Symphony*, DVD, dir. Jason Starr, Video Artists International VAI 4267, 2003.
7. See *Gustav Mahler*, BBC Great Composers series, 1997, dir. Kriss Rusmanis, Starr, *What the Universe Tells Me*, and Scheffer, *L'Attrazione d'Amore* and *Conducting Mahler/I have Lost Touch with the World*, Allegri Film BV 1996/2004.
8. See ML, p. 221.
9. See 'Gustav Mahler: in Memoriam' in Leonard Stein (ed.), *Style and Idea. Selected Writings of Arnold Schoenberg*, trans. Leo Black, London, Faber & Faber 1975, pp. 447–8; and 'Gustav Mahler' in *ibid.*, pp. 449–72, esp. pp. 455–6. See also, pp. 42, 82, and 136 of *Style and Idea*.
10. See Stein (ed.), *Style and Idea*, pp. 245, 256, 277, 399, 425–6, 459–62.
11. *Ibid.*, pp. 447–62, *passim*.
12. See *ibid.*, p. 450, and ML, pp. 256–7 and 325–6.
13. *Gustav Mahler. Der fremde Vertraute*, Vienna, Paul Zsolnay, 2003, p. 870.
14. Stein (ed.), *Style and Idea*, pp. 155 and 450.
15. Peter Brooks, *The Melodramatic Imagination. Balzac, Henry James, Melodrama and the Mode of Excess*, New Haven and London, Yale University Press, 2nd edn, 1995, p. 15.
16. Richard Heuberger, 1899 review of the Second Symphony, *Neue freie Presse*, cited in HLGE1, p. 507.
17. See 'Marginalia on Mahler' in Leppert (ed.), *Essays on Music*, pp. 612–18, esp. p. 616.
18. Adorno, 'Mahler Today', p. 604. See also Scheit and Svoboda, *Feindbild Gustav Mahler*, p. 268.
19. *The Whole Equation. A History of Hollywood*, London, Abacus, 2006, p. 98. I am indebted to Peter Franklin for bringing this book to my attention.
20. Adorno, 'Marginalia', p. 617.
21. Berio, in *Voyage to Cythera*, and Simon Rattle on the Seventh Symphony, in *Conducting Mahler*.

1 Socio-political landscapes: reception and biography
1. Laird M. Easton, *The Red Count. The Life and Times of Harry Kessler*, Berkeley and Los Angeles, University of California Press, 2002, p. 147.
2. *Ibid.*, p. 258.
3. *Ibid.*, p. 270.
4. See Bruno Walter, *Theme and Variations*, London, Hamish Hamilton 1947 (2nd impression 1948), p. 249.
5. Hans Pfitzner, *Die neue Aesthetik der musikalischen Impotenz*, Munich, Verlag der Süddeutschen Monatshefte, 1920; see also Peter, Franklin, 'Audiences, Critics and the Depurification of Music. Reflections on a 1920s Controversy', *Journal of the Royal Musical Association*, 114 (1989), 80–91.
6. In his typically angry but cogent review of a performance of the Third Symphony in Vienna in 1909, Hirschfeld had protested 'The great symphonists feel and reveal the grandeur, the strengths, the nobility and the integrity – not the negative features – of their time. Yet how frivolous, childish and without strength our epoch appears in Mahler's symphonies'; see Peter Franklin, *Mahler Symphony No. 3*, Cambridge University Press 1991, p. 32.
7. Iwan Sollertinski, *Gustav Mahler – Der Schrei ins Leere* (translated from Russian into German by Reimar Westendorf), *ssm 8 studia slavica musicologica*, Berlin, Verlag Ernst Kuhn, 1996, pp. 10 and 75 (author's translation).

8. Bernstein's open-air performance of the Second Symphony in 1967, following the Nine Days' War, was one of the many examples of Israeli unease with Mahler's 'Germanness' discussed in an illuminating paper by Yulia Kreinin of the Hebrew University of Jerusalem ('Mahler's Reception in Israel: The Fourth Homeland?') in the Third Biennial International Conference on Twentieth-Century music at the University of Nottingham, 26–9 June 2003. Uri Caine's initial 1997 Mahler arrangements (others have followed) were issued on the CD *gustav mahler/uri caine: urlicht/primal light*, Winter and Winter 910 004–2 New Edition, Munich, Germany 1997.

9. My allusion is to Richard Leppert, *The Sight of Sound. Music, Representation, and the History of the Body*, Berkeley, Los Angeles and London, University of California Press, 1993/1995. When they enter four bars after rehearsal figure 1, the trumpets are described as 'In sehr weiter Entfernung aufgestellt'. Five bars before figure 2, that direction is modified to 'in weiter Entfernung'.

10. Specific references to biographical details here inevitably rely on facts selected from my own short study: Peter Franklin, *The Life of Mahler*, Cambridge University Press, 1997; all biographical work on Mahler must, however, rely to some degree on the work of Henry-Louis de La Grange (see the bibliography for full details of these volumes).

11. In the third movement, at figure 6, the direction reads: 'Die Becken sind an dieser Stelle an der grossen Trommel anzuhängen und Becken- und Trommelstimme sind von einem und demselben Musiker zu schlagen'.

12. Track 5 on *gustav mahler/ uri caine: urlicht/ primal light* (see note 8 above).

13. For an account of Mahler's semi-public disavowal of symphonic 'programmes' in October 1900, following a Munich performance of his Second Symphony, see NBLG, pp. 170–1.

14. The 'Imperial Manifesto' (or 'Declaration') 'An meiner Völker!' was published on 21 October 1860; it is printed in facsimile and described in Kurt Blaukopf (ed.), *Mahler. A Documentary Study*, London, Thames and Hudson, 1976, Plate 5 and p. 148.

15. For a brief summary of the situation obtaining when Mahler returned to Vienna in 1897, see Peter Franklin, 'A Stranger's Story: Programmes, Politics and Mahler's Third Symphony' in Donald Mitchell and Andrew Nicholson (eds.), *The Mahler Companion*, Oxford University Press, 1999, pp. 178–9.

16. *Dionysian Art and Populist Politics in Austria*, New Haven and London, Yale University Press, 1974.

17. Kurt Blaukopf and Herta Blaukopf (eds.), *Mahler. His Life, Work and World*, London, Thames and Hudson 1991, p. 149.

18. From Mahler's letter of 13 December 1901 to his sister Justine, extract from Stephen McClatchie (ed. and trans.), *The Family Letters of Gustav Mahler*, New York, Oxford University Press, 2006, p. 364.

19. ML, p. 213.

20. In NBLE, p. 44. For the German text, see NBLG, p. 40.

21. ML, p. 214.

22. See HLGE2, p. 232.

23. For key statements on this by Mahler, as recorded by Bauer-Lechner, see NBLE, pp. 61–2.

24. See ML, p. 82, and McGrath, *Dionysian Art*, pp. 222–5.

25. The information about the Adagietto as Mahler's 'love-song' to Alma comes from Willem Mengelberg; see HLGE2, p. 538, n. 19. For the Finale's reference to the Adagietto theme, see Fifth Symphony, '5. Rondo-Finale', 14 bars after figure 7 (*Grazioso*).

26. See Richard Specht, *Gustav Mahler*, Berlin and Leipzig, Schuster und Loeffler, 1913, p. 304.

27. A valuable collection of accounts and reviews will be found in Zoltan Roman, *Gustav Mahler's American Years. A Documentary History*, Stuyvesant NY, Pendragon, 1989.

28. *The Etude*, May 1911, 301–2. There is no more recently published transcription of the complete text, but for this passage see Norman Lebrecht, *Mahler Remembered*, London, Faber, 1987, p. 292.

29. Bruno Walter, *Gustav Mahler*, trans. James Galton (with a biographical essay by Ernst Krenek) [originally 1941], New York, Vienna House, 1973, p. 59.

30. In his edition of the much-abbreviated English translation of Alma Mahler's memoir of her life with the composer, Donald Mitchell effectively dismissed the 'many intimate, lyrical affirmations of Mahler's love for her' ('highly personal' and 'well-nigh impossible to translate') along with the annotations on the manuscript of the Tenth Symphony which were transcribed in the German edition ('It is better to consult these in the facsimile edition of the sketches.') See ML, pp. 332 (n.) and xl.

31. ML, p. 135. See also Michael Kennedy, *Mahler*, The Master Musicians Series, London, Dent, 1974, p. 158, n. 5.

2 The literary and philosophical worlds of Gustav Mahler

1. See Norman Lebrecht, *Mahler Remembered*, London, Faber & Faber, 1987. For Horn's comments, see ML, pp. 103–4.

2. See Bruno Walter, *Theme and Variations*, trans. James A. Galston, repr. edn, Westport, CT, Greenwood Press, 1981, p. 86.

3. *Ibid.* (translation slightly amended). The scientist in question was no doubt Arnold Berliner.

4. GMB2, p. 141.

5. Bruno Walter, *Gustav Mahler*, Wilhelmshaven, Florian Noetzel Verlag, 1989, p. 99.

6. 17 and 18 June 1879; SLGM, p. 54.

7. Letter to Bruno Walter, December 1909, GMB2, p. 396. The literary allusion is to a book entitled *Todtenfeier* (see note 47). The passage in question, page 152, stems from the last section of the book, where, in a moment of absolute desperation, the protagonist curses the despotic whims of heaven.

8. Mahler in a letter to Max Marschalk on 26 March 1896; translation cited in Edward R. Reilly, '*Todtenfeier* and the Second Symphony' in Donald Mitchell and Andrew Nicholson (eds.), *The Mahler Companion*, Oxford University Press, 1999, p. 93; for an overview of the programmes to the Second Symphony, see *ibid.*, pp. 123–5.

9. For two standard works on this time and place, see Carl E. Schorske, *Fin-de-siècle Vienna*, New York, Vintage Books, 1981, and William J. McGrath, *Dionysian Art and Populist Politics in Austria*, New Haven, Yale University Press, 1974.

10. Mahler attended the University of Vienna for three semesters between the autumn of 1877 and the winter of 1880; see Herta Blaukopf, 'Mahler an der Universität' in Günther Weiß (ed.), *Neue Mahleriana*, Berne, Peter Lang, 1997, pp. 1–16.

11. Richard Kralik quoted in McGrath, *Dionysian Art*, p. 101.

12. 'Über die Elemente einer Erneuerung religiöser Ideen in der Gegenwart', Vienna: 'im Selbstverlage des Vorstandes des Lesevereines der deutschen Studenten Wiens', 1878, pp. 9 and 14. A few years previous, Lipiner's epic poem, *Der unfesselte Prometheus*, solicited the admiration of Friedrich Nietzsche, a much-admired and widely read figure in the circles Mahler frequented. As Bruno Walter later recalled: 'Nietzsche had a significant but not lasting influence on [Mahler]. As far as [Nietzsche's *Also sprach*] *Zarathustra* is concerned, one could say that he was attracted to the poetic fervour of the work yet put off by the essence of its thinking' (*Gustav Mahler*, p. 102).

13. Mahler had often expressed that besides Wagner in his essay 'Beethoven' only Schopenhauer in *The World as Will and Representation* had anything valuable to say about the essence of music; see GMB2, p. 124.

14. Letter to Anna von Mildenburg regarding the Third Symphony, 28[?] June 1896 in GMB2, p. 187.

15. See NBLG, pp. 25–6 and 33–4; note, too, Mahler's 'conversion' to vegetarianism immediately after reading Wagner's essay 'Religion und Kunst' in the autumn of 1880 (letter to Emil Freund in GMB2, pp. 39–40).

16. For a compilation of Mahler's poems (with English translation), see Appendix 4 in HLGE1.

17. For a sense of the content of Mahler's library, see Jeremy Barham, 'Mahler the Thinker: The Books of the Alma Mahler-Werfel Collection' in Jeremy Barham (ed.), *Perspectives on Gustav Mahler*, Aldershot and Burlington, VT, Ashgate, 2005, pp. 37–151.

18. See GMLW, pp. 50, 70, 72, 168–9 and 307; NBLG, pp. 32 and 34; and Donald Mitchell, *Gustav Mahler. The Wunderhorn Years*, Berkeley, University of California Press, 1980, pp. 225–35.

19. One should be cautious in referring to the composer's literary taste as simply 'romantic'. See Mahler's lengthy quote from Goethe on this subject in GMB2, p. 137.

20. GMLW, p. 81 (trans. amended); see also p. 116.

21. *Ibid.*, p. 168.

22. *Ibid.*, pp. 259–60 (trans. amended).

23. This point was not lost on some of his contemporaries: 'He did not take up any of the fashionable topics, not even the ever-popular topic of sex with which artists have earned so much money in the last decades. He saw everything in the light of a more pure world, one that is permeated by a superhuman, godly force, by a sacred, all-pervasive life-giving spirit.' (Georg Göhler, 'Gustav Mahler' in *Der Kunstwart* (July 1910, 2nd vol.), reprinted in Henry-Louis de La Grange and Günther Weiß (eds.), *Ein Glück ohne Ruh'. Die Briefe Gustav Mahlers an Alma*, Berlin: Siedler, 1995, p. 483 (translation mine).

24. NBLG, p. 62; on page 161 we read: 'Our modern impressionist poets want this so much: to express such moods and feelings, which – apart from that they are bumbling amateurs – they will never achieve in words'.

25. From the diary entry of 5 February 1904 in Martin Machatzke (ed.), *Gerhart Hauptmann. Tagebücher 1897 bis 1905*, Berlin, Propyläen, 1987, p. 386; see also HLGE2, p. 701.

26. Herta Blaukopf, 'Arthur Schnitzler's Response to Mahler. A Review Based on the Writer's Diaries', *News About Mahler Research*, 24 (October 1990), 4–6. Schnitzler had more to say about Mahler in his diary, calling him 'the greatest living composer' and a person 'surrounded by an air of genius'; see Herta Blaukopf, 'Witness to the Mahler Era: Arthur Schnitzler. "He is not doing so well. . ."', *News About Mahler Research*, 28 (October 1992), 13–14.

27. GMLW, p. 60 (trans. amended).

28. For a recent analysis of the peculiar mix of science and irrationalism in Vienna in the late nineteenth century, see David S. Luft, *Eros and Inwardness in Vienna. Weininger, Musil, Doderer*, University of Chicago Press, 2003, pp. 1–42.
29. Bruno Walter in Lebrecht, *Mahler Remembered*, p. 129.
30. See, for instance, Mahler's rendering of the first law of thermodynamics (quotation, p. 34), his discussion of gravitational theory (GMB2, pp. 283 and 342, respectively), and his mention of the spectral analysis of stars (GMLW, p. 57); note also the complete writings of Hermann von Helmholtz (1821–94) in Mahler's library (see Herta Blaukopf, 'Metaphysik und Physik bei Mahler' in Eveline Nikkels and Robert Becqué (eds.), *A 'Mass' for the Masses. Proceedings of the Mahler VIII Symposium Amsterdam 1988*, Rotterdam: Universitaire Pers, 1992, pp. 37–41, n. 1).
31. For more on Mahler's interest in science see Blaukopf, 'Metaphysik' and 'Musik als Wissenschaft und umgekehrt' in Friedrich Stadler (ed.), *Wissenschaft als Kunst. Österreichs Beitrag zur Moderne*, Vienna, Springer Verlag, 1997, pp. 119–32.
32. Mahler praised Rosegger in conversation with the critic Ernst Decsey (Lebrecht, *Mahler Remembered*, p. 255) and delighted in receiving some volumes of the writer's works in 1910 (GMLW, p. 369); for an account of Mahler's chance meeting with Rosegger in 1905, see ML, p. 98.
33. Mahler was particularly moved and somewhat repulsed by Tolstoy's account of his search for life's meaning in *A Confession*: 'Awfully sad and barbarically self-destructive, distorted questions and thus boundless destruction of all that is won by the heart and soul' (GMLW, p. 162 (trans. amended): see also p. 166). For Mahler's reflections on Dostoyevsky and especially his profound admiration of *The Brothers Karamazov*, see Inna Barsova, 'Mahler and Russia' in Mitchell and Nicholson (eds.), *The Mahler Companion*, pp. 517–30, and Lebrecht, *Mahler Remembered*, pp. 185, 194, 220, and 240–1.
34. See, for instance, GMLW, p. 207, and GMB2, pp. 198 and 444, n. 85.
35. See GMLW, pp. 168 (1904) and 249 (1906), respectively.
36. Letter to Strauss, 11 October 1905 in Herta Blaukopf (ed.), *Gustav Mahler–Richard Strauss Briefwechsel 1888–1911*, rev. edn, Munich, R. Piper, 1988, p. 106.
37. Letter to Alma of 12 January 1907 in GMLW, pp. 257–8. It should be noted that the comic scurrilousness of the last scene, set in the afterlife, bears a strong resemblance to Mahler's own tendency to combine humour with the deeply serious.

38. Embarking on a hermeneutic reading of any Mahler symphony is fraught with pitfalls. The following merely serves as an illustration of the various ways in which the composer lends extra-musical dimensions to a single work.
39. Letter from Mahler to Arthur Seidl, 17 February 1897, in GMB2, p. 223.
40. Mahler's alteration of this text – in which all souls are forgiven – is, however, hardly doctrinaire.
41. Mahler in a letter to Ludwig Karpath on 2 March 1905 in GMB2, p. 322.
42. There is a deep and largely overlooked connection between Mahler and Nietzsche in section 6 of *The Birth of Tragedy* in which the philosopher similarly praises the folk song as 'the musical mirror of the world' and explicitly points to *Des Knaben Wunderhorn*.
43. Bruno Walter, *Gustav Mahler*, p. 103. See, for instance, Mahler's amusement at Don Quixote's tilting at the windmills (*ibid.*, p. 31); Cervantes's novel came to Mahler's attention as a boy (see NBLG, p. 83) and would remain a lifelong favourite.
44. See, for instance, Reilly, '*Todtenfeier* and the Second Symphony', p. 94.
45. The passage comes at the end of Book 4 (before the Appendix critiquing Kant) that concluded the first version of the tome (published 1819); later editions were published with a substantial second volume of supplements to the first (2nd edn, 1844).
46. Arthur Schopenhauer, *The World as Will and Representation*, trans. E. F. J. Payne, New York, Dover Publications, 1966, 2 vols., vol. I, § 71, p. 411.
47. See programme notes in a letter to Alma, 14 December 1901, in GMLW, pp. 64–5. Note, too, that the title originally given to this first movement is taken from a book by Adam Mickiewicz (1798–1855) published in a German translation as *Todtenfeier* (*Funeral Rite*) in 1887 by Mahler's friend, Siegfried Lipiner (entitled *Dziady* [*Forefathers' Eve*] (1823–32) in the original Polish).
48. See Theodor W. Adorno, *Mahler. A Musical Physiognomy*, trans. Edmund Jephcott, University of Chicago Press, 1992, especially chapter 2.
49. Letter from Mahler to Max Marschalk, 22 June 1901, in GMB2, pp. 283–4; English translation, SLGM, pp. 251–2 (amended).
50. As one commentator has put it: '[Mahler] spoke the language of our time, but with the words of the previous century'. (Friedrich Heller in the commentary to Heinrich Kralik, *Gustav Mahler*, Vienna, Lafite, 1968, p. 17, cited in Walter, *Gustav Mahler*, p. 123.)

3 Music and aesthetics: the programmatic issue

1. Alexander Gottlieb Baumgarten, *Aesthetica* (2 vols.), Frankfurt a. Oder, Traiecti cis Viadrum, I. C.Kleyb, 1750, 1758 (rpt. Hildesheim, G. Olms, 1970). Text taken from Hans Rudolf Schweitzer, *Ästhetik als Philosophie der sinnlichen Erkenntnis*, Basel and Stuttgart, Schwabe & Co., 1973, p. 106.
2. *The Beautiful in Music*, ed. Morris Weitz, trans. Gustav Cohen, Indianapolis, Bobbs-Merrill Comp., 1957, p. 8.
3. *Aesthetic Theory*, ed. Gretel Adorno and Rolf Tiederman, trans. Robert Hullot-Kentor, Minneapolis, University of Minnesota Press, 1997, p. 333.
4. *Esthetics of Music*, trans. William Austin, Cambridge University Press, 1982, p. 10.
5. See E. T. A. Hoffmann, 'Beethoven's Instrumental Music (1813)', trans. Oliver Strunk in Leo Treitler (ed.), *Strunk's Source Readings in Music History*, rev. edn, New York, W. W. Norton, 1998, pp. 1193–4.
6. See HLGF1, pp. 88, 116, 162–3, and Donald Mitchell, *Gustav Mahler. The Wunderhorn Years*, Berkeley and Los Angeles, University of California Press, 1980, pp. 236–7.
7. *Ästhetic oder Wissenschaft des Schönen*, vol. 2, Bassenge, 1842, p. 269, cited in Dahlhaus, *Esthetics*, pp. 29–30.
8. See letter to Arthur Seidl, 17 February 1897, in SLGM, pp. 213 and 412, n. 105 (b); GMB2, p. 124.
9. *The world as will as representation* (vol. 2, ch. 39), cited in Dahlhaus, *Esthetics*, p. 42.
10. Terry Eagleton, *The Ideology of the Aesthetic*, Oxford, Blackwell Publishing, 1990, p. 167.
11. Letter of 26 March 1896 to Max Marschalk, in SLGM, p. 179.
12. See William McGrath, *Dionysian Art and Populist Politics*, New Haven, Yale University Press, 1974, pp. 120–6, and the studies by La Grange and Mitchell.
13. Dahlhaus, *Esthetics*, p. 43.
14. See McGrath, *Dionysian Art*; Peter Franklin, *Mahler. Symphony No. 3*, Cambridge University Press, 1991; Eveline Nikkels, *'O Mensch! Gib Acht!' Friedrich Nietzsches Bedeutung für Gustav Mahler*, Amsterdam, Rodopi, 1989; and HLGF1, pp. 105–11.
15. Friedrich Nietzsche, *The Birth of Tragedy and The Case of Wagner*, trans. Walter Kaufmann, New York, Vintage Books, 1967, p. 55. See also 'On Music and Words' of 1871, trans. Walter Kaufmann in Carl Dahlhaus, *Between Romanticism and Modernism. Four Studies in the Music of the Later Nineteenth Century*, trans. Mary Whittall, Berkeley, University of California Press, 1980, pp. 106–19.
16. Ed. Walter Kaufmann, trans. Walter Kaufmann and R. J. Hollingdale, New York, Vintage Books, 1968, p. 428.
17. *Aesthetic Theory*, p. 332.
18. See Liszt, 'Berlioz and his *Harold* Symphony' in Treitler (ed.), *Strunk's Source Readings*, pp. 1158–74.
19. Hanslick, *The Beautiful in Music*, pp. 47–8.
20. For detailed examples of 'absolute' versus 'programmatic' terminology see Vera Micznik, 'Meaning in Gustav Mahler's Music', unpublished Ph.D. dissertation, State University of New York at Stony Brook, 1989, and 'Is Mahler's Music Autobiographical: A Reappraisal', *Revue Mahler Review*, 1 (1987), 47–63.
21. ' "Swallowing the Programme": Mahler's Fourth Symphony' in Donald Mitchell and Andrew Nicholson (eds.), *The Mahler Companion*, Oxford University Press, 2002, p. 196.
22. Amy Edmonds, 'Instructor's Manual and Test-Item File' for Donald Grout and Claude Palisca, *A History of Western Music*, 6th edn, and Palisca (ed.), *The Norton Anthology of Western Music*, 4th edn, New York and London, W. W. Norton, 2001, p. 156.
23. 'Thesen über Programmusik' in Dahlhaus (ed.), *Beiträge zur musikalischen Hermeneutik*, Regensburg, Bosse, 1975, p. 204.
24. See Hans-Georg Gadamer, *Truth and Method*, 2nd rev. edn, trans. rev. by Joel Weinsheimer and Donald G. Marshall, New York, Continuum, 2000, pp. 190–9.
25. *Aesthetic Theory*, p. 191.
26. *Etudes d'art étranger*, Paris, Mercure de France, 1906, p. 280, cited in HLGF2, p. 134.
27. Cited in HLGF2, p. 137. For more reviews reproaching Mahler for the absence of an explicit programme see *ibid.*, pp. 134, 137 and 212–14, and Micznik, 'Meaning in Gustav Mahler's Music', pp. 3–5.
28. See Charles Youmans, 'The Private Intellectual Context of Richard Strauss's *Also sprach Zarathustra*', *19th -Century Music*, 22/2 (Fall 1998), 102–4.
29. 'Tchaikovsky's "Symphonie Pathétique" (1895)' in Henry Pleasants (ed. and trans.), *Hanslick's Music Criticisms*, New York, Dover, 1988, p. 303.
30. *Gustav Mahler. Eine biographisch-kritische Würdigung*, Leipzig, Herman Seeman Nachfolger, 1901, p. 13. This and all the following translations from German or French are mine, unless stated otherwise.
31. 'A Stranger's Story: Programmes, Politics, and Mahler's Third Symphony' in Mitchell and Nicholson (eds.), *The Mahler Companion*, p. 172.
32. HLGF1, p. 965. See also Stephen McClatchie, 'The 1889 Version of Mahler's First Symphony: A New Manuscript Source', *19th-Century Music*, 20/2 (Fall 1996), 100–1.
33. HLGF1, p. 965.

34. These and subsequent quotes translated from *ibid.*, pp. 306–7.

35. Review, dated 21 November 1889, cited in Mitchell, *The Wunderhorn Years*, pp. 151–5.

36. *Ibid.*, p. 153.

37. See HLGF1, pp. 965–9, and NBLE, p. 239.

38. NBLE, p. 30.

39. Letter to Arthur Seidl, 17 February 1897, in SLGM, p. 212.

40. *Gustav Mahler*, Berlin and Leipzig, Schuster & Loeffler, 1913.

41. 'The Ninth Symphony' in Mitchell and Nicholson (eds.), *The Mahler Companion*, p. 469.

42. Letter to Max Marschalk, 17 December 1895, in SLGM, p. 172.

43. Stephen E. Hefling, 'Mahler: Symphonies 1–4' in D. Kern Holoman (ed.), *The Nineteenth-Century Symphony*, New York, Schirmer, 1997, p. 370.

44. See Raymond Knapp, *Symphonic Metamorphoses: Subjectivity and Alienation in Mahler's Re-Cycled Songs*, Middletown, CT, Wesleyan University Press, 2003.

45. SLGM, p. 207.

46. See Mitchell, *The Wunderhorn Years*, p. 267.

47. Ludwig Schiedermair, *Gustav Mahler*, Leipzig, Hermann Seeman, 1901, pp. 13–14, cited in Kurt Blaukopf (ed.), *Mahler. A Documentary Study*, New York and Toronto, Oxford University Press, 1976, p. 225.

48. 'Thesen über Programmusik', p. 204.

49. 'Mahler's "Todtenfeier" and the Problem of Program Music', *19th-Century Music*, 12/1 (Summer 1988), 27–53.

50. Herta Blaukopf, 'Jean Paul, die erste Symphonie und Dostojewski' in Erich Partsch (ed.), *Gustav Mahler. Werk und Wirken. Neue Mahler-Forschung aus Anlass des vierzigjährigen Bestehens der Internationale Gustav Mahler Gesellschaft*, Vienna, Vom Pasqualatihaus, 1996, pp. 35–42.

51. *Paratexts. Thresholds of Interpretations*, trans. Jane E. Lewin, Cambridge University Press, 1997, pp. 1–2.

52. *Ibid.*, pp. 1 and 371–403.

53. Hugh J. Silverman, 'The Language of Textuality' in *Textualities. Between Hermeneutics and Deconstruction*, New York, London, Routledge, 1994, pp. 83–5. See also Roland Barthes, 'From Work to Text' in *Image, Music, Text*, trans. Stephen Heath, New York, Hill and Wang, 1976, pp. 157–8, and Jacques Derrida, *Limited Inc.*, trans. Samuel Weber, Evanston, IL, Northwestern University Press, 1988.

54. 'Text and Subjectivity' in *The Sense of Music. Semiotic Essays*, Princeton University Press, 2000, pp. 147–95.

55. See Richard Leppert, 'Paradise, Nature, and Reconciliation, or, a Tentative Conversation with Wagner, Puccini, Adorno, and the Ronettes', *Echo*, 4/1 (Spring 2002), www.echo.ucla.edu.

56. 'Narrative Archetypes and Mahler's Ninth Symphony' in Steven Paul Scher (ed.), *Music and Text. Critical Inquiries*, Cambridge University Press, 1992, pp. 118–36.

57. See Robert Samuels, *Mahler's Sixth Symphony. A Study in Musical Semiotics*, Cambridge University Press, 1995, and Carolyn Abbate, *Unsung Voices. Opera and Musical Narrative in the Nineteenth Century*, Princeton University Press, 1991.

58. *Mahler. A Musical Physiognomy*, trans. Edmond Jephcott, University of Chicago Press, 1992, pp. 3–4.

4 Juvenilia and early works: from the first song fragments to *Das klagende Lied*

1. See HLGF1 (chapters 1–5); NBLG, pp. 17, 55 and 69–70; NBLE, pp. 23 and 57–8; Kurt Blaukopf and Herta Blaukopf (eds.), *Mahler. His Life, Work and World*, London, Thames and Hudson, 1991, pp. 24–5 and 29–31; and Donald Mitchell, *Gustav Mahler. The Early Years*, rev. edn, Berkeley and Los Angeles, University of California Press, 1980.

2. Mitchell, *The Early Years*, pp. 116–20 and 322–4; HLGF1, pp. 915–17; Mitchell, *Gustav Mahler. The Wunderhorn Years*, Berkeley, University of California Press, 1980, pp. 51–82; and Paul Banks, 'The Early Social and Musical Environment of Gustav Mahler', unpublished D.Phil. thesis, University of Oxford, 1980, pp. 305–18.

3. Cited by Renate Hilmar-Voit in Manfred Wagner-Artzt (ed.), *Gustav Mahler Sämtliche Werke. Kritische Gesamtausgabe, Supplement Band III. Klavierquartett 1. Satz*, Vienna, Universal Edition, 1997, pp. viii–ix.

4. NBLE, pp. 23 and 57.

5. Cited in Paul Banks, 'An Early Symphonic Prelude by Mahler?' *19th-Century Music*, 3/2 (1979), 141–9; quote on p. 142.

6. Richard Specht, 'Gustav Mahler', *Die Musik*, 7/15 (1907–8), 153.

7. ML, p. 63.

8. Ludwig Karpath, *Begegnung mit dem Genius*, Vienna, Fiba, 1934, p. 62, cited in Banks, 'The Early Social and Musical Environment', p. 201.

9. See Banks, 'An Early Symphonic Prelude'.

10. See Banks, 'The Early Social and Musical Environment', pp. 275–85, and E. Mary Dargie, *Music and Poetry in the Songs of Gustav Mahler*, Berne, Peter Lang, 1981, pp. 54–5.

11. Mitchell, *The Early Years*, pp. 127–8.

12. See NBLG, p. 55, and NBLE, p. 58.

13. Cited in HLGF1, pp. 1068–70.

14. See Zoltan Roman (ed.), *Gustav Mahler Sämtliche Werke. Kritische Gesamtausgabe Band XIII, Teilband 5. Verschiedene Lieder für eine Singstimme mit Klavier*, Mainz, Schott, 1990.

15. See Jiri Rychetsky, 'Mahler's Favourite Song', *The Musical Times*, 130 (December 1989), 729; Banks, 'The Early Social and Musical Environment' (esp. pp. 1–68); and Vladimír Karbusický, *Gustav Mahler und seine Umwelt*, Darmstadt, Wissenschaftliche Buchgesellschaft, 1978.

16. SLGM, p. 393.

17. See NBLE, pp. 43–4.

18. See my review of the critical edition (Manfred Wagner-Artzt (ed.), *Gustav Mahler Klavierquartett 1. Satz*), *Music & Letters*, 80/1 (February 1999), 163–5, and 'Mahler's First Compositions: Piano Quartet and Songs' in Donald Mitchell and Andrew Nicholson (eds.), *The Mahler Companion*, rev. edn, Oxford University Press, 2002, pp. 597–607.

19. See Dika Newlin, 'Gustav Mahler's Piano Quartet in A minor', *Chord and Discord*, 2/10 (1963), 180–3; Peter Ruzicka, 'Editorial Remarks' in Ruzicka (ed.), *Gustav Mahler. Klavierquartett*, Hamburg, Sikorski, 1973, pp. 3 and 31, and 'Gustav Mahlers Klavierquartett von 1876', *Musica*, 28/5 (September–October, 1974), 454–7; HLGF1, pp. 933–5; Banks, 'The Early Social and Musical Environment', pp. 336–43; Klaus Hinrich Stahmer, 'Mahlers Frühwerk – Eine Stiluntersuchung' in Stahmer (ed.), *Form und Idee in Gustav Mahlers Instrumentalmusik*, Wilhelmshaven, Heinrichshofen, 1980, pp. 10–28; Mitchell, *The Early Years*, pp. 123–7; Renate Hilmar-Voit, 'Foreword' in Wagner-Artzt (ed.), *Gustav Mahler Klavierquartett 1. Satz*, pp. vii–xi; and Barham, 'Mahler's First Compositions'.

20. See NBLG, p. 55.

21. *Gustav Mahler. Eine Studie über Persönlichkeit und Werke*, Munich, Piper, 1912, pp. 29–30.

22. Newlin, 'Gustav Mahler's Piano Quartet', p. 183; Stahmer, 'Mahlers Frühwerk', p. 28; and Mitchell, *The Early Years*, p. 126.

23. Stahmer, 'Mahlers Frühwerk', p. 25; see Barham, 'Mahler's First Compositions', pp. 598–603.

24. Banks, 'The Early Social and Musical Environment', p. 339.

25. The F–F♯ false relation results from errors in Banks's transcription of bars 103–5 ('The Early Social and Musical Environment', ex. 65, vol. 1, p. 209) derived in part from Ruzicka's 1973 edition of the movement.

26. Barham, 'Mahler's First Compositions', p. 600.

27. See *News About Mahler Research*, 31 (March 1994), 28, and Barham, 'Mahler's First Compositions', p. 603.

28. See Barham, 'Mahler's First Compositions', pp. 605–7.

29. See Reinhold Kubik, 'Foreword' to the critical edition, *Gustav Mahler Sämtliche Werke. Kritische Gesamtausgabe Supplement Band IV. Das klagende Lied. Erstfassung in drei Sätzen (1880)*, Vienna, Universal Edition, 1997, p. x.

30. See n. 29 and my review of this edition in *Music & Letters*, 83/1 (February 2002), 177–80.

31. See Mitchell, '"Waldmärchen": the Unpublished First Part of *Das klagende Lied*', *The Musical Times*, 111 (1970), 375–9, *The Wunderhorn Years*, pp. 56–68, and '*Das klagende Lied*. Mahler's "Opus 1"', *Muziek & Wetenschap*, 7/1 (1999), 33–42; HLGF1, pp. 943–54; Wolf Rosenberg, 'Gustav Mahlers *Klagendes Lied*. Versuch einer Deutung', *Musica*, 26/2 (1972), 119–22; Edward Reilly, '*Das klagende Lied* Reconsidered' in Stephen Hefling (ed.), *Mahler Studies*, Cambridge University Press, 1997, pp. 25–52; Alfred Rosé cited in Jack Diether, 'Notes on Some Mahler Juvenilia', *Chord and Discord*, 3/1 (1969), 3–100, quote on p. 14; Banks, 'The Early Social and Musical Environment', pp. 302, 345 and 366; and John Williamson, 'The Earliest Completed Works: a Voyage Towards the First Symphony' in Mitchell and Nicholson (eds.), *The Mahler Companion*, pp. 39–61.

32. Jack Diether, 'Notes'; Martin Zenck, 'Mahlers Streichung des "Waldmärchens" aus dem *Klagenden Lied*. Zum Verhältnis von philologischer Erkenntnis und Interpretation', *Archiv für Musikwissenschaft*, 38 (1981), 179–93; and Kubik, '*Das klagende Lied*. Geschichte, Quellen, Fassungen', *Muziek & Wetenschap*, 7/1 (1999), 19–32.

33. See Barham, review, p. 180.

34. For further details see Richard Fiske, 'Mahler's *Das klagende Lied*: a Conductor's Analysis of the Original Tripartite Manuscript and its Bipartite Revisions', unpublished Ph.D. dissertation, Indiana University, 1983, pp. 127–244.

35. See Banks, 'The Early Social and Musical Environment', pp. 291–302.

36. See HLGF1, pp. 35–6 and 67, and ML, pp. 63–4.

37. For a related view of 'Waldmärchen' see Hans Holländer, 'Ein unbekannter Teil von Gustav Mahlers "Klagendem Lied"', *Der Auftakt*, 14/11–12 (1934), 200–2.

5 Song and symphony (I). *Lieder und Gesänge*
Volume 1, *Lieder eines fahrenden Gesellen* and
the First Symphony: compositional patterns
for the future

1. Only a later, clean autograph copy of 'Hans
und Grete' is extant, possibly dating from
1888–91. The best guess for 'Frühlingsmorgen',
'Erinnerung', 'Serenade' and 'Phantasie' is
1882–3, though there is some suggestion that the
last two were composed in 1887.

2. The critical edition of the first volume of
Lieder und Gesänge is in Zoltan Roman (ed.),
*Verschiedene Lieder, Gustav Mahler. Sämtliche
Werke. Kritische Gesamtausgabe*, Volume XIII,
Fascicle 5, Mainz/Vienna, Schott/Internationale
Gustav Mahler Gesellschaft, 1990.

3. For present purposes, the term designates
pieces that include one or more variations of two
or more themes, not ordered according to
strophic or rondo form.

4. For fuller details, see Roman, 'From
Collection to Cycle: Poetic Narrative and Tonal
Design in Mahler's *Lieder eines fahrenden
Gesellen*', *Revista de Musicología*, 16 (1993)
[published in 1997], 3595–602, and my critical
edition of the cycle in *Gustav Mahler. Sämtliche
Werke. Kritische Gesamtausgabe*, Volumes XIII
and XIV, Fascicle 1, London/Vienna, Josef
Weinberger/Internationale Gustav Mahler
Gesellschaft, 1982.

5. GMB2, p. 57; all translations are mine.

6. For the three poems, see E. Mary Dargie,
Music and Poetry in the Songs of Gustav Mahler,
Berne, Peter Lang, 1981, pp. 79–82; this excerpt
on p. 80.

7. So in the pianoforte edition; the orchestral
version has 'Dezember, (1883)'.

8. Implied in another, undated, letter to Löhr,
probably written in April 1884, referring to the
previous Christmas, in GMB2, p. 52.

9. Judging from Mahler's letters, the final break
with Johanna took place late in spring 1885; it may
well have prompted him to set the poems to music.

10. The letter is in Mathias Hansen (ed.), *Gustav
Mahler. Briefe*, 2nd edn, Leipzig, Reclam, 1985,
pp. 139–40.

11. NBLG, p. 39.

12. To facilitate comparison, the Second
Symphony's keys are transposed up a major
second.

13. *Gustav Mahler*, Vienna, Universal Edition,
1916, pp. 99 and 101.

14. GMB2, pp. 92–3. Though undated, the letter
refers to the recent birth of the Löhrs' first child
in early March. Based on this letter, and on a
miscellany of variously specific and reliable
sources, Constantin Floros believes that Mahler
wrote the entire work between 20 January and
the end of March (*Gustav Mahler III. Die*

Symphonien, Wiesbaden, Breitkopf & Härtel,
1985, p. 22).

15. GMB2, p. 172.

16. NBLG, p. 35.

17. *Ibid.*, p. 26.

18. GMB2, pp. 171 and 215.

19. *Ibid.*, p. 169. Reasoning from the 'uncannily'
accurate characterization of the music by a
German-language critic following the première,
Floros questions Mahler's veracity (*Gustav
Mahler III*, p. 27).

20. *Ibid.*, p. 222.

21. Monika Tibbe, *Lieder und Liedelemente in
instrumentalen Symphonisätzen Gustav Mahlers*,
2nd edn, Munich, Katzbichler, 1977, p. 132. The
Internationale Gustav Mahler Gesellschaft plans
to publish an edition of the five-movement
Hamburg version of the Symphony as
Supplemental Volume V, edited by Reinhold
Kubik.

22. References are to the revised critical edition,
Sander Wilkens (ed.), *Symphonie Nr. 1. Sämtliche
Werke. Kritische Gesamtausgabe*, Vol. I, Vienna,
Universal Edition/IGMG, 1992.

23. To the general indifference of contemporaries and later observers, Fritz Stiedry (Mahler's
protégé in his youth) also designated this as the
beginning of the 'recapitulation' in his analytical
introduction to the study score of the revised
edition (London, Boosey & Hawkes, 1943, p. 2).

24. *Gustav Mahler*, London, Gollanz, 1965,
p. 40.

6 Song and song-symphony (I). *Des Knaben
Wunderhorn* and the Second, Third and Fourth
Symphonies: music of heaven and earth

1. SLGM, p. 284.

2. ML, p. 93.

3. Letter from summer 1895, housed in the
Austrian Theatermuseum, Vienna, Sign. A
29091.

4. See Renate Hilmar-Voit, 'Symphonic Sound
or in the Style of Chamber Music? The Current
Performing Forces of the *Wunderhorn* Lieder and
the Sources', *News About Mahler Research*, 28
(October 1992), 8–12.

5. NBLG, p. 185.

6. NBLE, p. 68.

7. Christian Martin Schmidt, ' "O Röschen rot" –
Lied und Symphonie' in Bernd Sponheuer and
Wolfram Steinbeck (eds.), *Gustav Mahler und das
Lied*, Bonner Schriften zur Musikwissenschaft 6,
Frankfurt am Main, Peter Lang, 2003, p. 134.

8. Henry Louis de La Grange, 'Music about
Music in Mahler' in Stephen Hefling (ed.),
Mahler Studies, Cambridge University Press
1997, p. 139.

9. NBLE, p. 154.

10. *Ibid.*
11. SLGM, p. 212.
12. *Ibid.*, p. 180.
13. *Ibid.*
14. NBLE, p. 131.
15. Hans Heinrich Eggebrecht, *Die Musik Gustav Mahlers*, 2nd edn, Munich, Piper, 1986, p. 68.
16. NBLE, p. 68.
17. Cited in Edward E. Reilly, '*Todtenfeier* and the Second Symphony' in Donald Mitchell and Andrew Nicholson (eds.), *The Mahler Companion*, Oxford University Press, 2002, p. 86.
18. NBLE, p. 43.
19. ML, p. 213.
20. See also Reilly, '*Todtenfeier*', 94. For a contrasting view, see Stephen Hefling, 'Mahler's "Totenfeier" and the Problem of Program Music', *19th-Century Music*, 12 (1988), 27–53.
21. Downward curve of intensity.
22. Bernd Sponheuer, *Logik des Zerfalls. Untersuchungen zum Finalproblem in den Symphonien Gustav Mahlers*, Tutzing, Hans Schneider, 1978, p. 110.
23. *Mahler. A Musical Physiognomy*, trans. Edmund Jephcott, University of Chicago Press, 1992, p. 45.
24. Sudden change of fortune.
25. See Mahler's apocalyptic description of the work in NBLE, pp. 43–4.
26. Adorno, *A Musical Physiognomy*, p. 6.
27. SLGM, p. 180.
28. *Ibid.*
29. Gunter Gebauer and Christoph Wulf, *Mimesis Kultur – Kunst – Gesellschaft*, Reinbek bei Hamburg, Rowohlt, 1992, p. 185.
30. Eggebrecht, *Die Musik Gustav Mahlers*, p. 94.
31. Wilhelm J. Revers, *Psyche und Zeit*, Salzburg and Munich, Anton Pustet, 1985, p. 10.
32. Matthias Hansen, *Gustav Mahler*, Stuttgart, Philipp Reclam jun., 1996, p. 92.
33. Federico Celestini, 'Die Unordnung der Dinge. Die musikalische Groteske in der Wiener Moderne (1885–1914)', Habilitationsschrift, Karl Franzens-Universität Graz, 2004, p. 68.
34. Eggebrecht, *Die Musik Gustav Mahlers*, p. 181.
35. Friedhelm Krummacher, *Gustav Mahlers III. Symphonie. Welt im Widerbild*, Kassel, Bärenreiter, 1991, p. 113.
36. *Humor als Formkonzept in der Musik Gustav Mahlers*, Stuttgart and Weimar, Metzler, 1995, p. 135.
37. *Irony, Satire, Parody and the Grotesque in the Music of Shostakovich*, Aldershot, Ashgate, 2000, p. 15.
38. Krummacher, *Gustav Mahlers III. Symphonie*, p. 96.
39. See Donald Mitchell, *Gustav Mahler. The Wunderhorn Years*, London, Faber & Faber, 1975, pp. 311–15, and Raymond Knapp,

Symphonic Metamorphoses, Middletown, CT, Wesleyan University Press, 2003, p. 26.
40. NBLE, p. 151.
41. *Ibid.*, p. 40.
42. *Ibid.*, p. 66.
43. Adorno, *A Musical Physiognomy*, p. 77.
44. 'Mahler and Freud: the Dream of the Stately House' in Rudolf Klein (ed.), *Gustav Mahler Kolloquium 1979*, Kassel, Bärenreiter, 1981, pp. 40–51.
45. See Mahler's performance instructions for the corresponding bars 64 and 68.
46. Claudia Maurer Zenck, 'Die "dünne Hülle" über dem Kopfsatz der Dritten Symphonie', in Bernd Sponheuer and Wolfram Steinbeck (eds.), *Gustav Mahler und die Symphonik des 19. Jahrhunderts*, Frankfurt am Main, Bonner Schriften zur Musikwissenschaft 5, Peter Lang, 2001, p. 90.
47. Krummacher, *Gustav Mahlers III. Symphonie*, p. 74.
48. NBLE, p. 151.
49. Bernhard R. Appel, 'Humoreske' in *Die Musik in Geschichte und Gegenwart* (2nd edn), Sachteil, vol. 4, Kassel, Bärenreiter, 1996, Spalte 455.
50. NBLE, p. 152.
51. Constantin Floros, *Gustav Mahler. The Symphonies*, Aldershot, Scolar Press, 1994, p. 124.
52. See Berlioz–Strauss, *Instrumentationslehre*, Frankfurt am Main, C. F. Peters, 1905, p. 65.
53. NBLE, p. 153.
54. James Zychowicz, *Mahler's Fourth Symphony*, Oxford University Press, 2000, p. 18.
55. Hansen, *Gustav Mahler*, p. 105.
56. Rudolf Stephan, *Gustav Mahler. IV. Sinfonie G-Dur*, Munich, Wilhelm Fink, 1966, p. 24.

7 Song and symphony (II). From *Wunderhorn* to Rückert and the middle-period symphonies: vocal and instrumental works for a new century

1. Berlin, 1921; repr. Tutzing, Schneider, 1969, pp. 178 and 232–3.
2. Adler, *Gustav Mahler*, Vienna, Universal Edition, 1916, trans. in Edward R. Reilly, *Gustav Mahler and Guido Adler. Records of a Friendship*, Cambridge University Press, 1982, pp. 69 and 37; Walter, *Gustav Mahler*, trans. James Galston, New York, Vienna House, 1941, pp. 119–21.
3. 'ein schlecter Jasager'; Theodor W. Adorno, *Gustav Mahler. Eine musikalische Physiognomik*, Frankfurt, Suhrkamp, 1960, pp. 180–1; trans. Edmund Jephcott as *Gustav Mahler. A Musical Physiognomy*, University of Chicago Press, 1992, pp. 137–8.
4. Adorno, *A Musical Physiognomy*, p. 135.
5. HLGE2, p. 334.

6. Bruno Walter, *Briefe 1894–1962*, ed. Lotte Walter Lindt, Frankfurt, S. Fischer, 1969, p. 53.

7. *Gustav Mahler. A Life in Crisis*, New Haven, Yale University Press, 2004, chapter 5.

8. NBLE, pp. 172–4. Hereinafter the four independent Rückert settings will be called simply 'the Rückert Lieder'.

9. NBLE, p. 154.

10. Adorno, *A Musical Physiognomy*, pp. 53–4; Hefling, 'Mahler: Symphonies 1–4' in D. Kern Holoman (ed.), *The Nineteenth-Century Symphony*, New York, Schirmer Books, 1997, esp. from pp. 397 and 407; Hefling, 'Techniques of Irony in Mahler's Œuvre' in André Castagné, Michel Chalon and Patrick Florençon (eds.), *Gustav Mahler et l'ironie dans la culture viennoise au tournant du siècle. Actes du Colloque Gustav Mahler Montpellier 1996*, Castelnau-le-Lez, Editions Climats, 2001, esp. pp. 113–22.

11. Bekker, *Gustav Mahlers Sinfonien*, pp. 175–8; Bekker's observation has been pursued by numerous later writers.

12. See also Hefling, 'The Rückert Lieder' and 'Das Lied von der Erde' in Donald Mitchell and Andrew Nicholson (eds.), *The Mahler Companion*, Oxford University Press, 2002, esp. pp. 342–3 and 442–3, as well as Hefling, 'Mahler: Symphonies 1–4', pp. 369–416, esp. 387–91.

13. ML, p. 226; see also Alexander Odefey, *Gustav Mahlers Kindertotenlieder. Eine semantische Analyse*, Frankfurt, Peter Lang, 1999, pp. 204–7.

14. The sketch for the song is dated 9 June; Mahler arrived in Maiernigg for the summer on 5 June, and Natalie tells us that he began working on the third day thereafter (HLGE2, pp. 358 and 361; NBLE, p. 168).

15. Herta Blaukopf (ed.), *Gustav Mahler Richard Strauss. Correspondence 1888–1911*, trans. Edmund Jephcott, Chicago University Press, 1984, pp. 78–9, and Renate Hilmar-Voit, 'Symphonic Sound or in the Style of Chamber Music? The Current Performing Forces of the *Wunderhorn* Lieder and the Sources', *News about Mahler Research*, 28 (October 1992), 8–12; apparently Mahler used a string section no larger than 10–8–8–6–4.

16. Further on Mahler and pentatonicism, see Hefling, *Mahler. Das Lied von der Erde*, Cambridge University Press, 2000, pp. 84–6 and 144–5, n. 9.

17. See also Donald Mitchell, *Gustav Mahler. Vol. III. Songs and Symphonies of Life and Death*, London, Faber & Faber, 1985, pp. 57–68.

18. See also Mitchell, *Songs and Symphonies*, p. 74.

19. NBLE, pp. 174 and 39.

20. Feder, *A Life*, pp. 73–4.

21. HLGE2, pp. 368–9.

22. Bloom, *The Anxiety of Influence. A Theory of Poetry*, 2nd edn, Oxford University Press, 1997.

23. Reinhard Gerlach, *Strophen von Leben, Traum und Tod. Ein Essay über Rückert-Lieder von Gustav Mahler*, Wilhelmshaven, Heinrichshofen, 1982, p. 103.

24. NBLE, p. 174.

25. *Ibid.*, pp. 152–3; Walter, *Briefe*, p. 52.

26. The published orchestration is by Max Puttman; see also Hefling, 'The Rückert Lieder', pp. 360–5.

27. See Christopher O. Lewis, 'On the Chronology of the Kindertotenlieder', *Revue Mahler Review*, 1 (1987), 21–45, and HLGE2, pp. 826–8. Having examined the relevant sources carefully, I concur with this chronology. Odefey, *Mahlers Kindertotenlieder*, pp. 29–86, adduces additional arguments in its favour, some of which are persuasive.

28. Feder, 'Gustav Mahler, Dying', *International Review of Psycho-Analysis*, 5 (1978), 130–2; see also HLGE2, pp. 828–30.

29. Schopenhauer, *The World as Will and Representation*, trans. E. F. J. Payne, New York, 1969, vol. 1, pp. 275–6, 330–1; see also Hefling, 'Symphonies 1–4', pp. 370–4.

30. Peter Russell, *Light in Battle with Darkness. Mahler's 'Kindertotenlieder'*, Berne, Peter Lang, 1991, esp. pp. 55–61, 81–2.

31. NBLG, pp. 192–3; see also p. 158 (NBLE, pp. 172 and 147), August 1901. Claims that the first song is a compressed symphonic first movement seem misguided: there is no structural modulation away from D, and the third strophe hardly behaves like a symphonic development section. Only in the first movement of *Das Lied von der Erde* does Mahler undertake the synthesis of song and sonata form, with extraordinary success – and we have direct evidence of how he went about it (see Hefling, '*Das Lied von der Erde*: Mahler's Symphony for Voices and Orchestra – or Piano', *Journal of Musicology*, 10 (1992), 303–10).

32. This revoiced 'Tristan' chord occurs in bars 8, 10, 28 and 71, and in an incomplete form in bars 27, 49, 51 and 70.

33. See NBLG, p. 168 (not in NBLE); the glockenspiel stroke Mahler probably had in mind is at fig. 3 in 'Urlicht'.

34. Mitchell, *Songs and Symphonies*, p. 80; see also Russell, *Light in Battle*, pp. 102 and 45.

35. 'Mutter Schoß' is the wording in both the piano-vocal and orchestral autograph scores (New York, Pierpont Morgan Library, Lehman Deposit); it was changed only in the *Stichvorlage*, just prior to printing (Vienna, Internationale Gustav Mahler Gesellschaft); see also Edward F. Kravitt, 'Mahler's Dirges for His Death: February 24, 1901', *Musical Quarterly*, 64 (1978), 335–8.

36. Feder, *A Life*, pp. 70–2.

37. See Mitchell, 'Eternity or Nothingness? Mahler's Fifth Symphony' in Mitchell and Nicholson (eds.), *The Mahler Companion*, pp. 236–40, and Bekker, *Gustav Mahlers Sinfonien*, p. 178; see also NBLG, p. 193 (NBLE, p. 173).

38. Hans and Rosaleen Moldenhauer, *Anton von Webern: A Chronicle of His Life and Work*, New York, Random House, 1979, pp. 75–6. It is noteworthy that among Mahler's pursuits in the summer of 1901 was a thorough immersion in the music of Bach, the 'highest of all schools' (NBLG, p. 189; NBLE, p. 170).

39. NBLG, pp. 192–3 (NBLE, p. 172), 5 August 1901; see also ML, p. 92.

40. The spatial analogy is Adorno's: 'Mahler. Centenary Address 1960' in *Quasi una fantasia. Essays on Modern Music*, trans. Rodney Livingstone, London, Verso, 1992, p. 101. On Mahler's struggles with orchestration of the Fifth, see Paul Banks, 'The Publication of Mahler's Fifth Symphony' in Donald Mitchell and Henriette Straub (eds.), *New Sounds, New Century. Mahler's Fifth Symphony and the Royal Concertgebouw Orchestra*, Bussum, Royal Concertgebouw Orchestra, 1997, pp. 64–7; see also Mitchell's shortened version of 'Eternity or Nothingness: Mahler's Fifth Symphony' in the latter volume.

41. The plan for the Fourth is reproduced, *inter alia*, in Bekker, *Gustav Mahlers Sinfonien*, pp. 144–5.

42. NBLG, p. 193 (NBLE, p. 173). Regarding Mahler's sketches for the scherzo see Edward R. Reilly, 'The Manuscripts of Mahler's Fifth Symphony' in Mitchell and Straub (eds.), *New Sounds, New Century*, pp. 58–63.

43. Henry-Louis de La Grange and Günther Weiß (eds.), *Ein Glück ohne Ruh'. Die Briefe Gustav Mahlers an Alma*, Berlin, Siedler, 1995, p. 221 (14 October 1904) (ML, p. 243). In *Gustav Mahler und seine Umwelt* (Darmstadt, Wissenschaftliche Buchgesellschaft, 1978, pp. 93–4), Vladimir Karbusicky claims these lines were inspired by Jean Paul, yet offers no specific references.

44. Walter Kaufmann, translator's introduction to *The Gay Science*, New York, Vintage Books, 1974, p. 7; see also p. 257, n. 54. Alma's claim that Mahler instructed her to burn her complete works of Nietzsche (ML, pp. 18–19) does not indicate he rejected Nietzsche: the books were probably the gift of Max Burckhard, director of the Burgtheater and a potential rival as Mahler began courting Alma (see her *Mein Leben*, Frankfurt, Fischer, 1960, pp. 21–2, as well as Eveline Nikkels, *'O Mensch! Gib Acht!' Friedrich Nietzsches Bedeutung für Gustav Mahler*,

Amsterdam, Rodopi, 1989, pp. 100–1). In 1906, Mahler declared that *Zarathustra* is 'born of the spirit of music, absolutely "symphonic" in its construction'; see Norman Lebrecht, *Mahler Remembered*, London, Faber & Faber, 1987, p. 210.

45. *Thus Spake Zarathustra*, trans. Walter Kaufmann in *The Portable Nietzsche*, New York, Viking, 1954, pp. 153 and 129.

46. Richard Specht, *Gustav Mahler*, Berlin, Gose und Tetzlaff, 1905, pp. 44–5; see also Constantin Floros, *Gustav Mahler. The Symphonies*, trans. Vernon Wicker, Aldershot, Scolar Press, 1994, pp. 153–4, and Mitchell, 'Eternity or Nothingness?' pp. 302–4. On Mahler's approval of Specht's text see HLGE3, pp. 20–1, and GMB2, p. 318, autumn 1904. Bekker's commentary on the Fifth is also laced with Nietzschean parlance (*Gustav Mahlers Sinfonien*, for example pp. 186–8 and 200–3).

47. Nicholas Boyle, *Goethe. The Poet and the Age*, Oxford, Clarendon Press, 1991, pp. 193–4.

48. Translation from Richard Wigmore, *Schubert. The Complete Song Texts*, London, Gollancz, 1992, p. 52. Mahler undoubtedly knew Schubert's setting (D. 369).

49. *Zarathustra*, p. 310; see also, for example, pp. 126–8.

50. Floros, *Gustav Mahler II. Mahler und die Symphonik des 19. Jahrhunderts in neuer Deutung*, 2nd edn, Wiesbaden, Breitkopf and Härtel, 1987, pp. 176–8 and 381–4.

51. For more detailed attempts to analyse the scherzo (which do not agree with each other), see Floros, *The Symphonies*, p. 150, and HLGE2, pp. 813–16. Mahler's sketches indicate the second trio beginning at fig. 10 + 9.

52. *The Gay Science*, p. 273.

53. NBLG, p. 193 (NBLE, p. 173).

54. Although such an allusion might initially seem specious, in subsequent permutations of the triplet motive it becomes unmistakable – for example, first mvt., fig. 15, second mvt., fig. 8 + 5.

55. Cf. the composer's performance in *Mahler Plays Mahler. The Welte-Mignon Piano Rolls* (Golden Legacy Recorded Music GLRS 101, licensed to the Pickwick Group), also reproduced in Mitchell and Straub (eds.), *New Sounds, New Century*.

56. See Mitchell, 'Eternity or Nothingness?' pp. 287–93; Mitchell rightly notes (pp. 285–6) that despite the claims of several writers, the Fifth's second movement is not a sonata form.

57. Nietzsche, *Zarathustra*, pp. 170, 225–7, 250–3 and 268–70.

58. Karel Philippus Bernet-Kempers, 'Mahler und Willem Mengelberg' in Erich Schenk (ed.), *Bericht über den Internationalen Musikwissenschaftlichen Kongress Wien*,

Mozartjahr 1956, Graz, Hermann Bohlau, 1958, p. 44.

59. See Knud Martner, *Gustav Mahler im Konzertsaal. Eine Dokumentation seiner Konzerttätigkeit 1870–1911*, Copenhagen, 1985, p. 101.

60. Paul Banks, 'Aspects of Mahler's Fifth Symphony: Performance Practice and Interpretation', *The Musical Times*, 130 (May 1989), 261–4; Gilbert E. Kaplan, 'From Mahler with Love' in Kaplan (ed.), *Gustav Mahler, Adagietto. Facsimile, Documentation, Recording*, New York, The Kaplan Foundation, 1992, pp. 11–29.

61. Reproduced *inter alia* in Kaplan, 'From Mahler with Love', p. 20, whose essay provides further documentation of Mengelberg's claim. See also Mitchell, 'Eternity or Nothingness?', pp. 315–17.

62. See also Floros, *The Symphonies*, p. 155.

63. On cyclic connections in the Fifth, see Rainer Boss, 'Symphonic Construction and Fugue. Analytical Remarks on Form and Structure in Mahler's Fifth Symphony', *News About Mahler Research*, 41 (Autumn 1999), 3–30, and HLGE2, pp. 819–23.

64. *Zarathustra*, p. 435.

65. In addition to Adorno (see n. 4 above), this is the viewpoint of Bernd Sponheuer in *Logik des Zerfalls. Untersuchungen zum Finalproblem in den Symphonien Gustav Mahlers*, Tutzing, Hans Schneider, 1978, pp. 219–79.

66. *Zarathustra*, p. 435. See also Floros, *The Symphonies*, p. 211.

67. *Ibid.*, from p. 340. See also Floros, *ibid*. The first three parts of *Zarathustra* were published well before the fourth.

68. HLGE2, p. 825.

69. See SLGM, p. 28, and ML, p. 70.

70. HLGE2, pp. 808–41, provides a useful overview of literature on the Sixth.

71. ML, p. 70.

72. Adorno, *A Musical Physiognomy*, pp. 128–9; Wolfgang Stresemann, 'Bruno Walter' in *Große deutsche Dirigenten: 100 Jahre Berliner Philharmoniker*, Berlin, 1981, p. 133; Reilly, *Mahler and Adler*, pp. 59–60.

73. From a 1908 interview with Edgar Istel, cited by Floros, *Gustav Mahler II*, p. 323; shorter versions are found in Specht, *Gustav Mahler*, Berlin, Schuster & Loeffler, 1913, p. 282, and Adler, trans. Reilly in *Mahler and Adler*, p. 58.

74. See Warren Darcy, 'Rotational Form, Teleological Genesis, and Fantasy-Projection in the Slow Movement of Mahler's Sixth Symphony', *19th-Century Music*, 25 (2001), 50, n. 4.

75. See Robert Samuels, *Mahler's Sixth Symphony. A Study in Musical Semiotics*, Cambridge University Press, 1995, pp. 151–4.

76. ML, pp. 99–101; HLGE2, pp. 410–12.

77. Esp. Jerry Bruck and Reinhold Kubik in Gilbert Kaplan (ed.), *The Correct Movement Order of Mahler's Sixth Symphony*, New York, The Kaplan Foundation, 2004. See also HLGE4, App.II.

78. See especially Samuels, *Mahler's Sixth Symphony*, pp. 119–31.

79. ML, p. 70.

80. Adorno, *A Musical Physiognomy*, p. 107, translation modified (German edn, p. 142).

81. Commentators have long differed regarding the movement's structure; for a review of the literature, see Darcy, 'Rotational Form', 50–1. Darcy posits four 'rotations', commencing at bar 1 and figs 48, 55 and 60–1.

82. See, for example, Terry Eagleton, *Sweet Violence. The Idea of the Tragic*, Oxford, Blackwell, 2003, esp. chapter 5.

83. Schopenhauer, *The World*, vol. 2, p. 433.

84. Nietzsche, *The Birth of Tragedy*, trans. Kaufmann, New York, Vintage Books, 1967, p. 104; see also Eagleton, *Sweet Violence*, p. 56.

85. Nietzsche, *Twilight of the Idols*, trans. Kaufmann, in *The Portable Nietzsche*, pp. 562–3.

86. Bruno Walter, 'Mahlers Weg, ein Erinnerungsblatt', *Der Merker*, 3/5 (1912), 166–71, trans. in Lebrecht, *Mahler Remembered*, p. 129; see also Bekker, *Gustav Mahlers Sinfonien*, pp. 210–11.

87. Schopenhauer, *The World*, vol. 2, p. 433.

88. At bar 9, figs. 129, 140, 164 + 10, 143 + 11; the first is less distinctly marked than the others (Vienna, Gesellschaft der Musikfreunde). See also Hans-Peter Jülg, *Gustav Mahlers Sechste Symphonie*, Munich, Katzbichler, 1986, pp. 30 and 41.

89. *The Birth of Tragedy*, pp. 104–5.

90. Adorno, *A Musical Physiognomy*, p. 126.

91. ML, p. 100.

92. See Timothy L. Jackson, 'The Tragic Reversed Recapitulation in the German Classic Tradition', *Journal of Music Theory*, 40 (1996), 61–111.

93. Deryck Cooke, *Gustav Mahler. An Introduction to His Music*, London, Faber Music, 1980, p. 88.

94. Letter to Alma Mahler of [8 June] 1910, in ML, p. 328.

95. Adorno, *A Musical Physiognomy*, p. 101; Walter, *Mahler*, p. 121.

96. Letter of 17 October 1909 to Johanna Jongkindt, cited in Eduard Reeser (ed.), *Gustav Mahler und Holland. Briefe*, Vienna, Universal Edition, 1980, pp. 31–2. Dutch composer Alphons Diepenbrock (1862–1921) attended Mahler's performances of the Seventh in Holland in 1909 and discussed the work with him.

97. HLGE2, p. 861; see also Peter Davison, 'Nachtmusik I: Sound and Symbol' in James L. Zychowicz (ed.), *The Seventh Symphony of*

Gustav Mahler, The University of Cincinnati, 1990, pp. 69–70.

98. Peter Davison, 'Nachtmusik II: "Nothing but Love, Love, Love"?' in Zychowicz (ed.) *The Seventh Symphony*, p. 93.

99. Adorno, *A Musical Physiognomy*, p. 96; Davison, 'Nachtmusik II', p. 89. As noted below, the θ7 plays a rather different role in the opening of the first movement.

100. Davison, 'Nachtmusik II', pp. 95 and 94–5.

101. This movement is clearly the ancestor of the unfinished Tenth Symphony's second scherzo, another sardonic waltz that Mahler inscribed 'The devil is dancing it with me'; see, for example, Colin Matthews, 'The Tenth Symphony' in Mitchell and Nicholson (eds.), *The Mahler Companion*, pp. 491–507, esp. plate 21.4 on p. 506.

102. See Talia Pecker Berio, 'Perspectives of a Scherzo' in Zychowicz (ed.), *The Seventh Symphony*, pp. 74–88, esp. p. 78, and HLGE2, pp. 864–5.

103. See also Adorno, *A Musical Physiognomy*, p. 104.

104. Specht, *Gustav Mahler*, 1913, p. 299.

105. Hefling, '"Ihm in die Lieder zu blicken": Mahler's Seventh Symphony Sketchbook' in Hefling (ed.), *Mahler Studies*, Cambridge University Press, pp. 203 and 209.

106. Adorno, *A Musical Physiognomy*, pp. 100–1. For more detailed discussion of the Seventh's musical language see esp. John Williamson, 'The Structural Premises of Mahler's Introductions: Prolegomena to an Analysis of the First Movement of the Seventh Symphony', *Music Analysis*, 5 (1986), 29–57; Williamson, 'Mahler and Episodic Structure: The First Movement of the Seventh Symphony' in Zychowicz (ed.), *The Seventh Symphony*, pp. 27–46; and Serge Gut, 'Consonance et dissonance dans le premier mouvement de la Septième Symphonie de Gustav Mahler', in *ibid.*, pp. 47–67.

107. See Donald Mitchell, 'Reception', commentary to *Facsimile Edition of the Seventh Symphony*, Amsterdam, Rosbeek, 1995, pp. 39, 43 and 48.

108. See HLGF3, p. 360.

109. See John Williamson, 'Deceptive Cadences in the Last Movement of Mahler's Seventh Symphony', *Soundings* [Cardiff, Wales], 9 (1982), 87–96; Martin Scherzinger, 'The Finale of Mahler's Seventh Symphony: A Deconstructive Reading', *Music Analysis*, 14 (1995), 69–88; and Jonathan Kramer, 'Postmodern Concepts of Musical Time', *Indiana Theory Review*, 17 (1996), 30–8.

110. Floros, *The Symphonies*, p. 211.

111. Scherzinger, 'The Finale of Mahler's Seventh', 78.

112. Nietzsche, *Zarathustra*, p. 269, translation modified.

113. Williamson, 'Mahler and Episodic Structure', 27.

114. Specht, 'Thematische Novitäten-Analysen: I. Mahlers Siebente Symphonie', *Der Merker*, 1/2 (1909), 1; and Specht, *Gustav Mahler*, 1913, p. 283.

115. Walter, *Mahler*, p. 129.

8 The 'greatest' and the 'most personal': the Eighth Symphony and *Das Lied von der Erde*

1. SLGM, p. 157.

2. *Ibid.*, p. 165.

3. *Ibid.*, p. 294.

4. GMLW, p. 348.

5. Henry-Louis de La Grange and Günther Weiss (eds.), *Ein Glück ohne Ruh'. Die Briefe Gustav Mahlers an Alma*, Berlin, Siedler, 1995, p. 424. Note that on p. 357 of GMLW Beaumont translates 'bis das Größte fertig war' as 'until the work was all but finished'.

6. SLGM, p. 326.

7. Richard Specht, *Gustav Mahler*, Berlin, Schuster & Loeffler, 1913, p. 252.

8. Richard Specht, 'Zu Mahlers Achter Symphonie', *Tagespost*, 59/150 (14 June 1914), 9.

9. Erich Trunz, 'Anmerkungen und Zeilenkommentar zu Goethes Faust' in Trunz (ed.), Johann Wolfgang von Goethe, *Faust. Der Tragödie erster und zweiter Teil*, vol. 3 of *Hamburger Ausgabe in 14 Bänden*, Munich, C. H. Beck, 1996 and 1998, p. 462.

10. Specht, 'Zu Mahlers Achter Symphonie'.

11. See NBLE, p. 150, and La Grange and Weiss (eds.), *Ein Glück ohne Ruh'*, p. 424.

12. SLGM, p. 292.

13. Ernst Decsey, 'Stunden mit Mahler. Notizen', *Die Musik*, 10/18 (1911), 352–6, and 10/21, 143–53; quote on pp. 353–4.

14. Bruno Walter, *Thema und Variationen*, Frankfurt am Main, S. Fischer, 1988, pp. 239–40; see also Walter, *Theme and Variations*, trans. James A. Galston, London, Hamish Hamilton, 1947, p. 206 (trans. amended).

15. For a discussion of this early plan, first published by Alfred Rosenzweig in *Der Wiener Tag* on 4 June 1933, see Christian Wildhagen, *Die Achte Symphonie von Gustav Mahler. Konzeption einer universalen Symphonik*, Frankfurt am Main, Peter Lang, 2000, pp. 46–56.

16. Specht, 'Zu Mahlers Achter Symphonie', cited in Wildhagen, *Die Achte Symphonie*, p. 15.

17. For further details of these preparations and the critical response to the performance see Wildhagen, *Die Achte Symphonie*, pp. 108–48.

18. Otto Klemperer, *Meine Erinnerungen an Gustav Mahler*, Freiburg and Zurich, Atlantis, 1960, pp. 11 and 15; see also Peter Heyworth (ed.), *Conversations with Klemperer*, rev. edn, London, Faber & Faber, 1985, p. 34 (trans. amended).

19. See Wildhagen, *Die Achte Symphonie*, pp. 135–56.

20. 12 September 1910.

21. Cited in ML, p. 342. See also Mann's letter to Heinrich Mann of 18 September 1910 in Thomas Mann, *Briefe I (1889–1913)*, ed. Erika Mann, Frankfurt am Main, Fischer, 1961–2, p. 464.

22. See Wildhagen, *Die Achte Symphonie*, pp. 114–17, for a discussion of this title.

23. Cited in Norman Lebrecht, *Mahler Remembered*, London, Faber & Faber, 1987, p. 218.

24. Thomas Mann, 'Richard Wagner und *Der Ring des Nibelungen*' in Erika Mann (ed.), *Wagner und unsere Zeit*, Frankfurt am Main, Fischer, 1986, p. 144.

25. Hans and Rosaleen Moldenhauer, *Anton von Webern. Chronik seines Lebens und Werkes*, Freiburg and Zurich Atlantis, 1980, p. 121.

26. ML, pp. 320–1 (trans. amended).

27. SLGM, p. 329.

28. Bruno Walter, *Gustav Mahler*, trans. Lotte Walter Lindt, London, Quartet Books, 1990, pp. 108–9.

29. ML, p. 106.

30. See *ibid.*, pp. 120–2.

31. Walter, *Mahler*, p. 55.

32. For further details of the origins of the texts see HLGF3, pp. 1121–64; Donald Mitchell, *Gustav Mahler. Volume III. Songs and Symphonies of Life and Death*, London, Faber & Faber, 1985, pp. 435–443; Kii-Ming Lo, 'Chinesische Dichtung als Text-Grundlage für Mahlers *Lied von der Erde*' in Matthias Vogt (ed.), *Das Gustav Mahler-Fest Hamburg 1989. Bericht über den Internationalen Gustav-Mahler-Kongress*, Kassel, Bärenreiter, 1991, pp. 509–28; Fusako Hamao, 'The Sources of the Texts in Mahler's *Das Lied von der Erde*', *19th-Century Music*, 19 (1995), 83–95; Eberhard Bethge, 'Hans Bethge und *Das Lied von der Erde*', *News About Mahler Research*, 35 (April 1996), 15–21, esp. 17–19; and Margarete Wagner, '*Chinesische Flöte* versus *Lied von der Erde*. On Different Forms of Text Adaptation', *News About Mahler Research*, 51 (Winter 2004/05), 20–35.

33. ML, p. 123.

34. Mitchell, *Songs and Symphonies*, p. 165; Stephen E. Hefling, *Mahler. Das Lied von der Erde*, Cambridge University Press, 2000, pp. 31 and 139, n. 14.

35. Facsimile in Hefling, *Das Lied von der Erde*, p. 50.

36. See Stephen E. Hefling, '*Das Lied von der Erde*: Mahler's Symphony for Voices and Orchestra – or Piano', *Journal of Musicology*, 10 (1992), 293–340.

37. See Alma Mahler's description of this process in ML, p. 139.

38. See Constantin Floros, *Gustav Mahler I. Die geistige Welt Gustav Mahlers in systematischer Darstellung*, 2nd edn, Wiesbaden, Breitkopf & Härtel, 1987, pp. 105–7.

39. Walter argued against the baritone version in *Theme and Variations*, p. 213.

40. See *Allgemeine musikalische Zeitung*, 38/48 (1912), 1230.

41. Cited in Renate Ulm (ed.), *Gustav Mahlers Symphonien. Entstehung – Deutung – Wirkung*, Kassel, Bärenreiter, 2001, p. 260. See also Friedrich Wildgans, 'Gustav Mahler und Anton Webern', *Österreichische Musikzeitschrift*, 15/6 (1960), 302–6.

42. Cited in Hermann Danuser, *Gustav Mahler. Das Lied von der Erde*, Meisterwerke der Musik, vol. 25, Munich, Fink, 1986, pp. 114–15.

43. See Hefling, *Das Lied von der Erde*, pp. 86–8.

44. See Franz Willnauer, *Gustav Mahler und die Wiener Oper*, Vienna, Löcker, 1993, p. 230.

45. For further discussion of Mahler's blending of generic traditions in this movement, see Elisabeth Schmierer, 'The First Movement of Mahler's *Das Lied von der Erde*: Genre, Form and Musical Expression' in Jeremy Barham (ed.), *Perspectives on Gustav Mahler*, Aldershot, Ashgate Press, 2005, pp. 253–9.

46. See Floros, *Gustav Mahler. The Symphonies*, trans. Vernon Wicker, Aldershot, Scolar Press, 1994, pp. 248–9.

47. See Hefling, *Das Lied von der Erde*, pp. 92–3.

48. Joseph Venantius von Wöss, *Gustav Mahler. Das Lied von der Erde. Thematische Analyse*, Leipzig and Vienna, Universal Edition, 1912, p. 27.

49. Cited in Mitchell, *Songs and Symphonies*, p. 339.

50. Cited in Detlef Gojowy, *Dimitri Schostakowitsch*, Reinbek, Rowohlt, 1983, pp. 63–4.

9 The last works

1. ML, pp. 115, 152 and 187.

2. For a summary, see Constantin Floros, *Gustav Mahler. The Symphonies*, trans. Vernon Wicker, Aldershot, Scolar Press, 1994, pp. 272–5.

3. SLGM, p. 341.

4. See Jörg Rothkamm, '"Kondukt" als Grundlage eines Formkonzepts. Eine Charakteranalyse des ersten Satzes der IX. Symphonie Gustav Mahlers', *Archiv für Musikwissenschaft*, 54/4 (1997), 269–83, which also includes discussion of several earlier analyses of the movement.

5. Erwin Ratz (ed.), *Gustav Mahler, IX. Symphonie. Partiturentwurf der ersten drei Sätze. Faksimile nach der Handschrift*, Vienna, Universal Edition, 1971.

6. Alban Berg, *Briefe an seine Frau*, Munich/Vienna, Langen/Müller, 1965, p. 238.

7. See Floros, *The Symphonies*, pp. 284–6, and Floros, *Gustav Mahler II. Mahler und die Symphonik des 19. Jahrhunderts in neuer Deutung*, 2nd edn, Wiesbaden, Breitkopf & Härtel, 1987, pp. 171–8.

8. Compare the analyses of the movement's structure in Floros, *The Symphonies*, pp. 285–6, and Stephen Hefling, 'The Ninth Symphony' in Donald Mitchell and Andrew Nicholson (eds.), *The Mahler Companion*, Oxford University Press, 1999, pp. 467–90, esp. p. 480.

9. See Peter Andraschke, *Gustav Mahlers IX. Symphonie. Kompositionsprozess und Analyse*, Wiesbaden, Franz Steiner, 1976, pp. 59–70, and Colin Matthews, *Mahler at Work. Aspects of the Creative Process*, London, Garland, 1989, pp. 158–62.

10. See Willem Mengelberg's annotations to his conducting score, reproduced in Andraschke, *Gustav Mahlers IX. Symphonie*, pp. 81–3.

11. Bruno Walter, *Gustav Mahler*, trans. Lotte Walter Lindt, London, Quartet Books, 1990, p. 110.

12. Compare Floros, *The Symphonies*, pp. 287–8, with Hefling, 'The Ninth Symphony', p. 484.

13. Floros, *The Symphonies*, pp. 287–8.

14. See Floros, *Mahler und die Symphonik*, pp. 151–9.

15. Floros, *The Symphonies*, p. 291.

16. Peter Revers, *Gustav Mahler. Untersuchungen zu den späten Symphonien*, Hamburg, Karl Dieter Wagner, 1985, p. 159.

17. Mathias Hansen, *Gustav Mahler*, Stuttgart, Reclam, 1996, p. 198.

18. See Jörg Rothkamm, *Gustav Mahlers Zehnte Symphonie. Entstehung, Analyse, Rezeption*, Frankfurt, Peter Lang, 2003, p. 18 and n. 15 on p. 19.

19. Gustav Mahler, *Zehnte Symphonie, [Faksimile-Ausgabe des Manuskriptes]. Einführende Bemerkungen von Richard Specht*, Berlin, Vienna and Leipzig, Zsolnay, 1924; Gustav Mahler, *X. Symphonie. Faksimile nach der Handschrift*, ed. Erwin Ratz, Munich/Meran, Ricke/Laurin, 1967; Kunstmuseum Basel (ed.), *Musikhandschriften in Basel aus verschiedenen Sammlungen. Ausstellung im Kunstmuseum Basel vom 31. Mai bis zum 13. Juli 1975*, Basel, Kunstmuseum, 1975, p. 75; Gustav Mahler, *A Performing Version of the Draft for the Tenth Symphony Prepared by Deryck Cooke in Collaboration with Berthold Goldschmidt, Colin Matthews, David Matthews*,

New York/London, Associated Music Publishers/Faber, [1976], 1989, pp. xxvii–xxxi; Frans Bouwman, 'Editing Mahler 10. Unfinished Business', *The Musical Times*, 142 (2001), 43–51 (see p. 48, ex. 4b); Rothkamm, *Gustav Mahlers Zehnte Symphonie*, pp. 20–5; Bayerische Staatsbibliothek (ed.), *Gustav Mahler. Briefe und Musikautographen aus den Moldenhauer-Archiven in der Bayerischen Staatsbibliothek*, Patrimonia 157, Munich, Bayerische Staatsbibliothek und Kulturstiftung der Länder, 2003, pp. 199–220.

20. See Jörg Rothkamm, *Gustav Mahlers Zehnte Symphonie*, pp. 101–2.

21. *Ibid.*, p. 21.

22. GMLW, p. 381.

23. Rothkamm, *Gustav Mahlers Zehnte Symphonie*, pp. 24 and 158.

24. GMLW, p. 375.

25. See Rothkamm, *Gustav Mahlers Zehnte Symphonie*, pp. 205–98.

26. See Jörg Rothkamm, *Berthold Goldschmidt und Gustav Mahler. Zur Entstehung von Deryck Cookes Konzertfassung der X. Symphonie*, Musik im 'Dritten Reich' und im Exil 6, Hamburg, von Bockel, 2000, and Deryck Cooke, 'The History of Mahler's Tenth Symphony' in Mahler, *A Performing Version of the Draft for the Tenth Symphony*, pp. xiii–xviii.

27. Mahler, *A Performing Version of the Draft for the Tenth Symphony*, p. xvii.

10 Mahler as conductor in the opera house and concert hall

1. See NBLG, p. 119.

2. The first teacher of this conducting class was Franz Schalk, whom Mahler had brought to the Vienna Opera in 1901.

3. Kurt Blaukopf, *Gustav Mahler. Sein Leben, sein Werk und seine Welt in zeitgenössischen Bildern und Texten*, Vienna, Universal Edition, 1976, p. 167. See also HLGE1, pp. 108–9.

4. Franz Willnauer, *Gustav Mahler und die Wiener Oper*, Vienna, Löcker, 1993, p. 246.

5. *Laibacher Zeitung*, 8 September 1881.

6. *Laibacher Zeitung*, 4 October 1881.

7. SLGM, 1979, p. 68.

8. Recollections of the singer Jacques Manheit, cited in Kurt Blaukopf and Herta Blaukopf (eds.), *Mahler. His Life, Work and World*, London, Thames & Hudson, 1991, p. 43.

9. Letter from the personal file on Mahler in the Kassel Theatre superintendent's office, cited in Blaukopf and Blaukopf (eds.), *Mahler*, p. 46.

10. SLGM, p. 74.

11. Repertoire according to Hans Joachim Schaefer, *Gustav Mahler in Kassel*, Kassel, Bärenreiter, 1982, p. 28.

12. On Mahler's conducting in Kassel see Knud Martner, 'Mahler's Activities in Kassel from a New Perspective', *News About Mahler Research*, 21 (March 1989), 7–11.

13. Blaukopf and Blaukopf (eds.), *Mahler*, p. 57.

14. Schaefer, *Gustav Mahler*, p. 64.

15. See SLGM, p. 346.

16. Recollections of the singer Jacques Manheit, cited in Blaukopf and Blaukopf (eds.), *Mahler*, p. 45.

17. Langegasse 18.

18. Ernst Schulz, *Erinnerungen eines Prager Musikers*, Prague, Selbstverlag H. Schulz, A. G., n.d., p. 59.

19. Anna Bahr-Mildenburg, *Erinnerungen*, Vienna, Literarische Anstalt, 1921, p. 15.

20. Bruno Walter, *Gustav Mahler*, trans. Lotte Walter Lindt, London, Quartet Books, 1990, p. 25.

21. *Ibid.*, p. 81 (trans. amended).

22. Marie Gutheil-Schoder, *Erlebtes und Erstrebtes*, Vienna, Rudolf Krey, 1937, p. 53.

23. See Willnauer, *Gustav Mahler*, p. 39.

24. Max Graf, *Wagner-Probleme und andere Studien*, Vienna, Wiener Verlag, n.d. [1900], p. 124.

25. SLGM, p. 316.

26. See HLGE2, pp. 323–49, for an account of Mahler's increasingly hostile reception amongst critics and players, and the events leading up to his resignation.

27. SLGM, p. 348.

28. See Zoltan Roman, *Gustav Mahler's American Years, 1907–1911. A Documentary History*, Stuyvesant, Pendragon Press, 1989, p. 380.

29. For a thorough study of Mahler's travelling performances with the New York Philharmonic, see Mary H. Wagner, 'Gustav Mahler and his Tours with the New York Philharmonic Orchestra (1909–1911)', unpublished Ph.D. thesis, Kent State University (Ohio), 2002.

30. NBLE, pp. 92–3 (text supplemented with additional material from NBLG, pp. 89–90).

31. Ferdinand Pfohl, *Gustav Mahler. Eindrücke und Erinnerungen aus den Hamburger Jahren*, ed. K. Martner, Hamburg, Karl Dieter Wagner, 1973, p. 48.

32. NBLE, p. 94.

33. *Ibid.*, p. 109.

34. *Fremdenblatt*, 131, 12 May 1897.

35. See Kay Knittel, '"Ein hypermoderner Dirigent": Mahler and Anti-Semitism in *Fin-de-Siècle* Vienna', *19th-Century Music*, 18/3 (1995), 257–76, for these and many other visual representations of Mahler conducting.

36. *Neue Freie Presse*, 11752, 12 May 1897.

37. Peter Heyworth (ed.), *Conversations with Klemperer*, London, Faber & Faber, 1985, pp. 30 and 31.

38. See NBLE, pp. 35–6.

39. Gunter Hempel, 'Gustav Mahler in Leipzig', *Musik und Gesellschaft*, 17 (November 1967), 784–5, cited in Blaukopf and Blaukopf (eds.), *Mahler*, p. 69.

40. NBLE, p. 35.

41. Howard Shanet, 'Notes on the Programs', February 1960, cited in Roman, *Mahler's American Years*, p. 423. The CD recording produced by the Kaplan Foundation 'Mahler Plays Mahler. The Welte-Mignon Piano Rolls' (Pickwick Group Ltd., Golden Legacy of Recorded Music, GLRS 101, 1993) contains recorded conversations with orchestral musicians who played under Mahler.

42. Kurt Blaukopf, *Werktreue und Bearbeitung*, Karlsruhe, Braun, 1968, p. 7.

43. David Pickett, 'Gustav Mahler as Interpreter. A Study of his Textural Alterations and Performance Practice in the Symphonic Repertoire', Ph.D. thesis, University of Surrey, 1988 p. 28.

44. SLGM, p. 345.

11 Arrangements and *Retuschen*: Mahler and *Werktreue*

1. Ferdinand Pfohl, *Gustav Mahler. Eindrücke und Erinnerungen aus dem Hamburger Jahren*, Hamburg, Karl Dieter Wagner, 1973, p. 29.

2. *Ibid.*, p. 30.

3. Josef Foerster, *Der Pilger. Erinnerungen eines Musikers*, Prague, Artia, 1955, p. 386. For listings of all Mahler's concerts see Knud Martner, *Gustav Mahler im Konzertsaal*, Copenhagen, KM-Privatdruck, 1985.

4. *Allgemeine Zeitung, Abendblatt* No. 85, 26 March 1897, 1.

5. NBLE, pp. 78–9.

6. Clemens Hellsberg, *Demokratie der Könige: die Geschichte der Wiener Philharmoniker*, Zurich, Schweizer Verlagshaus AG, 1992, p. 290.

7. *Ibid.*, p. 290.

8. See HLGE2, pp. 116 ff. for details of the intrigues behind Richter's resignation and Mahler's appointment.

9. Edward Dent, *Ferruccio Busoni. a Biography*, Oxford University Press, 1933, reprinted by Ernst Eulenburg Ltd, 1974, pp. 110–11.

10. Ferruccio Busoni, *Sketch of a New Esthetic of Music*, trans. T. Baker in *Three Classics in the Aesthetics of Music*, New York, Dover Publications, 1962, pp. 84–6.

11. See Richard Wagner, 'Performing Beethoven's Ninth Symphony', trans. R. L. Jacobs in *Three Wagner Essays*, London, Eulenburg Books, 1979, p. 99.

12. *Ibid.*, pp. 97–127.

13. Richard Wagner, 'On Conducting', trans. R. L. Jacobs in *Three Wagner Essays*, London, Eulenburg Books, 1979, pp. 49–93.

14. *The Musical Courier*, New York, 24 Nov. 1909, 53.

15. Richard Strauss, 'Notes on the Interpretation of Beethoven's Symphonies', trans. L. Wurmser, *Recorded Sound*, 25 (January 1967), 137.

16. Felix Weingartner, 'On the Performance of Beethoven's Symphonies', trans. J. Crosland in *Weingartner on Music & Conducting*, New York, Dover Publications, 1969, p. 209.

17. Weingartner, *Ueber das Dirigiren*, Berlin, S. Fischer Verlag, 1896.

18. Pfohl, *Gustav Mahler*, p. 40. (A *Quartaner* is a thirteen-year-old schoolboy.) Pfohl also relates that Mahler's opinion of Weingartner's book did not prevent him from taking his place in the front row at the first of Weingartner's appearances as confirmed leader of the Hamburg 'Bülow Concerts' and ostentatiously leading the applause.

19. The full text of Mahler's essay is reproduced in Kurt and Herta Blaukopf (eds.), *Mahler. His Life, Work and World*, London, Thames and Hudson, rev. edn, 1991, pp. 144–5.

20. Egon and Emmy Wellesz, *Egon Wellesz Leben und Werk*, Vienna, Zsolnay, 1981, p. 32.

21. Foerster, *Der Pilger*, p. 385.

22. See Ernst Hilmar, 'Mahler's Beethoven-Interpretation' in Rudolf Stephan (ed.), *Mahler-Interpretation. Aspekte zum Werk und Wirken von Gustav Mahler*, Mainz, Schott, 1985, p. 31.

23. For further details of Mahler's string reductions in Beethoven, See Hilmar, 'Mahler's Beethoven-Interpretation'.

24. For further details of Mahler's conducting and his *Retuschen* see David Pickett, 'Mahler as an Interpreter', unpublished Ph.D. thesis, University of Surrey, 1988.

25. Elliott Galkin wrote that 'the first statement of the theme of the Trio was played by three horns located to his [Mahler's] extreme left, behind the violins; at its repetition the three other horns responded antiphonally from the far right of the orchestra' ('Gustav Mahler as Conductor', *Journal of the Conductors' Guild*, 8/1 (Winter 1987), p. 24); but when I spoke to Dr Galkin about this he was unable to quote a verifiable source of his information, and I have found none since.

26. Bruno Walter, *Thema und Variationen*, Frankfurt, S. Fischer Verlag, repr. edn of 1988, p. 117. This paragraph, which was omitted from the English version of Walter's autobiography, is quoted here from Kurt Blaukopf, *Gustav Mahler*, trans. Inge Goodwin, London, Allen Lane, 1973, p. 249.

27. Walter, *Thema und Variationen*, p. 117.

28. A score of Mahler's 'version' of Beethoven's Ninth Symphony is in preparation for publication in the Mahler Complete Edition.

29. *New York Daily Tribune*, 13 Dec. 1909, 7. For more information on Mahler's Beethoven *Retuschen* see also Pickett, 'Rescoring in Beethoven's Symphonies' in Robin Stowell (ed.), *Performing Beethoven*, Cambridge University Press, 1994, pp. 212–16.

30. See Bernd Schabbing, *Gustav Mahler als Konzert- und Operndirigent in Hamburg*, Berlin, Verlag Ernst Kuhn, 2002.

31. See Zoltan Roman, *Gustav Mahler and Hungary*, Budapest, Akadémiai Kiadó, 1991.

32. See the series of articles, Robert Werba, 'Mahlers Mozart Bild', *Wiener Figaro*, 42–6 (1975–9). *Zaïde* was conducted by Walter.

33. NBLE, p. 92.

34. See Erwin Stein, *Mahler and the Vienna Opera* in *The Opera Bedside Book*, London, Gollancz, 1965, p. 305. This is also quoted in Donald Mitchell, *Gustav Mahler. Vol. II. The Wunderhorn Years*, Berkeley, University of California Press, rev. edn 1995, p. 381.

35. The published score of this scene is reproduced in Mitchell, *The Wunderhorn Years*, pp. 419–22.

36. See Stein, *Mahler and the Vienna Opera*, p. 305.

37. Several New York critics claimed that Mahler had the single flute part played by four players in some passages, but evidence of this is not found in the surviving orchestral materials, and when Krehbiel in his obituary wrote of Mahler 'doubling the flutes in Mozart's G minor Symphony', he had clearly forgotten that there is only one flute part.

38. Wagner, *On Conducting*, pp. 83–4.

39. The horn part and many of the features of Mahler's performances of Mozart's last two symphonies may be heard in Bruno Walter's recordings of 1959 and 1960 respectively (Mozart, Symphony Nos. 40 & 41, Columbia Symphony, CBS/Sony MK 42028).

40. Donald Tovey, *Essays on Musical Analysis, Vol. I*, Oxford University Press, 1935, pp. 207 and 209.

41. The examples given in this section are also typical of Mahler's practice in other works.

42. For more details see Pickett, 'Gustav Mahler as Interpreter', pp. 484–520, and Peter Andraschke, 'Die Retuschen Gustav Mahlers an der 7. Symphonie von Franz Schubert', *Archiv für Musikwissenschaft*, 32/2 (1975), 106–20.

43. In Schumann's Third Symphony, for instance, Stock completely recomposed the bass-line and harmony as early as bars 6/7, the first four bars of the third movement are totally

recomposed for strings and horns alone, and an additional bar of a woodwind E♭ minor chord introduces the fourth movement. See score reproductions in Asher Zlotnik, 'Orchestration Revisions in the Symphonies of Robert Schumann', unpublished Ph.D. thesis, Indiana University, 1972, pp. 631–5.

44. This cymbal crash appears in no score and only in a single-page part carefully written out by an unknown person with the instruction 'Becken mit schwamschlägel [sic] *fff*' and 'Tacit le rest', from which it would be reasonable to assume that it was prepared in New York, perhaps by the player.

45. Erwin Stein, 'Mahler's Rescorings' in *Orpheus in New Guises*, London, Rockliffe, 1953, pp. 25–30. Mosco Carner, 'Mahler's Rescoring of the Schumann Symphonies' in *Of Men and Music*, London, Joseph Williams, 1944, pp. 115–28.

46. NBLE, p. 142.

47. Ernst Hilmar, '"Schade, aber es muß(te) sein": zu Gustav Mahlers Strichen und Retuschen insbesondere am Beispiel der V. Symphonie Anton Bruckners', *Bruckner-Studien* (1974), 187–201.

48. When Mahler donated the royalties on his own works to pay for the publication of Bruckner's Symphonies by Universal Edition he was probably unaware that he was supporting corrupt scores.

49. Interview with Herman Martonne in *I Remember Mahler*, a programme compiled by William Malloch and broadcast on KPFK, Los Angeles, California, 7 July 1964. Issued in *The Mahler Broadcasts 1942–1982*, New York Philharmonic, 1998.

50. *Die Wage*, 1/3 (1899), 50. Quoted more fully in Hilmar, '"Schade, aber es muss(te) sein" '.

51. NBLE, pp. 122–3.

52. The scores (Schubert/Mahler, *String Quartet in D minor*, D. 810 and Beethoven/Mahler, *String Quartet in F minor*, Op. 95) are published by Josef Weinberger Ltd. There are over twenty recordings of the Schubert and nine of the Beethoven: see www.mahlerrecords.com; but given that Mahler conducted these works with a complement of eighteen first violins, the numerous recordings with chamber orchestra can safely be disregarded as a representation of his intentions.

53. For further discussion of Mahler's Schubert Quartet, see Wolfgang Birtel, '"Eine ideale Darstellung des Quartetts". Zu Gustav Mahlers Bearbeitung des Streichqaurtetts d-Moll D 810 Schubert', *Neue Zeitschrift dur Musik*, 149/2 (Feb. 1988), 13–17.

54. The title page of the Third Suite published by Bartolf Senff, Leipzig reads: 'Neue Ausgabe für die Aufführungen im Gewandhause zu Leipzig genau bezeichnet u. herausgegeben von Ferdinand David. Die Clarinetten und die drei Trompeten aus den für die jetzigen Insrumente nicht ausführbaren Bach'schen Trompeten, für die Aufführungen im Gewandhause zu Leipzig arrangirt von Felix Mendelssohn Bartholdy' ('New edition meticulously notated and edited for the performances in the Leipzig Gewandhaus by Ferdinand David. The clarinets and the three trumpets arranged from the currently not practicable Bach trumpet parts by Felix Mendelssohn Bartholdy.')

55. Volker Scherliess, '"Ganz nach Art der Alten". Mahler als Interpret Bachs – Ein Beitrag zur Rezeptionsgeschichte', *Neue Zeitschrift dur Musik*, 147/5 (May 1986), 6.

56. Gennady Rozdhestvensky, programme note for his recording of Mahler's Bach Suite, Leningrad Philharmonic Symphony Orchestra, Melodiya LP C10 08979 008, 1977.

57. The notes given as 'Continuo' in the score are actually just the cello/bass part.

58. ML, pp. 154–5.

59. In modern performances of Mahler's Bach Suite, the problem of an appropriate instrument for the clavicembalo part is very acute.

60. For further discussion and illustration of Mahler's Bach Suite, see Mitchell, *The Wunderhorn Years*, pp. 350–60.

61. Julius Bittner, 'Instrumentations-Retouchen bei Beethoven', *Der Merker*, 11/24 (15 Dec. 1920), 569.

62. Ernst Decsey, 'Stunden mit Mahler', *Die Musik*, 10/21 (Aug. 1911), 149.

63. *The Evening Post*, 2 April 1910, 4.

64. Tovey, *Essays in Musical Analyis, Vol. II*, Oxford University Press, 1935, p. 159.

12 Issues in Mahler reception: historicism and misreadings after 1960

1. See Hermann Danuser and Friedhelm Krummacher (eds.), *Rezeptionsgeschichte in der Musikwissensschaft*, Laaber-Verlag, 1991.

2. *Foundations of Music History*, trans. J. B. Robinson, Cambridge University Press, 1983, pp. 39 and 162–3.

3. See, for example, Christoph Metzger, *Mahler-Rezeption. Perspektiven zur Rezeption Gustav Mahlers*, Wilhelmshaven, Florian Noetzel, 2000, pp. 143–202.

4. See Kurt Blaukopf, 'Mahlers materielle Existenz' in Matthias Vogt (ed.), *Das Gustav Mahler-Fest Hamburg 1989. Bericht über den Internationalen Gustav-Mahler-Kongress*, Kassel, Bärenreiter, 1991, pp. 83–8.

5. Christian von Borries, 'Willem Mengelberg. Ein vergessener großer Dirigent zwischen Mahler und Hitler', *Die neue Schweizerische Musikzeitzeitschrift*, 51 (February 1997), 1–4.

6. Hellmuth Christian Wolff, Art: Hugo Riemann (ed. Friedrich Blume) in: *MGG – Musik in Geschichte und Gegenwart*, Kassel, Bärenreiter-Verlag 1963, DTV 1989 Bd. 11, Sp. 483.

7. Hugo Riemann, *Riemann Musiklexikon*, 12th edn in 3 vols., ed. W. Gurlitt, Mainz, Schott, 1961.

8. See Karen Painter, 'Contested Counterpoint: Jewish Appropriation and Polyphonic Liberation', *Archiv fur Musikwissenschaft*, 58/3 (2001), 1–30.

9. Riemann, *Musiklexikon*, 6th edn, Leipzig, 1905, p. 800.

10. Riemann, *Musiklexikon*, 10th edn, Leipzig, 1922, p. 859.

11. See Metzger, *Mahler-Rezeption*, pp. 143–56, for discussion of the entries written in reference books up to the 1950s by leading musicologists such as Hermann Kretzschmar, Arnold Schering, Hermann Abert, Johannes Wolf, Hans Joachim Moser, Otto Schumann, Paul Bekker and Guido Adler.

12. See Metzger, *Mahler-Rezeption*, pp. 157–8.

13. 'Why Mahler Too?' *Chord and Discord*, 2/2 (November 1940), 13–15; quotations on p. 14.

14. See Metzger, *Mahler-Rezeption*, pp. 205–6.

15. Hermann Danuser, *Gustav Mahler und seine Zeit*, 2nd edn, Laaber-Verlag, 1996, p. 275.

16. See Gabriel Engel, 'New Symphonic Horizons', *Chord and Discord*, 1/1, (1933) 1–4.

17. *Ibid.*, p. 1.

18. *Ibid.*, p. 2.

19. For further details see Metzger, *Mahler-Rezeption*, pp. 212–14.

20. Anon., ' "23" – A Viennese Magazine', *Chord and Discord*, 1/4 (October 1933), 20. Cited in Metzger, *Mahler-Rezeption*, p. 213.

21. Hans Tischler, 'The Symphonic Problem in Mahler's Works', *Chord and Discord*, 2/3 (December 1941), 15–21, quotation on p. 15.

22. Oscar Thompson, 'An American School of Criticism', *The Musical Quarterly*, 22 (1937), 430.

23. *Ibid.*, p. 433.

24. The following articles, in chronological order, are representative of this: Gabriel Engel, 'New Symphonic Horizons', 1/1 (February 1932), 1–4; Gabriel Engel, 'Mahler's Musical Language', 1/1 (February 1932), 12–14; Bruno Walter, 'Back to Romanticism!', 1/3 (March 1933), 1–2; Robert G. Grey, 'The New Audience', 1/3 (March 1933), 3–5; William Parks Grant, 'Mahler's Use of the Orchestra', 1/10 (January 1939), 15–24; Tischler, 'The Symphonic Problem'; and Warren Storey Smith, 'Some Mahlerian Misconceptions', 2/4 (1947), 61–4.

25. Volume 3 no. 1 and no. 2 (the final issue) were published respectively in 1969 and 1998.

26. See Metzger, *Mahler-Rezeption*, pp. 162–75.

27. Theodor W. Adorno, *Mahler. A Musical Physiognomy*, trans. Edmund Jephcott, University of Chicago Press, 1992, p. 3.

28. *Ibid.*, p. 4.

29. *Ibid.*, p. 20.

30. *Ibid.*, p. 71.

31. See Metzger, *Mahler-Rezeption*, p. 245.

32. Adorno, *A Musical Physiognomy*, p. 19.

33. Heinz-Klaus Metzger, live recording of the second panel discussion on 5 September 1989 in the Gustav-Mahler-Fest, Hamburg 1989, in Vogt (ed.), *Das Gustav Mahler-Fest*, pp. 424–5.

34. Helmut Lachenmann, 'Antworten auf fünf Fragen des Herausgebers' in Peter Ruzicka (ed.), *Mahler. Eine Herausforderung, ein Symposion*, Wiesbaden, Breitkopf & Härtel, 1977, pp. 54–5.

35. *Ibid.*, p. 64.

36. *Ibid.*

37. *Die Musik Gustav Mahlers*, rev. edn, Munich and Zurich, R. Piper, 1986, p. 8.

38. See Metzger, *Mahler-Rezeption*, p. 179; Guido Adler, *Gustav Mahler*, Vienna, Universal Edition, 1916; Adler (ed.), *Handbuch der Musikgeschichte*, Frankfurt am Main, Frankfurter Verlags-Anstalt, 1924; and Paul Bekker, *Gustav Mahlers Sinfonien*, Berlin, Schuster, 1921.

39. Adorno, *A Musical Physiognomy*, pp. 22 and 23.

40. Herbert Schnädelbach, *Geschichtsphilosophie nach Hegel. Die Probleme des Historismus*, Freiburg and Munich, Alber, 1974, pp. 20–1.

41. See Christoph Metzger, 'Korrelationen musikwissenschaftlicher Rezeptionsforschung mit der Aufführungsgeschichte am Beispiel Gustav Mahlers' in Kathrin Ebel and Wolfgang Ruf (eds.), *Musikkonzepte – Konzepte der Musikwissenschaft, Bericht über den Internationalen Kongress der Gesellschaft für Musikforschung, Halle (Saale) 1998*, Kassel, Bärenreiter, 2000, pp. 591–5.

42. *Musikgeschichte als Geschichte der musikalischen Formenwandlungen*, Berlin and Leipzig, Deutsche Verlag Anstalt, 1926, repr. Hildesheim and New York, 1976.

43. Dahlhaus, *Foundations*, pp. 162–3.

44. Jiri Fukac, 'Gustav Mahlers Musikalische Gestaltungsprinzipien. Eine verpasste Sternstunde der Mahler–Rezeption' in Vogt (ed.), *Das Gustav Mahler-Fest*, pp. 225–6.

45. 'Mahler-Berichterstattung der Neuen Zeitschrift für Musik zwischen 1889 und 1991' in Vogt (ed.), *Das Gustav Mahler-Fest*, pp. 199–214.

13 The history of the International Gustav Mahler Society in Vienna and the Complete Critical Edition

1. See Clemens Hellsberg, 'Gustav Mahler und die Wiener Philharmoniker' in Erich Wolfgang Partsch (ed.), *Gustav Mahler, Werk und Wirken. Neue Mahler-Forschung als Anlaß des*

vierzigjährigen Bestehens der Internationalen Gustav Mahler Gesellschaft, Vienna, Vom Pasqualatihaus, 1996, pp. 64–72.

2. See Clemens Hellsberg, *Demokratie der Könige. Die Geschichte der Wiener Philharmoniker*, Zurich, Vienna and Mainz, Schweizer Verlagshaus, 1992.

3. All letters cited in this essay are to be found in the IGMG archive.

4. See Erich Wolfgang Partsch, 'Zur Geschichte der Internationalen Gustav Mahler Gesellschaft' in Partsch (ed.), *Gustav Mahler*, pp. 11–33, esp. p. 15.

5. English edn, *Gustav Mahler*, trans. Inge Goodwin, London, Allen Lane, 1973.

6. Trans. as *Gustav Mahler and Guido Adler. Records of a Friendship*, Cambridge University Press, 1982.

7. Trans. as *Gustav Mahler–Richard Strauss. Correspondence 1888–1911*, London, Faber & Faber, 1984.

8. *Gustav Mahler Briefe*, Vienna, Zsolnay, 1982, rev. edn 1996; unknown letters trans. as *Mahler's Unknown Letters*, London, Victor Gollancz, 1986.

9. Partsch, 'Zur Geschichte', 15.

10. A term used to describe an edition which incorporates the last known revisions of the composer.

11. Reinhold Kubik, 'Analysis versus History. Erwin Ratz and the Sixth Symphony' in Gilbert Kaplan (ed.), *The Correct Movement Order in Mahler's Sixth Symphony*, New York, The Kaplan Foundation, 2004, pp. 37–43.

12. SLGM, p. 372.

13. See Reinhold Kubik (ed.), *Das klagende Lied. Erstfassung in drei Sätzen (1880)*, Critical Edition, Supplement Band IV, Vienna, Universal Edition, 1999, p. xi and Plate 1.

14 Musical languages of love and death: Mahler's compositional legacy

1. Alastair Williams, 'Adorno and the Semantics of Modernism', *Perspectives of New Music*, 37 (1999) 31, 36. Adorno's 1960 'musical physiognomy' can be read as a reassertion of Mahler's contemporary relevance, as a 'defensive effort to secure Mahler for the future of modernism' (Leon Botstein, 'Whose Mahler? Reception, Interpretation and History' in Karen Painter (ed.), *Mahler and His World*, Princeton University Press, 2002, pp. 3–4, 17 and 19). Theodor W. Adorno, *Mahler. A Musical Physiognomy*, trans. Edmund Jephcott, University of Chicago Press, 1992.

2. Donald Mitchell, 'The Modernity of Gustav Mahler' in Gunther Weiß (ed.), *Neue Mahleriana*, Berne, Peter Lang, 1997, pp. 183 and 187.

3. For Hans Keller, Mahler is significant as the 'first to develop a consistent, "ruthlessly" self-observing as well as expressive' music, what he characteristically called 'superego music'. Keller concluded that 'the diagnosis, however tentative, cannot be avoided that it was in fact Mahler, rather than the more revolutionary Schoenberg, who was the widest influence on twentieth-century music – just because he was less of a revolutionary'. 'The Unpopularity of Mahler's Popularity' [1971] in Christopher Wintle (ed.), *Essays on Music*, Cambridge University Press, 1994, pp. 69–70.

4. See Paul Banks, 'Mahler and Viennese Modernism' in Philip Read (ed.), *On Mahler and Britten*, Woodbridge, Boydell Press, 1995, p. 14.

5. Schoenberg, 'My Evolution' in Leonard Stein (ed.), *Style and Idea. Selected Writings*, trans. Leo Black rev. edn, London, Faber, 1984, p. 82. On the op. 8 songs see Robert R. Holzer, 'Schoenberg sets Petrarch: Schopenhauer, Mahler, and the Poetics of Resignation' in Charlotte M. Cross and Russell A. Berman (eds.), *Schoenberg and Words. The Modernist Years*, New York, Garland, 2000, pp. 76–7.

6. See Peter Franklin, *The Idea of Music. Schoenberg and Others*, London, Macmillan, 1985, pp. 77–90.

7. Schoenberg, 'Gustav Mahler', *Style and Idea*, p. 450.

8. Schoenberg, letter to Mahler of 29 December 1909, in ML, p. 325.

9. See Walter Frisch, 'The Refractory Masterpiece: Towards an Interpretation of Schoenberg's Chamber Symphony, op. 9' in Juliane Brand and Christopher Hailey (eds.), *Constructive Dissonance. Arnold Schoenberg and the Transformations of Twentieth-Century Culture*, Berkeley, University of California Press, 1997, pp. 87–99.

10. See HLGE3, pp. 610–16 and 791–2.

11. Arnold Schoenberg, *Theory of Harmony*, trans. Roy Carter, London, Faber, 1983, p. 402.

12. On these Mahler links to Op. 14 no.1 and Op. 19 see Bryan R. Simms, *The Atonal Music of Schoenberg*, Oxford University Press, 2000, pp. 31–2 and 85.

13. Reinhold Brinkmann, 'The Compressed Symphony: On the Historical Content of Schoenberg's Op. 9', trans. Irene Zedlacher in Walter Frisch (ed.), *Schoenberg and His World*, Princeton University Press, 1999, pp. 141–61.

14. See Jan Maegaard, 'Schoenberg's Incomplete Works and Fragments' in *Constructive Dissonance*, pp. 140–1.

15. Simms, *The Atonal Music of Schoenberg*, pp. 108, 154–8 and 203–9.

16. Adorno, 'Mahler: A Centenary Address' in *Quasi una Fantasia. Essays on Modern Music*, trans. Rodney Livingstone, London, Verso, 1992, pp. 83–4.

17. Adorno, *Alban Berg, Master of the Smallest Link*, trans. and ed. Juliane Brand and Christopher Hailey, Cambridge University Press, 1991, pp. 13–14, 20, 73–6 and 82–3.

18. Derrick Puffett, 'Berg, Mahler and the Orchestral Pieces Op. 6 (1914–15)' in Anthony Pople (ed.), *The Cambridge Companion to Berg*, Cambridge University Press, 1997, pp. 111–44.

19. George Perle, *The Operas of Alban Berg vol. 1. Wozzeck*, Berkeley, University of California Press, 1980, pp. 73 and 171–2.

20. Allen Forte, 'The Mask of Tonality: Alban Berg's Symphonic Epilogue to *Wozzeck*' in David Gable and Robert P. Morgan (eds.), *Alban Berg. Historical and Analytical Perspectives*, Oxford, Clarendon Press, 1991, pp. 151–200.

21. Adorno, 'Vienna', *Quasi una Fantasia*, p. 215.

22. Judy Lochhead, 'Lulu's Feminine Performance' in Pople (ed.), *The Cambridge Companion to Berg*, pp. 227–44.

23. Douglas Jarman, *Alban Berg: 'Lulu'*, Cambridge University Press, 1991, pp. 87 and 89.

24. Julian Johnson, *Webern and the Transformation of Nature*, Cambridge University Press, 1999, p. 205 and *passim*.

25. Anton Webern, *The Path to the New Music*, ed. Willi Reich, trans. Leo Black, London, Universal Edition, 1975, pp. 34–5 and 52.

26. Arnold Whittall, 'Webern and Atonality: The Path from the Old Aesthetic', *The Musical Times*, 124 (1983), 733–7.

27. Adorno, 'Zemlinsky', in *Quasi una Fantasia*, pp. 113, 120 and 122.

28. Puffett, 'Transcription and Recomposition: the Strange Case of Zemlinsky's Maeterlink Songs' in Craig Ayrey and Mark Everist (eds.), *Analytical Strategies and Musical Interpretation. Essays on Nineteenth- and Twentieth-century Music*, Cambridge University Press, 1996, p. 479.

29. On the 'moment' in Austro-German music see Berthold Hoeckner, *Programming the Absolute*, Princeton University Press, 2002. Mahler is discussed in pp. 252–65.

30. Anthony Beaumont, *Zemlinsky*, London, Faber, 2000, pp. 315–19.

31. Robert P. Morgan, 'The Eternal Return: Retrograde and Circular Form in Berg' in Gable and Morgan (eds.), *Alban Berg*, p. 148.

32. Adorno, 'Mahler Today' (1930) in *Essays on Music*, ed. Richard Leppert, trans. Susan Gillespie, Berkeley, University of California Press, 2002, p. 610.

33. *Die Musik*, 22 (Feb. 1930), trans. in David Drew, booklet notes to CD Weill *Kleine Dreigroschenmusik*, etc. (London Sinfonietta/ David Atherton) DG 423 255–2.

34. Franklin, *The Idea of Music*, pp. 101–2.

35. Humphrey Carpenter, *Benjamin Britten. A Biography*, London, Faber 1992, p. 36. For a later reflection on his encounter with Mahler's Fourth see Britten's essay 'On Behalf of Gustav Mahler' (1942) in Paul Kildea (ed.), *Britten on Music*, Oxford University Press, 2003, pp. 38–9.

36. Christopher Mark, 'Juvenilia (1922–32)' in Mervyn Cooke (ed.), *The Cambridge Companion to Britten*, Cambridge University Press, 1999, p. 31.

37. Philip Rupprecht, *Britten's Musical Language*, Cambridge University Press, 2001.

38. Donald Mitchell, 'What Do We Know About Britten Now?' in Christopher Palmer (ed.), *The Britten Companion*, London, Faber, 1984, p. 31.

39. Donald Mitchell, *Britten and Auden in the 1930s. The Year 1936*, London, Faber, 1981, p. 31.

40. Wilfrid Mellers, 'Mahler and the Great Tradition' in Donald Mitchell and Andrew Nicholson (eds.), *The Mahler Companion*, rev. edn, Oxford University Press, 2002, p. 573.

41. See Christopher Mark, *Early Benjamin Britten*, New York, Garland, 1995, p. 131.

42. Eric Roseberry, 'The Concertos and Early Orchestral Scores: Aspects of Style and Aesthetic' in Cooke (ed.), *The Cambridge Companion to Britten*, p. 236.

43. Arnold Whittall, *The Music of Britten and Tippett. Studies in Themes and Techniques*, Cambridge University Press, 1982, pp. 104 and 109.

44. Carpenter, *Benjamin Britten*, p. 387.

45. Arved Ashby, 'Britten as Symphonist' in Cooke (ed.), *The Cambridge Companion to Britten*, pp. 223–5, 229 and 232.

46. Eric Roseberry, 'A Debt Repaid? Some Observations on Shostakovich and his Late Period Reception of Britten' in David Fanning (ed.), *Shostakovich Studies*, Cambridge University Press, 1995, pp. 229–53.

47. Ludmilla Kovnatskaya, 'Notes on a Theme from *Peter Grimes*' in Philip Read (ed.), *On Mahler and Britten*, pp. 172–85.

48. Eric Roseberry, 'Tonal Ambiguity in *Death in Venice*: a Symphonic View' in Donald Mitchell (ed.), *Benjamin Britten. 'Death in Venice'*, Cambridge University Press, 1987, pp. 93–4.

49. Carpenter, *Benjamin Britten*, p. 73.

50. Hans Werner Henze, *Language, Music and Artistic Invention*, trans. Mary Whittall, Aldeburgh, Britten-Pears Library, 1996, p. 7.

51. Henze, '*The Bassarids*: (2), Psychology in Music' in *Music and Politics*, trans. Peter Labanyi, London, Faber, 1982, p. 151. For more see my 'Hans Werne Henze as Post-Mahlerian: Anachronism, Freedom, and the Erotics of Intertextuality', *Twentieth-century music*, 1/ii (2004), pp. 179–207.

52. See Roseberry, 'A Debt Repaid?' See also Lyudmilla Kovnatskaya, 'Shostakovich and Britten: Some Parallels' in Rosamund Bartlett

(ed.), *Shostakovich in Context*, Oxford University Press, 2000, pp. 175–89.

53. See Inna Barsova, 'Mahler and Russia' in Mitchell and Nicholson (eds.), *The Mahler Companion*, pp. 517–30, and Pauline Fairclough, 'Mahler Reconstructed: Sollertinsky and the Soviet Symphony, *The Musical Quarterly*, 85/2 (Summer 2001), 367–90.

54. Richard Taruskin, 'Shostakovich and Us', *Shostakovich in Context*, pp. 16, 25–6.

55. Eric Roseberry, *Ideology, Style, Content, and Thematic Process in the Symphonies, Cello Concertos, and String Quartets of Shostakovich*, New York, Garland, 1989, pp. 394–419.

56. Taruskin, 'Shostakovich and Us', p. 25.

57. Sollertinsky, cited in Roseberry, *Ideology*, pp. 512 and 532–3. For a comparison of 'satirizing techniques' in Mahler and Shostakovich see Esti Sheinberg, *Irony, Satire, Parody and the Grotesque in the Music of Shostakovich. A Theory of Musical Incongruities*, Aldershot, Ashgate, 2000, pp. 94–7.

58. See David M. Schiller, *Bloch, Schoenberg, and Bernstein. Assimilating Jewish Music*, Oxford University Press, 2003, pp. 127–66.

59. The seminal article is Robert P. Morgan, 'Ives and Mahler: Mutual Responses at the End of an Era', *19th-Century Music*, 2 (1978), 72–81.

60. Leon Botstein, 'Innovation and Nostalgia: Ives, Mahler, and the Origins of Modernism' in J. Peter Burkholder (ed.), *Charles Ives and His World*, Princeton University Press, 1996, pp. 35–74.

61. Alfred Schnittke, 'Polystilistic Tendencies in Modern Music' (c. 1971), and 'On Concerto Grosso no.1' in Alexander Ivashkin (ed.), *A Schnittke Reader*, Bloomington, Indiana University Press, 2002, pp. 45 and 87–90.

62. Lisa Brooks Robinson, 'Mahler and Postmodern Intertextuality', unpublished Ph.D. thesis, Yale University, 1994, pp. 177–229.

63. Alexander Ivashkin, 'Shostakovich and Schnittke: the Erosion of Symphonic Syntax' in Fanning (ed.), *Shostakovich Studies*, pp. 257–9 and 266–8.

64. Robinson, 'Mahler and Postmodern Intertextuality', pp. 212, 226 and 227.

65. Georg Borchardt, 'Alfred Schnittke and Gustav Mahler' in George Odam (ed.), *Seeking the Soul. The Music of Alfred Schnittke*, London, Guildhall School of Music and Drama, 2002, pp. 28–37.

66. Ivashkin, 'Shostakovich and Schnittke'; the review of the Sixth Symphony is by Peter David, New York, 1994.

67. Richard Taruskin, 'After Everything' in *Defining Russia Musically*, Princeton University Press, 1997, pp. 99–104.

68. Schnittke, 'The Third Movement of Berio's *Sinfonia*: Stylistic Counterpoint, Thematic and Formal Unity in Context of Polystylism, Broadening the concept of Thematicism' in Ivashkin (ed.), *A Schnittke Reader*, pp. 216–24.

69. See David Osmond Smith, *Playing on Words. Berio's Sinfonia*, London, Royal Musical Association, pp. 39–71.

70. David Metzer, *Quotation and Cultural Meaning in Twentieth-Century Music*, Cambridge University Press, 2003, pp. 130 and 134.

71. György Ligeti and Clytus Gottwald, 'Gustav Mahler und die musikalische Utopie', *Neue Zeitschrift für Musik*, 135 (1974), 7–11, 288–91, 292–5.

72. Richard Steinitz, *György Ligeti. Music of the Imagination*, London, Faber, 2003, pp. 160 and 184.

73. Alastair Williams, *New Music and the Claims of Modernity*, Aldershot Ashgate, 1997, p. 84.

74. *Ibid.*, pp. 136–9.

75. Karlheinz Stockhausen, 'Introduction' (1972) to HLGE1, pp. xxi and xxii.

76. For discussion see Metzer, *Quotation and Cultural Meaning*, pp. 139–55.

77. Pierre Boulez, 'Stravinsky: Style or Idea? – In Praise of Amnesia' [1971] in *Orientations*, ed. Jean-Jacques Nattiez, trans. Martin Cooper, London, Faber, 1986, pp. 358–9.

78. Boulez, 'Mahler: Our Contemporary?' [1979] in *Orientations*, pp. 295–303.

79. Dieter Schnebel, '*Brouillards*. Tendenzen bei Debussy', *die Riehe*, 6 (1960), 'Musik und Sprache', trans. in *die Riehe* 6 'Music and Language', Bryn Mawr, Theodor Presser, 1964, pp. 30–5. See M. J. Grant, *Serial Music, Serial Aesthetics*, Cambridge University Press, 2001, p. 126.

80. Kurt Weill, 'Gustav Mahler: 9. Symphonie', *Der deutsche Rundfunk*, 4/25 (20 June 1926), 1723–7; trans. in Kowalke, *Kurt Weill in Europe*, Ann Arbor, UMI Research Press, 1979, p. 155.

81. Stephen Pruslin, 'Second Taverner Fantasia' (1965), *Peter Maxwell Davies. Studies from Two Decades* [*Tempo* Booklet No. 2], London, Boosey & Hawkes, 1979, pp. 27 and 31.

82. Pruslin, 'Nel mezzo del cammin – In Mid-flight' (1977) in *Peter Maxwell Davies. Studies from Two Decades*, p. 4.

83. Pruslin, ' "One if by the land, Two if by the Sea": Maxwell Davies the Symphonist', *Tempo*, 153 (1985), 2–6.

84. Arnold Whittall, 'Comparatively Complex: Birtwistle, Maxwell Davies and Modernist Analysis', *Music Analysis*, 13 (1994), 139–59 (esp. 141–9).

85. Robinson, 'Mahler and Postmodern Intertextuality', pp. 93, 108, 115 and 130.

86. George Rochberg, 'On the Third String Quartet' (1974) in *The Aesthetics of Survival*, Ann Arbor, UMI, 1984, p. 239.

87. Metzer, *Quotation and Cultural Meaning*, pp. 113 and 122–3.
88. See Mark Berry, 'Music, Postmodernism, and George Rochberg's Third String Quartet' in Judy Lochhead and Simon Auner (eds.), *Postmodern Music/Postmodern Thought*, London, Routledge, 2002, pp. 235–47.
89. Jonathan Harvey, *In Quest of Spirit. Thoughts on Music*, Berkeley, University of California Press, 1999, pp. 28–31, 35, and 72–3.
90. This discussion of Smalley owes much to knowledge generously shared by my colleague Chris Mark.
91. Richard Toop, 'Four Facets of "The New Complexity"', *Contact*, 32 (Spring 1988), 15–17.
92. Roger Redgate, 'The Chamber Music' in Henrietta Brougham, Christopher Fox and Ian Pace (eds.), *Uncommon Ground. The Music of Michael Finnissy*, Aldershot, Ashgate, 1997, p. 167.

15 Mahler conducted and recorded: from the concert hall to DVD
1. See HLGE1, pp. 635–6, 645–57; HLGE2, pp. 98–9, 140–1, 145–6, 307–12 and 100–1; Deryck Cooke, *Gustav Mahler. An Introduction to His Music*, London, Faber, 1980, pp. 3–4; Jonathan Carr, *The Real Mahler*, London, Constable, 1997, pp. 5–6 and 65; Hans F. Redlich, *Bruckner and Mahler*, London, Dent, 1963, p. 125.
2. Symphonic movements are abbreviated as follows: *III (ii)* signifies the second movement of the Third Symphony.
3. HLGE2, pp. 528–9.
4. *Ibid.*, pp. 473–6.
5. *Ibid.*, pp. 671–2, 639 and 726–7.
6. Truus de Leur, 'Gustav Mahler in the Netherlands' in Donald Mitchell (ed.), *Gustav Mahler. The World Listens*, Programme Book of the 1995 *MahlerFeest* in Amsterdam, Haarlem, TEMA Uitgevers, 1995, pp. 1 and 15.
7. The following abbreviations will be used: ASO (Atlanta Symphony Orchestra), BBCSO (BBC Symphony Orchestra), BoSO (Bournemouth Symphony Orchestra), BPO (Berlin Philharmonic Orchestra), BSO (Boston Symphony Orchestra), CO (Cleveland Orchestra), CPO (Czech Philharmonic Orchestra), CSO (Chicago Symphony Orchestra), DG (Deutsche Grammophon), DNRSO (Danish National Radio Symphony Orchestra), DSO (Dallas Symphony Orchestra), LSO (London Symphony Orchestra), MSO (Minneapolis Symphony Orchestra), NPO (New Philharmonia Orchestra), NRSO (Netherlands Radio Symphony Orchestra), NYPO (New York Philharmonic Orchestra), PSO (Pittsburgh Symphony Orchestra), PO (Philadelphia

Orchestra), RCO (Royal Concertgebouw Orchestra), RSSO (Russian State Symphony Orchestra), SFSO (San Francisco Symphony Orchestra), SPO (Stockholm Philharmonic Orchestra), SoPO (Sofia Philharmonic Orchestra), SWGRO (SW German Radio Orchestra), TSO (Tokyo Symphony Orchestra), USO (Utah Symphony Orchestra), VPO (Vienna Philharmonic Orchestra), VPMO (Vienna Pro Musica Orchestra), VSO (Vienna Symphony Orchestra) and VSOO (Vienna State Opera Orchestra).
8. See Erik Ryding and Rebecca, Pechefsky, *Bruno Walter. A World Elsewhere*, Yale University Press, 2001, pp. 18–19, and Andreas Kluge, booklet notes to Walter's 1961 recording of Symphony No. 9 (Sony SM2K 64452), p. 7.
9. Ryding and Pechefsky, *Bruno Walter*, pp. 62–3.
10. Cited in *ibid.*, p. 18.
11. *Ibid.*, p. 162.
12. Antony Beaumont, *Zemlinsky*, Ithaca, Cornell University Press, 2000, p. 224.
13. Hans and Rosaleen Moldenhauer, *Anton von Webern, a Chronicle of his Life and Work*, London, Gollancz, 1978, p. 183.
14. See *ibid.*, pp. 244 and 290–2.
15. Cited in *ibid.*, pp. 382–3.
16. *Ibid.*, p. 465.
17. See Peter Heyworth, *Otto Klemperer. His Life and Times, Volume 1: 1885–1933*, Cambridge University Press, 1983, p. 25.
18. *Ibid.*, p. 307.
19. See Peter Heyworth (ed.), *Conversations with Klemperer*, London, Gollancz, 1973, pp. 3 and 144.
20. 'Gustav Mahler, the Musician-Philosopher' cited in the booklet notes to Scherchen's 1960 performance of the Third Symphony on the Tahra label (101), pp. 20–2.
21. See Tony Duggan, 'The Mahler Symphonies: a Synoptic Survey: Symphony No. 7', www.musicweb.uk.net/Mahler/Mahler7.htm.
22. Smoley, Lewis, *Gustav Mahler's Symphonies. Critical Commentary on Recordings Since 1986*, Westport, CT, Greenwood, 1996, p. 249.
23. Information provided by Mark Kluge.
24. *The Mahler Broadcasts 1948–1982, The New York Philharmonic*, booklet, New York Philharmonic Special Edition NYP 9801/12 (1998), pp. 84–5 and 89.
25. See the recent review in *The Gramophone*, February 1998, 52–3.
26. Alan Sanders, booklet notes to Barbirolli's recording of the Second Symphony on Testament SBT2 1320, p. 4.
27. Cited in Michael Kennedy, booklet notes to Barbirolli's 1969 recording of the Third Symphony, p. 6.
28. Reid, *John Barbirolli. A Biography*, London, Hamilton, 1971, p. 331.

29. Broadcast on 7 February 1960 over the CBS Television Network; prod. by Roger Englander, and issued by Kultur (D1503) as part of a nine-DVD set of Young People's Concerts.

30. Rec. 1985 and issued by Kultur (1444); it includes excerpts from Bernstein's recordings from the 1970s and 1980s.

31. Rec. at the Berlin Philharmonie in 1971 and issued by Kultur (1570).

32. See *The Unanswered Question. Six Talks at Harvard by Leonard Bernstein*, rec. by Kultur (1570).

33. See Joan Peyser, *Bernstein. A Biography*, New York, Beech Tree Books, 1987, p. 298.

34. See John Steane, review of Haitink's Ninth and *Das Lied von der Erde* in *The Gramophone*, April 1999, 64.

35. See John Steane, review of Tennstedt's complete Mahler cycle in *The Gramophone*, January 1999.

36. Ole Kristian Ruud/Norrköping Symphony.

37. Zsolt Hamar/Pannon Philharmonic Orchestra (Pécs, Hungary).

38. The first recording, under Gary Bertini (RCA Victor PRL3 9063) is out of print. In 2004, Naxos released Paolo Arrivabeni's inferior performance.

39. See the review in *The Gramophone*, June 1986.

40. See reviews in *The Gramophone* of March 1985; September 1985 (Richard Osborne); June 1986; October 1987; December 1987; November 1990; September 1992 (Edward Seckerson); December 1992; January 1997; November 1998; August 1998; June 1998 (Edward Seckerson); May 2000 (David Gutman); January 2002 (Richard Osborne).

41. Review of the Berlin Fifth, *The Gramophone*, January 2002; review of the Berlin Tenth, *The Gramophone*, May 2000.

42. See Mark Swed, review in *The Gramophone*, January 1989, 1117 and 1154.

43. See Andrew Farach-Colton, review in *The Gramophone*, January 2003, 36–7.

44. 'What the Universe Tells Me. Unraveling the Mysteries of Mahler's Third Symphony', dir. Jason Starr (Video Artists International, 2003); 'Conducting Mahler' and 'Mahler – I have Lost Touch with the World', dir. Frank Scheffer (Allegri Film BV, 1996/2004).

16 New research paths in criticism, analysis and interpretation

1. Raymond Monelle, 'Mahler and Gustav' in *The Sense of Music. Semiotic Essays*, Princeton University Press, p. 172.

2. Max Paddison, *Adorno's Aesthetics of Music*, Cambridge University Press, 1993, p. 279.

3. *Ibid.*, p. 259.

4. NBLE, p. 146; see also Stephen McClatchie, 'Hans Rott, Gustav Mahler and the "New Symphony": New Evidence for a Pressing Question', *Music & Letters*, 81 (2000), 392–401, which argues for Mahler's knowledge of Rott's symphony as early as 1890 or 1891.

5. ML, p. 233.

6. Explication of Adorno's texts from the point of view of their formal categories, on the other hand, has been a prominent activity in English-language Mahler studies; see, for example, James Buhler, '"Breakthrough" as Critique of Form: The Finale of Mahler's First Symphony', *19th-Century Music*, 20 (1996–7), 125–43.

7. Hans Tischler, 'Key Symbolism versus "Progressive Tonality"', *Musicology*, 2 (1949), 383–8, and 'Mahler's Impact upon the Crisis of Tonality', *Music Review*, 12 (1951), 113–21.

8. Peter Bürger, *Theory of the Avant-Garde*, trans. Jochen Schulte-Sasse, Minneapolis, University of Minneapolis Press, 1999, p. 51.

9. Martin Geck, *Von Beethoven bis Mahler: Die Musik des deutschen Idealismus*, Stuttgart and Weimar, J. B. Metzler, 1993, p. 418.

10. Theodor W. Adorno, *Mahler. A Musical Physiognomy*, trans. Edmund Jephcott, University of Chicago Press, 1992, p. 5.

11. Peter Franklin, '"... his fractures are the script of truth." – Adorno's Mahler' in Stephen Hefling (ed.), *Mahler Studies*, Cambridge University Press, 1997, p. 291.

12. Kofi Agawu, *Playing with Signs: A Semiotic Interpretation of Classic Music*, Princeton University Press, 1991, pp. 51–79.

13. Stephen Hefling, 'Techniques of Irony in Mahler's Œuvre' in André Castagné, Michel Chalon and Patrick Florençon (eds.), *Gustav Mahler et l'ironie dans la culture au tournant du siècle. Actes du colloque de Montpellier 16–18 Juillet 1996*, Castelnau-le-Lez, Climats, 2001, p. 99.

14. Hans Heinrich Eggebrecht, *Die Musik Gustav Mahlers*, Munich, Piper, 1982, p. 268.

15. *Ibid.*

16. Geck, *Von Beethoven bis Mahler*, p. 410.

17. Eggebrecht, *Die Musik Gustav Mahlers*, pp. 37–8 and 166–7.

18. Ute Jung-Kaiser, 'Die wahren Bilder und Chiffren "tragischer Ironie" in Mahlers "Erster"' in Günther Weiß (ed.), *Neue Mahleriana. Essays in Honour of Henry-Louis de La Grange on his Seventieth Birthday*, Berne, Peter Lang, 1997, pp. 101–52.

19. Siegfried Oechsle, 'Autonomie, Immanenz, und Bruch: Mahlers Erste Symphonie und die Geschichte der Gattung' in Bernd Sponheuer and Wolfram Steinbeck (eds.), *Gustav Mahler und die Symphonik des 19. Jahrhunderts. Referate des Bonner Symposions 2000*, Frankfurt am Main, Peter Lang, 2001, p. 47.

20. Eckard Roch, '"Wie ein Naturlaut . . .":
Ästhetik des Uneigentlichen in der Symphonik
Gustav Mahlers' in *Gustav Mahler und die
Symphonik des 19. Jahrhunderts*, p. 144.

21. Raymond Monelle, *The Sense of Music*, p. 80.

22. At its best in Donald Mitchell, 'Mahler and
Smetana: Significant Influences or Accidental
Parallels?' in Hefling (ed.), *Mahler Studies*,
pp. 110–21.

23. Henry-Louis de La Grange, 'Music about
Music in Mahler: Reminiscences, Allusion, or
Quotations?' in Hefling (ed.), *Mahler Studies*,
pp. 122–68.

24. Paul Thissen, *Zitattechniken in der
Symphonik des 19. Jahrhunderts*, Sinzig, Studio,
1998.

25. Hans-Joachim Hinrichsen, 'Bruckners
Wagner-Zitate' in Albrecht Riethmüller (ed.),
*Bruckner-Probleme. Internationales Kolloquium
7.–9. October 1996 in Berlin*, Stuttgart, Franz
Steiner, 1999, pp. 124–5.

26. Kofi Agawu, 'Prolonged Counterpoint in
Mahler' in Hefling (ed.), *Mahler Studies*,
pp. 217–47.

27. Paul Bekker, *Gustav Mahler Sinfonien*, repr.
Hans Schneider, Tutzing, 1969, p. 219.

28. Norman Del Mar, *Mahler's Sixth Symphony.
A Study*, London, Eulenburg, 1980, pp. 23–5 and
34–40; HLGE3, p. 812; Bernd Sponheuer, *Logik
des Zerfalls. Untersuchungen zum Finalproblem in
den Symphonien Gustav Mahlers*, Tutzing, Hans
Schneider, 1978, pp. 281–2.

29. For example, Hans-Peter Jülg, *Gustav
Mahlers Sechste Symphonie*, Munich and
Salzburg, Emil Katzbichler, 1986, pp. 42–55.

30. Martin Geck, 'Zur Final-Idee in Mahlers
Sechster Symphonie' in Sponheuer and
Steinbeck (eds.), *Gustav Mahler und die
Symphonik*, p. 163.

31. Robert Samuels, *Mahler's Sixth Symphony. A
Study in Musical Semiotics*, Cambridge
University Press, 1995, p. 155.

32. Eveline Nikkels, *'O Mensch! Gib Acht!'
Friedrich Nietzsches Bedeutung für Gustav
Mahler*, Amsterdam and Atlanta, Ga., Rodopi,
1989.

33. For example, Ursula Kirkendale, 'The Source
for Bach's *Musical Offering*', *Journal of the

American Musicological Society*, 33 (1980),
88–141.

34. Adorno, *A Musical Physiognomy*, pp. 61–80.

35. *Ibid.*, p. 69.

36. Eggebrecht, *Die Musik Gustav Mahlers*,
p. 169.

37. Jörg Rothkamm, '"Kondukt" als Grundlage
eines Formkonzepts: Eine Charakteranalyse des
ersten Satzes des IX. Symphonie Gustav
Mahlers', *Archiv für Musikwissenschaft*, 54
(1997), 269–83.

38. Eggebrecht, *Die Musik Gustav Mahlers*,
pp. 34, 67, 251, and 277.

39. An overview of various theories can be found
in Peter Andraschke, *Gustav Mahlers IX.
Symphonie: Kompositionsprozess und Analyse*,
Wiesbaden, Franz Steiner, 1976, pp. 32–58;
needless to say, there have been other approaches
since he wrote his excellent monograph.

40. Warren Darcy, 'Rotational Form,
Teleological Genesis, and Fantasy-Projection in
the Slow Movement of Mahler's Sixth
Symphony', *19th-Century Music*, 25 (2001–2),
49–74.

41. Anthony Newcomb, 'Narrative Archetypes
and Mahler's Ninth Symphony' in Steven Scher
(ed.), *Music and Text: Critical Inquiries*,
Cambridge University Press, 1992, pp. 118–36;
Vera Micznik, 'The Farewell Story of Mahler's
Ninth Symphony', *19th-Century Music*, 20
(1996–97), 144–66.

42. Allen Forte, 'Middleground Motives in the
Adagietto of Mahler's Fifth Symphony', *19th-
Century Music*, 8/2 (1985), 153–63.

43. Darcy, 'Rotational Form', 51.

44. Samuels, *Mahler's Sixth Symphony*, p. 59; for
Tischler, see above, n. 7.

45. Samuels, *Mahler's Sixth Symphony*, p. 157.

46. *Ibid.*, p. 163.

47. Roland Barthes, *Elements of Semiology*, trans.
Annette Lavers and Colin Smith, New York, Hill
and Wang, 1967, p. 91.

48. Forte, 'Middleground Motives', 163.

49. As opposed to defend it: see Peter
Franklin, '". . . his fractures are the script of
truth." – Adorno's Mahler' in Hefling (ed.),
Mahler Studies, pp. 271–94.

50. Monelle, 'Mahler and Gustav', *passim*.

Bibliography

Abbate, Carolyn, *Unsung Voices. Opera and Musical Narrative in the Nineteenth Century* (Princeton University Press, 1991).

Adler, Guido, *Gustav Mahler* (Vienna: Universal Edition, 1916).

   Gustav Mahler, trans. in Edward Reilly, *Gustav Mahler and Guido Adler. Records of a Friendship* (Cambridge University Press, 1982), pp. 15–73.

Adorno, Theodor, Mahler. *Eine musikalische Physiognomik* (Frankfurt: Suhrkamp, 1960).

   Gesammelte Schriften in zwanzig Bänden, ed.Rolf Tiedemann in collaboration with Gretel Adorno, Susan Buck-Morss and Klaus Schultz (Frankfurt: Suhrkamp, 1970–86).

   Aesthetic Theory, trans. C. Lenhardt (London: Routledge and Kegan Paul, 1984).

   Mahler. A Musical Physiognomy, trans. E. Jephcott (University of Chicago Press, 1992).

   Quasi una Fantasia. Essays on Modern Music, trans. Rodney Livingstone (London: Verso, 1992).

   Aesthetic Theory, ed. Gretel Adorno and Rolf Tiederman, trans. Robert Hullot-Kentor (Minneapolis: University of Minnesota Press, 1997).

   'Mahler Today' [1930] in Richard Leppert (ed.), *Essays on Music. Theodor W. Adorno*, trans. Susan Gillespie (Berkeley: University of California Press, 2002), pp. 603–11.

   'Marginalia on Mahler' [1936], in Richard Leppert (ed.), *Essays on Music. Theodor W. Adorno* trans. Susan Gillespie (Berkeley and Los Angeles: University of California Press, 2002), pp. 612–18.

Agawu, V. Kofi, 'Tonal Strategy in the First Movement of Mahler's Tenth Symphony', *19th-Century Music*, 9/3 (1986), 222–33.

Andraschke, Peter, 'Die Retuschen Gustav Mahlers an der 7. Symphonie von Franz Schubert', *Archiv für Musikwissenschaft*, 32/2 (1975), 106–20.

   Gustav Mahlers IX. Symphonie. Kompositionsprozess und Analyse (Wiesbaden: Franz Steiner, 1976).

Bahr-Mildenburg, Anna, *Erinnerungen* (Vienna: Literarische Anstalt, 1921).

Banks, Paul, 'An Early Symphonic Prelude by Mahler?' *19th-Century Music*, 3/2 (1979), 141–9.

   'The Early Social and Musical Environment of Gustav Mahler' (unpublished D.Phil. dissertation, University of Oxford, 1980).

   'Aspects of Mahler's Fifth Symphony: Performance Practice and Interpretation', *The Musical Times*, 130 (May 1989), 258–65.

Barham, Jeremy, 'Mahler's Third Symphony and the Philosophy of Gustav Fechner: Interdisciplinary Approaches to Criticism, Analysis and Interpretation' (unpublished Ph.D. dissertation, University of Surrey, 1998).

   'Mahler's First Compositions: Piano Quartet and Songs', in Donald Mitchell and Andrew Nicholson (eds.), *The Mahler Companion*, rev. edn (Oxford University Press, 2002), pp. 597–607.

Barham, Jeremy (ed.), *Perspectives on Gustav Mahler* (Aldershot and Burlington, VT: Ashgate Press, 2005).

Barry, Barbara, 'The Hidden Program in Mahler's Fifth Symphony', *The Musical Quarterly*, 77/1 (1993), 47–66.

Bauer-Lechner, Natalie, *Mahleriana*, unpublished manuscript housed in the collection of Henry-Louis de La Grange, Bibliothèque Musicale Gustav Mahler, Paris. *Erinnerungen an Gustav Mahler* (Vienna: E. P. Tal & Co., 1923).

Bayerische Staatsbibliothek (ed.), *Gustav Mahler. Briefe und Musikautographen aus den Moldenhauer-Archiven in der Bayerischen Staatsbibliothek*, Patrimonia 157 (Munich: Bayerische Staatsbibliothek und Kulturstiftung der Länder, 2003).

Bekker, Paul, *Die Symphonie von Beethoven bis Mahler* (Berlin: Schuster & Loeffler, 1918; rev. repr. in *Neue Musik, Gesammelten Schriften*, Stuttgart and Berlin: Deutsche Verlags-Anstalt, 1923). *Musikgeschichte als Geschichte der musikalischen Formenwandlungen* (Berlin and Leipzig: Deutsche Verlag Anstalt, 1926; repr. Hildesheim and New York, 1976). *Gustav Mahlers Sinfonien* (Berlin: Schuster & Loeffler, 1921; repr. Tutzing: Schneider, 1969).

Berg, Alban, *Briefe an seine Frau* (Munich/Vienna: Langen/Müller, 1965).

Berry, Mark, 'Music, Postmodernism, and George Rochberg's Third String Quartet' in Judy Lochhead and Simon Auner (eds.), *Postmodern Music/ Postmodern Thought* (London: Routledge, 2002), pp. 235–47.

Bethge, Eberhard, 'Hans Bethge und *Das Lied von der Erde*', *News About Mahler Research*, 35 (April 1996), 15–21.

Bittner, Julius, 'Instrumentations-Retouchen bei Beethoven', *Der Merker*, 11/24 (15 Dec. 1920), 567–70.

Blaukopf, Herta (ed.), *Gustav Mahler. Unbekannte Briefe* (Vienna: Zsolnay, 1983).

Blaukopf, Herta, 'Arthur Schnitzlers Mahler-Rezeption. Ein Befund aufgrund der Tagebücher des Schriftstellers', *Nachrichten zur Mahler Forschung*, 24 (October 1990), 4–6. ' "Es geht ihm nicht so gut . . .". Zeuge der Mahler-Zeit: Arthur Schnitzler', *Nachrichten zur Mahler Forschung*, 28 (October 1992), 13–14. 'Metaphysik und Physik bei Mahler' in Eveline Nikkels and Robert Becqué (eds.), *A 'Mass' for the Masses. Proceedings of the Mahler VIII Symposium Amsterdam 1988* (Rotterdam: Universitaire Pers, 1992), pp. 37–41. 'Jean Paul, die erste Symphonie und Dostojewski' in Erich Partsch (ed.), *Gustav Mahler. Werk und Wirken. Neue Mahler-Forschung aus Anlass des vierzigjährigen Bestehens der Internationale Gustav Mahler Gesellschaft* (Vienna: Vom Pasqualatihaus, 1996), pp. 35–42. 'Mahler an der Universität' in Günther Weiß (ed.), *Neue Mahleriana: Essays in Honour of Henry-Louis de La Grange on his Seventieth Birthday* (Berne: Peter Lang, 1997), pp. 1–16. *Gustav Mahler–Richard Strauss. Correspondence, 1888–1911*, trans. E. Jephcott (London: Faber & Faber, 1984). *Mahler's Unknown Letters*, trans. R. Stokes (London: Victor Gollancz, 1986). *Gustav Mahler–Richard Strauss Briefwechsel 1888–1911*, rev. edn (Munich: R. Piper, 1988).

(ed.), *Gustav Mahler Briefe*, 2nd edn (Vienna: Zsolnay, 1996).

Blaukopf, Kurt, *Werktreue und Bearbeitung* (Karlsruhe: Braun, 1968).

   Gustav Mahler oder der Zeitgenosse der Zukunft (Vienna, Munich and Zurich: Fritz Molden, 1969).

   Gustav Mahler, trans. Inge Goodwin (London: Allen Lane, 1973).

Blaukopf, Kurt (ed.), *Mahler. Sein Leben, sein Werk und seine Welt in zeitgenössischen Bildern und Texten* (Vienna: Universal Edition, 1976).

   Mahler. A Documentary Study (London: Thames & Hudson, 1976).

Blaukopf, Kurt and Blaukopf, Herta (eds.), *Mahler. His Life, Work and World* (London: Thames and Hudson, 1991).

Borchardt, Georg, 'Alfred Schnittke and Gustav Mahler' in George Odam (ed.), *Seeking the Soul. The Music of Alfred Schnittke* (London: Guildhall School of Music and Drama, 2002), pp. 28–37.

Borries, Christian von, 'Willem Mengelberg. Ein vergessener großer Dirigent zwischen Mahler und Hitler', *Die neue Schweizerische Musikzeitzeitschrift*, 51 (February 1997), 1–4.

Boss, Rainer, 'Symphonic Construction and Fugue. Analytical Remarks on Form and Structure in Mahler's Fifth Symphony', *News About Mahler Research*, 41 (Autumn 1999), 3–30.

Botstein, Leon, 'Innovation and Nostalgia: Ives, Mahler, and the Origins of Modernism' in J. Peter Burkholder (ed.), *Charles Ives and His World* (Princeton University Press, 1996), pp. 35–74.

   'Whose Gustav Mahler? Reception, Interpretation, and History' in Karen Painter (ed.), *Mahler and His World* (Princeton University Press, 2002), pp. 1–53.

Boulez, Pierre, 'Mahler: Our Contemporary?' [1979] in Jean-Jacques Nattiez (ed.), *Orientations*, trans. Martin Cooper (London: Faber, 1986), pp. 295–303.

Bouwman, Frans, 'Editing Mahler 10: Unfinished Business', *The Musical Times*, 142 (2001), 43–51.

Brand, Juliane and Hailey, Christopher (eds.), *Constructive Dissonance. Arnold Schoenberg and the Transformations of Twentieth-Century Culture* (Berkeley: University of California Press, 1997).

Britten, Benjamin, 'On Behalf of Gustav Mahler' [1942] in Paul Kildea (ed.), *Britten on Music* (Oxford University Press, 2003), pp. 38–9.

   Gustav Mahler. Beispiel einer deutsch-jüdischen Symbiose (Frankfurt am Main: Ner-Tamid Verlag, 1961).

Buhler, James, ' "Breakthrough" as Critique of Form: The Finale of Mahler's First Symphony', *19th-Century Music*, 20/2 (1996), 125–43.

Cardus, Neville, *Gustav Mahler: His Mind and His Music. Vol. 1: the First Five Symphonies* (London: Gollancz, 1965).

Carner, Mosco, *Of Men and Music* (London: Joseph Williams, 1944).

Carr, Jonathan, *The Real Mahler* (London:, Constable, 1997).

Castagné, André, Chalon, Michel and Florençon, Patrick (eds.), *Gustav Mahler et l'ironie dans la culture viennoise au tournant du siècle. Actes du colloque Gustav Mahler Montpellier 1996* (Castelnau-le-Lez: Editions Climats, 2001).

   Gustav Mahler. An Introduction to his Music (London: Faber Music, 1980).

Dahlhaus, Carl, 'Thesen über Programmusik' in Dahlhaus (ed.), *Beiträge zur musikalischen Hermeneutik* (Regensburg: Bosse, 1975), pp. 187–204.

Esthetics of Music, trans. W. Austin (Cambridge University Press, 1982).

Foundations of Music History, trans. J. Bradford Robinson (Cambridge University Press, 1983).

Danuser, Hermann, *Gustav Mahler. Das Lied von der Erde* (Munich: Fink, 1986).

Gustav Mahler und seine Zeit (Laaber-Verlag, 1991).

Danuser, Hermann and Krummacher, Friedhelm (eds.), *Rezeptionsgeschichte in der Musikwissensschaft* (Laaber-Verlag, 1991).

Darcy, Warren, 'Rotational Form, Teleological Genesis, and Fantasy Projection in the Slow Movement of Mahler's Sixth Symphony', *19th-Century Music*, 25/1 (2001), 49–74.

Dargie, E. Mary, *Music and Poetry in the Songs of Gustav Mahler* (Berne: Peter Lang, 1981).

Decsey, Ernst, 'Stunden mit Mahler', *Die Musik*, 10/18 (1911), 352–56 and 10/21 (1911), 143–53.

Del Mar, Norman, *Mahler's Sixth Symphony – A Study* (London: Eulenberg Books, 1980).

Diether, Jack, 'Notes on Some Mahler Juvenilia', *Chord and Discord*, 3/1 (1969), 3–100.

Downes, Stephen, 'Hans Werne Henze as Post-Mahlerian: Anachronism, Freedom, and the Erotics of Intertextuality', *Twentieth-century music*, 1/2 (2004), 179–207.

Eggebrecht, Hans Heinrich, *Die Musik Gustav Mahlers*, 2nd edn (Munich: Piper, 1986).

Engel, Gabriel, 'Mahler's Musical Language', *Chord and Discord*, 1/1 (February 1932), 12–14.

'New Symphonic Horizons', *Chord and Discord*, 1/1, (1933), 1–4.

Fairclough, Pauline, 'Mahler Reconstructed: Sollertinsky and the Soviet Symphony', *The Musical Quarterly*, 85/2 (Summer 2001), 367–90.

Feder, Stuart, 'Gustav Mahler Dying', *International Review of Psychoanalysis*, 5 (1978), 125–48.

Gustav Mahler. A Life in Crisis (New Haven: Yale University Press, 2004).

Fischer, Jens Malte, *Gustav Mahler. Der fremde Vertraute* (Vienna: Paul Zsolnay, 2003).

Fiske, Richard, 'Mahler's *Das klagende Lied*: a Conductor's Analysis of the Original Tripartite Manuscript and its Bipartite Revisions' (unpublished Ph.D. dissertation, Indiana University, 1983).

Floros, Constantin, *Gustav Mahler III. Die Symphonien*, Wiesbaden: Breitkopf & Härtel, 1985).

Gustav Mahler I. Die geistige Welt Gustav Mahlers in systematischer Darstellung, 2nd edn (Wiesbaden: Breitkopf & Härtel, 1987).

Gustav Mahler II. Mahler und die Symphonik des 19. Jahrhunderts in neuer Deutung, 2nd edn (Wiesbaden: Breitkopf & Härtel, 1987).

Gustav Mahler. The Symphonies, trans. Vernon Wicker (Aldershot: Scolar Press, 1994).

Foerster, Josef Bohuslav, *Der Pilger. Erinnerungen eines Musikers* (Prague: Artia, 1955).

Forte, Allen, 'Middleground Motives in the Adagietto of Mahler's Fifth Symphony', *19th-Century Music*, 8/2 (1984), 153–63.

Franklin, Peter, *The Idea of Music. Schoenberg and Others* (London: Macmillan, 1985).

    Mahler. Symphony No. 3 (Cambridge University Press, 1991).

    The Life of Mahler (Cambridge University Press, 1997).

    'A Stranger's Story: Programmes, Politics and Mahler's Third Symphony' in Donald Mitchell and Andrew Nicholson (eds.), *The Mahler Companion* (Oxford University Press, 1999), pp. 171–86.

Franklin, Peter (ed.), *Recollections of Gustav Mahler by Natalie Bauer-Lechner*, trans. Dika Newlin (London: Faber Music, 1980).

Fülöp, Peter, *Mahler Discography* (New York: The Kaplan Foundation, 1995).

Geck, Martin, *Von Beethoven bis Mahler. Die Musik des deutschen Idealismus* (Stuttgart and Weimar: J. B. Metzler, 1993).

Genette, Gérard, *Paratexts. Thresholds of Interpretation*, trans. J. E. Lewin (Cambridge University Press, 1997).

Gerlach, Reinhard, *Strophen von Leben, Traum und Tod. Ein Essay über Rückert-Lieder von Gustav Mahler* (Wilhelmshaven: Heinrichshofen, 1982).

Glanz, Christian (ed.), *Wien 1897. Kulturgeschichtliches Profil eines Epochenjahres* (Frankfurt: Peter Lang, 1999).

Graf, Max, *Wagner-Probleme und andere Studien* (Vienna: Wiener Verlag, n.d. [1900]).

Grant, William Parks, 'Mahler's Use of the Orchestra', *Chord and Discord*, 1/10 (January 1939), 15–24.

Gutheil-Schoder, Marie, *Erlebtes und Erstrebtes* (Vienna: Rudolf Krey, 1937).

Hamao, Fusako, 'The Sources of the Texts in Mahler's *Das Lied von der Erde*', *19th-Century Music*, 19 (1995), 83–95.

Hansen, Mathias (ed.), *Gustav Mahler Briefe*, 2nd edn (Leipzig: Reclam, 1985).

    Gustav Mahler (Stuttgart: Philipp Reclam, 1996).

Hanslick, Eduard, *The Beautiful in Music*, ed. Morris Weitz, trans. Gustav Cohen (Indianapolis: Bobbs-Merrill, 1957).

Hefling, Stephen, 'Mahler's "Todtenfeier" and the Problem of Program Music', *19th-Century Music*, 12/1 (1988), 153–63.

    '*Das Lied von der Erde*: Mahler's Symphony for Voices and Orchestra – or Piano', *Journal of Musicology*, 10 (1992), 293–340.

    Mahler. Das Lied von der Erde (Cambridge University Press, 2000).

Hefling, Stephen (ed.), *Mahler Studies* (Cambridge University Press, 1997).

Hellsberg, Clemens, *Demokratie der Könige. Die Geschichte der Wiener Philharmoniker* (Zurich: Schweizer Verlagshaus AG, 1992).

Hempel, Gunter, 'Gustav Mahler in Leipzig', *Musik und Gesellschaft*, 17 (November 1967), 784–5.

Heyworth, Peter (ed.), *Conversations with Klemperer* (London: Faber & Faber, 1985).

Hilmar, Ernst, '"Schade, aber es muß(te) sein": zu Gustav Mahlers Strichen und Retuschen insbesondere am Beispiel der V. Symphonie Anton Bruckners', *Bruckner-Studien* (1974), 187–201.

'Mahlers Beethoven-Interpretation' in Rudolf Stephan (ed.), *Mahler-Interpretation. Aspekte zum Werk und Wirken von Gustav Mahler* (Mainz: Schott, 1985), pp. 29–44.

Hilmar-Voit, Renate, 'Symphonic Sound or in the Style of Chamber Music? The Current Performing Forces of the *Wunderhorn* Lieder and the Sources', *News About Mahler Research*, 28 (October 1992), 8–12.

Hilmar-Voit, Renate (ed.), *Des Knaben Wunderhorn. Gesänge für eine Singstimme mit Orchesterbegleitung, Kritische Gesamtausgabe* vol. 14/2 (Vienna: Universal Edition, 1998).

Hoeckner, Berthold, *Programming the Absolute* (Princeton University Press, 2002).

Holländer, Hans, 'Ein unbekannter Teil von Gustav Mahlers "Klagendem Lied"', *Der Auftakt*, 14/11–12 (1934), 200–2.

Closure and Mahler's Music: the Role of Secondary Parameters (Philadelphia: University of Pennsylvania Press, 1990).

Johnson, Julian, *Webern and the Transformation of Nature* (Cambridge University Press, 1999).

'The Sound of Nature? Mahler, Klimt and the Changing Representation of Nature in Early Viennese Modernism' in Christian Glanz (ed.), *Wien 1897. Kulturgeschichtliches Profil eines Epochenjahres* (Frankfurt: Peter Lang, 1999), pp. 189–204.

Jülg, Hans-Peter, *Gustav Mahlers Sechste Symphonie* (Munich and Salzburg: Musikverlag Emil Katzbichler, 1986).

Kaplan, Gilbert (ed.), *Gustav Mahler, Adagietto. Facsimile, Documentation, Recording* (New York: The Kaplan Foundation, 1992).

The Correct Movement Order of Mahler's Sixth Symphony (NewYork: The Kaplan Foundation, 2004).

Kaplan, Richard, 'Temporal Fusion and Climax in the Symphonies of Mahler', *Journal of Musicology*, 14 (1996), 213–32.

Karbusicky, Vladimir, *Gustav Mahler und seine Umwelt*, Impulse der Forschung 28 (Darmstadt: Wissenschaftliche Buchgesellschaft, 1978).

Karpath, Ludwig, *Begegnung mit dem Genius* (Vienna: Fiba, 1934).

Kennedy, Michael, *Mahler* (London: Dent, 1974; 2nd edn, 1990).

Killian, Herbert (ed.), *Gustav Mahler. Erinnerungen von Natalie Bauer-Lechner* (Hamburg: Karl Dieter Wagner, 1984).

Klein, Rudolf (ed.), *Gustav Mahler Kolloquium 1979*, Beiträge der Österreichischen Gesellschaft für Musik 2 (Kassel: Bärenreiter, 1981).

Klemperer, Otto, *Erinnerungen an Gustav Mahler* (Freiburg and Zurich: Atlantis, 1960).

Knapp, Raymond, *Symphonic Metamorphoses: Subjectivity and Alienation in Mahler's Re-Cycled Songs* (Middletown, CT: Wesleyan University Press, 2003).

Knittel, Kay, '"Ein hypermoderner Dirigent": Mahler and Anti-Semitism in *Fin-de-Siècle* Vienna', *19th-Century Music*, 18/3 (1995), 257–76.

Kralik, Heinrich, *Gustav Mahler* (Vienna: Lafite, 1968).

Kramer, Lawrence, *Music as Cultural Practice: 1800–1900* (Berkeley & Los Angeles: University of California Press, 1990).

Kravitt, Edward, 'Mahler's Dirges for his Death: February 24, 1901', *Musical Quarterly*, 64 (1978), 329–53.

Krebs, Dieter, *Gustav Mahlers Erste Symphonie. Form und Gehalt*, Musikwissenschaftliche Schriften vol. 31 (Munich: Musikverlag Katzbichler, 1997).

Krenek, Ernst, 'Gustav Mahler', in Bruno Walter, *Gustav Mahler* (New York: Vienna House, 1941), pp. 155–220.

Krummacher, Friedhelm, *Gustav Mahlers III. Symphonie. Welt im Widerbild* (Kassel: Bärenreiter, 1991).

Kubik, Reinhold, 'Das klagende Lied. Geschichte, Quellen, Fassungen', *Muziek & Wetenschap*, 7/1 (1999), 19–32.

Kubik, Reinhold (ed.), *Gustav Mahler Sämtliche Werke. Kritische Gesamtausgabe Supplement Band IV. Das klagende Lied. Erstfassung in drei Sätzen (1880)* (Vienna: Universal Edition, 1997).

La Grange, Henry-Louis de, *Mahler. Vol. 1* (New York: Garden City, 1973).
  Mahler. Vol. 1 (London: Gollancz, 1974).
  Gustav Mahler, Chronique d'une Vie. Vol. I. Vers la Gloire (1860–1900) (Paris: Fayard, 1979).
  Gustav Mahler, Chronique d'une Vie. Vol. II. L'âge d'or de Vienne (1900–1907) (Paris: Fayard, 1983).
  Gustav Mahler, Chronique d'une Vie. Vol. III. Le Génie foudroyé (1907–1911) (Paris: Fayard, 1984).
  Gustav Mahler. Vol. 2. Vienna: the Years of Challenge (1897–1904) (Oxford University Press, 1995).
  Gustav Mahler. Vol. 3. Vienna: Triumph and Disillusion (1904–1907) (Oxford University Press, 1999).

La Grange, Henry-Louis de and Weiß, Günther (eds.), *Ein Glück ohne Ruh'. Die Briefe Gustav Mahlers an Alma* (Berlin: Siedler, 1995).
  Gustav Mahler. Letters to his Wife, rev. and trans. Antony Beaumont (London: Faber & Faber, 2004).

Lebrecht, Norman (ed.), *Mahler Remembered* (London: Faber & Faber, 1987).

Lewis, Christopher O., *Tonal Coherence in Mahler's Ninth Symphony* (Ann Arbor: UMI Research Press, 1984).

Ligeti, György and Gottwald, Clytus, 'Gustav Mahler und die musikalische Utopie', *Neue Zeitschrift für Musik*, 135 (1974), 7–11, 288–91, 292–5.

Lipiner, Siegfried, 'Über die Elemente einer Erneuerung religiöser Ideen in der Gegenwart' (Vienna: im Selbstverlage des Vorstandes des Lesevereines der deutschen Studenten Wiens, 1878).

Luft, David S., *Eros and Inwardness in Vienna. Weininger, Musil, Doderer* (University of Chicago Press, 2003).

Machatzke, Martin (ed.), *Gerhart Hauptmann. Tagebücher 1897 bis 1905* (Berlin: Propyläen, 1987).

Mahler, Alma (ed.), *Gustav Mahler Briefe 1879–1911* (Vienna: Paul Zsolnay, 1924).
  Gustav Mahler. Erinnerungen und Briefe (Amsterdam: Allert de Lange, 1940).
  Gustav Mahler. Memories and Letters, trans. Basil Creighton, ed. Donald Mitchell (London: John Murray, 1968/1973).

Gustav Mahler. Erinnerungen und Briefe, ed. Donald Mitchell (Frankfurt, Berlin and Vienna: Propyläen, 1971).

Gustav Mahler. Memories and Letters, trans. B. Creighton, ed. Donald Mitchell and Knud Martner (London: Cardinal, 1990)

Mahler, Gustav, 'The Influence of Folk-Song on German Musical Art', interview in *The Etude* (May 1911), 301–2.

Zehnte Symphonie [Faksimile-Ausgabe des Manuskriptes]. Einführend Bemerkungen von Richard Specht (Berlin, Vienna and Leipzig: Zsolnay, 1924).

X. Symphonie. Faksimile nach der Handschrift, ed. Erwin Ratz (Munich/Meran: Ricke/Laurin, 1967).

A Performing Version of the Draft for the Tenth Symphony, ed. Deryck Cooke (New York/London: Associated Music Publishers/Faber Music, 1976).

A Performing Version of the Draft for the Tenth Symphony, ed. Deryck Cooke, 2nd edn (London: Faber Music, 1989).

Facsimile Edition of the Seventh Symphony, 2 vols. (Commentary and Facsimile) (Amsterdam: Rosbeek Publishers, 1995).

Mahler-Werfel, Alma (1959), *And the Bridge is Love*, in collaboration with E. B. Ashton (London: Hutchinson, 1959). [Also New York: Harcourt, Brace & Co., 1958].

Mein Leben (Frankfurt am Main: Fischer Taschenbuch, 1960, repr. 2000).

Tagebuch-Suiten 1898–1902, ed. Antony Beaumont and Susanne Rode-Breymann (Frankfurt am Main: S. Fischer, 1997).

Diaries 1898–1902, selected and trans. A. Beaumont (London: Faber & Faber, 1998).

Malloch, William, *I Remember Mahler* (programme broadcast on KPFK, Los Angeles, California, 7 July 1964); NYP *The Mahler Broadcasts 1942–1882* CD, 1998, Nos. 11 and 12.

Mann, Thomas, *Briefe I (1889–1913)*, ed. Erika Mann (Frankfurt am Main: Fischer, 1961–2).

Wagner und unsere Zeit, ed. Erika Mann (Frankfurt am Main: Fischer, 1986).

Martner, Knud, *Gustav Mahler im Konzertsaal: eine Dokumentation seiner Konzerttätigkeit 1870–1911* (Copenhagen: KM-Privatdruck, 1985).

'Mahler's Activities in Kassel from a New Perspective', *News About Mahler Research*, 21 (March 1989), 7–11.

Martner, Knud (ed.), *Selected Letters of Gustav Mahler*, trans. Eithne Wilkins, Ernst Kaiser and Bill Hopkins (London: Faber & Faber, 1979).

Matthews, Colin, *Mahler at Work*. Aspects of the Creative Process (New York and London: Garland Publishing, 1989).

McClatchie, Stephen, 'The 1889 Version of Mahler's First Symphony: a New Manuscript Source', *19th-Century Music*, 20/2 (1996), 99–124.

'Hans Rott, Gustav Mahler and the "New Symphony": New Evidence for a Pressing Question', *Music & Letters*, 81 (2000), 392–401.

McClatchie, Stephen (ed. and trans.), *The Mahler Family Letters* (Oxford University Press, 2006).

McGrath, William, *Dionysian Art and Populist Politics in Austria* (New Haven and London: Yale University Press, 1974).

'Mahler and Freud: the Dream of the Stately House' in Rudolf Klein (ed.), *Gustav Mahler Kolloquium* 1979, Beiträge der Österreichischen Gesellschaft für Musik 2 (Kassel: Bärenreiter, 1981), pp. 40–51.

Metzger, Christoph, *Mahler-Rezeption. Perspektiven zur Rezeption Gustav Mahlers* (Wilhelmshaven: Florian Noetzel, 2000).

'Korrelationen musikwissenschaftlicher Rezeptionsforschung mit der Aufführungsgeschichte am Beispiel Gustav Mahlers' in Kathrin Ebel and Wolfgang Ruf (eds.), *Musikkonzepte – Konzepte der Musikwissenschaft, Bericht über den Internationalen Kongress der Gesellschaft für Musikforschung, Halle (Saale) 1998* (Kassel: Bärenreiter, 2000), pp. 591–5.

Micznik, Vera, 'Is Mahler's Music Autobiographical? A Re-appraisal', *Revue Mahler Review*, 1 (February 1987), 47–63.

'Meaning in Gustav Mahler's Music: A Historical and Analytical Study Focusing on the Ninth Symphony' (unpublished PhD dissertation, State University of New York at Stony Brook, 1989).

'The Farewell Story of Mahler's Ninth Symphony', *19th-Century Music*, 20 (1996–97), 144–66

'Music and Narrative Revisited: Degrees of Narrativity in Beethoven and Mahler', *Journal of the Royal Musical Association*, 126/2 (2001), 193–249.

Mitchell, Donald, *Gustav Mahler. The Early Years* (London: Rockliff, 1958).

'"Waldmärchen": the Unpublished First Part of *Das klagende Lied*', *The Musical Times*, 111 (1970), 375–9.

Gustav Mahler. Vol. II. The Wunderhorn Years (Berkeley and Los Angeles: University of California Press, 1980).

Gustav Mahler. Vol. I. The Early Years, rev. edn, ed. Paul Banks and David Matthews (Berkeley and Los Angeles: University of California Press, 1980).

Gustav Mahler. Vol. III. Songs and Symphonies of Life and Death (London: Faber & Faber, 1985).

Gustav Mahler, Vol. II. The Wunderhorn Years, rev. edn (Berkeley: University of California Press, 1995).

'Eternity or Nothingness? Mahler's Fifth Symphony', in Mitchell and Nicholson, *The Mahler Companion* (Oxford University Press, 2002), pp. 236–325.

'*Das klagende Lied*. Mahler's "Opus 1"', *Muziek & Wetenschap*, 7/1 (1999), 33–42.

Mitchell, Donald, (ed.), *Gustav Mahler. The World Listens*, Programme Book of the 1995 MahlerFeest in Amsterdam (Haarlem: EMA Uitgevers, 1995).

Mitchell, Donald and Nicholson, Andrew (eds.), *The Mahler Companion*, rev. edn (Oxford University Press, 2002).

Mitchell, Donald and Straub, Henriette (eds.), *New Sounds, New Century. Mahler's Fifth Symphony and the Royal Concertgebouw Orchestra* (Bussum: Royal Concertgebouw Orchestra, 1997).

Moldenhauer, Hans and Rosaleen, *Anton von Webern. A Chronicle of His Life and Work* (New York/London: Random House, 1979/Gollancz, 1978). [German edn, Zurich and Freiburg: Atlantis, 1980].

Monelle, Raymond, *The Sense of Music. Semiotic Essays* (Princeton University Press, 2000).

Morgan, Robert P., 'Ives and Mahler: Mutual Responses at the End of an Era', *19th-Century Music*, 2 (1978), 72–81.

Murphy, Edward, 'Sonata-rondo Form in the Symphonies of Gustav Mahler', *The Music Review*, 36/1 (1975), 54–62.

'Unusual Forms in Mahler's Fifth Symphony', *The Music Review*, 47/2 (1986), 101–9.

Newcomb, Anthony, 'Narrative Archetypes in Mahler's Ninth Symphony' in Steven Paul Scher (ed.), *Music and Text: Critical Inquiries* (Cambridge University Press, 1992), pp. 118–36.

Newlin, Dika, 'Gustav Mahler's Piano Quartet in A minor', *Chord and Discord*, 2/10 (1963), 180–3.

Bruckner, Mahler, Schoenberg (London: Marion Boyars, 1979).

Nietzsche, Friedrich, *The Birth of Tragedy and The Case of Wagner*, trans. Walter Kaufmann (New York: Vintage Books, 1967).

The Will to Power, trans. and ed. Walter Kaufmann and R. J. Hollingdale (New York: Vintage Books, 1968).

The Gay Science (New York: Vintage Books, 1974).

'On Music and Words' [1871], trans. Walter Kaufmann, in Carl Dahlhaus, *Between Romanticism and Modernism. Four Studies in the Music of the Later Nineteenth Century*, trans. Mary Whittall (Berkeley: University of California Press, 1980), pp. 106–19.

Nikkels, Eveline, *'O Mensch! Gib Acht!' Friedrich Nietzsches Bedeutung für Gustav Mahler* (Amsterdam: Rodopi, 1989).

Nikkels, Eveline and Becqué, Robert (eds.), *A 'Mass' for the Masses. Proceedings of the Mahler VIII Symposium. Amsterdam 1988, Rijswijk* (Rotterdam: Universitaire Pers, 1992).

Odefey, Alexander, *Gustav Mahlers Kindertotenlieder. Eine semantische Analyse* (Frankfurt: Peter Lang, 1999).

Olsen, Morten S., 'Culture and the Creative Imagination: the Genesis of Gustav Mahler's Third Symphony' (unpublished Ph.D. dissertation, University of Pennsylvania, 1992).

Op de Coul, Paul (ed.), *Fragment or Completion? Proceedings of the Mahler X Symposium Utrecht 1986* (The Hague: Nijgh & Van Ditmar, 1991).

Paddison, Max, *Adorno's Aesthetics of Music* (Cambridge University Press, 1993).

Painter, Karen (ed.), *Mahler and His World* (Princeton: Princeton University Press, 2002).

Partsch, Erich Wolfgang (ed.), *Gustav Mahler, Werk und Wirken. Neue Mahler-Forschung als Anlaß des vierzigjährigen Bestehens der Internationalen Gustav Mahler Gesellschaft* (Vienna: Vom Pasqualatihaus, 1996).

Pfohl, Ferdinand, *Gustav Mahler. Eindrücke und Erinnerungen aus den Hamburger Jahren*, ed. Knud Martner (Hamburg: Karl Dieter Wagner, 1973).

Pickett, David, 'Gustav Mahler as Interpreter. A Study of his Textural Alterations and Performance Practice in the Symphonic Repertoire' (unpublished Ph.D. dissertation, University of Surrey, 1988).

'Rescoring in Beethoven's Symphonies' in Robin Stowell (ed.), *Performing Beethoven* (Cambridge University Press, 1994), pp. 212–16.

Puffett, Derrick, 'Berg, Mahler and the Orchestral Pieces Op. 6 (1914–15)' in Anthony Pople (ed.), *The Cambridge Companion to Berg* (Cambridge University Press, 1997), pp. 111–44.

Ratz, Erwin (ed.), *Zehnte Symphonie: Faksimile nach der Handschrift* (Munich: Walter Ricke; Meran: Laurin, 1967) [Second of the two facsimiles of Mahler's manuscript of the Tenth Symphony.]

Gustav Mahler, IX. Symphonie. Partiturentwurf der ersten drei Sätze. Faksimile nach der Handschrift (Vienna: Universal Edition, 1971).

Read, Philip (ed.), *On Mahler and Britten* (Woodbridge: Boydell Press, 1995).

Redlich, Hans, *Bruckner and Mahler* (London: Dent, 1963).

Reeser, Eduard, *Gustav Mahler und Holland: Briefe* (Vienna: Bibliothek der Internationale Gustav Mahler Gesellschaft, 1980).

Reilly, Edward, *Gustav Mahler and Guido Adler. Records of a Friendship* (Cambridge University Press, 1982).

'*Das klagende Lied* Reconsidered' in Stephen Hefling (ed.), *Mahler Studies* (Cambridge University Press, 1997), pp. 25–52.

'*Todtenfeier* and the Second Symphony' in Donald Mitchell and Andrew Nicholson (eds.), *The Mahler Companion* (Oxford University Press, 1999), pp. 84–125.

Revers, Peter, *Gustav Mahler. Untersuchungen zu den späten Symphonien* (Hamburg: Karl Dieter Wagner, 1985).

Mahlers Lieder. Ein musikalischer Werkführer (Munich: C. H. Beck, 2000).

Ritter, William, *Etudes d'Art étranger* (Paris: Mercure de France, 1906).

Robinson, Lisa Brooks, 'Mahler and Postmodern Intertextuality' (unpublished Ph.D. dissertation, Yale University, 1994).

Roman, Zoltan, *Gustav Mahler's American Years. A Documentary History* (Stuyvesant, NY: Pendragon, 1989).

Gustav Mahler and Hungary (Budapest: Akadémiai Kiadó, 1991).

'From Collection to Cycle: Poetic Narrative and Tonal Design in Mahler's *Lieder eines fahrenden Gesellen*', *Revista de Musicología*, 16 (1993), 3595–602.

Roman, Zoltan (ed.), *Gustav Mahler. Lieder eines fahrenden Gesellen. Sämtliche Werke. Kritische Gesamtausgabe, Vols. XIII and XIV* (London and Vienna: Josef Weinberger/Internationale Gustav Mahler Gesellschaft, 1982).

Gustav Mahler Sämtliche Werke. Kritische Gesamtausgabe Vol. XIII/5. Verschiedene Lieder für eine Singstimme mit Klavier (Mainz: Schott, 1990).

Rosenberg, Wolf, 'Gustav Mahlers *Klagendes Lied*. Versuch einer Deutung', *Musica*, 26/2 (1972), 119–22.

Rosenzweig, Alfred, 'Wie Mahler seine "Achte" plante. Die erste handschriftliche Skizze', *Der Wiener Tag*, 3607 (4 June 1933), 27–8.

Gustav Mahler. New Insights into his Life, Times and Work, ed. and trans. Jeremy Barham (Aldershot, Burlington, VT and London: Ashgate Press/Guildhall School of Music and Drama, 2007).

Rothkamm, Jörg, '"Kondukt" als Grundlage eines Formkonzepts. Eine Charakteranalyse des ersten Satzes der IX. Symphonie Gustav Mahlers', *Archiv für Musikwissenschaft*, 54/4 (1997), 269–83.

Berthold Goldschmidt und Gustav Mahler. Zur Entstehung von Deryck Cookes Konzertfassung der X. Symphonie, Musik im 'Dritten Reich' und im Exil Vol. 6 (Hamburg: von Bockel, 2000).

Gustav Mahlers Zehnte Symphonie. Entstehung, Analyse, Reception (Frankfurt am Main: Peter Lang, 2003).

Ruzicka, Peter, 'Editorial Remarks' in Ruzicka (ed.), *Gustav Mahler. Klavierquartett* (Hamburg, Sikorski, 1973), pp. 3 and 31.

'Gustav Mahlers Klavierquartett von 1876', *Musica* 28/5 (September–October, 1974), 454–7.

Ruzicka, Peter (ed.), *Mahler. Eine Herausforderung, ein Symposion* (Wiesbaden: Breitkopf & Härtel, 1977).

Samuels, Robert, *Mahler's Sixth Symphony. A Study in Musical Semiotics* (Cambridge University Press, 1995).

Schabbing, Bernd, *Gustav Mahler als Konzert- und Operndirigent in Hamburg* (Berlin: Verlag Ernst Kuhn, 2002).

Schadendorff, Mirjam, *Humor als Formkonzept in der Musik Gustav Mahlers* (Stuttgart and Weimar: Metzler, 1995).

Schaefer, Hans Joachim, *Gustav Mahler in Kassel* (Kassel: Bärenreiter, 1982).

Scheit, Gerhard and Svoboda, Wilhelm, *Feindbild Gustav Mahler. Zur anti-semitischen Abwehr der Moderne in Österreich* (Vienna: Sonderzahl, 2002).

Scherliess, Volker, '"Ganz nach Art der Alten" Mahler als Interpret Bachs – Ein Beitrag zur Rezeptionsgeschichte', *Neue Zeitschrift dur Musik*, 147/5 (May 1986), 4–8.

Scherzinger, Martin, 'The Finale of Mahler's Seventh Symphony: A Deconstructive Reading', *Music Analysis*, 14 (1995), 69–88.

Schiedermair, Ludwig, *Gustav Mahler. Eine biographisch-kritische Würdigung* (Leipzig: Hermann Seemann Nachfolger, 1901).

Schmierer, Elisabeth, *Die Orchesterlieder Gustav Mahlers* (Kassel and London: Bärenreiter, 1991).

Schoenberg, Arnold, 'Gustav Mahler: in Memoriam' [1912] in Leonard Stein (ed.), *Style and Idea. Selected Writings of Arnold Schoenberg*, trans. Leo Black (London: Faber & Faber 1975), pp. 447–8.

'Gustav Mahler', lecture MS [1912, rev. 1948] in Leonard Stein (ed.), *Style and Idea. Selected Writings of Arnold Schoenberg*, trans. Leo Black (London: Faber & Faber 1975), pp. 449–72.

Schorske, Carl E., *Fin-de-siècle Vienna: Politics and Culture* (New York: Vintage Books, 1981).

Smith, Warren Storey, 'Why Mahler Too?' *Chord and Discord*, 2/2 (November 1940), 13–15.

'Some Mahlerian Misconceptions', *Chord and Discord*, 2/4 (1947), 61–4.

Smoley, Lewis, *Gustav Mahler's Symphonies. Critical Commentary on Recordings Since 1986* (Westport, Conn.: Greenwood, 1996).

Sollertinski, Iwan, *Gustav Mahler – Der Schrei ins Leere* (trans. from Russian into German by Reimar Westendorf), *ssm 8 studia slavica musicologica* (Berlin: Verlag Ernst Kuhn, 1996).

Specht, Richard, *Gustav Mahler* (Berlin: Gose und Tetzlaff, 1905).

'Gustav Mahler', *Die Musik*, 7/15 (1907–8), 149–71.

'Thematische Novitäten-Analysen: I. Mahlers Siebente Symphonie', *Der Merker*, 1/2 (1909), 1.

Gustav Mahler (Berlin: Schuster & Loeffler, 1913; rev. edns, 1918 and 1922).

'Zu Mahlers Achter Symphonie', *Tagespost*, 59/150 (14 June 1914), 9.

Sponheuer, Bernd, *Logik des Zerfalls. Untersuchungen zum Finalproblem in den Symphonien Gustav Mahlers* (Tutzing: Hans Schneider, 1978).

Sponheuer, Bernd and Steinbeck, Wolfram (eds.), *Gustav Mahler und die Symphonik des 19. Jahrhunderts*, Bonner Schriften zur Musikwissenschaft 5 (Frankfurt am Main: Peter Lang, 2001).

Gustav Mahler und das Lied, Bonner Schriften zur Musikwissenschaft 6 (Frankfurt am Main: Peter Lang, 2003).

Stadler, Friedrich (ed.), *Wissenschaft als Kunst. Österreichs Beitrag zur Moderne* (Vienna and New York: Springer Verlag, 1997).

Stahmer, Klaus Hinrich, 'Mahlers Frühwerk – Eine Stiluntersuchung' in Stahmer (ed.), *Form und Idee in Gustav Mahlers Instrumentalmusik* (Wilhelmshaven: Heinrichshofen, 1980), pp. 10–28.

Stefan, Paul, *Gustav Mahler. Eine Studie über Persönlichkeit und Werk*, 4th edn (Munich: Piper, 1912).

Gustav Mahler. A Study of his Personality and Work, trans. T. E. Clark (New York: G. Schirmer, 1913).

Stein, Erwin, *Orpheus in New Guises* (New York: Rockliff, 1953).

Stephan, Rudolf, *Gustav Mahler. IV. Sinfonie G-Dur* (Munich: Wilhelm Fink, 1966).

Stephan, Rudolf (ed.), *Gustav Mahler: Werk und Interpretation. Autographe, Partituren, Dokumente* (Cologne: Arno Volk, 1979).

Mahler-Interpretation. Aspekte zum Werk und Wirken von Gustav Mahler (Mainz: Schott, 1985).

Strauss, Richard, 'Notes on the Interpretation of Beethoven's Symphonies', trans. L. Wurmser, *Recorded Sound*, 25 (January 1967), 135–9.

Tibbe, Monika, *Über die Verwendung von Liedern und Liedelementen in instrumentalen Symphoniesätzen Gustav Mahlers*, 2nd edn (Munich: Katzbichler, 1977).

Tischler, Hans, 'The Symphonic Problem in Mahler's Works', *Chord and Discord*, 2/3 (December 1941), 15–21.

'Key Symbolism versus "Progressive Tonality"', *Musicology*, 2 (1949), 383–8.

'Mahler's Impact upon the Crisis of Tonality', *Music Review*, 12 (1951), 113–21.

Ulm, Renate (ed.), *Gustav Mahlers Symphonien. Entstehung – Deutung – Wirkung* (Kassel: Bärenreiter, 2001).

Vogt, Matthias Theodor (ed.), *Das Gustav-Mahler-Fest, Hamburg 1989. Bericht über den Internationalen Gustav-Mahler-Kongreß* (Kassel: Bärenreiter, 1991).

Wagner, Margarete, '*Chinesische Flöte* versus *Lied von der Erde*. On Different Forms of Text Adaptation', *News About Mahler Research*, 51 (Winter 2004/2005), 20–35.

Wagner, Mary H., 'Gustav Mahler and his Tours with the New York Philharmonic Orchestra (1909–1911)' (unpublished Ph.D. dissertation, Kent State University, Ohio, 2002).

Wagner, Richard, *Three Wagner Essays*, trans. R. L. Jacobs, (London: Eulenburg Books, 1979).

Wagner-Artzt, Manfred (ed.), *Gustav Mahler Sämtliche Werke. Kritische Gesamtausgabe, Supplement Band III. Klavierquartett 1. Satz* (Vienna: Universal Edition, 1997).

Walter, Bruno, 'Mahlers Weg. Ein Erinnerungsblatt', *Der Merker*, 3/5 (1912), 166–71.

   Gustav Mahler (Vienna: Herbert Reichner, 1936).

   Gustav Mahler, trans. James Galston (London: Kegan Paul, Trench, Trubner & Co., 1937).

   Gustav Mahler (New York: Vienna House, Inc., 1941).

   Theme and Variations, trans. James Galston (London: Hamish Hamilton, 1947).

   Briefe 1894–1962, ed. Lotte Walter Lindt (Frankfurt: S. Fischer, 1969).

   Gustav Mahler, trans. James Galton (New York: Vienna House, 1973).

   Thema und Variationen (Frankfurt am Main: S. Fischer, 1988).

   Gustav Mahler (Wilhelmshaven: Florian Noetzel Verlag, 1989).

   Gustav Mahler, trans. Lotte Walter Lindt (London: Quartet Books, 1990).

Weill, Kurt, 'Gustav Mahler: 9. Symphonie', *Der deutsche Rundfunk*, 4/25 (20 June 1926), 1723–7.

Weingartner, Felix, *Ueber das Dirigiren* (Berlin: S. Fischer Verlag, 1896).

   Weingartner on Music & Conducting, trans. J. Crosland, (New York: Dover Publications, 1969).

Weiß, Günther (ed.), *Neue Mahleriana. Essays in Honour of Henry-Louis de La Grange on His Seventieth Birthday* (Berne: Peter Lang, 1997).

Wellesz, Egon and Wellesz, Emmy, *Egon Wellesz, Leben und Werk* (Vienna: Paul Zsolnay, 1981).

Werba, Robert, 'Mahlers Mozart Bild', *Wiener Figaro*, 42–6 (1975–9).

Wildgans, Friedrich, 'Gustav Mahler und Anton Webern', *Österreichische Musikzeitschrift*, 15/6 (1960), 302–6.

Wildhagen, Christian, *Die Achte Symphonie von Gustav Mahler. Konzeption einer universalen Symphonik* (Frankfurt am Main: Peter Lang, 2000).

Wilkens, Sander (ed.), *Gustav Mahler Symphonie Nr. 1. Sämtliche Werke. Kritische Gesamtausgabe, Vol. I* (Vienna: Universal Edition/Internationale Gustav Mahler Gesellschaft, 1992).

Williamson, John, 'Deceptive Cadences in the Last Movement of Mahler's Seventh Symphony', *Soundings*, 9 (1982), 87–96.

   'The Structural Premises of Mahler's Introductions: Prolegomena to an Analysis of the First Movement of the Seventh Symphony', *Music Analysis*, 5/1 (1986), 29–57.

   'The Earliest Completed Works: a Voyage Towards the First Symphony' in Mitchell and Nicholson (eds.), *The Mahler Companion*, rev. edn (Oxford University Press, 2002), pp. 39–61.

Willnauer, Franz, *Gustav Mahler und die Wiener Oper* (Vienna: Löcker, 1993).

Wöss, Joseph Venantius von, *Gustav Mahler. Das Lied von der Erde. Thematische Analyse* (Leipzig and Vienna: Universal Edition, 1912).

Wunberg, Gotthart (ed.), *Die Wiener Moderne* (Stuttgart: Philipp Reclam, 1981).

Zenck, Martin, 'Mahlers Streichung des "Waldmärchens" aus dem *Klagenden Lied*. Zum Verhältnis von philologischer Erkenntnis und Interpretation', *Archiv für Musikwissenschaft*, 38 (1981), 179–93.

Zlotnik, Asher G., 'Orchestration Revisions in the Symphonies of Robert Schumann' (unpublished Ph.D. dissertation, Indiana University, 1972).

Zychowicz, James L. (ed.), *The Seventh Symphony of Gustav Mahler* (The University of Cincinnati, 1990).

   Mahler's Fourth Symphony, Studies in Musical Genesis and Structure (Oxford University Press, 2000).

Index

Numbers in italics indicate illustrations, figures or musical examples

Cambridge Companions to Music

Topics

The Cambridge Companion to Ballet
Edited by Marion Kant

The Cambridge Companion to Blues and
Gospel Music
Edited by Allan Moore

The Cambridge Companion to the Concerto
Edited by Simon P. Keefe

The Cambridge Companion to Conducting
Edited by José Antonio Bowen

The Cambridge Companion to Electronic Music
Edited by Nick Collins and Julio D'Escriván

The Cambridge Companion to Grand Opera
Edited by David Charlton

The Cambridge Companion to Jazz
Edited by Mervyn Cooke and David Horn

The Cambridge Companion to the Lied
Edited by James Parsons

The Cambridge Companion to the Musical,
second edition
Edited by William Everett and Paul Laird

The Cambridge Companion to the Orchestra
Edited by Colin Lawson

The Cambridge Companion to Pop and Rock
Edited by Simon Frith, Will Straw and John Street

The Cambridge Companion to the String Quartet
Edited by Robin Stowell

The Cambridge Companion to Twentieth-
Century Opera
Edited by Mervyn Cooke

Composers

The Cambridge Companion to Bach
Edited by John Butt

The Cambridge Companion to Bartók
Edited by Amanda Bayley

The Cambridge Companion to Beethoven
Edited by Glenn Stanley

The Cambridge Companion to Berg
Edited by Anthony Pople

The Cambridge Companion to Berlioz
Edited by Peter Bloom

The Cambridge Companion to Brahms
Edited by Michael Musgrave

The Cambridge Companion to Benjamin Britten
Edited by Mervyn Cooke

The Cambridge Companion to Bruckner
Edited by John Williamson

The Cambridge Companion to John Cage
Edited by David Nicholls

The Cambridge Companion to Chopin
Edited by Jim Samson

The Cambridge Companion to Debussy
Edited by Simon Trezise

The Cambridge Companion to Elgar
Edited by Daniel M. Grimley and Julian Rushton

The Cambridge Companion to Handel
Edited by Donald Burrows

The Cambridge Companion to Haydn
Edited by Caryl Clark

The Cambridge Companion to Liszt
Edited by Kenneth Hamilton

The Cambridge Companion to Mahler
Edited by Jeremy Barham

The Cambridge Companion to Mendelssohn
Edited by Peter Mercer-Taylor

The Cambridge Companion to Mozart
Edited by Simon P. Keefe

The Cambridge Companion to Ravel
Edited by Deborah Mawer

The Cambridge Companion to Rossini
Edited by Emanuele Senici

The Cambridge Companion to Schubert
Edited by Christopher Gibbs

The Cambridge Companion to Schumann
Edited by Beate Perrey

The Cambridge Companion to Sibelius
Edited by Daniel M. Grimley

The Cambridge Companion to Verdi
Edited by Scott L. Balthazar

Instruments

The Cambridge Companion to Brass
Instruments
Edited by Trevor Herbert and John Wallace

The Cambridge Companion to the Cello
Edited by Robin Stowell

The Cambridge Companion to the Clarinet
Edited by Colin Lawson

The Cambridge Companion to the Guitar
Edited by Victor Coelho

The Cambridge Companion to the Organ
Edited by Nicholas Thistlethwaite and Geoffrey
Webber

The Cambridge Companion to the Piano
Edited by David Rowland

The Cambridge Companion to the Recorder
Edited by John Mansfield Thomson

The Cambridge Companion to the Saxophone
Edited by Richard Ingham

The Cambridge Companion to Singing
Edited by John Potter

The Cambridge Companion to the Violin
Edited by Robin Stowell